Contents

Contemporary Spanish Film from Fiction

Thomas G. Deveny

The Scarecrow Press, Inc.
Lanham, Maryland, and Oxford

SCARECROW PRESS, INC.

Published in the United States of America
by Scarecrow Press, Inc.
A Member of the Rowman & Littlefield Publishing Group
4501 Forbes Blvd., Suite 200, Lanham, MD 20706
www.scarecrowpress.com

PO Box 317
Oxford
OX2 9RU, UK

Copyright © 1999 by Thomas G. Deveny
First paperback edition 2003

British Library Cataloguing in Publication Information Available

The hardback edition of this book was previously cataloged by the Library of
Congress as follows:

Deveny, Thomas G., 1950–
    Contemporary Spanish film from fiction / Thomas G. Deveny.
      p. cm.
    Filmography: p.
    Includes bibliographical references and index.
    ISBN 0-8208-3635-1 (cl. : alk. paper)
      1. Motion pictures—Spain—History. 2. Spanish literature—Film
    and video adaptations. 3. Film adaptations. I. Title.
PN1993.5.S7D49   1999
791.43'0946—DC21   99-11960
                                                            CIP

☉™ The paper used in this publication meets the minimum requirements of
American National Standard for Information Sciences—Permanence of
Paper for Printed Library Materials, ANSI/NISO Z39.48-1992.
Manufactured in the United States of America.

ISBN: 0-8108-4692-6   (paper)

Acknowledgments

I would like to express my appreciation to the staff at the Filmoteca Nacional in Madrid for the assistance that they gave me in research. In particular, I would like to thank Dolores Devesa and her staff at the library of the Filmoteca for their suggestions, as well as technicians Juan Peña, Pepe Fernández, and María García. I am grateful to the Spanish film producers who furnished me with stills and information for the illustrations for this study. I am deeply indebted to my friends Gerardo Pastor and Rosario Sánchez for their generosity and hospitality. Thanks to Francisco Frisuelos for his suggestions about the manuscript, and to my wife Isabel for her support throughout this project.

Research for this study was made possible from a Faculty Development Grant from Western Maryland College.

Portions of this study have appeared in "Cinematographic Adaptations of Two Novels by Camilo José Cela," *Film/Literature Quarterly* 16,4 (1988); "From Page to Screen: Contemporary Spanish Cinema," *The Spanish Civil War in Literature*, edited by Janet Pérez and Wendell Aycock, Lubbock, Tex: Texas Tech University Press, 1990; "Cela on Screen: *La colmena*," *Camilo José Cela: Homage to a Nobel Prize*, edited by Joaquín Roy, Coral Gables, Fla.: University of Miami Press, 1991; "Recuperation of a Novel: Screen Adaptation of *El bosque animado.*" *Romance Languages Annual* 3 (1991); "The Libidinous Gaze: Screen Adaptation of Crónica del rey pasmado." In *Cine-Lit II. Essays on Hispanic Film and Fiction.* Edited by George Cabello-Castellet, Jaume Martí Olivella, and Guy H. Wood. Corvallis, Oreg.: Portland State Univ., Oregon State Univ., and Reed College, 1996; "The Mirror and the Mask: Cinematographic Adaptation of Juan Marsé's *El amante bilingüe.*" *Post Script* 16,1 (Fall 1996); "Contemporary Spanish Women Writers and the Silver Screen." In *Estudios en honor de Janet Pérez: El sujeto femenino en escritoras hispánicas.* Edited by Luis A. Jiménez, Oralia Preble-Niemi, and Susana A. Cavallo. Potomac, Md: Scripta Humanística, 1998. Reprinted with permission.

Introduction

Alfred Hitchcock used to tell about two goats in a garbage dump who were eating a roll of movie film that they had found; one goat suddenly stopped chewing, turned to the other goat and said, "I liked the book better." This anecdote captures the often dependent yet often contentious relationship between cinema and literature in which filmmakers "retell the tale" of a novel in the language of the seventh art. Nevertheless, there continues to be a lively debate about the relative merits of adapting novels to the screen and the success of individual adaptations, among authors, directors, critics, and filmgoers around the globe. Some authors and filmmakers have a negative opinion of the entire process. Even in the nineteenth century, French author Gustave Flaubert did not want illustrations of any kind to accompany his texts: "Never, as long as I live, shall I allow anyone to illustrate me, because the most beautiful literary description is eaten up by the most wretched drawing . . . the idea is closed, complete, and every sentence becomes useless" (Miller, *Subsequent* 213). Ironically, four versions of *Madame Bovary* have been filmed to date. Authors such as Virginia Woolf and Norman Mailer have expressed adamant opinions against cinematographic adaptations of literary material. Some film directors, such as François Truffaut —known for his famous cry "Down with litera-ture"—or Ingmar Bergman also believe that film and literature are totally incompatible; the Swedish filmmaker states that "Film has nothing to do with literature; the character and substance of the two art forms are usually in conflict" (Glassco 165).

Nevertheless, the fact remains that film industries around the world rely perennially on novels as "raw material." The reasons for this appropriation are both cultural and economic. We must never lose sight of the fact that movies are products of the film industry, and studio executives want to make profits.

1

Novels provide them with "proven property," but as Boyum points out, they are more than just that, "for to adapt a prestigious work was to do more than merely borrow its plot, its characters, its themes: in the eyes of the movie industry, it was—and in fact still is—to borrow a bit of that work's quality and stature" (4-5). For the audience, too, there are rewards, since they receive "the promise of a relatively painless appropriation of a culturally valued text" (Orr 4) by seeing the film version instead of reading the original novel.

Making Meaning and Narrativity

Studies by Panofsky, Fell, and Cohen manifest the debts that cinema has to other media, such as theater, painting, and photography, but the analogy between two narrative forms —film and novel—is the most compelling. The pioneering Russian movie director and film theoretician Sergei Eisenstein described how early filmmakers were inspired by novels—particularly those of Dickens—for their major innovations. He found examples of analogies in Dickens's prose to the montage, the dissolve, the close-up, the pan, and so on (195-255). A fundamental commonality between the two narrative forms is their visual quality. In 1897, novelist Joseph Conrad stated in the preface to *The Nigger of the Narcissus*, "My task . . . is, by the power of the written word, to make you hear, to make you feel—it is before all, to make you see" (xiv). In 1945, Herbert Read offered advice to writers that also applies to film: "If you asked me to give you the most distinctive quality of good writing, I would give it to you in this one word: VISUAL. Reduce the art of writing to its fundamentals, and you come to this single aim: to convey images by means of words. But to convey images. To make the mind see. . . . That is a definition of good literature. . . . It is also a definition of the ideal film" (230-231). Early director D. W. Griffith's statement about his aims as a filmmaker echoed those of novelist Joseph Conrad. The director stated, "The task I'm trying to achieve above all is to make you see" (Jacobs 119).

Nevertheless, there is a question about the difference in the receptive process of novels and films. Monaco states, "The reader of the page invents the image, the reader of a film does not, yet both readers must work to interpret the signs they receive in order to complete the process of intellection" (125). Various critics theorize about the differences in this process of interpretation, and their opinions tend to reflect preferences toward one medium over the other. Leon Edel states that it requires imagination to read, but not to view a film ("Camera vision cripples the use of the mind's eye . . . It is all there for us to see, not to imagine" [182]), and Wolfgang Iser believes that "the reader of *Tom Jones* is able to visualize the hero virtually for himself, and so his imagination senses the vast number of possibilities; the moment the possibilities are narrowed down to one complete and immutable picture, the imagination is put out of action, and we feel we have somehow been cheated" (283). On the other hand, Seymour Chatman dismisses Iser's contention that a reader forms myriad images, and he says, "though visual imagination may be less stimulated by a film than a novel, the conceptual imagination may be very much stimulated by, say, a face filled with emotion that goes unexplained by dialogue or diegetic context" (162). Robert Scholes points out that "the cinematic world invites—even requires conceptualization. The images presented to us . . . are narrational blueprints for a fiction that must be constructed by the viewer's narrativity" (293).

The shared narrativity of novels and films, then, is a key linking factor in the adaptation from page to screen: "both words and images are sets of signs that belong to systems and, at a certain level of abstraction, these systems bear resemblances to one another. More specifically within each such system there are many different codes (perceptual, referential, symbolic). What makes possible, then, a study of the relation between two separate sign systems, like novel and film, is the fact that the same codes may re-appear in more than one system" (Cohen, *Film* 4).

According to Dudley Andrew, "One would have to hold that while the material of literature (graphemes, words, and sentences) may be of a different nature from the materials of cinema (projected light and shadows, identifiable sounds and forms, and represented actions), both systems may construct in their own way, and at higher levels, scenes and narratives that are indeed commensurate" (*Concepts* 101). He also notes that "narrative codes, then, always function at the level of implication or connotation. Hence they are potentially comparable in a novel and a film" ("Well-Worn" 14). Consequently, "the story can be the same if the narrative units (character, events, motivations, consequences, context, viewpoint, imagery and so on) are produced equally in two works. Now this production is, by definition, a process of connotation and implication. The analysis of adaptation, then, must point to the achievement of equivalent narrative units in the absolutely different semiotic systems of film and language" (Andrew, *Concepts* 103).

Critics theorize about a fundamental question regarding reception: how does the brain process these differing sets of signifiers? Morrissette states, "just as written texts have always been assumed to produce in the imagination an accompaniment of visual, or at least sensorial, images, more or less clear or confused, so the apparently 'final' surface of the film image is quickly transferred into the imaginary realm, where it becomes productive of inner images, pseudomemories, associative, parasitic recalls, and conjectures" (*Novel* 26).

This imaginary realm again is based on the element of narrativity. Christian Metz indicates that the "role of the story is so powerful that the image, which is said to be the major constituent of film, vanishes behind the plot it has woven" (*Film Language* 45).

Indeed, film directors often approach the seventh art through the narrative. Italian director Antonioni says of filmmaking, "it is the story which fascinates me most. The images are the medium through which a story can be understood" (Beja 54). Cohen also notes that "narrativity is the most solid median link between novel and cinema, the most pervasive tendency of both verbal and visual languages. In both novel and cinema, groups of signs, be they literary or visual signs, are apprehended consecutively through time; and this consecutiveness gives rise to an unfolding structure, the diegetic whole that is never fully *present* in any one group yet always *implied* in each such group" (*Film and Fiction* 92).

A Question of Fidelity

An inescapable issue in cinematographic adaptation studies is the question of fidelity. Filmgoers who have read the novel upon which a movie is based almost inevitably compare the screen adaptation to the original. What does fidelity mean? How does one judge fidelity? Several critics envision a topology of relationships between the original novelistic narrative and its cinematographic adaptation. This topology is often based on a bipartite or tripartite model.

Morris Beja limits himself to two classifications: "If we oversimplify for the sake of discussion, there are probably two basic approaches to the whole question of adaptation. The first approach asks that the integrity of the original work—the novel, say—be preserved, and therefore that it should not be tampered with and should in fact be uppermost in the adapter's mind. The second approach feels it proper and in fact necessary to adapt the original work freely, in order to create—in the different medium that is now being employed—a new, different work of art with its own integrity" (82).

Geoffrey Wagner, however, prefers a tripartite division, noting three levels of fidelity. His first category is "transposition—in which a novel is directed given on the screen, with the minimum of apparent interference. This has been the most dominant and most pervasive method . . . it has also been the least satisfactory. . . and typically puerile." The second level is commentary: "This is where an original is taken and either purposely or inadvertently altered in some respect. It could also be called a re-emphasis or re-structure. . . . This seems to represent more of an infringement on the work of another than an analogy which may simply take a fiction as a point of departure. Yet film can make authentic reconstructions in the spirit of so many cinematic footnotes to the original." His third category is analogy: "to judge whether or not a film is a successful adaptation of a novel is to evaluate the skill of its makers in striking analogous attitudes and in finding analogous rhetorical techniques . . . analogy must represent a fairly considerable departure for the purpose of making another work of art . . . an analogy cannot be indicated as a violation of a literary original since the director has not attempted (or has minimally attempted) to reproduce the original" (222-31). Wagner offers many examples of these three modes: Minnelli's *Madame Bovary* would be an example of transposition; Nichols's *Catch 22* would be a commentary; and Fosse's *Cabaret* would be a case of analogy.

Dudley Andrew also uses a tripartite division, calling for three modes of relationship between film and text: borrowing, intersecting, and transforming (*Concepts* 98-104). Borrowing, the most frequent mode of adaptation, occurs when the artist "employs, more or less extensively, the material, idea, or form of an earlier, generally successful text" (98); intersecting occurs when "the uniqueness of the original text is preserved to such an extent that it is intentionally left unassimilated in adaptation," and Andrew is of the opinion that Robert Bresson's *Diary of a Country Priest* is "the novel as seen by cinema" (*Concepts* 99); in transformation "it is assumed that the task of adaptation is the reproduction in cinema of something essential about an original text" (*Concepts* 99). Regarding fidelity to the "letter" and the "spirit," Andrew (*Concepts* 100) believes that cinema can emulate in an almost mechanical fashion aspects of the text's letter, which includes "characters and their inter-relationships,the geographical, sociological, and cultural information providing the fiction's context, and the basic narrative aspects that determine the point of view of the narrator (tense, degree of participation and knowledge of the storyteller, etc.)." He adds, however, "more difficult is fidelity to the spirit, to the original's tone, values, imagery, and rhythm, since finding stylistic equivalents in film for these intangible aspects is the opposite of a mechanical process" (Andrew, *Concepts* 100).

Michael Klein and Gillian Parker's analysis of film adaptations of the English novel likewise is based on a three-tiered level of fidelity: (1) faithful, that is literal, translations; (2) one that "retains the core of the structure of the narrative while significantly re-interpreting, or in some cases, de-constructing the source text"; and (3) one that "regards the source merely as raw material, as simply the occasion for an original work" (9-10).

Spanish critic Luis Quesada, whose study *La novela española y el cine* offers a panoramic view of Spanish screen adaptations likewise uses a tripartite model consisting of (1) a "transfer of the original text from written language to the cinematographic image, by means of a faithful illustration, reconstructing in photography and in sound the scenes, actions, and even the dialogues of the book"; (2) "recreation of the original text through the means and elements of filmic language, conserving its spirit, but introducing changes, if necessary, like the elimination or creation of characters and scenes, as a means of adapting the situations that are expressed through the written word to the cinematographic image"; and (3) "capturing certain situations, scenes, characters, etc. in the original novel as a point of departure in order to create a work which is totally or partially different, varying the focus and the central concept of the novelist" (11-12).

In any transformation from one medium to another, changes are inevitable, and this is certainly the case in screen adaptations of novels. Consequently, critics theorize about what is meant by fidelity in this process. Pere Gimferrer offers the opinion that "a faithful adaptation should consist of one that, with the means that are appropriate to it—the image—the film is able to produce in the spectator an analogous effect to that which the verbal material of the novel—the word—had on the reader" (61). Bazin notes, "For the same reasons that render a word-by-word translation worthless and a too free translation a matter for condemnation, a good adaptation should result in a restoration of the essence of the letter and the spirit" (Bazin 67). However, Larsson makes an important observation regarding the latter concepts postulated by Bazin when he raises the question, "Faithful to *what*? Like the Law, novels are said to have a 'letter' and a 'spirit,' and it is considered better to be faithful to the spirit than to engage in a 'slavish' following of the original text. The 'spirit' of the novel, though, is precisely what changes in the historical matrix within which we read the novel . . . [yet] faithfulness to the 'letter' may be impossible because it *is* the letter. . . . To ask 'Faithful to *what*?' also requires a recognition that most adaptations are made to assure a profit" (75, 76).

Some recent critics tend to dismiss the classification of the relationship between the original narrative and the adaptation. Joy Gould Boyum is of the opinion that categories are not particularly useful, and that "the only truly meaningful way to speak of any given film's 'fidelity' is in relation to the quality of its implicit interpretation of its source," which holds true even for the freest of adaptations (71), and she believes that the adaptation is subject to criteria such as "consistency and coherence, sensitivity and nuance" (73). Boyum asserts that "In assessing an adaptation, we are never really comparing book with film but an interpretation with an interpretation—the novel that we ourselves have re-created in our imaginations, out of which we have constructed our own individualized 'movie,' and the novel on which the film maker has worked a parallel transformation. For just as we are readers, so implicitly is the film maker, offering us, through his work, his ·perceptions, his vision, his particular insight into his source. An adaptation is always, whatever else it may be, an interpretation" (61-62). Consequently, the director's "reading" of the original novel must be subject to the same criteria applied to other readings. Boyum notes, "though a literary work can admit countless readings, the inescapable fact is that some readings are better than others . . . an interpretation must be consistent with the facts of a given text . . . it must be capable of support with evidence from the text itself" (71-72).

The adaptation is an independent aesthetic work, a "new object" (Linden 163), "a work of art that relates to the book from which it derives, yet is also independent, an artistic achievement that is in some mysterious way the 'same' as the book but also something other: perhaps something less but perhaps something more as well" (Beja 88). Consequently, the film adaptation must be judged first and foremost as a film. Luhr and Lehman stress importance of the integrity of the new work (the adaptation): "the basic aesthetic imperative is to approach a work through the attributes of the work itself and not to assume it to be in any important sense derivative because it bears resemblance to a prior work. If it is derivative, if it makes no sense without recourse to a prior text . . . then it is not aesthetically realized. If it is aesthetically realized, then its use of

source material is of historical, not aesthetic interest" (223).
And Francisco Ayala goes so far as to say:

> When a film is announced as an adaptation of a novel or a
> drama, it is hard to resist the temptation to establish a
> comparative judgment between the two productions and
> measure the cinematography with the criteria of literature.
> There is nothing more false, however, than this point of view.
> The adapted novel or play serves as a basis for the film in the
> same way and with the same scope as an original plot, a
> popular legend, an event taken from History or an event found
> in a journalistic story. The novel simply loans material to the
> film, and the only thing that could distinguish it from any other
> plot, its artistic quality, cannot be transferred to the cinemato-
> graphic version. The base novel is (or tries to be) a work of art,
> and the film based on it will be another distinct work of art.
> Each one has its corresponding aesthetic intents, and even when
> they coincided in the intended artistic problem, the different
> media will lead to different creations. (128-29)

For Millecent Marcus there is "a continuum of literature-
film relations ranging from faithful adaptations, to free
adaptations that rise above the limits of their textual origins,
to entirely original cinematic creations," and she states that
"the good adapter, aware of the unique properties of literary
and cinematic form, must first infer from the textual source a
preliterary idea—one that stands prior to its written expression . . . the adapter must then deduce its cinematically
appropriate form according to Pudovkin's notion of the 'plastic
material' that bodies forth the abstractions and sentiments of
the precursor text" (*Filmmaking* 8, 15).

If the adaptation is, as Boyum (110) says, "rather than
mere re-creation, something nearer creation itself," then to
what extent can the director change the original narrative?
Keith Cohen calls for a radical response with regard to the
original literary material, which he refers to as "subversive
adaptations." Adaptation is a truly artistic feat only when the
new version "carries with it a hidden criticism of its model, or
at least renders implicit (through a process we should call
'deconstruction') certain key contradictions implanted or
glossed over in the original. . . . The adaptations must subvert
its original, perform a double and paradoxical job of masking an
unveiling its source, or else the pleasure it provides will be

nothing more than that of seeing words changed into images"
("Eisenstein's" 245). Furthermore, the specificities of the new
sign system . . . require that reproduction take full cognizance of
the change of sign. For it is these specificities that make
possible the truly radical reproduction that exploits the
semiotic transformation in order to redistribute the formative
materials of the original and to set them askew" (245, 255) We
should note, however, that the subversive adaptation that
Cohen holds up as a model—Sergei Eisenstein's Marxist
reading of capitalist class relationships in Theodore Dreiser's
An American Tragedy—was never actually filmed. Subversion
can be incompatible with a generally conservative, capitalist
industry such as film.

Bazin also speaks of the fact that there is something to be
gained by the "consumption" of both: "It is not a question of free
inspiration with the intention of making a duplicate. It is a
question of building a secondary work with the novel as
foundation. In no sense is the film 'comparable' to the novel or
'worthy' of it. It is a new aesthetic creation, the novel so to
speak multiplied by the cinema. . . . The aesthetic pleasure we
derive . . . includes all the novel has to offer plus, in addition,
its refraction in the cinema" (Bazin 39-40). Of course, publishing houses often take advantage of the relationship between
the screen adaptation and the original narrative by including
an image from the film on the cover of the latest edition of the
novel (especially if it is a photograph of famous actors), thus
encouraging the public to "consume" the novel as well.

Novel and Film: A Comparative Analysis?

What is the best approach when undertaking a comparative analysis of a novel and its cinematographic adaptation?
We can focus on specific areas of what Joy Gould Boyum refers to
as the "rhetoric of adaptation," including point of view; style
and tone; metaphor, symbol, allegory; interiors: thought,
dream, inner action. For Robert Giddings, an analysis of film
adaptations of literary texts should focus on specific problems
of transfer: point of view,time, imagery, psychological realism,
and "selective perception" (13). Likewise, Stuart McDougal

considers the following areas pertinent to a comparative analysis: plot and structure; character; point of view; the world of inner experience; figurative discourse; symbol and allegory; and time. Morrissette lists ten points to be considered: objective viewpoint, subjective viewpoint, transitions, chronology, problems of film versus literary "language," cinematic versus novelistic "universe," projection and empathy in novel reader and film spectator, verbal versus visual "description," presence or absence of the narrator in film and novel, and the "double register" (image and sound) in film versus the single register in the novel (*Novel* 18). As Metz points out, film has more than a double register. He indicates five "channels of information" that convey meaning in cinema: (1) images that are photographic, moving, and multiple; (2) graphic traces which include all written material that we read on the screen; (3) recorded speech; (4) recorded music; and (5) recorded noise or sound effects (Andrew, *Concepts* 218).

An important feature of novelistic narratives is point of view, but the variety of possibilities that exists in the novel is more limited in film narrative. Indeed, one of the most frequent problems in screen adaptations is how to deal with a first-person novelistic narrative. Directors have attempted to meet the problematic nature of first-person narrative with a variety of different solutions: Montgomery's *Lady in the Lake* (1947) is a classic example of how an attempt to show everything through the eyes of the protagonist—Philip Marlowe was essentially kept off screen—proved to be unsatisfactory. More frequently, filmmakers recur to voice-over narration to establish the first person narrator, and this has had mixed results in capturing the tone of the original. Film narratives, then, are preeminently in the third person: "the camera acts as third-person 'narrator' while still establishing the controlling vision as a subjective one—identifying it as that of one of the characters shown to us on screen" (89). Bruce Morissette notes, "the camera becomes an 'existence' that appropriates and becomes in the film a point of view outside any mental content within a character or narrator or neutral 'third observer.' The point of view passes in a way to the spectator himself, who becomes with the aid of the camera, a new kind of fictional god: one who, if not omniscient, can nevertheless move about with seemingly magical powers" (93). Other techniques used by many directors to approximate a first person narrative are voice-overs by the protagonist, point of view shots, choices of angles, and the relative closeness of the camera (especially in the use of strategic close-up shots).

Another crucial issue with regard to cinematographic adaptations is temporality. An important initial consideration in the comparison of the two texts is the "discourse time," that is, the amount of time it takes to either read a novel or view a film (Chatman 62). Discourse time for film has been established at approximately two hours, although in recent years the running time of feature films has declined. Exceptions do exist—Erich von Stroheim's forty-two-reel *Greed*, or novels made into television miniseries (some Spanish films from novels, such as *La Plaça del Diamant*, have been filmed in two versions, feature length and miniseries). Nevertheless, as Morris Beja points out, "when a three-hundred-page novel is made into a two or three-hour movie, a great deal will have to be sacrificed" (84). By the same token, adaptations of short stories may require the addition of narrative material in order to have a feature length film of standard length. Does it follow, then, that there is an optimal size narrative for the most successful screen adaptation?

Generally, this results in emphasis and selection on the part of script writers and directors (MacFarlane 7). Bazin (107) borrows a metaphor from Baudelaire, and has likened the literary source to a dazzling chandelier, while comparing the film version to the beam of a movie usher's flashlight. Martin (179) elaborates on this metaphor, saying, "in these terms, the film adaptation represents not only a simplification—the usher's flashlight leaves most of the theater in the dark—but also a narrowing and sharpening of focus." Yet are there any criteria for streamlining, for the process of selectivity? Are there essential features that cannot be sacrificed when undertaking a cinematographic adaptation?

Luhr and Lehman use Tomashevsky's definition of "motif," ("the meaning behind an irreducible part of the work") as a fundamental concept in studying adaptation. Tomashevsky distinguishes between "bound motifs" which cannot be omitted without disturbing the chronological chain of events, and "free motifs" which may be omitted in a summary (68). Luhr and Lehman are of the opinion that an adaptation usually includes all the bound motifs, but may omit free motifs (174). Similarly, Barthes refers to a major narrative event as a *kernel* [noyau]; it "advances the plot by raising and satisfying questions...kernels cannot be deleted without destroying narrative logic" (Chatman 53). A minor plot event is a *satellite*, which "can be deleted without disturbing the logic of the plot, though its omission will, of course, impoverish the narrative aesthetically (Chatman 54).

Another important aspect of time also related to the concept of selectivity and emphasis is story-time, or "the duration of the purported events of the narrative" (Chatman 62). Although often filmmakers need to condense the original narrative material, at times they have to expand on it. In either case, the story-time of the film narrative does not necessary conform to the story-time of the novel. When these changes occur, it is important to maintain narrative logic. Robert Scholes notes that "our primary effort in attending to a narration is to construct a satisfying order of events. To do this we must locate or provide two features: temporality and causality" (422-423). Consequently, we must keep in mind the difference between *plot* and *story*. Tomashevsky (66) defines story as the causal-temporal sequence of narrated events which indicates causality: because of A, then B. In other words, the story represents the chronological order in which the narrated events would occur in real life. The fragmentation of the story in the novel (or film) is what Tomashevsky defines as plot: the aesthetic distortion or defamiliarization that constitutes the process of telling the story (66-67). Quite often a change in the structure of the plot, as well as an extension of or limitation of the story-time when going from page to screen is an aesthetic choice that serves to foreground an aspect of the original narrative. And often this choice is the result of another important area to be considered when studying screen adaptations: the analysis of the differences in the contexts of production and consumption of the two works.

Films in Context

Panofsky contends that film "developed less from 'high-brow' literature than out of diverse media with a popular body of established conventions that tended toward melodrama. These conventions have continued to dictate the shape of mass-market motion pictures. At the least, to violate these patterns is to tamper with the public expectations and taste—and to threaten the all-determining box office" (Peary and Shatzkin, 6). But to what extent do expectations and taste differ from country to country? It is important to note when considering filmic conventions that film is at once a universal medium, and a medium consisting of national cinemas that also manifest their own aesthetic and thematic tendencies in an international marketplace dominated by American cinema. Does spectator response differ among nationalities? For example, do American audiences have different reactions and expectations regarding happy endings in comparison, say, with a European audience? How does the dominance of American films in other countries affect the aesthetics of their national cinemas?

Both a synchronic and a diachronic analysis of expectations and taste is necessary to arrive at a complete understanding of a national cinema such as that of Spain. Dudley Andrew believes that a crucial question is, "What conditions exist in film style and film culture to warrant or demand the use of literary prototypes? The choices of the mode of adaptation and the prototypes suggests a great deal about the cinema's sense of its role and aspirations from decade to decade. Moreover, the stylistic strategies developed . . . not only are symptomatic of a period's style, but may crucially alter that style" (*Concepts* 104). Larsson emphasizes that adaptations must be analyzed in the context of three broad areas: (1) the "historical matrix within which the text has its origin, its popular reception, its critical study, and its conversion into film"; (2) "the aesthetic intent of the adaptor in conjunction with market pressures to produce a saleable commodity"; and (3) the "ideological constraints, both covert, manifest in sociological and psychological subtexts, and overt, resulting from direct pressures to bring a text into conformity with dominant moral and political pressures" (71). Consequently, it is important to keep in mind the observation made by Christopher Orr, who views "the changes that occur in the passage from novel to film as privileged sites from which to reconstruct the ideological processes at work in the production of the film text" (2). Especially in the case of a national cinema, such as that of Spain, a diachronic study of the relationship of film to society is crucial.

Contemporary Spanish Cinema

Following the Spanish civil war, Spanish cinema was completely dominated by the political and religious values of the Franco regime. Censorship of both national and foreign films was the rule of the day. Hooper points out that "the Church was involved in official censorship for deciding on matters of sexual propriety" and that "the cinema was of particular concern to the Church. Fr. Angel Ayala, the founder of the Catholic pressure group ACNP, described it as 'the greatest calamity that has befallen the world since Adam—a greater calamity than the flood, the two World Wars or the atomic bomb'" (152-153). Travellers to Spain during the 1950s and 1960s such as James Michener saw warnings posted by priests on church doors about the dangerous nature of certain films: "This should be seen only by those ninety-four and above" (Michener 61). Ana Mariscal humorously depicts the moral state of affairs regarding cinema during the 1940s and early 1950s in her 1965 film adaptation of Miguel Delibes's novel, *El Camino*, in which parish women try to cover the projector lens and stop the projection of a "risque" Latin American movie.

The Franco regime's moral values also included attitudes toward the Spanish nation, and this is reflected on screen during the period. Besas (19) notes that the film *Raza* (*Race*, 1941) was the "major landmark of the period" and "marked the first direct intervention of the government in film production." The script was written by none other than General Franco, under the pseudonym of Jaime de Andrade, and although the film extols the patriotism of the Churruca family, there are strong autobiographical elements in it, so tacitly it is the *caudillo* himself (as Franco was known) who was the object of praise. The major Spanish film production company, Cifesa, monopolized movie production during the 1940s, and Besas estimates that "about 80% of Cifesa's films at that time were 'society' comedies, a politically safe genre which could be shot at relatively low cost" (26). In the late forties and early fifties, Cifesa produces a series of historical epics that promoted patriotic values such as *La princesa de los Ursinos* (1947) and *Agustina de Aragón* (1950).

In the 1950s, the situation slowly began to change, mainly due to the efforts of two film directors, Luis García Berlanga and Juan Antonio Bardem. The former's *Bienvenido, Mr. Marshall (Welcome, Mr. Marshall)* won an Honorable Mention at the 1953 Cannes film festival, and Bardem's 1954 film, *Muerte de un ciclista (Death of a Cyclist)*, which shows the influence of Italian neo-realist directors such as Rossellini, won the International Critics Award in 1955.

That year also saw an important conference on Spanish film sponsored by the University of Salamanca. The document that resulted from these "Cinematographic Conversations" as they were called, began by stating, "Current Spanish cinema is 1. Politically ineffective. 2. Socially false. 3. Intellectually abject. 4. Aesthetically null and void. 5.Industrially stunted" (Castro 439). Director Juan Antonio Bardem issued the battlecry, "Spanish cinema is dead. Long live Spanish cinema" (Besas 41). A renewed interest in Spanish film as manifested by these "Conversations" led to the founding of magazines dedicated to this topic, such as *Film ideal* (begun in 1956). García Berlanga and Bardem continued to direct important films, such as *Calabuch* (1956) and *Los jueves, milagro* (*A Miracle Every Thursday*, 1957) by the former, and *Calle mayor* (*Main Street*, 1956) by the latter.

Cinematographic adaptations of literary works during the 1940s and 1950s consisted mainly of screen versions of nineteenth-century novels or earlier classics of Spanish literature: works by Galdós (*Marianela*; *Nazarín*—which Buñuel filmed in Mexico), Pardo Bazán (*Viaje de novios*), Alarcón (*El Capitán Veneno*; *El sombrero de tres picos*), and Generation of 98 authors

Pío Baroja (*Las inquietudes de Shanti Andia; Zalacaín el aventurero*). Ardavín filmed the award-winning *Lazarillo de Tormes* in 1960, and *Don Quixote* was adapted to the screen by Rafael Gil in 1948 and by Eduardo García Maroto in 1961. Although it is possible that this choice of classics for film material corresponds to the Spanish film industry's broader intent to portray a reality that had nothing to do with Spanish reality of the moment (Garía Fernández 119), and perhaps in this way the Franco regime wanted to develop film as an art form for cultural exportation. However, there is no doubt that nineteenth-century narratives have continued to attract the attention of directors in many national cinemas. In France, there have been adaptations of Flaubert and Zola, and filmmakers in Great Britain and the United States have done screen versions of works by authors such as Henry James, Jane Austen, James Fenimore Cooper, and Nathaniel Hawthorne. Adaptations of nineteenth-century Spanish works (as well as earlier classics) have continued in recent decades with works such as *Fortunata y Jacinta, Tristana, Doña Perfecta, Los pazos de Ulloa (The Palaces of Ulloa)*, and *El buscón (The Swindler)*, as well as Manuel Gutiérrez Aragón excellent adaptation of *Don Quixote* for Spanish television in 1992. Indeed, although there was a paucity of adaptations of contemporary novels in the early 1970s, Buñuel's adaptation of *Tristana* in 1970 might have inspired Spanish filmmakers to bring classic literary works to the screen, since the main examples of the transformation from novel to screen from this period are mainly nineteenth-century works: Galdós's *Marianela, Tormento (Torment)*, and *El abuelo (The Grandfather*, called *La duda [Doubt]* in its screen version); Alas's *La regenta (The Regentess)*, and Valera's *Pepita Jiménez*.

Prior to 1965, few contemporary narratives made their way to the screen. In the late 1940s and early 1950s, narratives by Concha Espina (*La esfinge maragata, La niña de Luzmela*, and *Dulce nombre*) were adapted, and in 1947, Edgar Neville made a screen version of Carmen Laforet's *Nada* a mere three years after its publication. Although adapting such recent narratives represented an anomaly at that time, in recent decades it has become the norm.

In 1962, under the direction of Manuel Fraga Iribarne, minister of information, there was a certain liberalizing movement in Spanish culture. This was at a time when Spain was undergoing fundamental social transformations, with Opus dei technocrats in government posts and an influx of foreign tourists who brought not only foreign currency but foreign mores, as well. Michener (395-396) notes that Spaniards referred to the changes as the "revolution of the *Sueca*," in which Swedish women who flocked to sunny Spain changed the psychology of both Spanish men and women.

With the naming of José María García Escudero as undersecretary of cinema, there were important changes in that industry. In February of 1963, the Norms of Film Censorship were published, and they represented a liberalization of the artistic climate because from that moment directors at least had written guidelines within which they could work. In the following year, legislation created the "special interest" category for films, which entitled movies that qualified to receive larger state subsidies and set distribution quotas for foreign and domestic films. In 1963, Luis García Berlanga directed *El verdugo* (*The Executioner*), a compelling film about capital punishment and the individual's role in modern society, which represented Spain at the Venetian film festival and caused a scandal because of the reaction of the Spanish ambassador, Sánchez Bella, who called the film "one of the greatest libels ever perpetrated against Spain" (Besas 79). In addition to García Berlanga and Juan Antonio Bardem, several young directors began to be active in Spain in the 1960s. Many of them were products of the "Escuela Oficial de Cinematografía" (EOC), and they received government subsidies for their productions. Thus, under the protection of García Escudero, the movement known as the "New Spanish Cinema" was born. The two main innovations of the movement were, according to José Angel Rodero (7), a spirit of "renovation with regards to all that earlier Spanish cinema meant" and an aesthetics "capable of shaping a real vision of our society with its problems, its people, its circumstances." By the middle of the decade, directors such as Carlos Saura (*La caza* [*The Hunt*]) and Basilio Martín Patino (*Nueve cartas a Berta* [*Nine Letters to Berta*]), as well as screen adaptation of novels by directors Mario Camus (*Con el viento solano* [*With the Easterly Wind*]), and Ana Mariscal (*El camino* [*The Road*]) were having an important impact on Spanish cinema.

Franco's death on November 20, 1975 marked a watershed date for Spanish society. Spain's transition to democracy was seen on screen as much as in the rest of society. Spanish cinema, never divorced from Spanish history and politics, has found new avenues of expression and new perspectives on cultural, historical, and political matters. Many of the changes in Spanish movies over the past two decades are due to radical transformations in Spanish society, and the relationship between the government, the Catholic church, and the film industry. There is no more state censorship of films, and no longer does the Catholic church have the control over Spanish society's morals that it once did, determining what films were appropriate for Spaniards to view.

In November of 1977 censorship laws regarding Spanish cinema were abrogated, and the end of censorship meant that the two main topics that were the targets of the censors' pens—sex and politics—began to appear on the Spanish screen. Freed from prior constraints, the Spanish film industry produced during the 1980s and the first years of this decade a wide variety of movies of excellent quality that achieved both critical and popular acclaim on the international scene. On this side of the Atlantic, Spanish film festivals in New York and Washington have met with great success in recent years. Festivals dedicated exclusively to Spanish cinema have been held in Miami and Buenos Aires, and Spanish films have also appeared in festivals in Chicago, Los Angeles, and Toronto. The prizes won at these festivals together with those from Cannes and Berlin, as well as the Oscars for best foreign film in 1983 to José Luis Garci's *Volver a empezar* (*To Begin Again*) and to Fernando Trueba's *Belle epoque* in 1994 attest to the quality of current production in the cinema industry in Spain.

In addition to ending censorship and the establishing an official school of cinematography, there are other ways in which the Spanish government has had an important impact on the film industry. In 1977, the new legislation that abolished censorship and introduced an "S" classification for pornographic and violent films also established a new screen quota in which for every two days of screening dubbed foreign films, there had to be one day of Spanish films. However, as Miró (28) notes, this attempt to protect and give impulse to the Spanish film industry did not function as planned, since distributors dusted off old national films to fulfill their legal obligation. In 1979, the Spanish Supreme Court struck down the quota, and the following year the quota changed to a 1-to-3 ratio, with the distribution based on a quarterly basis.

That same year, the Spanish government began a massive subsidy campaign in collaboration with Spanish television that brought 13 billion pesetas to the production of Spanish films, which, after two years of exhibition in movie theaters, would be shown on the small screen. The government called for movies based on important works by Spanish writers, and several important novels were adapted to the screen: *La Plaza del Diamante* (1982), *Valentina* (1982), *La colmena* (1982), *Bearn o la sala de muñecas* (1982), *1919-Crónica del alba* (1983), *Ultimas tardes con Teresa* (1984), and *Los santos inocentes* (1984). This initiative in the 1980s represents the culmination of the development of a cultural mode of production in order for Spanish cinema to gain attention in international festivals and markets that had been in place since the middle of the Franco regime.

The Socialist victory at the polls in late 1982 marked the beginning of a new period in Spanish history. With President Felipe González at the helm, Spain would undergo a period of modernization and integration into Europe, with Spain joining both NATO and the Common Market (later European Union). González appointed film director Pilar Miró (whose film *Crimen de Cuenca* had caused her to face a military tribunal) as Directora General de Cinematografía. The number of Spanish films produced at that time was artificially high, since Miró (31) estimates that one-third of the production consisted of "S" films, and another third was films that were "false co-productions" only made to fulfill the quota law. Under her leadership, there was an attempt to solidify the remaining segment of the Spanish film industry, bringing subventions into line with those of other European nations. Spanish films then could receive a subvention up to fifty percent of the budget. Nevertheless, the expected recovery did not materialize, and Hopewell remarks that her critics "gloat over the fact that under her leadership, Spanish box-office takings have gone down drastically precisely at the time when Spanish advance subsidies have gone up drastically" (117). Part of this problem, however, is based on a marked increase in video consumption during the 1980s in Spain, as well as a huge expansion in television viewing based on both greater broadcast time by Spanish state television and the advent of private television in Spain. Hopewell (118) also notes that the number of cinemas in Spain declined rapidly during the 1980s—from 2,640 in 1986 to 1,882 in 1988, thus making it difficult for Spanish films to compete against an already American-dominated market.

Payan (21) notes that in 1981 the Spanish government developed a plan of credits backed by a major Spanish bank, the Banco de Crédito Comercial, and that the Ministry of Culture established a "Protection Fund" that provided 1.2 billion pesetas per year. However, aside from the special subsidy in 1979 when the Ministry of Culture called for films based on Spanish novels, screen adaptations do not regularly receive preferential treatment regarding subsidies. Thus, for example, in 1986, of the almost 1.5 billion pesetas in subsidies, only 367 million went to films based on Spanish novels. Beginning in 1987, the government administered these subsidies on a tri-yearly basis. Not all members of the film community hailed this program, however. Director Luis G. Berlanga denounced the "progressive nationalization" of Spanish cinema (Payan 35), and figures seemed to confirm his claim: in 1985, 69 percent of Spanish films were produced without any subsidies, but by 1987, that figure had decreased to 28 percent. In 1989, the Semprún decree aimed at reducing state support with the idea of inducing more private investment in the Spanish film industry, and the result was a radical decline in the number of films. In 1990, of forty-seven films, only nine received prior subsidy (subvención anticipada). The following year also proved to be a difficult one for Spanish cinema, since Spanish television (TVE), showing deficits and facing new competition, refused to invest 2 billion pesetas in the industry that it had promised.

Currently, percentages of subventions are again high; in 1995, thirty-nine films were completed and another thirty-nine received subsidies for future production. There has been a modification in screen quotas and dubbing licences so that Spanish films are included with others from the European Union in a new 1-to-2 ratio—one European film must be shown for each non-European (i.e. Hollywood) film in cities with populations over 125,000 (in smaller cities, the ratio is 1 to 3). Although there is talk of the Aznar government radically reducing subsidies to the Spanish film industry, movies produced in Spain have other avenues of funding: from regional governments, from advanced sales to television, as well as grants from European commissions such as Euro-Image. In addition, many of Spain's important films that are intended to transcend their national audience, both through entry into global film festivals as well as distribution abroad, are international co-productions.

During the 1980s, Spanish audiences drifted away from the products of their own cinema industry. Although Spanish films captured 21 percent of national audiences in 1981, by 1991, that figure had declined to a mere 11 percent. Production between 1985 and 1994 fell 43 percent (from seventy-seven to forty-four films). In spite of those dire statistics, Spanish film seems to be recovering of late. In 1995, production increased by 27 percent to fifty six films, and sales of Spanish films abroad increased from 2.7 to 4 billion pesetas. New directors (Julio Medem, Alex de la Iglesia, Iciar Bollain) and new actors (Carmelo Gómez, Javier Bardem, Penélope Cruz, Silke) appear to be attracting a younger audience.

Parameters

Two basic parameters of this study are related to the dates of appearance of the works of art in question—the novels and their screen adaptations. The original works are post-civil-war narratives written in Spanish, and this study covers three decades of Spanish cinema, analyzing feature-length films that have had their debuts from 1965 to 1995. Within these parameters, I have attempted to provide a comprehensive survey of film adaptations, including analyses of both masterpieces as well as lesser-known works, in order to provide a complete picture of this enterprise. For ease of reference, the analyses of individual film adaptations appear under the alphabetical listing of authors whose works have been adapted to the screen.

There are thus several Spanish screen adaptations that fall outside the parameters of this study. These include contemporary films are based on earlier "classics," such as Galdos's *Tristana, Fortunata y Jacinta, Marianela*, and *Tormento*, Alas's *La Regenta*, Valera's *Pepita Jiménez*; screen adaptations of Latin American narratives, such as Sábato's *El túnel*, even if these adaptations are done by Spanish directors; or novels and films that both linguistically and culturally pertain to regional areas in Spain (most significantly, Catalonia)—*Bearn, La Plaça del Diamant*, etc.—since they are worthy of a separate study.

My analysis follows earlier critics' studies of ten-year cycles in recent Spanish culture. Evans and Fiddian (2-3) note the practical value of "the conventional historiographic tool of analysis-by-decade," which focuses on "crucial turning points in contemporary Spanish affairs." I view Franco's death in 1975 as the single most important turning point for the recent changes in Spanish society. I consequently examine films from the decade prior to the *caudillo*'s death and the two decades after the end of the dictatorship. Kinder (3-6) believes that there are three important phases in New Spanish Cinema based on roughly ten-year cycles: (1) between 1951-1961, beginning with an Italian film week and including the Salamanca Congress in 1955;(2) from 1962-1972, a period of cultural opening when Manuel Fraga Iribarne was head of the Ministry of Information and Tourism, with the development of the Escuela Oficial de Cinematografía and a subvention of films that were deemed of "Special Interest" (based on their aesthetic dimension), with a swing to the right (including more rigorous censorship and a cut in government subventions following the Matesa scandal); and (3) from 1973-1982, which includes the move to the post-Franco period, with an end of censorship and more international recognition of Spanish cinema. The Socialist victory in 1982 began a period of power that lasted until March of 1996, when the Partido Popular under the leadership of José María Aznar ousted Felipe González and the socialists from power. My study, therefore, focuses on thirty important years in contemporary Spain in which important transitions marked the middle of each decade.

Novel to Film: A Healthy Relationship?

Lester Asheim calculates that between 1935 and 1947, 17 percent of films released by major studios were adapted from novels (Giddings 21). Morris Beja indicates that between 20 and 30 percent of American films released each year are based on novels, three-quarters of the best Academy Awards have gone to adaptations, and that of the twenty top money-earners as of 1977, fourteen were derived from novels (74). In recent years, *Driving Miss Daisy*, *Dances With Wolves*, *Silence of the Lambs*, *Schindler's List*, *Forrest Gump*, and *The English Patient*—all films based on novels —have won the Oscar for best film of the year.

In Spain, many of the most important post-civil war novels have been made into movies. Authors such as Delibes, Marsé, and Cela have all had multiple works transformed to the screen. Some of contemporary Spanish cinema's most critically acclaimed films have been adaptations: *El sur*, *Los santos inocentes*, *La colmena*, *Pascual Duarte*, etc. Spain's National Academy of Cinema has awarded Goyas to screen adaptations such as *El viaje a ninguna parte* (best film, best director, best script, 1987); *El bosque animado* (five Goyas, including best film, 1988); *Si te dicen que caí* (Jorge Sanz, best actor, 1991); *Las edades de Lulú* (María Barranco, best supporting actress, 1992); *El rey pasmado* (seven Goyas in 1993); *Días contados* (best film, 1995); and *Más allá del jardín* (Mari Carrillo, best supporting actress; Ingrid Rubio, best new actress, 1997).

Spanish cinema has also seen adaptations of works other than contemporary Spanish novels. Fernando Trueba's film adaptation of Christopher Frank's novel, *El sueño del mono loco*, won the Goya for best film in 1990, and his 1995 film *Two Much*, starring Antonio Banderas, Melanie Griffith, and Daryl Hannah, is based on the novel by Donald Westlake. Carlos Saura's *¡Ay Carmela!*, which virtually swept the Goya awards in 1992, is a screen adaptation of the play by Sanchis Sinisterra. And screen adaptations are almost perennially among the top-grossing national films in Spain.

Since numbers of movie ticket sales far exceed numbers of book sales for an given adapted title, the fact is that the majority of filmgoers have not read the original work. However, Boyum says that "many would contend that such an 'innocent' viewer [one who hasn't read the book] is indeed the ideal one, that ideally novel and film should be regarded as independent entities" (64). Without bringing previous knowledge of the original narrative, this "ideal" spectator can judge the film simply as film. Eventual comparisons of the two narratives, however, seem inevitable.

Orr points out that "the process of adapting a narrative content from another medium inevitably involves the construction of two hypothetical spectators. That is, the adaptation attempts to satisfy the first spectator's desire for repetition by maintaining the illusion of fidelity while at the same time remaining intelligible to the spectator unfamiliar with the film's source. Moreover, in the case of a conflict between the desire of the first spectator for fidelity and the desire of the second for an intelligible text, the usual practice is to accommodate the latter" (Orr 4). Bazin makes these comments regarding viewers' reactions toward a screen adaptation: "either they will be satisfied with the film which is as good as most, or they will want to know the original, with the resulting gain for literature. This argument is supported by publishers' statistics that show a rise in the sale of literary works after they have been adapted to the screen. No, the truth is that culture in general and literature in particular have nothing to lose from such an enterprise" (Bazin 65). Other critics also cite evidence that film adaptations cause a renewal of interest in the original novels (Bluestone 4-5; Beja 87-8). Certainly many people—both critics and the general public—read the novel and see the film, or are spurred to read the literary work after their viewing the cinematographic version of the narrative. Since, in the words of Géloin (141), an adaptation "is always a discourse that brings in the process a dialogic dimension," the two versions of the narrative will interact with each other in our perception. If telling tales is an inexorable component of *homo ludens*, then telling the tale a second time on screen should provide twice the fun, or at least the basis for spirited discussions.

Ignacio Aldecoa

Ignacio Aldecoa (1925-1969) was a novelist whose untimely death at age forty-four deprived Spain of one of the most important writers of his generation. Aldecoa's style of realism was based on a desire for complete narrative objectivity and the attempt to portray the lives of lower-class segments of Spanish society: sailors (a profession that Aldecoa had tried), miners, gypsies.

Con el viento solano (*With the Easterly Wind*), directed by Mario Camus and based on Aldecoa's novel from 1962, was filmed in 1965 and had its commercial debut in 1967. The narrative is the story of Sebastián Vázquez (Antonio Gades), a gypsy who gets drunk, kills a civil guard and flees, and finally turns himself in to the police. Navales (120) notes that Sebastián's fleeing is a pretext to present a gallery of minor characters, a technique that links the novel to the Spanish picaresque tradition. In this existential narrative, the inevitability of Sebastián's capture leads us to transcend the protagonist's fear of death, and concentrate on his fear of life.

Both novel and film have a biblical epigraph that provides the title of the narrative.[1] The pistol shot, the sound of blowing wind, and the jerky dance shots of Antonio Gades that precede the epigraph in the film portend a lyrical dimension to the film that would parallel that of the novel, but the screen adaptation never captures the full poetic element of the original narrative. Aldecoa's novel is imbued with an often lyrical style: frequent use of similes, anaphora—usually having to do with places (Plaza Mayor . . .), time (At four o'clock), or about the easterly wind that gives the title to the narrative (45)—and with a symbolic structure in which each chapter corresponds to a day of the week that has a symbolic

---

[1]The biblical citation from the Old Testament's Book of Haggai v. 18 often refers to "blight" instead of "wind" in most English translations: "I struck all the works of your hands with blight." The *New International Version Study Bible* does clarify in a note that the blight was "probably caused by a scorching easterly wind," which corresponds to the Spanish rendition.

saint's name (Borau 27-28). Camus maintains this lyrical style of original in the filmic language of his adaptation.

The world of the protagonist Sebastián is imbued with elements of machismo: a bullfighter friend that he will go to see at a fair, the pistol that he shows off to friends at the bar, the girlfriend who suffers his verbal abuse and whose loyalty is unquestioned from the beginning of the narrative—"Yo voy contigo donde y cuando tú quieras"—(I'll go with you wherever and whenever you want)—and the liquor that leads to his tragedy. His girlfriend Lupe (María José Alfonso) warns him in their initial encounter in the bar, "No bebas mucho" (Don't drink very much), but it is to no avail. When drunk at a fair, Sebastián mocks a farmer who asks for a soda, saying, "¿Por qué no traga usted saliva?" (Why don't you swallow some spit?) The barman grabs Jacinto (José Manuel Martín), and Sebastián reacts: he grab a glass, breaks it and slashes him, and then flees. The mixture of alcohol, gypsy bravado, and fear lead to his tragic mistake: the fatal wounding of a civil guard.

The visual metonymy that Camus uses for the flight scene—shots of Sebastián's feet as he runs—and the frequent dissolves underscore the duration and the anguish of his flight, and add to the lyrical dimension of the film. Camus briefly uses rythmic montage to capture the spatial and psychological separation of the protagonist from his girlfriend: Sebastián's flight—as he asks for water from a shepherd, or throws his pistol into a river—contrasts with the interrogation of Lupe by the civil guard, and her departure to find Sebastián.

The theme of friendship and solidarity among the gypsies occurs in relation to several characters in the film. However, the film depicts this marginalized community in Spanish society as often reluctant to help a fugitive criminal for fear of repercussions. Sebastián takes the train to Madrid, and he asks his friend Francisco Vázquez (Fernando Sánchez Polak) for money. He is reluctant to make the loan, but offers a watch instead; his possession of four watches indicates that Sebastián's world is one of petty criminals. Vázquez's reaction when he discovers the reason for Sebastián's need for money is fear—"A mí me van a preguntar. Se enteran de todo" (They are going to ask me. They find out about everything)—and a metaphorical reference to the fate that dominates the atmosphere of the narrative: "Mal viento te ha traído, Sebastián" (A bad wind brought you here, Sebastián). Sebastián's pride and sense of protectiveness motivate him to return the watch to Vázquez, but the latter's sense of solidarity prompts him to give Sebastián money, after all. In Madrid, Sebastián seeks protection from other gypsies who are likewise reluctant to assist him: a dance teacher (a character not in the novel, tailored to Antonio Gades's background as a flamenco dancer), and a gypsy leader, Don Baldomero, who complains that helping Sebastián would make himself an accomplice. Ironically, the character in Madrid who shows the greatest sympathy to Sebastián is José Cabeda, the elderly man with whom he shares a room at the boarding house.

Camus downplays the sociopolitical component of this character who spent eighteen years in Franco's prisons (the reference to his old revolutionary friend Hernández is omitted), although the movie does maintain the politically charged language of the original when Cabeda tells Sebastián, "Por favor, llámeme compañero" (Please call me comrade cf. 112). Cabeda's poverty magnifies his generosity with Sebastián; his solidarity with the gypsy comes because he sees Sebastián as a victim—like himself—and knows from experience the difficult times that await him: "Lo vas a pasar muy mal, muchacho" (You're going to have a rough time, boy). As Sebastián eats alone, the footsteps heard off screen announce the arrival of a woman, and the camera pans up to show that Lupe has found him. Sebastián realizes that his life has inexorably changed, however, and that punishment awaits him—a punishment that he must face alone.

Sebastián continues to flee, and goes to Alcalá de Henares near Madrid, where he has family. Even blood ties, however, do not help the fugitive. His Uncle Manuel (Antonio Ferrandis) rejects him and provides both a deterministic analysis of Sebastián's situation as well as a fatalistic prognostication when Sebastián refuses to take a seat: "Siempre bravo como tu padre. Ahora lo vas a pagar" (Always filled with bravado like your father. Now you're going to pay). When his cousin closes the gate on Sebastián, the camera pans to the expelled fugitive, whose gesture of pounding the outside wall captures his inner despair. Sebastián continues his journey to the village of Cogolludo in order to see his mother (played by the most famous star of the Spanish screen in the 1930s and 1940s, Imperio Argentina).

The chiaroscuro lighting that Camus uses when Sebastián is seated on the floor of an abandoned building where he took shelter captures the inner division of the man who is tragically trapped. He leaves his girlfriend's name written four times on the wall—the repetition underscores the futility of the relationship and Sebastián's despair. His mother elicits sympathy for this marginalized segment of society—"Ay, lo que he sufrido. Los pobres tenemos que ir dónde nos lleva el hambre" (Oh, how I have suffered. We poor folk have to go wherever hunger takes us). Nevertheless, her son's confession, "Vengo con sangre" (I come with blood [on my hands]) prompts the same metaphorical rejection that Sebastián received before: "Que mal viento te ha traído" (A bad wind brought you), since she, too, fears that other members of her family will suffer the repercussions of his presence. It is too late for Sebastián to change, and he repeats his earlier behavior as he squanders the money that his mother generously gives him on booze.

In his drunken stupor, he recalls events from the past days. The montage sequence best approximates the first-person point of view of the original novel, where Sebastián's memories, imagination, and inner fears are interwoven with descriptions of cinematographic style (cf. 79, 113, 182). As Sebastián crosses the plaza, the high-angle shot of him falling at the foot of the Spanish flag poetically captures his surrender to the State. He turns himself in to the civil guard; the vital statistics of the prisoner together with the close up of his handcuffed hands metonymically capture the fate that has awaited him from the moment of his tragic act. The final shot of the civil guard's cap and cape hanging on the wall not only symbolizes the authority of the State that finally dominates, but also recalls (through the disembodiment of the hanging clothes) the very act that sealed his fate: the killing of the civil guard.

Although Quesada (414) believes that Camus did not

achieve the same degree of penetration of Sebastián's inner being as in the novel by Aldecoa, the screen adaptation of *Con el viento solano* is "a film of marvelous lyrical sweep" (Hopewell 68) and one of the better Spanish films of the mid-1960s. The film's social theme, and in particular, its treatment of a marginalized segment of Spanish society, helps mark a new direction for Spanish cinema. This is Camus's third film and it solidified his reputation as one of Spain's most promising young directors. It also is the first in a series of important film adaptations done by this director whose career develops in large measure by bringing important literary works to the screen.

The title of another Mario Camus film, *Los pájaros de Baden-Baden* (*The Birds of Baden-Baden*, 1976) comes from a saying by the Marqués de Valdivia, according to whom "Madrid in August, with money in one's pocket, was like Baden-Baden, the famous German spa" (Besas 252). The opening credits state that it is a "free version" of the short story by Ignacio Aldecoa. Set in contemporary Madrid during August, *Los pájaros de Baden-Baden* is a film about an amorous relationship that ends in tragedy because of the rigidity of social hierarchies. Elisa (Catherine Spaak), a thirty-year-old professor from an affluent Spanish family, first rejects the amorous propositions of her friend Ricardo (Carlos Larrañaga), who is taking advantage of the fact that his wife and family are on vacation. As part of her research, however, she visits the home of a photographer, Pablo (Frederick de Pascuale), and is attracted to him. When she visits a bookstore, Elisa looks for a copy of the book that Pablo is reading, and its title foreshadows the outcome of their own relationship: Pío Baroja's *Dos amores tardíos* ("Two Late Loves"; the adjective of the title can connote "too late," which is the case here). Whereas in the original narrative, Pablo rejects Elisa because he does not want to be tied down by her love, in the film, they become lovers, with Elisa providing a happiness for both the photographer and his son Andrés that they have not known for some time. When Elisa asks her uncle David (Andrés Mejuto) for advice about the relationship, we see the inevitable conflict between romance and the values of Spanish bourgeois society in the waning days of the Franco regime: "Tus padres pondrán el grito en el cielo . . . no es lo que ellos han soñado para ti" (Your parents will hit the roof . . . he is not what they dreamed of for you). Although the kind uncle sides with Elisa, advising her not to give him up, the die has already been cast. A party at David's house manifests Pablo's incompatibility with Elisa's world: the photographer gets into a fight with other guests. The summer comes to an end, as symbolized by the noisy traffic heard off screen, and the women who exchange stories of their respective amorous adventures of the summer. Elisa, who has grown apart from Pablo, returns to visit him, only to discover that he has committed suicide.The film ends with a close-up shot of Elisa in tears and an epilogue from Ernest Hemingway's *Death in the Afternoon*.

Script writers Camus and Manuel Merinero take considerable liberties with the original text, notably the consummation of Elisa and Pablo's relationship, and the later frustration and suicide of the photographer. Quesada (416) notes that while the short story centers on seemingly unimportant daily activities that shape the characters' lives into a gray existence, the film version includes more melodramatic elements and creates a narrative in which Camus possibly wanted to analyze the confrontation between two worlds, that of the powerful bourgeoisie and that of a frustrated and hopeless intellectual—worlds that can only come together under the special circumstances of a summer vacation.

Aldecoa's *Gran sol*, published in 1957, was brought to the screen by Ferrán Llagostera in 1989. The film received financial backing from six different producers mainly from Catalonia and the Basque country, and it was released in three different language versions, thus making it another example of regionalism in contemporary Spanish cinema. The narrative follows Aldecoa's concept of the novel, in which he wanted to make an epic out of the daily labor of humble jobs (Sanz Villanueva, 110). In this case, the work is fishing, as the novel tell the story of the men on the "Aril" who go to the Great Sole fishing bank off the coast of Ireland.

The solitary life of a sea captain: Luis Iriondo in Ferrán Llagostera's *Gran sol. Courtesy Centre Promotor de la Imatge S.A.*

For the average reader, one problematic element of Aldecoa's novel is the technical terminology and maritime jargon. Names of fish (pollack, cuckoo, carnival, spotted dogfish), birds (petrel, arrendajo = a type of jay), parts of the ship (amura = the beam at one eighth of its length from the bow), tools of the trade (scoop net or purse seine = a large fishing net weighted along the bottom), or even types of work on board (to veer around, to top a yard) are all unfamiliar to the non-sailor, and proved so daunting that one early reviewer, M. Fernández Almagro, even suggested that a vocabulary list would have been helpful at the end of the novel (Fernández Heliodoro 49). The film version of the narrative, however, obviates this problem due to the distinct nature of the sign systems of the two narratives. Film uses a broader range of signifiers (speech, image, etc.) and this combination can provide support and clarity. This is due to the fact, as Christian Metz comments, that the image discourse in film provides cinematographic specificity: "an image is not the

Monotony on board: Agustín González and Carlos Lucena in Ferrán Llagostera's *Gran sol. Courtesy Centre Promotor de la Imatge S.A.*

indication of something other than itself, but the pseudo-presence of the thing it contains" (76). Since we *see* the mass of swarming fish on deck, and do not need to match linguistic signifier with signified, or since the meaning of an enigmatic signifier, such as in the command, "Bring in the scoop net right away" (160) is visually contextualized, it is immediately understood.

In order to overcome the problem of viewing the fishermen, as does García Viño (155), as "insignificant characters" who constitute an "amorphous mass," Llagostera individualizes them from the beginning of the film by showing an "album" of stills over the names of the characters, together with the names of the actors. In the first chapter of the novel, Aldecoa narrates the last-minute preparation of the "Aril" (the actual ship used in the film was the "Lagunak") in port before sailing, as well as the bar scene in which the fishermen share the final moments with their families before departing. In the film version, Llagostera places this segment before the credits, thus formally giving this spatial component of the narrative a secondary or merely introductory status.

The sea as protagonist: Ferrán Llagostera's *Gran sol. Courtesy Centre Promotor de la Imatge S.A.*

The other spatial components of the narrative are the relative confinement of the ship, the vastness of the ocean, and a brief visit to the port city of Bantry, Ireland. The different zones of the ship's space correspond to its different working and living areas: the bridge, where captain Simón Orozco is at the helm or communicating by radio; the mess, where cook Macario Martín, el Matao, serves the food; the engine room, where machinist Domingo Ventura and mechanic Gato Rojo work amid an infernal noise;[2] the main deck, where fishermen Juan Ugalde, Venancio Artola, and the others separate the myriad fish from their catch; and the living quarters, below deck, where the men pass their hours in trivial conversations. The cinematographic version of the novel does not convey a sense of claustrophobia, however, since the visual space ranges from

---

[2]This infernal noise comes across much more vividly in the film version; other diegetic and nondiegetic elements of the soundtrack that enhance the film version of the narrative include the ominous beep of the horn of a large ship passing in the fog, and the accordion music that lends a salty tone to the film.

close-up shots of Paulino Castro's log or of Captain Simón Orozco's hand on the ship's wheel, to medium shots of the fishermen in the mess area, high-angle long shots of the men working on deck, or extreme long shots of the ship at sea. The descriptions of the ocean make it virtually another character in the novel, and the vastness, power, and mystery of the sea are augmented in the film, as the visual representation on the big screen of the eery and dangerous fog, or of the crashing waves and whipping rain leaves the viewer spellbound. Of course, this also caused difficulties in filming Gran sol; in one stormy sequence, the camera lens is covered with water.

Asís (142) notes that one of the main points of interest in the novel is the rich psychological portraits of the characters, and Llagostera captures the characters through a faithful rendition of the novel's dialogue—conversations about women, jokes among the men (when Macario complains that his mattress is wet because water is coming in, Afá retorts, "You must have peed your pants" [Aldecoa, Gran sol 37]), telling of tall tales, etc. Their actions, from their hard labor to close-ups of Macario tenderly wiping the brow of his dying captain, are also faithful to the original. However, perhaps the most telling paragraph in the novel that captures life at sea is the one that simply consists of the three-word sentence that cannot successfully be shown on screen: "Idleness on board" (54).

There is constant tension caused by the difficult life at sea that takes its toll on the sailors. Captain Orozco's long, seventeen-hour days at the helm are hard on an older man: in one scene, Orozco rubs his legs while he contemplates (in a voice-over): "I didn't used to get tired on the bridge. You have to be young, with strong legs." The sailors complain about their food and their work. El Matao feels unappreciated as ship's cook—"Being a cook on a ship is the worst thing in the world"—and Joaquín Sas's retort, "Your obligation is to do things well," (47) indicates an underlying tension that exists among the crew. Indeed, Sas is a bitter man who constantly complains about the captain, and refuses to do work unless directly ordered. Afá also complains about the captain: "The son of a gun doesn't let anyone rest" (66). The economic misery of the profession causes the subject of wages to surface time and again. The comment made in the initial bar scene in the film, "We might not even bring home enough to cover our expenses" and Joaquín Sas's final comment before the credits, "I hope we have luck," constitute a synthesis of Aldecoa's text in which luck can be both good and bad (15) and which serves as a foreshadowing of the captain's untimely death.

Even the respite that the sailors receive when they take to port in Bantry, Ireland, is not without difficulties. Drinking and dancing provide relief from their labors during their brief sojourn on land, but all is not happiness, as questions of self-esteem, a surfacing of old tensions, and a visit to the graves of Spanish sailors in the Bantry cemetery provide reminders of the difficulties of a sailor's life. The diversion for the sailors comes in the form of a local dance, and there is a shift from iterative narrative to singulative narrative when going from page to screen.[3] Although they are in port on a Saturday, and Matao comments, "habrá baile" (there will be a dance 110) and Paulino Castro later reiterates, "In the dance hall there is a party," 115), Aldecoa never shows the sailors dancing except in the iterative: "The women of Bantry, even the married women, used to dance with the sailors" (120). Llagostera, however, incorporates this narrative in the concrete, singulative form.from their labors during their brief Another slight liberty that he takes in this sequence is based on the dichotomy of showing and telling or scene and summary (Booth 8, 154). What begins on a humorous note—Matao's barking like a dog in the bar—takes a downward turn after Mr. O'Hallahan jokingly tells him that he could be in a circus. Matao's injured self-esteem seeks refuge in alcohol, and his drunkenness causes the running tension between the cook and Sas to surface. Sas's comment, "Stop barking, you mangy dog," leads to fisticuffs, and Llagostera shows the fight between the two sailors, whereas the novel only provides a summary after the fact: when the sailors return to the ship, Paulino Castro inquires what happened, and Afá responds, "Nothing important

---

[3]See Gerard Genette, *Narrative Discourse: An Essay in Method*, 114-116. For an application of Genette's theories to cinematographic narrative, see Kinder, "The Subversive Potential of the Pseudo-Iterative."

happened, skipper. A few punches. Nothing important" (117).
In both cases, Llagostera's decision to represent these in concrete
visual terms as singulative narrative serves to liven up the film
version of *Gran sol*.

The accident that causes Simón Orozco's death is the only
truly dramatic action in the story. The crew has difficulty
bringing in the net which is bulging with over a ton of fish. The
novel implies a certain sense of camaraderie and sacrifice that
seems absent in the film, since his death is the result of an
attempt to save a sailor from danger (179). Llagostera imbues
the film version with suspense in this scene as he shows the
overloaded net in a low angle shot, the straining cable in close-
up, and the breaking of the cable and crushing of the captain in
slow motion. Of course, there is a certain irony in the fact that
what Orozco had hoped to be his last voyage turns out
tragically to be so.

The predominant use of dissolves during the two cemetery
scenes—when Orozco visits the grave of his friend Zugasti, and
during the burial of Orozco at the end of the film—underscores
the tenuousness of the sailors' lives and the finality of their
deaths. Llagostera also underscores this theme in his change in
the dedication. Aldecoa's dedication, which comes before the
text of the novel, reads, "I dedicate this novel to the men who
work on the fishing banks that are between 48 and 56 degrees
north and between 6 and 14 west, the sea of the Great Sole" (7).
Llagostera's dedication, which fittingly appears at the end of
the film, is, "We dedicate this film to the men who have made
the sea their life, their work, their death." This film version
of Aldecoa's *Gran sol*, especially when seen on the big screen,
constitutes an epic vision that inspires a new respect for the sea
and its men.

Max Aub

Born in Paris of a German father, Max Aub (1903-1972) was active in the Republican governments during the 1930s. He collaborated with Malraux on the film *Sierra de Teruel*, and left Spain for exile with the film crew. After living briefly in France and Algeria, he fled to Mexico in 1942 and lived there until his death. Aub was a prolific writer, and many of his works have to do with the Spanish civil war. *Soldados* (*Soldiers*), the 1978 film by Alfonso Ungría, is an adaptation of Aub's *Las buenas intenciones* (*Good Intentions*, 1954).

Following the censorship that existed during the Franco regime, Spanish filmmakers began to challenge the official discourse created by the regime during almost four decades regarding the Spanish civil war. This is the first Spanish film to portray the point of view of the Republican side regarding the conflict. The film portrays the lives of Republican soldiers Agustín and Tellines, and two women in their lives, Remedios and Tula, both during and before the war. The novel follows a basically linear temporal progression from 1924 to 1939, and the civil war does not even appear until more than two-thirds into the narrative. Ungría significantly changed the narrative structure. He abandons linearity and begins in the middle of the war and then weaves a complex narrative through constant use of flashbacks and dream sequences. This important transformation in the narrative structure serves to focus our attention on the discourse itself, which Ungría, as Juan Hernández Les points out, elegantly carries out in this film ("Soldados" 25). The important transformation in narrative structure, together with the radical change in title, also serves to foreground the war.

The first protagonist, Agustín Amparo (Ovidi Montllor), is a Republican soldier who enters a small town with his comrades, only to be ambushed by local Nationalists. The point of view is immediately established in the film in this opening sequence, since the low-angle shots of the second-story windows, where the shooting that is killing many of the Republican soldiers originates, places the spectator at Agustín's side, in danger. After his escape from the ambush, a close-up of his eyes triggers the first flashback of the film. In a luxurious setting, a woman named Remedios informs us that her child was sired by Agustín Amparo, but we discover that the culprit was the lecherous Agustín père. In order not to endanger his ailing mother's health, the young Agustín offers to marry Remedios, and subsequent flashbacks develop the contrast between the moral character of the father and the son: while the father continues to attempt to seduce Remedios, the younger Agustín maintains a chaste relationship with her, treating her with kindness and tenderness. Remedios testifies to her husband's essential goodness in her good-bye note in which she says that he is a "most decent person." However, this love triangle constitutes an untenable situation for Agustín, and he suffers deep emotional problems because of it. One evening Remedios finds her husband crying on the floor near the entrance to their home, a scene artfully photographed by José Luis Alcaine with the camera at floor level to better capture Agustín's inner agony. After suffering from sexual impotence with a prostitute, Agustín manifests his subconscious anguish and hostility toward Remedios in a dream sequence in which he crucifies her. The discovery of the note announcing her departure is an existential limit point for Agustín, and in the next scene, as his tuxedo-dressed father returns home from an evening escapade, Agustín kills him with one shot to the head. Another male protagonist who has a violent past is Tellines, who after being rejected by gangster boss Don Rodolfo in his request for a job, decides to shoot up the nightclub where the boss does business. Tellines must later escape from Don Rodolfo's men who seek vengeance, and during the war he is a comrade in arms with Agustín.

Unlike these two characters, a third Republican soldier, Javier, brings an ideological dimension to the film. He is a Communist who meets and has an affair with Pilar, a somewhat older woman who runs a bookstore. Like Agustín, Javier is basically a decent person: after his first night with Pilar, he leaves her a note which says, "No soy un chulo" (I'm not a bastard). However, he is caught up in the historical circumstances, and after political discussions with some anarchists, he decides to leave for the front. This decision

A new perspective on the Civil War: Ovidi Montllor and Francisco Algora in Alfonso Ungría's *Soldados. Courtesy Filmoteca Nacional.*

devastates Pilar, who, in a fit of rage, kills her daughter, and ends up in an insane asylum. Javier's failure on a personal level mirrors that on the ideological level. Arriving for active duty with an armload of books results in a sharp rebuke on the part of his captain—"No aguantamos propaganda de ninguna clase" (We won't stand for propaganda of any type)—which the officer combines with the threat of a firing squad. On the front-line, amidst a pouring rain with persistent gunfire, Javier admits that the concept of revolution makes no sense there.

Like Remedios, who, after leaving Agustín goes to a brother to seek employment, the other female protagonist, Tula, also becomes a prostitute. Director Ungría interweaves the narrative strands of these characters' lives as they meet on the frontline and try to escape the Nationalist troops. As they attempt to cross a river, Tula desperately attempts to return to the water's edge to retrieve her missing treasure, but her friends restrain her. A close-up of her laughing face triggers the flashback that provides us with information about her past. As a young girl, her parents inform her that she will marry "master Vicente," but the relationship proves to be unsatisfactory. One night the pregnant Tula discovers her husband in bed with a prostitute, and she rushes out of her husband's house into a storm. After the resulting miscarriage, Tula abandons "el señorito Vicente" with the declaration, "Me marcho, pero no voy a morirme de hambre" (I'm leaving, but I'm not going to die of hunger). The following scenes artfully show how she kept her word: a brothel setting with close-ups bordered by dissolves of feminine hands which contain money or which place a pearl necklace into a jewelry box. This narrative information, taken in syntagmatic relationship with Tula's laughter at the river's edge, gives that wartime scene an acute sense of the absurd. After the dissolve following the brothel scene, the three protagonists are sleeping in an open field, an image which symbolizes their passive acceptance of their fate—their defeat. In their struggle to survive, however, Agustín kills a threatening soldier whom he later identifies as a fellow Republican. His reaction to this incident is both verbal and non-verbal: not only does he exclaim, "Estamos todos locos" (We're all crazy), but he abandons his rifle, a gesture that epitomizes the symbolism of his despair and of the absurd. His verbal response echoes Tula's comment from her first encounter with Agustín, which also manifests the absurdity of their situations. When Agustín fails to understand something that she says, Tula responds, "Eso es lo que pasa, que nadie entiende nada" (That is what is happening, nobody understands anything). When the three friends reach Alicante, port of departure for the Republican soldiers who are fleeing the onslaught of the Nationalist troops, Agustín decides that he will return to Madrid.

Ungría adds narrative information that heightens the sense of disillusionment and loss in each of the protagonists, and he takes considerable liberty with the end of the novel. In the film, Agustín follows Tula's recommendation of a brothel for shelter in the capital, and this leads him to a chance reuniting with Remedios and the consummation of their relationship. The length of this scene—with a change in camera angle in a tracking shot from the foot to the side of the bed—is justified by its importance in the film narration. It marks a contrast with both his earlier unhappiness and his impotency, and it forebodes (recalling the French concept of "la petite morte") his subsequent death. After the Nationalist soldiers burst into the brothel and capture him, they take him on a "stroll" and assassinate him. Both the sexual encounter and the assassination manifest how Ungría visually expands on the terse, connotative prose of Aub. The novelist's description of the sexual act is simply "Cumplieron, ella sabía su oficio" (They were fulfilled, she knew her profession, 273), and the change in this scene is clearly a manifestation of the new freedom allowed by the abolishment of censorship. After Agustín's arrest, he was to be taken to prison, and we learn of his assassination only through the comment, "No llegaron" (They didn't arrive, 280). The penultimate shot of the film, a close-up of the dead Agustín's head with the camera at ground level, parallels the earlier crying scene. The form of assassination of the prisoner also culminates the wanton violence portrayed throughout the film, such as the initial assassination of the village mayor and the killing of the civilian driver when the Republican soldiers commandeer an automobile.

The characters all move from pre-war situations of frustration and failure to end-of-war situations of defeat and death. The despair and frustration portrayed in the film are also the result of the social and artistic climate in which Ungría worked. He has stated that this tremendous frustration was the result of having lost not just any war, but the Spanish civil war (Rentero, "Entrevista" 45). Although Ungría has referred to Soldados as simply a melodrama which manifests the "impossible search for goodness" (Cine español 281), Soldados is an excellent film on many counts. Superb acting by Ovidi Montllor, brilliant photography by José Luis Alcaine, and excellent direction by Alfonso Ungría add to its significance as the first Spanish film about the Spanish civil war to adopt the Republican point of view.

Manuel Barrios

Andalusian novelist Manuel Barrios (b. 1924) often lyrically portrays life in southern Spain. Roberto Fandiño directed the screen adaptation of his *La espuela* (*The Spur*, 1965) in 1976. Although the novel contains numerous references to spurs worn by Andalusian gentlemen, the meaning of the title is more metaphorical. The wealthy landowner and protagonist, Enrique Medina, explains, "Do you know why that last drink that you have at a gathering with friends is called a spur? Precisely because it's not really the last one, the last one for ever, but it could be" (27).

The novel presents a portrait of Enrique as the archetypical Andalusian "señorito," the wealthy aristocrat who loves wine, women, and song, and who acts like a feudal lord. Quesada (403) notes that the novel is a sort of roman à clef, in which some of the minor characters, such as the cook and the waiter at the famous "El Rinconcillo" tavern in Seville, have their real names. The novel has an interesting structure: it is a frame tale, with an introduction and an epilogue in italics in which the conversation of two civil guards opens and closes the narrative and provides crucial comments for its interpretation; it contains a narrative of the hours between midnight and eight in the morning on New Year's Day, with multiple flashbacks to before the Spanish civil war; and each chapter has a different main character who provides a new perspective on the life of Enrique. We see the landowner from the point of view of his son Luis, his right-hand man Manolo, his wife María Isabel, his lover Maruja, his foreman Lucas, his priest, Father Ignacio, and his physician, Dr. Avila. Each character provides new information about Enrique, and at the end of the novel, the reader must decide what type of a man he was.

Both Enrique's womanizing and social dominance are evident from the beginning of the film. At a party in an Andalusian wine cellar, he steals a younger man's girlfriend. Part of his erotic foreplay is to pour wine over her naked breasts, a ritual that repeats in the first flashback of the film: on his wedding night Enrique (Javier Escrivá) "baptizes" both his wedding bed and his bride María Isabel (Claudia Gravi) before he carries her in his arms and throws her on it. María

Isabel's voice-over speaks of the turbid events of that night when her illusions were transformed to despair. Her downward gaze connotes her shame and unhappiness, and the continued voice-over confirms her sense of solitude and humiliation. María Isabel later prohibits Enrique from entering their bedroom, and here the feudal lord has no dominion. Enrique finds other outlets for his sexual urges, however: when surveying his lands on horseback, he sees a girl cutting asparagus, and offers her a job at the ranch house. His son Luis (Mario Pardo) drives by on his motorcycle and sees his father's horse; his discovery of Enrique in flagrante delicto causes revulsion that is more on social than personal terms. Although Enrique defends himself saying, "Y tú, ¿no lo has hecho alguna vez?" (And haven't you done it yourself some time?), Luis denies having done so, and reproaches his father saying, "Yo no me aprovecho de nadie ofreciéndole trabajo" (I do not exploit anybody by offering them work).

Luis's negative response to his father is initially ambiguous, but it soon becomes clear that Fandiño grasps the mere allusion to Luis's homosexuality in the novel (124-125) and transforms it into an important narrative thread. Fandiño changes Lucas's comment concerning Luis from Barrios's work, "no anda muy derecho que digamos" (Let's just say he isn't exactly right, 171) to the much more blatant insult that he is "delicadilla" (very delicate—using the feminine form together with the diminutive to connote a condescending attitude toward gays), which elicits a violent response from Enrique. The landowner follows his son one night, and catches Luis and his boyfriend in flagrante delicto. Since homosexuality is not tolerated by the culture of machismo that Enrique represents, this relationship is doomed: on a hunting expedition, Enrique shoots and kills his son's lover, making it look like an accident. This scene substitutes for the episode of a heterosexual nature in the novel in which Enrique lets a young man who was courting one of his girlfriends drown (67, 107). It might seem odd that in the film version Luis's homosexuality receives the approval of Father Ignacio, given the Vatican's current stand on such matters. However, the overall treatment of sexuality in the film manifests the new freedom in Spain following the death of Franco. The film certainly includes nudity, and Quesada (404) notes that Fandiño augments the voyeurism of the episode in which Lucas spies María Isabel swimming in the reservoir, but the film seems to want to go beyond *destape* and condemn old sexual mores in favor of new ones.

The cinematographic adaptation of the novel contains several other differences from the original. Since Fandiño eliminates the pre-civil war episode with Lucas from the novel, it weakens the motivation for the foreman's desire for revenge against the landowner. This revenge consists of informing Enrique's wife of her husband's many infidelities, thus resulting in María Isabel not only terminating her physical relationship with her husband, but also making him a cuckold. Another transformation in the film regards the circumstances surrounding Enrique's death. Both versions contain the prognosis of major heart problems, but instead of poisoning himself at his lover's house, which provides a new meaning to the title and a harsh criticism of Enrique's way of life, in the film version he suffers angina at a party and goes to his lover's apartment to find her in bed with another man. The attempt to cover up the circumstances of his death results in Luis criticizing the shallow hypocrisy of his parents by exclaiming, "Pero qué clase de gente sois?" (But what kind of people are you?).

The structure of the novel leads to a Cervantine sense of perspectivism. The reader's negative opinion of Enrique begins to change with the ideas of Father Ignacio (134ff.), who presents the landowner in a positive light. The frame tale structure confirms the importance of perspectivism, when in the epilogue the civil guards leave some gypsies alone at the insistence of the older guard, who says "who knows if someone is good or bad?" Unfortunately, Fandiño loses this important element of the narrative in his film version. Although he keeps the temporal structure with multiple flashbacks, they turn out to be more confusing in the film than in the novel. At a time when regionalism in Spanish cinema was reappearing (Antoni Ribas's Catalan film *La ciutat cremada* was released the same year), Fandiño's attempt to portray Andalusia and to make the film version of this narrative commercially appealing was not successful.

Juan Benet

The novels of Juan Benet (1927-1994) are among the most important works in contemporary Spanish letters. His creation of a Faulkneresque provincial setting "Región," begins in his first novel, *Volverás a Región* (1968) and continues through his *Herrumbrosas lanzas* (1983). Since most of his novels are "dense, obscure, and quite hermetic" (Sanz Villanueva 165), it is perhaps not surprising that the only one to be converted to the screen is *El aire de un crimen* (*The Air of a Crime*, 1980), which director Antonio Isasi adapted in 1988. Although the title points to a narrative of the detective genre, both the novel and the film transcend traditional generic motifs.

There is no detective of the traditional type here. Although Alewy (67) calculates that only 10 to 20 percent of sleuths in the genre are official police detectives, the rest being amateurs. Winks (7) notes that in contemporary manifestations of the genre 'the detective is no longer an amateur . . . [nor] wholly of the middle or upper class" but could be a Navajo, an Australian aborigine, a male or female homosexual, or other marginal figure. In this case, it is an army captain with the help of a busybody former exile from the Spanish civil war who unwittingly unravel the mystery.

The action is set in Benet's imaginary Spanish city of Bocentellas in 1956, and it begins with the discovery of a crime. The high-angle shot of a barefoot man wearing a straw hat who is sitting with his back against the fountain in the square represents a certain mystery, since neither the peasant who comes to get water from the fountain nor the tavern owner recognizes him. The stranger is not merely sleeping off drunkenness, however, but has been shot dead. The information from the police report that the bullet entered his neck and exited the crown of his head is a narrative detail that later proves crucial to the plot, since as Kermode points out, 'although all [narratives] have hermeneutic content, only the detective story makes it preeminent" (181). The inability to reach the judge creates the problem of what to do with the corpse, which is now giving off a terrible stench. As the locals play dominos at the bar, they discuss who the dead man might be; a shallow-focussed close-up of a bottle of liquor with a lizard at the bottom is a key visual image since it provides a solution to the problem of the corpse. They take it to a wine cellar and submerge it in a huge earthen jar of wine in order to preserve it. That close-up also hints at a future event, since the image of Captain Medina (Chema Mazo) occupies the right-hand side of the frame, visually linking him with the liquor bottle in the left foreground.

When the judge finally arrives, they lift the cadaver from the wine jar; a boot falls off its foot into the wine, and close-up shots of the men in the wine cellar looking at each other with astonishment—together with the close-up shot of the dead man's feet and the voice off screen that proclaims, "Lleva botas" (He's wearing boots)—all underscore the element of surprise, since the original cadaver was barefoot. This revelation constitutes a narrative element that Erlich (178) calls 'deliberately impeded form" that is so crucial to detective fiction, which Porter defines as "an art of narrative that promotes the reader's pleasure through the calculation of effects of suspense on the way to a surprise denouement" (28). The forensic description of the new cadaver (the gunshot to the neck) corresponds to that of the old, so the mystery is heightened. Not only are there two murder victims, but the similarity of their deaths connotes a relationship between the two.

Director Isasi slowly reveals the mystery through the use of a flashback to fifty-three days earlier. This narrative thus manifests a prime aspect of detective fiction, which 'is preoccupied with the closing of the logico-temporal gap that separates the present of the discovery of crime from the past that prepared it" (Porter 29).

Medina leads a double life that causes him to be caught in the web that is slowly revealed to be spun by the criminals. This double life consists of his strict military comportment on the one hand, and the fulfilling of his sexual appetite on the other. The film narrative hints at this motif early on: as a truckload of soldiers passes the Bar Doria, prostitutes blow them kisses, and the close-up of Medina looking back—together with a later point of view low-angle shot of the lighted upper window in the bar—connotes a gaze of desire. When the captain visits the pensión in the town of Macerta dressed as a civilian, the landlady addresses him as Señor Vázquez, but it is not until later in the narrative that the importance of this element becomes clear. Medina has fallen in love with La Chiqui (Maribel Verdú), a prostitute at the bar, but the girl is merely a trap to keep the captain from blocking criminal activities in Bocentellas. These activities consist of shady real estate purchases by the representatives of a Señor Chaflán, as well as the fleeing of Luis Barceló and his friend Ventura Palacios from the military garrison. The fugitives can only elude capture and escape through the rugged terrain with the help of Amaro (Germán Cobos), but the violation of Amaro's retarded daughter by the fugitives causes him to seek vengeance: the abduction and violation of La Chiqui, as well as the murder of Chaflán's representative. After Amaro kills him, Amaro's helper asks his boss if he can have the dead man's shoes. Two close-up shots during this scene reveal important narrative information: the first is the shot of Amaro putting the pistol to the blond man's neck and pulling the trigger; the second is of the dead man's bare feet as they throw him across the back of a mule. These shots provide important pieces of the narrative puzzle, since these physical character- istics are taken in syntagmatic relationship with the earlier portion of the narrative and clarify the identity of the cadaver from the opening sequence.

The final segment of the film is the most interesting, both in terms of the revelation of the mysteries and the way in which director Isasi reveals them. The narrative technique involves a repetition of key previous segments, but their meaning is changed either because of the syntagmatic relation with other narrative information, or because Isasi slightly changes their presentation. The repetition of the captain's visit to the pensión (in the guise of Señor Vázquez) adds the accusation that La Chiqui is pregnant by him, thus closing the trap on the captain. Isasi repeats the earlier sequence when Medina returned to the barracks from the manhunt for the escaped soldiers, and found a note on his door—"Capitán. No se meta en camisas de once varas. No le conviene. Un amigo"

(Captain. Don't get involved. It won't be good for you. A friend). He then adds the repercussion of this action: Medina visits Coronel Olivera (Francisco Rabal), who tells him that he has fallen into the trap and is covered with shit. While Olivera insists that Medina must abandon his military career, the coronel's constant dunking of his pastries takes on a new meaning as the montage sequence associates the pastry going into the cup with the dead man being lowered into the wine jar; the interspersed close-ups of the captain connote the germination of an idea, and Medina puts his pistol on Olivera's neck and fires. The close-up of the the bullet hole in the crown of his head matches that of the earlier victim, and provides Medina with a way out of his crime. A brief scene of the captain cutting the rope that held the first body leads to the repetition of the key earlier scene in which the second cadaver is discovered.

Now, however, Isasi reveals more information. In the first sequence, the viewer could not identify the cadaver, since when he is laid on the floor, the view of him was only from above his head, and when the doctor examines him, the dead man's face is discreetly blocked by the arm of another man. In this scene, we see the coronel's face not only as they lower him to the floor, but the camera location changes from the side of the doctor (in the earlier scene) to in back of the doctor, and from the earlier profile of the man who lights the match, to a close-up of the dead coronel. The final scenes—Captain Medina dictating the report that the coronel was missing, and a close-up of Medina with a subtle smirk on his face as he watches the burial of the "unknown" dead body—connote that he has successfully carried out his crime. Porter states that the traditional detective story "moves from mystery to solution and from crime to punishment or, if not to punishment, at least to arrest" (Porter 85) and that "works in the genre always take a stand in defense of the established societal order. . . . The deep ideological constant, therefore, is built into the action of investigation. The classic structuring question is always 'Whodunit' and secondarily, how will justice be done" (Porter 125). *El aire de un crimen* transcends these classic generic elements, and Navajas (228) notes that the novel's rupture from the genre occurs because the enigma is not resolved.

Clues in detective fiction are often discovered by sheer chance, and this is the case here. Medina's discovery of certain key information throughout is fortuitous, as it is revealed to him by minor characters: the captain learns from Ignacia (Rafaela Aparicio) that Chaflán and Coronel Olivera are friends (and therefore partners in crime) when she announces that she has sold her land to them, and the reaction shot of Medina shows his astonishment; the busybody Fayón (Fernando Rey), who makes it a point to overhear conversations, informs him about the visit to the coronel by the madam from the Bar Doria, thus confirming another thread of the criminal web. But ultimately, the spider is Medina, as this "detective" becomes the criminal in a marvellous twist on the detective genre in a film version by Antonio Isasi that is one of the best examples of its type in Spanish cinema.

Juan Antonio Cabezas

Juan Antonio Cabezas is an author from the northern region of Asturias, and he was a war correspondent for the Republic, which caused him to be incarcerated by the Franco regime for several years. His novel *La montaña rebelde* (*Rebel Mountain*, 1960) was adapted to the screen in 1972 by Ramón Torrado. The setting for the narrative is the northern Spanish region of Asturias in 1936, the first year of the Spanish civil war. This story of jealousy and vengeance is set among the beautiful mountains of that region. Here, the normal lover's triangle is expanded so that Rita is the object of three men's desire: her boyfriend Mingo, a local "vaqueiro" or cowhand; Abel, a physician who comes to the town of his forebears to practice medicine; and Tomás, the leader of a group of anarchists who prowl the mountains. A few months after the outbreak of the war, Abel must serve at a military hospital at the front. Tomás and his group take over the town, and the leader wants to have Rita. In spite of the fact that she marries, Tomás accosts her; Mingo defends Rita, killing the anarchist with his own pistol, and the other anarchists then take him away to be tried. However, following an attempted escape, the truck in which they are taking Mingo crashes, and it seems that everyone is killed. After the war, Abel convinces Rita that they should marry. Shortly thereafter, however, Mingo appears (surprise!) after being in France. Instead of seeking vengeance, he withdraws, tearfully telling the village priest, "No quiero tener otro crimen sobre mi alma" (I don't want to have another crime on my soul).

Filmed in the waning years of the Franco regime, it is not surprising that this film, set with the background of the Spanish civil war, portrays the enemies of Franco's nationalists (here, the anarchists, embodied in their evil leader, Tomás) in a negative light. Quesada (319) notes that the film did not enjoy success at the box office, and that its only saving grace is the beautiful scenery of Asturias.

Luis de Castresana

Basque novelist Luis de Castresana's *El otro árbol de Guernica* (*Guernica's Other Tree*) obtained the National Prize for Literature in 1968, and the following year, director Pedro Lazaga adapted it for the screen with a script written by Pedro Masó and Florentino Soria. The title obliquely refers to the tree of Guernica that has important historical significance. The principal reason that Franco chose this Basque town as the target of a bombing attack (which inspired Picasso's famous painting) is that when Spanish kings assumed the throne, they had to travel to Guernica to swear under an ancient tree that they would uphold local laws. Guernica thus was a symbol of regional autonomy in Spain. This movie deals with the problem of child refugees from the Basque country during the Spanish civil war. The narration centers on two young children, Santi and Begoña Celaya Fernández, whose parents decide to send them to Belgium from their native Bilbao for safety's sake. The film version is a faithful illustration of the novel. It maintains the fundamental narrative events of the original in the same chronological order.

As in other films about the civil war, children here perform the function of the ingenue who asks the difficult question of the adults, "¿Por qué hacen los hombres la guerra?" (Why do men wage war?) The occasion here is a beach scene after a boat delivers the children to Belgium, and one of them discovers a helmet from World War I in the sand. Santi poses the question to Don Segundo, the man who is escorting the children to their temporary new homes. His response, "Las guerras vienen muchas veces sin saber por qué" (Wars often come without knowing why), glosses over the reason for the conflict and constitutes an overly facile answer. Although one could justify it in the context of the narrative—young children cannot indeed always understand the complexities of the adult world—it seems to follow a pattern whereby certain Nationalist directors such as Lazaga dismiss the reasons for the war. The recurring motif that the war will end soon also appears on more than one occasion in this film; first, during the emotional departure of the children from their parents, and then at a point in the narration one year later when the children receive a letter from their parents in Spain. Sound effects of sirens and bombs off screen sometimes accompany the voice-over of the mother reading the letters, belying the hopes of the civilians.

The majority of the narrative deals with the children's relationship with their new environment. Although Begoña is content with her new family, Santi has difficulty accepting the kindness and hospitality of his hosts, the Defout family. When they give him a new bicycle and sign the card from "mamá" and "papá," Santi's negative outburst and crossing out those words of kindness cause an equally immature reaction in Madame Defout, and the young Spaniard must move to a boarding school. His life there also has its trials and tribulations, mainly due to the fact that Santi has confrontations with school personnel, Belgians that are portrayed with almost xenophobic zeal. When a small Spanish boy named Eusebio suffers from enuresis because of his psychological suffering, Madame Jacob calls him a "cochino español" (Spanish pig), to which Santi retorts, "Usted es una cochina belga" (You are a Belgian pig) in his defense. Madame Jacob's mean character surfaces again when Montse, Santi's little Catalan friend, has an altercation with a Belgian girl over a sweater. When Madame Jacob unjustly takes the sweater from Montse, Santi seeks refuge and solidarity with the other Spanish children under the giant tree in the school courtyard which reminds them of the famous tree of their homeland that provides the title of the movie. Santi then leads a successful protest to regain the sweater and their rights.

Even the Belgian children do not escape the xenophobic view of the director. The only one that is accepted by Santi and the other Spanish children is André, who, in order to gain the full confidence of the group, must become "Hispanified" through the name change of Andrés.

The worst confrontation between Belgians and Spaniards, however, occurs in Santi's history class when the Belgian professor lectures about how Spaniards killed Indians in the new world and makes the condescending remarks, "los españoles han sido, son y serán salvajes" (Spaniards have been, are, and will be savages) and "¿Qué esperas de un pueblo cuya fiesta nacional son los toros?" (What do you expect from a country whose national pastime is bullfighting?) Although Santi has an immediate reaction—calling the professor a liar and a coward—he later decides to escape the boarding school, not without leaving the proclamation "Viva España" written on the blackboard. This provides the opportunity for some brief "touristy" shots of Brussels, but luck would have it that the very next morning Santi sees that the headlines of the newspaper *Le matin* proclaim the end of the war in Spain. At this juncture, Lazaga includes the only other documentary footage in the film, that of Nationalist troops triumphantly marching into Madrid. The children return by boat to Spain, and the last scene contains a long shot of the port of Bilbao and the children singing on their joyous return to their homeland. This scene represents the only variation from the original narrative, in which the children return home by train.

Although the film seems to provide a more circular narrative structure and a more complete sense of resolution than the original narrative, no mention is made of the difficult times that lay ahead for these children of Basque and Catalan Republicans, and an epigraph that dedicates the film to all Spaniards attempts to strike a conciliatory note. Gubern points out the Nationalistic bias of the film, as it equates "Spanish" with Francoism and makes the countries that gave asylum to Republican children seem like places of sequestration (*1936* 150). *El otro árbol de Guernica* has problems with the script, but director Lazaga was able to obtain solid performances from the child actors, which help bolster the quality of the film.

Juan Luis Cebrián

Juan Luis Cebrián, director of Spain's most important daily newspaper, *El país*, published his first novel in 1986, and *La rusa* (*The Russian Woman*, 1987) is director Mario Camus's cinematographic adaptation of it. The narrative represents the period of political transition from dictatorship to democracy in Spain, and it interweaves sociopolitical problems of the time—negotiations with the Basque terrorist group, ETA, and the question of who is really in control of the country—with the personal life of the protagonist, Juan Altamirano (Didier Flamand), a political advisor on foreign affairs.

The voice-over with which the film begins lends an air of fatality to the narrative; Begoña (Angeli Van Os), now twenty-five, is not sorry for her relationship with Juan, since, as she says, "Jamás pretendí hacerle daño. Jamás lo hice (I never intended to harm him. I never did). (The transnational casting here occurs in many contemporary Spanish films as an attempt to increase their marketability in other European countries; this is sometimes a stipulation imposed by European producers in exchange for their financial support.) The crosscut close-ups of Juan and Begoña at a Socialist congress in Paris connote the beginning of the emotional relationship between the forty-year-old politician and the twenty-year-old student, and Juan's statement during a television interview that Spanish democracy is not strong connotes a fragility that will affect the personal, as well as the societal. Juan's pursuit of Begoña through the streets of the French capital contrasts with the allusive and cool relationship with his wife, Eva (Muntsa Alcañiz): Juan's personal life, his political ideals, and his work are all tarnished and empty. The young leftist, Begoña, represents a renewal for Juan, both sexually and ideologically; although Begoña manifests her independence and initially rejects the apartment that Juan gets for them—"No vivimos juntos, muchachito. Mi vida es solo mía" (We don't live together, sonny. My life is mine alone)—the only accoutrement in the apartment (the painting that she had admired in the gallery) convinces her of Juan's love.

Their trip to the gallery was marred, however, by the

Personal and sociopolitical problems intertwined : Didier Flamand and Angeli Van Os in Mario Camus's *La rusa. Courtesy Pedro Maso Producciones Cinematográficas, S. A.*

discovery that a man in the distance was following them, thus introducing an element of suspense in the narrative. The double plot twist that ensues leaves both the protagonist and the viewer in doubt: the pursuer turns out to be friendly and the beloved may be an enemy, as Juan's boss asserts when he gives him a confidential folder containing photos of him kissing Begoña, who—according to Juan's supervisor—is a KGB spy.

The narrative threads now begin to form a web, as Juan's personal life, his work, and national security issues all become intertwined. He adamantly rejects the allegations regarding Begoña, as well as his own victimization as a target of counter-espionage: "La libertad ya es norma en este jodido país" (Freedom is the norm now in this fucking country). Juan, however, is not free, since his search of his apartment resulted in the discovery of a microphone. His boss's later inquiry, "¿A quién pertenece el poder en este país?" (Who does power belong to in this country?) is the rhetorical question that constitutes the essence of the dilemma. Who is spying on Juan? He is involved with secret negotiations with members of ETA, and following his second encounter with his contact, the latter is assassinated by a hit-and-run automobile. Who carried out the assassination? And who will be their next victim? The letter written by a prodemocratic policeman that Juan obtains from a journalist friend tightens the web, as he accuses ultrarightist police as being the hitmen. If this is so, then virtually no one can be trusted. The fact that the assassination did not make the news means that some type of censorship is at work, even under the newly democratic system. Juan's attempt to escape everything by driving to a deserted beach with Begoña is only a transitory hiatus; the zoom in to the image of Picasso's *Guernica* following the dissolve that ends this sequence connotes a return to the theme of victimization on the political plane.

Juan is caught between his desire to leave with Begoña and his loyalty to his ideals and his mission. Begoña, however, always more independent, does depart, leaving behind the curt note, "No me busques. No me encontrarás" (Don't look for me. You won't find me). The discovery of evidence that the extreme Right killed the Basque negotiator not only puts Juan himself at risk, but allows Cebrián (through his journalist character) to echo the theme of the fratricidal conflict that haunts Spain: because of those who speak in the name of the past, "todavía hay guerras santas" (there are still holy wars). Juan inevitably falls victim to the assassins bullets, bullets that are of the caliber associated with ETA so as to shift the blame for the crime. Begoña's reappearance after a sojourn in Cuba allows her to see Juan one final time before his death.

The film follows the original novel quite faithfully, indeed too faithfully for critics such as Norberto Alcover, who believes that the script for *La rusa* lacked "soul."("*La rusa*" 227). The technical quality of the film has many merits, as Bayón notes of the love scenes that are meticulously filmed with "spectacularly framed shots" (138), yet the movie leaves him with a sense of coldness—a film whose themes demanded much more action than provided (138). The nature of the male protagonist is crucial in this regard, since his relative passivity is not only "an expression of a deep inner mortality" (Alcover 229), but because Juan Altamirano is not a professional spy or detective who, with cunning and bravery, actively solves a mystery, but merely someone with good intentions serving his country who has gotten into this "game" over his head. (Juan's realization of his predicament occurs after the assassination of his Basque contact, and his reaction is to vomit.) Like many of the other postmodern thriller/detective narratives in contemporary Spain, *La rusa* asks many questions and provides few answers.

Camilo José Cela

Camilo José Cela (b. 1916) is perhaps Spain's most internationally known contemporary novelist by virtue of his 1989 Nobel Prize for literature. Cela made a splash on the literary scene in postwar Spain with the publication of his first novel, *La familia de Pascual Duarte* (*The Family of Pascual Duarte*, 1942). The almost scandalous style of this work, which is referred to as *tremendismo* for its tremendous, shocking violence, contributed to Cela's immediate fame. Although Cela's novelistic output is now into its fifth decade, only two of his classic early works have been adapted for the screen. Ricardo Franco's film *Pascual Duarte* (1975), the cinematographic version of Cela's first novel, won several important awards, including the best actor award at the Cannes Film Festival in 1976 to José Luis Gómez for his portrayal of Pascual. Cela's 1951 novel *La colmena* (*The Hive*) was adapted in 1982 by Mario Camus.

Director Franco believed that *La familia de Pascual Duarte* was a very "literary" novel and decided to seek out the narrative line and discard its literary elements (Hernández Les and Gato 199). The elimination of the transcriber and the literary framework of the novel causes a shift in Pascual's character, since, as Vernon (93) notes, without Pascual's (written) words that explain his actions, he is used by Franco as a "physical eyewitness and narrative center" and that "with the elimination of any introspective, psychological motivation or justification of Pascual's actions, the more contextual, historical explanation comes to the foreground."

Pascual Duarte portrays the life of its protagonist, a poor peasant living in Extremadura in the years prior to the civil war, as he is caught up in webs of violence both of his own making and of society's making. The chronology of the film narrative begins in 1937 with Pascual arrested for homicide, and then a series of flashbacks alternate the narrative between the past—one of Pascual as a youth, with the rest as a young man in the 1930s—and the present of his incarceration, and finally, his execution. Kenworthy (56-57) details the change in the chronology in the transformation from page to screen: in the

60

latter version, Pascual commits his crimes not in 1922, but in 1931.

The first flashback commences with a young Pascual reading from the Bible to a priest: "Allí viviréis dichosos y sueltos y llamó Abrahán a los suyos . . ." (You will live happy and free there, and Abraham called his family members . . .). The fact that the flashback occurs while being taken away as a prisoner in an army truck conflates the importance of the church and the army in Pascual's life (Santoro 96). The choice of this text is significant: the script to the film indicates that this text shows "the concept of the promised land and of homeland . . . and the element of violence, even family violence" (Martínez Lázaro 35). Critic Hernández Les points out that "the biblical reference to the sacrifice of Abraham serves as a foreshadowing of a possible interpretation of the character. Pascual sacrifices, but he is also sacrificed" ("Pascual Duarte" 30).

The concept of land becomes one of the fundamental themes of the film because of the sociopolitical element with which director Franco imbues his cinematographic text. This begins in the sequence in which Pascual's father, Esteban, reads from the newspaper, Fusilados los de Reus" (Reus Criminals Executed by Firing Squad), followed by a close-up of the headline, Fusilamiento de Ferrer" (Ferrer Executed by Firing Squad), both of which refer to the social turmoil of the events of the Tragic Week" of 1909 and its aftermath in Barcelona. The following scene, in which Pascual and his father visit the rich landlord's farm and Esteban diagnoses a sick pig as having el mal rojo" (the red sickness) is certainly not fortuitous, and must be read metaphorically.

A later scene, which occurs at the landlord's, further emphasizes the sociopolitical element. When Pascual writes to his sister Rosario, who has abandoned the family and gone to Trujillo with her lover, "el Estirao" ("Stretch"), Pascual's mother mentions to him that he should thank her for the money that the sister sent by way of el Estirao" (who is also her pimp). A close-up of Pascual's letter, with the words "Otra vez a ver si este año algunos van a quedarse sin trabajo" (Let's see if some men are going to be left without work again this year), triggers the transition to the scene at the landlord's,

The determining factor of landscape: Ricardo Franco's *Pascual Duarte*, starring José Luis Gómez, Diana Pérez de Guzmán, Paca Ojea, and José Hinojosa. *Courtesy Elías Querejeta, P.C.*

where two men are fighting outside of the house. Don Jesús, the landlord, appears at the window to tell the laborers that there is no work for them, and that they should go away. The reverse low and high-angle shots visually underscore the social hierarchy of Spanish society, and the fistfight of the two laborers metonymically represents the strife among Spanish workers as a whole.

Two other brief scenes show the landlord's influence and importance in the community: after Don Jesús deposits his ballot in the transparent urn during the election scene, a low-angle shot captures him pronouncing that all should vote, since it is their obligation. In the next scene, Pascual's wedding to Lola, Don Jesús arrives on horseback, dismounts for a quick drink of wine to everyone's applause, but refuses to sit with the other guests. He then gives Pascual some money, with the wish Espero que todo os vaya bien" (I hope that everything will go well for you), and then leaves. Both scenes connote his power, wealth, and a certain condescending attitude toward the lower class, of which Pascual is certainly a member. Again, the juxtaposition of scenes is not fortuitous, and the next scene finds Pascual at night listening to a radio broadcast of the declaration of the Republic: Viva España y viva la República" (Long Live Spain and Long Live the Republic).

The animosity between Pascual and el Estirao" builds in a bar scene during which there is a type of singing contest. The first song, by an old man and directed metaphorically to the protagonist, further underscores the characterization of Pascual as victim:

> Ningún hombre debe ser
> a garrote sentenciado
> por meterse en un cercado
> a desprender un clavel.
> (No man should be sentenced to
> be garroted for getting into a
> fenced-in garden to cut free a
> carnation.)

El Estirao's" song contains a negative allusion to Pascual's shotgun marriage to Lola (Hay algunos que se casan / por cumplir una obligación [Some men get married to fulfill an obligation]), which causes Pascualito to attack el Estirao," and although he is restrained by others, it serves as a foreshadowing of the violent murder of el Estirao," which Franco considers a substitute homicide," since Pascual kills his brother-in-law instead of his sister (Balagué 14).

The matricide, preceded by a lengthy shot of Pascual shining his shotgun, which is the murder weapon, and the homicide of Don Jesús, the landowner, complete the cycle of violence. These both represent changes from the original narrative. Kovács (29) believes that the murder of his mother is more impersonal in the film, and Kenworthy (57) notes that in the novel, "Pascual never explains the circumstances of the crime for which he is executed," yet in the film Franco moves Don Jesús—and his homicide—"to center stage." This is part of Franco's political reading of the novel. Vernon (94-95) believes that the juxtaposition of the two murders "imposes a new interpretive context for both actions" in which there is an "interdependence of story and history." In addition, the use of the shotgun as the murder weapon (a radical change from the original novel) seems to implicitly link Pascual to the concept

Civil crimes in a militarized context: Ricardo Franco's *Pascual Duarte*, starring José Luis Gómez. *Courtesy Elías Querejeta, P.C.*

of armed struggle and the fratricidal conflict that was to follow.

The literary text is so tremendously violent that it caused critics to coin the term tremendismo to refer to Cela's style. The visual images of the film make the text even more so. Spanish critic Manolo Marinero praises how the film visually captures this style with its splendid photography and how Ricardo Franco obtained an ideal atmosphere for the "coarseness and barbarity of the story" (Pascual Duarte" 47), and Juan Carlos Rentero describes the film as having a latent, ferocious, savage, tremendous, incredible, but magnificently exposed violence, with an exasperating and destructive coldness" (Pascual Duarte" 38).

Part of the audience's reaction to the violence in the film is the result of a deliberate aesthetic distancing on the part of the director. Of course, the graphic images heighten the sense of violence in the film, but there is a deliberate lack of linkage or cause and effect with regard to some of the violent scenes, and Hernández Les reports that the resulting lack of a moral sanction or humanizing vision is precisely what caused the most repugnance among Spanish audiences (29). Thus, for example, in the novel, violence appears in the context of cause and effect: Pascual kills his mule after the animal threw Lola. In the film, however, there is a mere juxtaposition of scenes: after his mother calls Pascual away from the bar scene, we witness Lola in bed, unconscious, as Pascual looks on, horrified, and in the next scene (exterior, day), Pascual knifes his mule to death, a scene which caused an acute reaction in cinemas throughout Spain. Kovács (28) also notes that "the actor had to have really killed these animals [the dog and the mule], thereby violating the spectator-viewer covenant of permissible representations of violence in film." However, Angel A. Pérez Gómez considers that none of the violence in the film is gratuitous, since Pascual's decisions to kill el Estirao," his mother, and Don Jesús obey an unconscious desire to end the injustice of which he has been a victim. And by shooting at them, he is rebelling against a broader model: against the complete underdevelopment in which he is forced to live" (220). Kinder (192) likewise sees the murder of the landlord as the justified patricide of the politicized father.

The historical circumstances of the Spanish campesino during the 1930s constitute a harsh reality that foments frustration and social turmoil: daily wages for agricultural laborers of less than one peseta per day; clashes with civil guards in many small towns such as Casas Viejas (1933) that result in massacres; and Haro Tecglen points out that in Pascual Duarte, the schematic and almost silent biography of the protagonist and those who surround him is precisely an almost mathematical demonstration of the social pressures on Spanish country dwellers during the years that lead to the civil war" (28). Carmen de Elejabeitia and Ignacio F. de Castro note that this social pressure was due to the inequitable distribution of wealth—particularly land—and that this leads to a metonymical reading of the film: in a parallel way, Pascual Duarte's life leads to the garrote and his final desperate shout, and the history of the country leads to the civil war and its

Dragged to the garrote: Ricardo Franco's *Pascual Duarte*, starring José Luis Gómez. *Courtesy Elías Querejeta, P.C.*

dark night. In the story and in history, the cause that unchains the tragedy is money and landholding" (13).

Ricardo Franco's film version also emphasizes the harsh environment of Extremadura that shapes the destiny of the protagonist: frequent long shots of "the empty and endless road, the hot and sunlit village, the whitewashed houses form the basis for the mise-en-scène that dominates the characters and determines their actions" (Kovács 27).

Santoro (89) notes that the main aesthetic component of the film is minimalist hyperrealism comprised of a minimum of props, a minimum of actors, and a minimum of movement and speech" so that each element in the film becomes a kind of hypersign." She also points out the paucity of close-ups of characters' faces, and she contends that the emphasis on the distantiated image, rather than on dialogue and plot movement, is the real maker of meaning" in the film adaptation (Santoro 93). Certainly one of the most striking aesthetic elements of the film is the sparsity of dialogue. Although Franco does not use a voice-over to convey the words of Pascual's confession, Vernon believes that "the narrative logic of the film . . . can only be explained as Pascual's own rememoration of the events of his life" (90-91). In his interview with E. Balagué, Ricardo Franco states that the violence became the only viable language for a class that was stripped of any identity. Pascual only assumes his own life when he exercises this violence; he has no other means for communicating his frustration" (14). Kinder notes that in the novel this substitution of violence for normal language "is explicitly reversed, for when Pascual goes to Madrid he is astonished to see how city folk use language to substitute for violence . . . Thus the writing of his memoirs serves to exorcise and control the violent impulses that drive him. In the film, the memoirs are replaced by cinematic stylization, which calls attention to the issue of language and its paradoxical relation to violence" (188). Kinder also believes that in the film version of the narrative, "humor is acknowledged as an alternative to violence, another way of discharging the aggression and lust that have been repressed by the Francoist culture" and that "the discourse of laughter is linked with the expression of female desire" as Pascual and his sister go to the movies to see Buster Keaton's *Seven Chances*. As we see the comedian pursued through the streets by dozens of women, "the laughter that erupts in the theater is a displacement both for the incestuous desire of the siblings and for the greater violence to come" as well as a manifestation of the "misogynist fear of female sexuality" which is present in the novel (Kinder 192-193).

Although the homicide of el Estirao" results in Pascual's incarceration, the amnesty declared by the Republic allows Pascual to regain his freedom. An important deep shot from inside a train car shows Pascual returning home, and outside, written on a wall, are clear graffiti of a political nature: CNT" (Confederación Nacional del Trabajo or National Confederation of Labor, the anarchist union) and more importantly, Tierra y libertad" (Land and Freedom), which at once underscores the political emphasis with which Ricardo Franco has imbued the film text, and also manifests the principal source of conflict. The final homicides of the film cause Pascual to return to prison, this time to face the execution by garrote. Hernández Les contemplates the effect on Spanish audiences of the final gripping still shot of the film: it "inexorably provokes reflection in the spectator [and] a scream for our conscience as Spaniards" (30). *Pascual Duarte* is a superb film on many counts, a film that combines magnificent aesthetic qualities with an important sense of social theme.

Several critics have alluded to the cinematographic qualities of Camilo José Cela's 1952 novel, *La colmena*, and even the novelist himself has referred to the "photographer's little camera" with which he created the narrative (Cela, "La miel" 21). José María Castellet (33) points out that perhaps a better symbol would be a movie camera, and the montage technique used contributes to the objectivity of the narrative. Other critics concur: McPheeters speaks of a "cinematic effect" in the novel (88); Henn mentions the "camera-eye" of the narrative (142); and Sobejano uses the cinematographic term "montage" when discussing the structure of the novel (120).

Given the propensity of contemporary cinema to choose successful novels as a source for new films, it was not unexpected, then, that in 1982, Spanish director Mario Camus would undertake the cinematographic version of the novel. The film was a huge popular and critical success, winning the prestigious Golden Bear Award at the 1983 Berlin Film Festival, and it was the top-grossing national film in Spain during the year that it was released. Hans Burmann provided splendid photography for the film, and the musical score by Antón García Abril is a sometimes haunting, sometimes ironic complement to the narrative.

Although the narrative structure of the novel lends itself to a cinematographic treatment, a major obstacle to the adaptation is the huge number of characters in the novel, which would only confuse a film audience that would not have two basic advantages held by the novel's readers: the ability to interrupt the narrative in order to either reread a previous passage or to check the accompanying "census" of characters that appears with some editions.

The screenwriters, Camus and José Luis Dibildos, attempted to solve this problem by reducing the novel's almost three hundred characters to around sixty. This reduction is not as drastic as it might seem, however. Arquier shows that forty-five characters in the novel only appear once, and only seventeen appear six or more times; of these, significantly all but one (Señorita Elvira) appear in the "Final" chapter, and only eight characters, who appear more than eleven times each, become the collective protagonists: Visi; her daughter Julia; the latter's boyfriend Ventura; Doña Rosa, the owner of the café; Elvira; Roberto González; his wife Filo; and her brother Martín Marco (Villanueva 53). Camus filled the cast with stars of the Spanish screen, and even included a cameo appearance by the novelist, ironically cast as an "inventor of words." Twenty-eight actors receive top billing in alphabetical order. Some of these actors represent minor characters in the novel whose roles were given much more importance in the film adaptation. Such is the case of Paco Rabal, who is even featured in the photograph from the film on the cover of recent editions of the novel. He plays the poet Ricardo Sorbedo, a character who is so minor that he only appears on pages 237 to 242. Nevertheless, in the film version, Don Ricardo constitutes the nucleus of the café life, and he opens the film narrative with comments about the proper construction of a novel. His observation that without a plot with its proper denouement, all you have is "modernism and fraud" provides an ironic commentary on Cela's novel. It may also say something about Camus's film aesthetic. Dougherty notes that the filmic discourse, as opposed to the novelistic, seems to beg for a story with an ending, and he asks if Camus's reading corresponds to the demands of a medium that seeks to tell a coherent story (even though it might not exist) and to discover in it some stand-out roles for its stars (20).

Following Arquier's classification, the novel's eight protagonists receive varied treatment in the film, as Martín Marco (José Sacristán) is certainly first among equals; Julia (Victoria Abril), Ventura (Emilio Gutiérrez Caba), Doña Rosa (María Luisa Ponte), and Filo (Fiorella Faltoyano) are all important, whereas Visi (Elvira Quintilla) and Roberto

The screen adaptation of a classic with an all-star cast: Mario Camus's
La colmena, with Francisco Rabal, José Sacristán, Mario Pardo, and
Francisco Algora. *Courtesy Filmoteca Nacional.*

González (Ricardo Tundidor) are less so. Life in the cafés
perhaps grows in importance, as other important stars of the
Spanish screen play characters from these scenes in the original
narrative: Leonardo Meléndez (José Luis López Vázquez), Don
Mario de la Vega (Agustín Gonzalez), Don Ibrahím de Ostolaza
(Luis Escobar), Ramón Maello (Francisco Algora), Rubio
Antofagasta (Mario Pardo), Julián Suárez, "the Photographer"
(Rafael Alonso), Pepe "the Chip" (Antonio Resines), Tesifonte
Ovejero (José Sazatornil), Purita (Concha Velasco), and Doña
Matilde (Queta Claver). Likewise, Victorita (Ana Belén) and
Nati Robles (Charo López) have important roles in the film.
Using faces that were familiar to Spanish movie audiences
helped overcome the potential problem of confusion among so
many characters. Spanish film critic Juan Arribas offers the
following opinion: "if their faces were not familiar to us, it
would have generated a lot of confusion" (113).

In spite of this reduction in the number of characters, the film still has what Jesús Ruiz (43) calls a "choral structure" that shows us a slice of life from the 1940s, a comment that echoes the author's comments regarding the original novelistic narrative. In order to capture the atmosphere of the period, Camus went to great lengths to recreate the café "La Delicia" of the 1940s, attending to such details as magazines from the period, ration coupons, matchboxes and cigarette packages made after drawings of the originals, and three hundred bottles, half of which were authentic, behind the bar of the café (Pérez Ornia, "El café" 4). The same is true for the scenes at characters' homes, which feature portraits from the 1940s of Franco and the pope. Camus even included exterior footage of streetcars from the 1940s (as well as an old newsreel during a scene in a movie theater) in order to complement the interior scenes of the café and boarding houses.

The rhythm of the film follows that of the novel: a continuous montage of one short scene after another with shifts from the café "La Delicia" to street scenes, the bordello, the apartments of Doña Visi or Filo, and the boarding house provides a vertiginous sense of the characters' lives and of the passage of time. The film follows a more linear chronology than the original, but Camus basically follows the temporal framework of the novel. The end of each day is especially linked to Martín Marco; after an exterior night scene, we see the end of the first day as he gets into bed at Doña Jesusa's bordello. The next day ends in a similar fashion, except that before reaching the bordello on this second night, policemen stop Martín in the street and ask for his documentation. The poet's nervous response—that he does not have his documentation with him, but that he collaborates in the "Prensa del Movimiento," having just written an article about Isabel la Católica—ends with a circular tracking shot of a shaken Martín leaning against the wall. This shot beautifully captures in images the description of the novel: "He carries a dreadful fear within his body that you cannot explain" (209). The third night also ends in the bordello for Martín Marco, but he must now share a bed with the ailing Purita, since all of the other rooms are occupied.

Camus does take the liberty of developing the relationship between Martín and Purita a bit more than in the novel: Martín's recitation of verses by Juan Ramón Jiménez, which in the original takes place in their bed in the brothel (273), occurs during a walk in the park later that day. This does not go against the spirit of the original, however, since one of Martín's last thoughts in the novel has to do with furthering the relationship between the two: in a monologue statement, Martín says as he looks at a store window, "When I am working and earning money, I will buy some earrings for Filo. And for Purita" (292).

Asún (36) believes that the first thing that draws your attention in the novel is the chronological disorder, which creates a sense of simultaneity and synchronism that allow it to encompass the collectivity in distinct moments, and Guillot (41) states that these temporal jumps, which distinguish the novel from the realist tradition, constitute a fundamental narrative element that the film does not respect (38-39). Nevertheless, Guillot notes that Camus sometimes captures the simultaneity of the original, such as when the poets converse with Doña Rosa in the foreground and Don Mario de la Vega is smoking a gigantic cigar in the background (39-40). González also points out the visual importance of mirrors in the café in the temporal component of the film narrative: "semiotically, the mirror connotes the repetitiveness that makes each individual a reflection of the whole and thereby translates into visual imagery what is implied in the novel by means of the fragmented temporal structure" (99).

Overall, the film brilliantly captures what Gonzalo Sobejano has called the novel's "odor of misery." The hunger theme appears throughout, beginning with the intellectual clients of the café who are so impoverished that they often sit there without ordering anything at all, or who occasionally dupe the "almost" academician Don Ibrahím into reciting his boring acceptance speech to the academy, in return for which the elderly gentleman gregariously orders coffee for everyone at the table. A close-up shot shows Don Leonardo ingeniously stealing an egg by pinching a hole in the shell and sucking it out, and Leonardo and Tesifonte later eagerly open a package of food that has arrived for Ventura. Martín suffers humiliation when Doña Rosa orders him thrown out of the café for not paying, and as he passes the lady who sells roasted chestnuts, he cannot even afford this humble repast. Martín's Spain is that of soup lines, which Camus ironically portrays with martial music on the soundtrack.

Not everyone suffers from hunger and misery, of course: Doña Rosa is able to pontificate, "De grandes cenas, están las sepulturas llenas" (The sepulchers are full of those who had large suppers) precisely because she has the option of choosing to eat or not; Don Mario is a man of means who ostentatiously smokes cigars worth an entire "duro" (five pesetas).

The film thus captures the portrayal of a society divided between haves and have-nots, or what Francisco Carenas calls the dichotomy of "the humiliating and the humiliated" (232). The political framework for this dichotomy is that of victors and vanquished, as we see in the political undertones of the epithets that Doña Rosa uses when a waiter trips and falls: "bestia, rojo (you beast, red [commie]). These divisions also appear in a confrontation between Don Leonardo and Don Mario de la Vega, and in the relationship between Martín and his brother-in-law, and in a conversation between Visi and Filo. After Don Leonardo sells what he claims to be a Parker pen to Don Mario, the latter returns in a rage another day, saying that the pen leaked and ruined his suit. When he threatens to denounce Leonardo to the police, the latter counters by showing his medal from the war, which gives him moral authority, and by accusing Mario of being an "estraperlista" (black marketeer), thus concretizing the black market theme that is mentioned several times in the novel (12, 85, 171).

When Martín visits his sister, their discussion includes a comment about Roberto, Martín's brother-in-law, and his country ("su país"), with the use of the possessive adjective connoting a distinction between the Spain of Martín and that of Roberto, a distinction which is underscored in a later conversation between the two in which we see that they are men of different ideas and that the latter considers the poet a loafer. However, Martín is compelled to write articles on Carlos V, monk and soldier, surely not stuff that an "ultraísta" poet is normally made of, but an ideological capitulation to the political system that allows him to survive. Roberto's Spain is clearly connoted in a scene at night: he and his wife listen to the radio with its martial music and cries of "Viva Franco" and "Arriba España" (Up with Spain); the camera seeks out a photograph on the desk of Roberto in a soldier's uniform. The scene is charged with irony, however, because after the triumphant cries, the lights go out, and we see that electrical shortages are a common occurrence with Roberto's comment of "Sí que estamos buenos otra vez" (We're in fine shape again).

Camus amplifies the antagonism between Martín Marco and his brother-in-law by changing the latter's political affiliation. In the novel, he is described as a Republican supporter of Alcalá Zamora (84); in the film, Camus identifies him as a former Nationalist soldier. When Visi goes to Filo's house, it is to ask for a favor, since her husband is an "ex-combatant," and therefore someone with access to certain privileges. She asks for intercession in the case of her husband, Roque, who needs the "expediente de depuración" (purification record). We know of Roque's "questionable" background, since we have learned that he listens to the BBC at 6 o'clock and because he voted for Azaña in 1936. The shifts in camera angle and point of view in the scene of the conversation between the two women underscore the division of the haves and the have-nots.

This method of obtaining political favors through personal connections also appears when Don Leonardo tells Suárez that his friend Pepe will soon have employment in the government-run union. This is a good example of how Camus maintains a theme (in this case, "el enchufe") through synthesis: the theme in the novel appears when el Señor José promises Purita her brother will get a job because of the former's connections (255); José does not appear in the cinematographic version of the narrative.

The have-nots, it seems, must circumvent traditional morality in order to survive. Martín sleeps in an empty bed at a brothel when business there is slow. Leonardo conducts shady business deals. In order to obtain money for her tubercular boyfriend, Victorita finally overcomes her initial scruples and prostitutes herself to the wealthy Don Mario. Likewise, Martín's old girlfriend, Nati, now wears pearls, has a fancy cigarette lighter, and gives the poet a large sum to pay for their bill in a restaurant scene.

Camus often maintains fidelity to the original dialogue of the novel, and this stands out in several instances: Doña Rosa's famous expression, "Nos ha merengao" (We've been screwed), Purita's comment to Martín, "Con hombres como tú da gusto" (It is a pleasure with men like you), or the question put to Victorita, "¿Estás virgo?" (Are you a virgin?) come to mind. Sometimes Camus maintains the fidelity to the dialogue but slightly changes the setting to visually underscore thematic content. When Julita circumspectly tells her mother about her boyfriend, Doña Visi advises her daughter to conserve her virginity, and Julita responds, "Descuida, mamá" (Don't worry, Mama), in spite of the fact that she has already been to bed with Ventura. Camus films this scene in front of a mirror to capture the sense of duplicity in Julita. At other times, the transition from the language of the novel to that of cinema is more evident. In the novel, when Victorita surrenders herself to Don Mario, she coldly says, "Ande, lléveme usted a la cama" (Come on, take me to bed, 224); in the film, Camus shoots the scene using reverse-angle long and medium shots to underscore the emotional distance between the two characters; the silent image of an emotionless Victorita undressing magnificently portrays the anguish of the original.

Another aspect of adopting the novel to screen relates to the narrative dichotomy that Wayne Booth refers to with the terms "telling" and "showing" (3). Since the image is the main vehicle of the narrative in film, there is generally an emphasis on "showing" in cinema. Camus thus transforms the dry description of the tabletops in Doña Rosa's café (23) into a humorous scene manifesting the theme of deceptions unmasked through the technique of "showing," as Don Ricardo discovers that the marble table tops are really inverted tombstones, and to shouts of "profanadora de tumbas" (profaner of tombs) the entire establishment becomes an uproar as everyone inverts their table. Other examples of humor in the film have to do with the sexual relationship between Ventura and his girlfriend Julita, as Camus transforms and expands upon the ingenious message given to Alfonsito the messenger boy in the novel. When Ventura convinces Julita to visit him at a "safe" boarding house and give the password "Napoleon Bonaparte," she timidly enters the building but mistakenly calls at the wrong door, and they bluntly inform her, "La casa de citas es en el piso de arriba" (The whorehouse is in the apartment upstairs). This sequence also ends with a humorous note as the shirt which Ventura wrapped around the light bulb that hangs from the ceiling so as to accommodate Julita's sense of modesty bursts into flames and falls upon the couple. Although these scenes constitute a transformation from the original narrative, they exemplify the humor that is present in the novel, and they represent examples of what André Bazin calls the creativity necessary for a successful transition from page to screen (55).

The most important transformation between the novel and the film, however, has to do with the ending of the cinematographic narrative. In the novel, the news of Doña Margot's death comes about one-third of the way into the narrative (110-111); in the film it occurs near the end, and there is a similar chronological displacement for the apprehension of her son Julián Súarez and his friend Pepe (131-32). (In the film version, Doña Margot's death is attributed to suicide, thus following the condensation technique that maintains characteristics or motifs related to minor characters that have been eliminated.) Although Sobejano (123) notes that many characters are on the brink of suicide in the novel, this act of desperation only occurs with one, the man who smelled of onion.

The detention of Martín and subsequent simultaneous release of Martín, Julián, and Pepe represents the biggest discrepancy between novel and film. When they leave prison, they are identified by a guard (who represents the authority of the regime) as "dos maricones y uno que escribe" (two queers and a guy who writes). González (102) believes that this manifests the unequivocal message regarding "the precarious status of writing in a repressive society." The final image of the film is of the café, with a narrator off screen speaking the words at the end of chapter 6 of the novel: "La mañana, esa mañana eternamente repetida, juega un poco, sin embargo, a cambiar la faz de la ciudad, ese sepulcro, esa cucaña, esa colmena . . ." (The morning that eternally repeated morning, plays a bit, nevertheless, at changing the face of the city, that tomb, that greased pole, that hive, 277). In addition to giving the film a literary flavor, this voice-over performs the same function as in the novel: providing a sense of futile repetitiveness of daily activities in an attempt to simply survive.

Camus underscores this sense of repetitiveness in three ways: the final sequence of the film consists of a tracking shot in the café that moves from left to right, followed by a dissolve, and a tracking shot from right to left, thus indicating a sense of sameness and repetitiveness; the final image includes the revolving door of the café, which connotes circularity and repetitiveness; and the voice-over significantly changes the original novelistic text, repeating the phrase "esa mañana eternamente repetida" (that eternally repeated morning) twice. Nevertheless, ending the film here transforms what Sobejano (120) calls the open ending of the narrative, and it diminishes the importance of Martín Marco's role in the "final" chapter, thereby negating both the threatening political undertones stemming from the mysterious reason for which the police are searching for the poet, as well as the sense of solidarity that his friends and relatives manifest on his behalf. With rereadings of the novel, the importance of this solidarity becomes clear; indeed, Villanueva (70) even refers to it as the principal theme of the novel. Consequently, the film omits a fundamental narrative kernel from the original narrative. Nevertheless, Camus's film adaptation of Cela's novel should be praised for its creative fidelity to the original.[1]

From the time of the film's debut in October of 1982 until the end of that year, more than 983,000 people saw the film

---

[1]Some critics object to the formal aspect of the filmic discourse. Dougherty says that "an overly-conventional film reading does not serve well a text whose narrative discourse consciously went against the norm" (20) and Guillot believes that the film betrays the novel, saying everything that makes Cela's novel innovative does not appear in Camus's film (37, 41).

version of *La colmena*; the following year the figure was almost 415,000, and in 1984 the figure was nearly 80,000; since then, countless thousands have seen the film on video. Even though the movie caused an increase in book sales (Deveny, *Cela* 95), the numbers of readers is negligible compared to the number of spectators, so for many Spaniards, Camus's film, which according to González (102) both corresponds to and reflects the 1980s as a "period of national reconciliation through the reevaluation of the native canon" is their *Colmena*.

Rosa Chacel

Rosa Chacel (1898-1994) participated on the Republican side during the civil war, and she had to leave Spain for exile in Argentina for many years. Many of her works have a strong autobiographical element, with a constant probing of memories related to her youth in Valladolid. This is certainly the case in her first novel, *Las memorias de Leticia Valle* (*The Memoirs of Leticia Valle*, 1946), which was adapted for the screen by Miguel Angel Rivas in 1979. As the title indicates, the novel is an intimate, first-person narrative in which the narrator records the crucial events of her adolescence. Rivas uses repeated voice-overs to capture this intimacy of the narrative voice, as well as flashbacks to capture the temporal distance between her act of remembering and recording in her diary, and the events that inexorably shaped her life.

Although Leticia's initial entry into her diary seems odd at first, it points to a temporal question that implies different levels of maturity: "El diez de marzo cumpliré catorce años, ¿y qué?, ¿qué me importa cumplir catorce años o cincuenta? (On March 10th, I will be fourteen. So what? What difference does it make if I'm fourteen or fifty?) As she continues in voice-over, she alludes to a mysterious event that haunts her: "Si pienso en lo que pasó, parece que estoy oyendo a mi padre . . ." (If I think about what happened, is seems like I am hearing my father say . . .). In addition, her father's voice off screen repeatedly says, "Es inaudito" (It's unheard of), and thus emphasizes through its repetition the mysterious event to which the rest of the narrative will lead.

A caption places the action in the Castilian town of Simancas (site of the historical archives of the Spanish Hapsburg kings) in June of 1911. Leticia (Emma Suárez) is a thirteen-year-old girl who lives with her father, a wounded war veteran, her aunt, and a maid. Since Leticia has a beautiful voice, her school teacher advises her to take singing lessons. The thunder in the background seems to portend a negative result to this decision, however. Leticia begins voice lessons from Luisa, and since she is not challenged at school, she subsequently begins private history lessons from Luisa's

husband, Daniel (Ramiro Oliveros), who is a historian at the
Simancas archives. Leticia grows fond of them, but a series of
intercut shots between the thirteen-year-old girl and her tutor,
with extreme close ups of Daniel's eyes and lips, connotes that
there is more than just a history lesson here.

A later lesson confirms the latent tension in the relationship. Among the papers and books on Daniel's desk, there is a
woodcut of his biblical namesake, and he augurs, "A mí me
comerán los leones" (The lions will eat me), a comment that is
followed by a second montage series of intercut close-ups of the
tutor and pupil. Daniel intuits that his feelings toward Leticia
will lead to his doom. Ribas uses the same technique to
underscore the emotional triangle that is developing between
Daniel, Luisa, and Leticia during the girl's poetry recital. An
accidental fall by Daniel's wife results in her being bedridden,
which gives Leticia an even greater opportunity to spend time
with them, since she is now not only a student, but a nurse. The
inner tension in the tutor causes him to treat Leticia's musical
talent with sarcasm, but his comment, "Realmente te creo capaz
de incendiar Roma" (I really believe that you are capable of
setting Rome on fire), reveals his true feelings toward her.
Following the next montage series of close-ups between Daniel
and Leticia, the erotic gaze leads to their physical possession
of one another. Director Rivas follows the elliptical treatment
of the original novel, as Daniel embraces her and caresses her
hair.

Although Leticia records in her diary, "Al día siguiente, no
sucedía nada" (The next day, nothing happened), thus denying
the ramifications of the liaison, her father discovers the affair
and gives Daniel half an hour to leave town. Her father's
repeated comment, "Es inaudito" (It's unheard of), brings the
narrative full circle. The repetition of Daniel's fatalistic
prediction in Leticia's memory connotes his tragic end for
transgressing the morals of turn-of-the-century Spanish culture.
Since her honor has been sullied, Leticia cannot remain in this
provincial town, and the narrative ends with her move to her
uncle's house in Switzerland.

Rivas's film version also captures many of the other events
in the life of this thirteen-year-old girl: the Christmas

shopping trip by carriage to Valladolid, the New Year's eve dinner, and the visit of her cousin Adriana when they dance together. The film has a slow rhythm, and Quesada (280) notes that some of its problems lie with its excessive fidelity to the original novel—especially in its artificial dialogues. Nevertheless, it is important to note that this is one of the few film adaptations of works by contemporary Spanish women authors. *Las memorias de Leticia Valle* is an attempt to bring a classic work by a grande dame of Spanish literature to the screen.

José Luis Coll

Benito Rabal made his directing debut with the 1986 film *El hermano bastardo de Dios* (*God's Bastard Brother*), the screen adaptation of the novel by José Luis Coll. This work is one of many contemporary narratives that reexamines the Spanish civil war.

Rabal divides the narrative into five segments: although it begins 1939, the next segment flashes back to the months before the war, followed by the beginning of the conflict, the end of the war, and finally returning to the opening scene to continue the action in 1939. The film's epigraph, which is dedicated to children or everyone that the government did not allow to be a child, indicates from the very beginning that the point of departure of this movie is a common one: the war seen from the perspective of a young person. Although the protagonist, Pepe Luis, is indeed a child, the perspective here is really that of the adult who remembers his childhood in the provincial city of Cuenca during the war, since the voice-over that conveys his thoughts is that of a grown man who has sought answers to philosophical questions and reflects upon the meaning of life. The early sequences—the discussion about the execution of Don Jacinto, the school teacher; the children killing the cat; or the close-up of a photograph of his grandparents—elicit the comment by the voice of his conscience (heard off screen): "Yo tenía pocos años, pero sabía lo que era la muerte" (I was young, but I knew what death was). Nevertheless, the reason for death's existence is a question that he pursues all his life.

Although there is no actual fighting in the film, death and suffering inevitably surface from the background. The child protagonist functions as the ingenue who does not understand the reasons for the outbreak of the conflict ("Nadie le aclara nada para un niño en semejantes circunstancias" [No one clears up anything for a child in circumstances like these]) and whose questions lay bare the inherent absurdity of war. Pepe Luis asks, "¿Qué hacen en el frente de batalla? (What do they do at the battle front?) and Trini responds, "Matarse" (Kill each other). The ingenue is unable to understand the subtleties of civil war—"No sabia distinguir rojos y nacionales" (I couldn't tell reds from Nationalists). Pepe Luis witnesses the suffering among the adults as Trini, who writes letters dictated by Alejandra to her son at the front, must now comfort her friend over her boy's death. Pepe Luis's uncle Julio returns from the front with a bad wound, and he must have his leg amputated. The family's visit to the hospital where Pepe Luis sees the suffering of his uncle and other patients causes the boy to reflect on God's goodness and conclude with a thought that serves as the film's title: "Solo el hermano bastardo de Dios podria permitir tales cosas" (Only God's bastard brother could permit such things to happen).

Among the many movies that deal with the Spanish civil war, this film handles the religious theme in a unique way. In a scene in the local grocery before the war breaks out, Ramona predicts, "Aquí va a pasar algo muy gordo" (Something really big is going to happen here), and she states, "La culpa es del clero y de la oligarquía" (The clergy and the oligarchy are to blame). She has special criticism for priests, speaking of "mucha sobrinita" (lots of nieces) with reference to the hypocrisy regarding their sexual behavior. The family of Pepe Luis, however, is Catholic. When they take down and put away a painting of the Virgin, the young Pepe Luis talks about religion with Trini, who explains, "Este gobierno que tenemos aqui prohibe que la gente crea en Dios" (This government that we've got prohibits people from believing in God). Although this statement is not accurate regarding the legal situation regarding religion under the Republic, it may reflect an individual Catholic's perspective of the *de facto* situation during the war. When the youngster plays with some companions in the stable, they discover hidden religious statues. A slow motion shot of the statues flying through the air to their destruction is a portent of later harassment that Pepe Luis's family will suffer. Near the end of the war, soldiers break down their door in search of a projector that they claim the family uses to communicate with the enemy. When Rosendo, the grandfather, protests that it is only a toy, a soldier hits him.

After the war, with the Nationalists now in power, Pepe Luis becomes an altar boy, and some of the weakest parts of the film are scenes imagined by Pepe Luis at mass, such as a cathedral in the sky accompanied by the voices of children singing. Director Rabal includes two other such scenes—when Pepe Luis is knocked unconscious by falling rocks in a cave and imagines Pilarina putting roses on his casket, and when he serves as an altar boy at a funeral and imagines that the dead man awakens and greets everyone.

Death is the key image in Pepe Luis's subconscious, and death seems to fill the entire atmosphere of the postwar period as well. The voice-over states, "Ya no se mataba en el frente; ahora se mata en los juzgados o poco juzgados" (There wasn't any more killing at the front; now they killed at the court of justice or injustice), a humorous but barbed criticism of injustices committed after the war by the Nationalists. In this regard, we return to the execution of the school teacher, Don Jacinto. At the beginning of the narrative, we discover that his sin consisted of being "liberal, ateo, de todo y de nada" (liberal, atheist, everything and nothing).

The lesson that he teaches his class near the end of the war concerning the lack of generosity of the Christians after the conquest of the Muslim kingdom of Granada in 1492 is a foreshadowing of the lack of generosity and clemency of the Franco regime. When civilians beat the prisoner on the way to his execution, he falls as if he were Christ on his way to Golgotha. The fact that unlike the others, Pepe Luis does not take pleasure in the poor man's suffering, points out one of the strengths of the film: its lack of a dogmatic, single-sided perspective. Making the protagonist the child of a Catholic family that fights for the cause of the Republic puts him in a somewhat ambiguous position. Although Pepe Luis never finds answers to many of the questions that the asks, *El hermano bastardo de Dios* poignantly records the memories of those questions of a child who lived through this fratricidal conflict.

Miguel Delibes

Miguel Delibes (b. 1920) began his literary career by winning the Nadal Prize in 1948 for his first novel, *La sombra del ciprés es alargada* (*The Cypress's Shadow Is Elongated*), and in 1993 he won the prestigious Cervantes Prize for his entire *oeuvre*. More of his novels have been adapted to the screen as feature-length films than those of any other contemporary Spanish author. These include *El camino* (*The Road*), *Mi idolatrado hijo Sisí* (*My Adored Son Sisí*), *El príncipe destronado* (*The Dethroned Prince*), *Los santos inocentes*(*The Holy Innocents*), *El disputado voto del señor Cayo* (*The Disputed Vote of Mr. Cayo*), and *El tesoro* (*The Treasure*), as well as *La sombra del ciprés es alargada*. One additional title, *Cinco horas con Mario*, is the "once-removed" source for Josefina Molina's *Función de noche*, since it is based on occurrences in the life of Lola Herrera, the actress who performed the monologue of the widow Carmen in the dramatic adaptation of Delibes's novel. Many of the works of this author from Valladolid deal with country life in Castile, or with issues regarding the nature of progress, and these are often manifested with a city/country dichotomy.

The first screen adaptation of a work by Delibes was his 1950 novel, *El camino* by Ana Mariscal, which had its debut in 1965.[1] This film portrays a "child's world, with its peculiar atmosphere that is at once ingenuous and malicious, unworried and observant" (Quesada 381). This child's world centers on an eleven-year-old boy in a small Castilian town whose parents are about to send him to the city to receive an education. The stills with which the film begins—shots of the town, the forest, the river—convey an atemporal, mythical idealization of life in rural Castile. The protagonist, Daniel, nicknamed "el Mochuelo" (the Owl, played by José Antonio Mejías), is the

---

[1]Confusion exists about the date of this film's debut. García Domínguez (241) lists it as being from 1962; the "Puntos de Información" from the Ministerio de Educación y Cultura lists it as being from 1964. The *Cine español* annual published by Uniespaña lists it as being presented to censors in 1965. The Instituto Cervantes has indicated to me that the date of its debut can be determined by its license number. The first four digits indicate the year that it actually appeared: 1965.

leader of a group of youths who likewise have nicknames, such as Germán "el Tiñoso" (Mangy, played by Jesús Crespo). The narrative voice of the novel is the first-person memories of Daniel, and Martin-Márquez (Bifurcaciones 37-38) notes that the voice-over narrative at the beginning of the film captures diverse thoughts from the first three chapters of the novel in order to establish our relationship with the young boy, and that director Mariscal often includes the free indirect narrative of the novel in the film's dialogue. The boys enjoy their camaraderie, swimming in the local stream together, and they often perpetrate youthful pranks, such as when they steal apples from "la Mica" (a nickname for Micaela, played by Mari Paz Pondal), throw spitballs in class, or forge a love letter from their teacher, Don Moisés (José Orjas), to the spinster Sara. The boys vacillate at first about stealing the apples, and when "la Mica" discovers them, the sound- track has church bells ringing. Martín-Márquez notes that this sound represents the values of the church and is an abstract reminder of their moral transgression (42-43).

Mariscal portrays this world with humorous images, such as that at the end of the episode in which the boys wait together in a tunnel for a passing train in order to be scared so much that they defecate. After they have had their fun, they look for their pants, and the close-up shot of the tattered shreds of their former garments in the bushes provides an unexpected comic note. Likewise, the scene in which they attempt to set a cat, who is sleeping in a store window, on fire by using a magnifying glass focused on his fur consists of delightful reverse-angle shots that add a picaresque note to the situation. Indeed, humor is one of the key ingredients of the film, as Mariscal captures the small town atmosphere with the gossipers who have a field day when Irene (Maruchi Fresno), known as "la Guindilla," (a nickname meaning a "hot pepper," due to her character [41]) runs off with Don Dimas (Adriano Domínguez), and again when she returns to the town in shame. Indeed, the sign in the door of their store, "Cerrado por Deshonra" ("Closed Due to Dishonor") sets the tone for the entire episode. Upon her return, her intolerant sister, Lola, hides her in the back room of their store in an attempt to cover up her dishonor and shame, but a string of neighbor women suddenly appears at the store in search of salt (with each arrival, the humor grows, especially since some ask for minuscule amounts, thus making their ruse even more transparent). The superficial and intolerant religiosity of Lola and other townsfolk is the brunt of humorous treatment in a sequence in which director Mariscal satirizes the film censorship that existed in Spain during the 1940s and1950s. When the townsfolk go to the movies, Lola and other parish women try to cover the projector's lens and stop the projection of a "risqué" Latin American film. Martin-Márquez points out that when the priest, Don José (Joaquín Roa), likewise attempts to block the images, Mariscal creates a touch of scandalous irony, since his hands symbolically caress the women on screen (Bifurcaciones 52). Martin-Márquez also notes that Mariscal's screen adaptation emphasizes the concept of spectacle in the narrative—the spectacle of cinema, the spectacle of the children observing (and partly creating) the amorous dialogue between Don Moisés and Sara, and the spectacle of the movie audience members that scandalizes several old women ("The Spectacle" 470-72).

Shot in black and white on a low budget, this first adaptation of a Delibes novel continues the neorealist aesthetic that directors such as Antonio Bardem and Luis García Berlanga espoused in their early films from the 1950s, and it corresponds to the style that critics such as López Martínez (83) and Umbral (59) attribute to Delibes's novel. It is an excellent film by one of Spain's first female directors.

Retrato de familia (*Family Portrait*, 1975) is an adaptation by Antonio Giménez Rico of Delibes's 1953 novel entitled *Mi idolatrado hijo Sisí* (*My Adored Son Sisí*). The change in title is a significant indication of the director's intention to portray a bourgeois family that is caught up in turbulent events in Spain in the 1930s. This family consists of Cecilio Rubes (Antonio Ferrandis), a prosperous merchant of bathroom fixtures, his wife Adela (Amparo Soler Leal), and one son, named Ceci (Miguel Bosé) after the father. Director Giménez Rico says that since the screen adaptation of such a long novel would be impossible in the normal format of around ninety

minutes without synthesizing too much and losing the essence of
the novel, he opted to concentrate on the third part of the
narrative while using flashbacks to capture the essential
moments that occur in parts one and two (García Domínguez
108).

The emphasis on the historical period from 1936 to 1938 is
evident in the chronology of the film narrative, as Giménez
Rico radically departs from the mainly linear depiction of
events that Delibes utilizes in the novel, whose opening line
places the action in 1917. Since the film narrative begins in
1936, all prior events are subordinated to that historical
present through seven major flashbacks that portray the
moment of Ceci's conception, the boy's rebellious youth, signs of
social unrest, and Ceci's death in the war.

The opening shot of a newspaper with headlines about the
elections of February 1936, and the following sequence of
political speeches and gangs of right-wing thugs who break up
meetings, place immediate emphasis on the political element
in the film narrative. Cecilio is an egotistical and vacuous
character whose sole motivation is that of self-interest, and in
this context, he chooses not to become involved in any of the
events sweeping across Spain. He praises neutrality, and tells
Adela, "La política no es todo en esta vida; donde hay una
buena copa . . ." (Politics isn't everything in this life; as long as
you can have a good drink . . .), and he later exclaims, "Lo mejor
es no comprometerse con nada ni con nadie" (The best thing to do
is not get involved with anything or anybody). Even when
events begin to strike close to home and his store windows are
broken, he only views the event in terms of his own benefit, as
he tells his assistant to augment the damage report, since
everything is completely insured.

His wife, in contrast, attempts to become involved in
political events, and wishes that her son Ceci would follow
suit. She works for the CEDA (Confederación Española de
Derechas Autónomas [Spanish Confederation of Rightist
Autonomous Parties]), giving speeches to women in which she
praises the values of the Right: "Dios, patria, familia, orden y
trabajo" (God, fatherland, family, order, and work). Although
she is worried about the Falangist activities of her son, she

tells her husband, "Por lo menos tiene ideales, cree en algo" (At least he has ideals, he believes in something). After the war breaks out, she tells Cecilio that her son will have to enlist. When he finally does so, she tells Ceci, "Cumple con tu deber" (Fulfill your obligation). Cecilio, however, is against his son's involvement, out of fear for his safety. The father unsuccessfully speaks with General López, who is a friend, in an attempt to obtain a safe, rear-guard post for his son. In a burst of emotions that both manifests his fears and foreshadows the tragic events to come, he exclaims to Adela, "Esta guerra, esta guerra, esta guerra—me cago yo en la guerra. Cualquier día se nos agarran al chico y lo llevan a morir como un perro" (This war, this war, this war—war sucks. One of these days, they're going to grab our boy and take him away to die like a dog).

The flashbacks constitute the narrative crux of the film. The first one occurs when Ceci first appears on screen, coming from his Falangist activities. He looks at his father, and after a close-up of Cecilio's face, we are taken back to the moment of Ceci's birth, with Adela's screams and entreaties to her husband, "Júrame que no tendremos más hijos" (Swear to me that we won't have any more children). The second flashback is signalled by a zoom-in to a pearl earring warn by a woman called Lina (Mónica Randall), who is Cecilio's lover. The chronological point of the narrative is when Ceci is a baby; the father explains to Lina that he has made a promise to God that in return for curing his sick son, he shall refrain from his sexual promiscuity. The next flashback begins with a shot of a victrola, an object that symbolically represents Lina (connoting the sensuous dance of forbidden lovers). Lina feels that she deserves to be the mother of Cecilio's child, and she has a great desire to at least see the boy. This is followed by a sequence in a park in which Lina casually encounters the Rubes family, and she views the baby in a carriage. The fourth flashback occurs when Ceci, who as a young man of twenty, has met Lina and has taken her on as a lover. The narrative jumps further back in time as it switches from a shot of Ceci in bed with Lina to the time when Ceci was thirteen and, rebelling against his mother ("Vete a la mierda, idiota" [Fuck off, idiot]) leaves the house to go on his first adventure with girls. During a ride in his car

Foregrounding the civil war: Antonio Giménez Rico's *Retrato de familia*, starring Antonio Ferrandis and Amparo Soler Leal. *Courtesy Filmoteca Nacional.*

at night, Cecilio witnesses several signs of civil unrest—a bonfire, gunshots, the graffito "Death to . . . ." The latter triggers a jump to a scene that shows the death of Cecilio's mother, another moment of rebellion for the thirteen-year-old Ceci: when his distraught father slaps him, the boy retorts, "No te acerques, idiota. Y no se te ocurra volver a tocarme" (Don't you come close to me, idiot. And don't ever try to touch me again). As a twenty year old, Ceci seems to have a real romantic interest in Elisita, a neighbor girl. As she plays the piano for him, the camera zooms in to a close-up of Ceci, and the piano is now that of a prostitute in a brothel as the thirteen-year-old Ceci looks on and accepts a cigarette from a friend. This sequence, with a prostitute who leads the young boy to her room and initiates him to sex, placing his hands on her bare breasts, created a scandal in Spain and was the object of most of the negative criticism about the film. The final flashback occurs after the death of Ceci, whose truck was bombed by an enemy plane. His father goes to the front to collect the remains, and during the return trip by car, his mind (manifested in his voice off screen) wanders back to the earliest point of the film story, the moment of his son's conception. The memory of the words, "¿Sabes lo que he pensado esta tarde? Que quiero tener un hijo" (You know what I thought about this afternoon? That I want to have a son), precedes his pulling back a curtain and the shot of a naked Adela, twenty years ago.

The death of his son has a profound effect on the bourgeois merchant. He becomes a recluse, and later irrationally demands that Adela give him another child. Time and again, we observe that he cannot comprehend his tragedy: when he collects his son's remains, he asks the general amid tears, "¿Por qué me has engañado? (Why have you deceived me?) and ¿Qué has hecho de mi hijo?" (What have you done with my son?) At home, he comments to Adela about the war, "Vosotros armáis la guerra para que paguemos los que no tenemos nada que ver con ella" (You start up a war just so we who don't have anything to do with it end up paying). Finally, when he goes to see Lina, his lover, who seeks consolation over Ceci's death in drink, we see his strongest statement set against a background of sirens, bombs, and blinking lights: "Cabrones, hijos de puta. ¿Qué habéis hecho de él? Tú, ella, ella entre todos lo habéis matado" (Bastards, sons of bitches. What have you done with him? You, her, above all her, you all have killed him). His combination of rage, depression, and lack of understanding leads to his final act: suicide, throwing himself from the window of Lina's apartment. Ironically, Cecilio and Ceci live on in Lina, who announces to the father in his final visit that she is pregnant by his son. Giménez Rico artfully captures this last tragic moment with a frozen shot of the drunken Lina as the final shot of the film.

Because of its sexual and political elements, censors initially rejected *Retrato de familia* in 1975, and even after its subsequent initial acceptance, the film was subjected to further cuts prior to its debut (García Domínguez 115-118). Fernando Méndez-Leite observes that *Retrato de familia* is the "first film of the post-Franco era that directly deals with the theme of the Spanish civil war" (16), and Gubern comments that the film demythifies the so-called "crusade" of the victorious side (168-69). *Retrato de familia* is an excellent depiction of the war's effect on one segment of Spanish society, and a portrait of an egotist whose destruction brings to mind Lenin's maxim that you do not have to seek war out, it will seek you out.

Antonio Mercero's 1977 box office hit, *La guerra de papá* (*Daddy's War*), is based on the Delibes short novel, *El príncipe destronado* (*The Dethroned Prince*). The narrative presents the portrayal of a family dominated by the values of the father who fought on the victorious side of the war. The emphasis on the bellicose appears even during the opening stills—a child's drawings include those of a tank and a boy with a pistol. Likewise, the opening scene shows Quico, a three year old played by child actor Lolo García, awakening in his crib with a cannon in his hand "para ir a la guerra de papá" (to go to Daddy's war).

The temporal setting is March of 1964, a full quarter of a century after the end of the civil war, but a moment in which the deep feelings that contributed to the conflict still reign. The father's role in the war appears both in the images of objects in his study—flags, a photograph of himself as a young soldier, and a pistol in his desk drawer—as well as in a dinner conversation wrought with tension due to the fact that the father (Héctor Alterio) wants Pablo, his sixteen-year-old son, to enter into the armed forces. The children question the father about the war, and terms such as "buenos" (good guys), "malos" (bad guys), and "cosa santa" (holy thing) clearly divide the ideological question into two clear-cut areas of black and white, with the father ("naturally") on the side of the good, who are, of course, the victors. He now tries to impose his ideology on his oldest son, saying, "Sus ideas—si las tiene —serán las mías, digo yo" (His ideas—if he has any at all —should be mine, as far as I'm concerned). The lack of response on Pablo's part leads to accusations by the father toward the mother (Teresa Gimpera), who does not support her husband. Her opinion about the righteousness of the cause is that "Esas cosas siempre suelen ser lo que nosotros queremos que sean" (Those things are usually just as we want them to be).

The military element in the film is also underscored by a song that Domi, a maid, sings to the children. Entitled, "El puñal de dos filos" ("The Two-Edged Knife"), it tells of a soldier who returns from Africa to find that his beloved Rosita has betrayed him. The final verses, "Y sacando un puñal de dos filos / En su pecho se lo atravesó" (And taking out a two-edged knife he stabbed it in her chest), is accompanied by a shot of Quico urinating in his pants in order to underscore the negative consequences of violence on the psyche of young children. The appearance of Femio, the boyfriend of a younger maid, Vito, also underscores the military element. He is in uniform because he is shipping out the next day for service in Africa, and he has come to say good-bye. Quico ingenuously asks him if he is going to kill Rosita Encarnada, the victim in the song, as well as a lot of "bad guys" (just as his father did). Finally, Pablo's decision to follow his father's wishes stems from a conversation that the youth had with Father Llanes of the Veterans' Association in which the priest explains that the only way to forget old animosities is to join together, "unidos los de un lado con los del otro" (those of one side united with those of the other). Nevertheless, instead of reconciliation, Pablo's decision represents the continuing oppression of the younger generation of Spaniards by the older, victorious generation. The final scene shows the end of the day, with the mother putting Quico to bed and reassuring him that "Ya no habrá más guerra de papá" (There won't be any more Daddy's war). The rest of the film consists of a series of mischievous acts carried out by Quico and his brother, including the playing with the father's pistol, which serves to further underscore the bellicose element and add a small note of tension to the film.

Aside from the fact that Spaniards generally adore children, and the fact that one could characterize child actor Lolo García as "cute," the incredible box office success of the film can only be attributed to the empathy that Spaniards felt toward the sociopolitical theme of the movie.

Josefina Molina's *Función de noche* (*Night Performance*, 1981) is not a screen adaptation in the traditional sense. If considered an adaptation at all (García Domínguez does not include it in his recent monograph on film adaptations of Delibes's novels, nor was it included in the 1993 retrospective dedicated to Delibes at the Valladolid Film Festival), we must say that it is a screen adaptation twice removed. Miguel Delibes's novel *Cinco horas con Mario* (1968) was adapted for the theater in a production directed by Josefina Molina. Actress Lola Herrera played the role of Carmen in an unusual theatrical monologue, as she addresses her dead husband Mario. The actress became very engrossed in the role, and it had such an emotional impact on her that during the opening performance, she fainted on stage in Barcelona. Lola was going through a midlife crisis of her own—an annulment of her marriage with actor Daniel Dicenta—and director Molina, who wanted to make a film about the search for identity by Spanish women, decided to film Lola and her husband conversing about their lives in a re-creation of Lola's dressing room. Martin-Márquez ("La literatura proyectada" 360) notes that in order to film these intimate conversations, Molina used eight cameras that she situated behind two-way mirrors. *Función de noche* intercuts footage of Lola acting in the theatrical adaptation of the Delibes novel, as well as Lola with other people in her life—her two children, Natalia and Daniel, a friend who walks with her down the street, a woman who reads cards, and a surgeon who discusses her breast operation—all of which mitigate the claustrophobic nature of the dressing room conversation. It is here, however, where we see the crux of the film, as two people in a great deal of pain open up to each other as perhaps they have never done before.

Martin-Márquez ("La literatura proyectada" 360) states it is appropriate that this film, which is inspired in an identity crisis, should begin with Lola sitting in front of a mirror, since as La Belle explains, "looking at oneself in a mirror can, in a disturbingly ambiguous way, bring up the whole question of the nature of identity" (41). In the opening shot of the film Lola speaks to the camera/mirror, which becomes a vehicle for painful self-recognition. Seated before the mirror, Lola later states, regarding her performance, "Surgen imágenes que corresponden a mi vida a nuestra vida." The theme that runs throughout the film is failure: the failure of their relationship on an individual level, and the failure of their generation and their society. Lola painfully asks Daniel questions such as

"When did you stop loving me?" and "What was I to you?" When she admits that she was never in love, he thanks her for her great sincerity, but the pain shows through. Lola wonders why Daniel was unfaithful to her, but one of the greatest sorrows of her life was what she considered a condescending attitude on his part because of what she deemed his cultural superiority, saying, "no tengo la culpa por no saber más" (I am not to blame for not knowing more [than I did]). Toward the end of the film she painfully recognizes that she had never been able to accept herself and had considered herself a "shit." Daniel, for his part, felt "swindled" when she declares that she has never been sexually satisfied in her life, since that means that the orgasms that he thought she was having with him were untrue. Although Lola declares that she "swindled" herself, these revelations blur the distinction between fiction (acting) and reality.

The use of montage in *Función de noche*, according to Martin-Márquez ("La literatura proyectada" 362), favors Lola and the feminist perspective, and Molina uses shots that prejudice Daniel, such as when he spits out some ice when Lola talks about his level of culture, or when we see him vainly looking into a mirror when Lola comments on his egoism. Nevertheless, there is no Manichean manipulation in the film—there is no clear division of good person/bad person or victim/victimizer. In contrast to the montage that puts Daniel in a bad light, his actions make the viewer empathize with him, or at least see him in a more positive light. Often when Lola expresses her pain, she is led to tears, and on several occasions Daniel reaches out to her to touch her, caress her, or kiss her, but her pain is so great that she often shrinks back from these gestures of love that are too late.

Both Lola and Daniel often mention the problem of gender roles imposed on them by society, and the failure of that society and their generation. As a young woman, Lola only saw one future—raising children—and she laments that she never had the freedom to live her own life for herself. In part, the problems stem from what she terms a horrendous postwar period. The montage of the couple's conversation and the theatrical performance also underscores the societal problem.

One of Carmen's lines deals with the male propensity toward freedom and permissiveness in Spanish society. After being married, "os largáis de parranda cuando os apetece y sanseacabó" (you go off on a spree whenever you feel like it, and that's it). Martin-Márquez ("La literatura proyectada" 362) notes the way that Molina has filmed Lola reciting these lines, with interruptions by male technicians and workers or by her son, symbolizes how men in Spanish society put restrictions on women and hinder their professional development. Lola returns to the societal problem at the end of the film, blaming her inferiority complex because "they educated us badly," concluding that "La vida nos ha estafado" (Life has swindled us). The annulment provides a new beginning of sorts, however, and the film ends on a somewhat positive note, with Lola declaring, "Tengo tantas cosas que hacer" (I have so many things to do).

Función de noche walks the fine line between fiction and documentary film. Martin-Márquez ("La literatura proyectada" 363) remarks that the "theatricality" of their conversation grows throughout the film and questions whether they are playing roles or are unmasking themselves. Perhaps when anyone is placed before a camera for a long period of time, they inevitably begin to act, and this must especially be the case for two professional actors. Be that as it may, *Función de noche* reveals a great deal of pain in the lives of two individuals and the society that produced them.

Los santos inocentes (*The Holy Innocents*), director Mario Camus's 1984 cinematographic version of the Delibes novel from 1981, is a masterpiece of Spanish cinema. This film achieved both critical acclaim, with Paco Rabal and Alfredo Landa sharing the best actor award at the Cannes Film Festival, as well as popular acclaim: it was the biggest box office hit of the year of its release. The film portrays life during the 1960s on a large ranch (cortijo) in Extremadura. The characters in the film are divided into two groups: the haves and the have nots, who live in different worlds. The first group consists of the landlords: the "señorito" (master) Iván (Juan Diego), and the Marquesa (Mari Carrillo) who visits the ranch on the occasion of the first communion of her grandson; although

Purita (Agata Lys) and her husband Don Pedro (Agustín González), the manager of the ranch, mainly pertain to the world of the haves, the latter in particular is also a victim of that world; the have-nots are the servants: Paco (Alfredo Landa) and his family—his wife Régula (Terele Pávez), their children Quirce (Juan Sánchez) and Nieves (Belén Ballesteros). Two special characters of this group are "la Niña Chica" (the Little Girl), the youngest child in the family who is infirm and who gives forth occasional heart-wrenching screams, and Azarías (Francisco Rabal), the brother of Régula who is not in possession of all his mental faculties.

The opening sequence of the movie is an evocative tracking shot that shows Azarías running through the woods at dusk as he "runs the tawny owl" to the accompaniment of the rustic music of tambourine, drums, and rebec, which is to become his motif in the film. This sequence must be taken in syntagmatic relationship with a later segment of the film, when this narrative element is repeated; its initial impact is to establish the importance of this character in the film narrative, and to manifest Azarías's love for birds as a central motivating force in his character. The still shot of Paco's family in front of their quarters at the big house also relates to a later moment of the narrative when a photographer who attends the first communion ceremonies stops to take a family portrait of them. This still shot begins as a negative that is overexposed and gradually grows darker. Instead of this process stopping at the point when the photograph would be perfectly exposed, however, it continues to a point when the photograph is underexposed and barely visible, thus foreshadowing the darkness that eventually overcomes the household.

The greatest transformation from page to screen is that director Camus frames Delibes's narrative with a temporal present that extends beyond the denouement of the novel. Camus also imbues the film with a high degree of literariness by dividing it into four distinct "chapters" whose titles refer to characters' names: "Quirce," "Nieves," "Paco, el bajo," and "Azarías." This contrasts somewhat with the chapter titles of the novel: "Azarías," "Shorty Paco," "The Goshawk," "The Hunting Assistant," "The Accident," and "The Crime." The latter two titles serve as foreshadowings of the major narrative events of the chapters, and in the film the framing device serves a similar function.

The narrative structure of the film, then, consists of a present, marked by Quirce as a soldier and his sister as a factory worker in Zafra, and four flashbacks, each of which is overtly marked by Camus. The first flashback to grammar lessons for Quirce in his stone hut is signalled by three shots (long, medium, and close-up) joined by dissolves of the young soldier leaning against a wall in Zafra. This structural unit terminates with the rustic music associated with Azarías and the lyrical refrain with which he greets his pet, "Milana bonita" (Beautiful goshawk). A fade to white signals the transition to the present, where Nieves accompanies Quirce to the bus station where he will depart to visit their parents. A succession of three stills that represent a zoom-in on Nieves, together with a chapter title with her name, signals the second flashback to the beginning of her service in the big house as a maid. Again Camus uses Azarías and the rustic music to close this narrative segment, and a long shot of Quirce in uniform approaching the stone hut returns us to the present. A medium shot of Paco cleaning a shotgun dissolves into a double image (followed by the title, "Paco, el bajo") to signal the commencement of the next chapter. Following a variant of the previous pattern, this flashback terminates with the tambourine music and a fade to white that brings us again to the present, with Quirce visiting his outcast and crippled father and aged mother in their isolated hovel. This final flashback is triggered by an object—a rosary that Régula gives to Quirce so that he can take it to her brother in the mental hospital. A poetic shot of Azarías holding the cross in the light of his hospital window precedes the title of the last chapter, which begins with a close-up of him holding the rosary and "la niña chica," (the youngest child who is mentally deranged and whose animal-like screams add a sense of helplessness and despair to the household) in his lap.

Although at the beginning of the story Paco and his family live in an isolated stone hut, they are called up to serve at the big house, and they must follow the wishes of the landowners.

The haves: Mario Camus's *Los santos inocentes*, with Juan Diego, Maribel Martín, Agata Lys, Mary Carrillo. *Courtesy Televisión Española.*

The servile attitude of the members of the lower class appears in their speech—both Paco and Régula repeat, "Lo que usted mande, Don Pedro" (Whatever you order, Don Pedro), and the woman servant underscores the attitude with her phrase, "A mandar, Don Pedro, para eso estamos" (Just order, Don Pedro, that's what we're here for), as well as in the visual images relating to their demeanor. José Miguel Carión considers that the face of Terele Pávez, who plays Régula, is a "pure symbol of bitterness . . . that the impotence of human submission produces" (93-94). Paco and Régula accept the move to the new house because they do not have any control over their own lives, even knowing that serving there dashes their hopes for a better future for their children. While at the stone hut, Paco gave Quirce grammar lessons by candlelight, and Régula wanted to send her children to school, commenting that "Con una pizca de conocimientos, podrán no ser pobres" (With a pinch of knowledge, they won't have to be poor). When they move next to the big house, and Don Pedro tells them that he wants Nieves to serve as a maid, shots of Paco and Régula exchanging furtive looks of profound disappointment and submission acutely capture the tone of the original narrative (45).

The privileged class wants the servants to have some education—but not too much—and they cannot hide their condescending attitude toward the workers. When Don Iván shows off the rudimentary writing skills of Paco and Régula to a visiting ambassador, he quips, "Ya no estamos en el '36 . . . hacemos todo lo posible para redimir a esta gente" (We're not in '36 any more . . . we do everything possible to redeem these people). The specific temporal reference here immediately brings the civil war to mind, and tacitly allies the landlords with the Franco regime. The close-up of the extremely child-like letters that Régula writes constitutes a fitting irony to Iván's contention that there is equality for women in modern Spain; the landlord's command to the couple, "Podéis largaros" (You can get out now), subtly completes the attitude of condescension in this scene.

Iván likewise treats Paco in a condescending fashion as he constantly calls him "maricón" (queer). When, during a hunting episode, Paco falls from a tree, Iván's egoism prevails as he snaps, "Serás maricón, por poco me aplastas" (You queer, you almost smashed me). When he discovers that Paco has broken his leg, his only reaction is that it is a "mariconada" (queer-assed thing to do) since it will interfere with his hunting. Iván's constant use of billingsgate, and especially his repetition of the term "maricón," marks his macho domination. One of the most telling scenes in the film occurs when Paco returns from the doctor's office with his leg in a cast, and he struggles in great pain to walk from Iván's land rover to the door of his house. As he is about to enter, Iván, who is standing next to his vehicle, calls Paco. The faithful servant painfully returns to his master, merely to be told by Iván that Azarías won't do as a hunting assistant. This scene acutely captures Iván's egoism and callousness.

The section of the film entitled "Nieves" begins with this character and her brother Quirce walking through the streets of Zafra, where Nieves now works in a factory. Márquez-

The have-nots: Mario Camus's *Los santos inocentes*, with Alfredo Landa, Terele Pávez, Belén Ballesteros, Juan Sánchez, Susana Sánchez. *Courtesy Televisión Española.*

Pribitkin notes that Camus takes Nieves out of the ranch in a way that does not follow the traditional path (i.e., marriage) and that her working in the factory corresponds to the changes in social attitude in Spain whereby only twenty-two percent of Spaniards believe that a woman's place is in the home (59, 61). Her comment that she left the ranch because she did not want to spend the rest of her life cleaning up other people's garbage clearly indicates that her departure from the ranch constitutes a type of liberation. When she asks Quirce if he knew that the Niña Chica had died, he responds that she had written him that information in the spring, further underscoring the fact that both siblings can now read and write. Their literacy is even a more important sign of their liberation, and is an element that relates syntagmatically to both the early grammar lesson and (in contrast) to the pathetic scene in which the señorito Iván makes Paco, Régula, and Ceferino sign their names in order to show the Spanish ambassador how much "these people" have progressed.

When the brother and sister arrive at the bus station, and Quirce leaves to visit his parents, the three shots of Nieves in long shot, medium shot, and close-up linked by dissolves again signal the jump to the past. The image in close-up of Nieves on the ranch contrasts with that of her in the bus station, especially with regard to her hair. In the present, her hair is loose, hanging down to her shoulders, whereas in the past it is pulled up tightly into a bun. This contrast in coiffure symbolizes her change in circumstances: on the ranch, she was restricted and oppressed; now working on her own in Zafra, she is liberated. Santoro (178) also notes that her "sparkling white uniform contrasts sharply with the dark clothes that she wears throughout the flashback segments as housekeeper in the Casa Grande. A close-up of a pile of dirty dishes indicates not only the type of work that she will have to do, but also reflects on the woman of the house, Doña Pura, the wife of the farm manager, Don Pedro. She is in bed filing her nails. The deep shot with Doña Pura's hands in the foreground and Nieves standing in the door in the background captures both the indolence and exploitation in this situation.

When the señorito Iván arrives and immediately goes hunting with Paco, the sounds of their rifles are in the distance and Camus uses this sound effect to link two spatial components of the narrative. In the big house, Doña Pura arranges flowers in a vase and walks over to the mirror, where she touches up her hair. This mirror shot constitutes both a cultural inscription of female beauty as well as a foreshadowing of her duplicity. She goes to the window and looks out at the countryside; her husband, Don Pedro, is walking outside the house, and a low-angle point of view shot shows him observing her as she looks out the window toward the countryside that echoes with shotgun blasts. That distant gunfire metonymically represents Iván, and this montage sequence subtly introduces the amorous triangle, since Pura's primping in front of the mirror is for the sake of Iván, not her husband Pedro. When Iván joins the manager and his wife for dinner, his jocose comment about Pura asking if he would like (chicken) breast sets the tone of sexual tension throughout the meal. After Don Pedro departs, the close-up of Pura's hand approaching Ivan's as they simultaneously use the ashtray increases the tension considerably. As Iván withdraws his hand, not allowing contact, he represents the epitome of machismo in a machista society: it is the male who must control and dominate, and he immediately does so by grabbing Pura's arm, pulling her into his lap, and passionately kissing her. When Nieves enters the room to serve tea, the camera captures the reflection of the couple in the mirror. Martin-Márquez notes that this represents "a splendid example of harmony between the filmic narrative and the characters," since "the camera imitates Nieves's discretion" (248). In addition, a mirror shot is a classic way to symbolize a split in personality or inner conflict: here it is the hypocrisy and adulterous behavior of Iván and Pura (whose name is supremely ironic).

The late arrival of Pura and Iván for Carlos Albertos first communion ceremony raises the ire of Don Pedro, and the fact that Iván is the only one of the family not to take communion underscores his adulterous behavior. Indeed, at the moment that the priest logically would have offered him communion, he turns and looks at Pura in a stare that represents a real existential choice. Her husband, Don Pedro, then, is a victim, as well—a cuckold, in spite of the fact that after Pura disappears from the ranch, Iván tells him, "tu frente está tan lisa como la palma de la mano, puedes dormir tranquilo" (your forehead is as smooth as the palm of your hand, you can sleep tranquilly; cf. 161) in a reference to his lack of "horns" (a symbol of being a cuckold). And yet, we do not feel compassion for Don Pedro because of his treatment of the have-nots—Paco, Régula, and their family. It is Don Pedro who stymies their hope for educating Nieves when he has the girl begin work at the big house. And when the Marquesa and her daughter Miriam (Maribel Martín) contemplate Nieves as a possible lady's maid, Don Pedro's comment to the Marquesa that these are her people and she can dispose of them as she wishes exemplifies a dehumanization of the have-nots. In a scene that Camus adds to the original narrative, Don Pedro catches Azarías stealing some grain so he can feed his goshawk, and he beats Azarías with his riding crop, a gesture symbolic of the general oppression of the have-nots. In addition, Martin-

The most innocent of all. Francisco Rabal as Azarías in Mario Camus's *Los santos inocentes. Courtesy Televisión Española.*

Márquez notes that there are several cage images throughout the film that connote imprisonment and oppression (Bifurcaciones 255-257).

Camus's use of montage during the first communion festivities beautifully underscores the contrast between the haves and the have-nots. While the ranch hands and servants enjoy a boisterous festivity with food, drink, music, and dancing outside the big house, a tracking shot of the haves eating dinner in silence—the only sound is the rattling of the silverware on the fine china—shows how essentially empty their lives are, in spite of their material affluence. The Marquesa, who is the matriarch of the family, comes from the city to attend her grandson's first communion. In medieval fashion, she treats the workers like little children, even referring to them as "hijos míos" (my children) when she addresses them from her balcony in a low-angle shot that underscores her authority and importance. As the laborers submissively form a line to receive a monetary present on this happy occasion, the Marquesa speaks to them individually. The combination of inquiring about one's family and one's pigs in the same breath, however, subtly equates these have-nots with mere animals. Another example of this attitude occurs when the physician examines Paco's broken leg: Iván insists that Paco is needed for a shoot on the 22d, and the doctor's response is "tu eres el amo de la burra" (you're the donkey's master, cf. 130), an expression that underscores the condescending attitude of the "haves" toward the "have-nots" as mere animals.

Although this equation of the servants with animals is degrading from the point of view of the landlords, it is certainly not so from the point of view of the lower class. Indeed, it represents a harmony with nature that is vital to their happiness and survival. Paco's skill at retrieving downed prey when assisting Iván at hunting is equated with that of the best bird-dog (cf. 92, 97, 98) and is a source of great pride for the hunter's assistant: in a marvelous tracking shot, Paco, on all fours, sniffs the trail of a wounded bird and leads his master to a lost prize. Azarías's love for birds constitutes the most important manifestation of harmony with nature in the narrative. This relationship begins with the opening sequence when Azarías runs the tawny owl, but is most important in his relationship with the goshawk. When the creature becomes sick, Azarías's pleas for help at the big house receive only disdainful rejection. The close-ups of Azarías crying when the bird dies are emotionally counterbalanced by the scene in which Camus uses contrasting high- and low-angle shots to show how the new goshawk flies to his shoulder when Azarías calls to him, "quiá." These two sequences that show Azarías sorrow and joy are underscored by the two contrasting musical motifs of the film.

The other scene that is related to this harmony between man and nature occurs at the end of the film when Azarías substitutes for the injured Paco as Iván's hunting assistant. With Azarías now in the tree with a decoy, the rage of the "señorito" over his bad luck leads to the denouement of the film: when Azarías signals the goshawk to come, Iván raises his shotgun and pays no heed to the servant's plea, "No tire, señorito, que es la milana" (Don't shoot, master, it's the goshawk, cf. 170). A circular tracking shot around the crying Azarías clutching the dead bird captures the emotions of this, the most innocent of all the characters. Again Camus uses the contrasting low- and high-angle shots in the counterbalancing scene: on the next outing, we see Azarías high in the tree with a rope in hand, and a shift in angle to show how he hangs the despised Iván is a shot filled with such emotion that it caused audiences in Spain to applaud in approbation.

The moment of his revenge against Don Iván—aptly set to the music of the tambourine—closes this segment with a fade to white before the epilogue: Azarías, in the mental hospital, repeats his refrain, "Milana bonita," and Quirce leaves him to contemplate a flock of birds passing by in the sky, which is a symbol of "freedom of movement, and in this case, the freedom to migrate in search of a better life" (Santoro 174). Varela also believes that with this image, Camus "conjoins the natural and social aspects of the narrative by linking nature symbolism to Quirce, the main carrier of social development and the ulti- mate opponent of Ivan's view of life" (643). Camus, then, gives Quirce added importance in the film version: from the signifi- cant close-up of Quirce writing a letter in the opening se- quence—his literacy is a symbol of his liberation from the oppression of the ranch—to the final shot of Quirce and the birds, symbol of the freedom of this younger generation. Martin- Márquez also notes that during his visit with his parents, Quirce's refusal to eat the birds that his father shot for him represents a rejection of the killing of free beings, an activity that cost his family so dearly (259). A syntagmatic reading of the framing shot of the final segment of the film allows for a new symbolic interpretation: Azarías holds the rosary with the crucifix hanging, and repeats his refrain, "milana bonita." The association of the goshawk with the crucifix is one of sacrifice and redemption. Only through the sacrifice of the goshawk (and of the holy innocent, Azarías) does the younger generation gain its redemption and liberation.

In addition to the early family photograph that darkens as a foreshadowing of the tragic denouement, there is an excellent use of visual metaphor by Camus that subtly guides the viewer to this ending: this occurs in the close-ups of excre- ment. Azarías, the innocent, does not distinguish between acceptable and unacceptable locations for relieving himself, and he defecates even on the grounds of the big house. The singling out of these remains by the camera lens visually symbolizes a fundamental expression of Spanish billingsgate, "Me cago en . . ." (I shit on . . .). His symbolic curse on those who oppress and exploit turns to reality at the end of the narration as he carries out his vengeance on Don Iván.

Although the political element does not receive overt emphasis in *Los santos inocentes*, the prominently displayed photograph of Franco in the big house overtly allies the landlords with the regime. In Iván's opinion, fighting—and winning—the civil war was a fundamental aspect of his family's well-being and indeed of Spanish society's well-being. He complains about Quirce, "Que los jóvenes de hoy no lucharon una guerra" (The young people of today didn't fight any war). His subsequent remark to the ambassador, "Todos tenemos que aceptar una jerarquía. Unos abajo, otros arriba. Es ley de vida, ¿no?" (We all have to accept a hierarchy. Some below, others on top. It's the law of life, isn't it?), manifests the fundamental social question of the film. *Los santos inocentes* beautifully captures the oppression of the lower classes in Spain during the second half of the Franco regime. Camus's screen adaptation of this Delibes novel is as much a classic as the original.

El disputado voto del señor Cayo (The Disputed Vote of Mr. Cayo, 1986) is director Antonio Giménez Rico's second film adaptation of a Delibes novel. The author indicated in *Un año de mi vida (A Year in My Life,* 34) that *El disputado voto del señor Cayo* would deal with Spanish *cainismo* (a tendency toward fratricidal conflict) as well as the problem of rural exodus in Castile. The narrative is placed during the elections of 1977, and centers on the encounter between politicians from the city and a country dweller. Giménez Rico (189) believes that unlike the adaptation of *Mi idolatrado hijo Sisí*, where the problem was of synthesis or capturing only a section of the original, the key to adapting this novel was in finding a way to extend the narrative, and he found that key by asking what became of the young, enthusiastic politicians ten years later.

After a nocturnal urban aerial shot during the credits, the film opens in black and white: Rafael (Iñaki Miramón), a parliamentary representative, receives a note in the middle of a debate. A close-up shot reveals the news that Víctor Velasco has died and will be buried tomorrow. After a rainy scene in the cemetery, the first of three flashbacks takes us to the main narrative thread of the film: the elections of 1977, which appears in color. The camera pans the local party headquarters of the PSOE (Partido Socialista Obrero Español), which is adorned with campaign posters of presidential candidate Felipe González and of Víctor Velasco. Indeed, this party propaganda serves as a foreshadowing of a later conflict in the film, as one party member complains that opposing parties cover up his posters with theirs. The sound off screen of breaking glass and shouts—"rojos, maricones de mierda" (reds, fucking queers)—further underscores the *cainismo* in the film: political hostilities that are the remnants of the fratricidal conflict of forty years ago.

A close-up of a map on the wall, in which the camera pans upward in a northerly direction from Burgos, indicates the geographical setting where the rest of the narrative is to occur. After exterior shots that include the city's gothic cathedral and evidence along the streets of the "poster war," the three socialist candidates, Rafa, Víctor (Juan Luis Galiardo), and Laly (Lydia Bosch), set forth to campaign in an isolated and poor region of rural Spain. Their vehicle, a red Simca, is not without symbolism, both in terms of its color and model: it seems the appropriate car to connote leftist proletariat ideals. The car does have a cassette player, however, which allows the differences between Víctor, in his forties, and a younger Rafa to become manifest: the former's musical tastes favor the *zarzuela* (light opera), while the latter listens to rock music, proclaiming in the modern urban slang that is his "signature," "mola cantidad" (it's really cool). A small ideological rift between Víctor and Laly is also evident: whereas the feminist Laly wants to speak about women's liberation, she cedes to Víctor, who wants to address the campaign theme of emigration. Aerial shots of the car travelling through the Castilian countryside and a long shot of a beautiful canyon add to the

A portrait of divided Spain: Antonio Giménez Rico's *El diputado voto del señor Cayo*, starring Francisco Rabal, Juan Luis Galiardo, and Ana Alvarez. *Courtesy Penélope, S.A.*

visual quality of the film. This countryside, however, becomes symbolic of the growing division between Víctor and Rafa; the former is in awe of its beauty, whereas the latter condescendingly remarks, "Está bien para ovejas" (It's okay for sheep). The cut to the black-and-white cemetery scene brings us back to the present. The restaurant dialogue between Rafa and Laly captures the former's disillusionment, as he admits that he has left his revolutionary dreams behind. The images attest to this change: in contrast to the casual look of the 1977 elections, Rafael now dresses in a suit, with hair neatly parted and dark-rimmed glasses. (One cannot help but compare this transformation with images of Felipe González in 1977 and in more recent elections.)

The second flashback begins with a 360-degree aerial shot of the candidates at the canyon's edge, and a repetition of the dialogue with which the first flashback ended. In this segment of the narrative, they arrive at a small town and meet Señor Cayo Fernández (Francisco Rabal), a seventy-four year old who is one of the last inhabitants of the village. Rabal in the role of a rustic and poorly clothed *campesino* cannot help bring to mind his outstanding performance as Azarías, in Mario Camus's 1984 film adaptation of another Delibes novel, *Los santos inocentes*. Although the physical appearance of the two characters is similar, Cayo has full use of his mental faculties, and indeed, shows on many occasions that his "country wisdom" is superior to that of the urban politicians. A close-up of his hand among a swarm of bees shows that Cayo, like Azarías, lives in harmony with nature, and he often shows the visitors his knowledge of the world around him: identifying the elder tree, showing how to catch crayfish, when is the best time for transplanting, or that mallows are used "para aligerar el vientre" (to clear out your innards). The dichotomy between Cayo and the urban visitors also occurs at a linguistic level. When Cayo, puffing smoke on his bees, asks Víctor to hand him "el humeón" (the fumigator), the latter queries, "¿El puchero?" (The smoke-pot?) Later, Rafa mistakenly uses the term "chova" (jay) to identify a "mirlo" (blackbird). The linguistic rift between the *campesino* and the urban politicians symbolizes the greater differences in values and lifestyles.

In spite of his knowledge, Cayo has in common with Azarías the trait of the ingenue, the outsider who functions to defamiliarize the narrative, and therefore subtly ridicule the sociopolitical pretensions of the visitors. When Víctor tells him about the great opportunity of the elections, saying, "Si la desaprovechamos, nos hundiremos sin remedio esta vez para siempre" (If we don't take advantage of it, we'll sink forever this time, with no remedy), the response of the ingenuous *campesino* is "¿Y dónde vamos a hundirnos?" (And where are we going to sink to?) Later, when Laly is aghast that he has no television, Cayo retorts, "¿Para qué?" (What for?) Although he did not learn of Franco's death until four weeks after the fact, he exclaims, "¿Qué prisa me corría?" (Was I in any hurry?)

Ultra-Rightists appear in town and use extremist rhetoric to scare the *campesino*, warning that if the Socialists win, they will take away his lands and set fire to the church. Cayo's ingenuous character continues in this new context: when the rightists assure him that they offer order, his response is,

"¿Orden, dice? Es aquí de más" (Order, you say? There's more than enough of that here). Although ultra-Rightists earlier attacked the Socialists' car, throwing stones at it, the confrontation in the small town before the incredulous eyes of Señor Cayo constitutes the culmination of the *cainismo* in the film. Their provocation of the Socialists comes from the "poster war" motif, as they cover over Víctor's propaganda. When Rafa tries to intervene, they stick glue in his mouth, and beat Víctor with a chain.

After meeting with Cayo, a Castilian "noble savage" who seems to have no need for politicians, and after the violence of his encounter with the ultra-Rightists, Víctor's disillusionment comes to a head. On the drive home, he tells Laly, "No sé lo que me pasa en los últimos tiempos. Todo por lo que he luchado y en lo que he creído se me va de las manos" (I don't know what's wrong with me lately. Everything that I have fought for and everything that I have believed in is slipping through my fingers). In a later scene in the present, we learn from Rafa that Víctor gave up politics altogether.

The conflict of the present is related to that of the past in the film. Cayo takes them to a grotto where he narrates that during the war the mayors of the town were killed, and everyone had to spend two weeks hiding inside the grotto until a shepherd informed them that the soldiers had left. Possible remnants of *cainismo* persist in the town in the relationship between Cayo and the only remaining neighbor, an unnamed man to whom Cayo disdainfully refers to as "ese" (that one). Cayo calls him an animal, saying that he hanged Cayo's cat, an act of spiteful violence that can only reflect a deep-seated hatred between these neighbors.

After Víctor's burial, Rafa returns to the village. The new Opel with a car telephone, and the *zarzuela* music that Rafa now listens to are all symbolic of the profound transformations in Rafa's character: the revolutionary idealist of the first trip has given way to the cynical bourgeois. Nevertheless, two final acts return us to the Rafa of earlier days. The politician finds a sickly and widowed Cayo, and he intervenes to get him proper medical attention (a close-up of the elder-tree flower, with its medicinal qualities that are now insufficient contrasts with the juxtaposed long shot of the ambulance taking the ailing *campesino* away). Rafa then paints on the wall, "Vote for V V"—the political slogan of the 1977 elections, and specifically that of the idealist candidate who later gave up politics "para dedicarse a no sé qué tipo de enloquecidas empresas" (in order to dedicate himself to I don't know what kind of crazy enterprises), according to Rafa. Although his attendance at Víctor's funeral (against the wishes of his superiors) and his subsequent trip to the village may have momentarily rekindled his idealism, the final image of the film, a long shot in the rearview mirror of the receding town, visually reinforces Rafa's definitive separation from the worlds of both Cayo and Víctor.

Giménez Rico's use of black and white for the narrative in the present constitutes an overly facile use of color symbolism (the drabness and shallowness of the current life of Rafa and Laly), and it breaks the aesthetic development of the rest of the narrative. Although the narrative in the present causes the viewer to witness the culmination of the theme of disillusionment that is hinted at in the narrative of the events of 1977, Giménez Rico also seems to use the present narrative and the transitions from present to past (repetitions of dialogue with changes in camera angle that signify a transformation in point of view) as filler: the film is only ninety-eight minutes long and would have been excessively short without these scenes.

El tesoro (*The Treasure*, 1990), directed by Antonio Mercero, is based on Delibes's novel from 1985. This work, which is about an archaeological dig in central Spain, is quite brief, and Mercero adds to and transforms the original narrative in order to heighten the dramatic tension of the confrontation between the archaeologists from Madrid and the townspeople from a small Castilian village who epitomize avarice and a close-minded attitude. Director Mercero (205) believes that the two innovative elements in the script are the creation of the female character, Marga, and the expansion of violence to make it the true protagonist of the film narrative. He sees the film as a "testimonial western," since the confrontation between "good guys" (the archaeologists) and the "bad guys" (the town folks) is based on an actual event that occurred to Professor Germán Delibes, the novelist's son.

The juxtaposition of the initial two sequences connotes the inevitable confrontation between greedy villagers and disinterested scholars: a farmer named Lino, using a metal detector, begins to dig in a field, in contrast with an archaeology class in which the professor, Jero Otero (José Coronado), admonishes his students about the correct way to conduct an excavation. Use of a metal detector precludes the "discoverer" from any monetary reward under Spanish law, but Lino lies in order to cash in on the fabulous Celtiberian treasure that he has encountered.

The tracking shot around the sign, "Excavations prohibited," which is posted near the discovery site, underscores its ominous message that is clearly aimed at the outsiders, and the brief montage sequence that follows it (shots that juxtaposes Jero and the students with the shepherd, the machine operator, and the town, set to a soundtrack that contains a drumbeat that lends a threatening air to the sequence) sets the stage for a confrontation. The film adaptation conserves the rustic billingsgate of the original novel in the shepherd's threat to the group: "Me cago en sos . . . La vais a pagar todos juntos, cacho cabrones, por venir a robar la mina" (Fuck you . . . You're all going to pay, you assholes, for coming to rob the mine). Although Jero dismisses him as a "poor lunatic," his threat of physical violence—hanging them from the oak tree—indicates resentment not only against the scientists from Madrid, but also against Lino and his female companion, Pelaya, who are also considered outsiders because they are not from Gamones. The film narrative contains a crescendo of suspense as threats turn to violence. Following the tractor burning sequence, the long shot of two bodies hanging from the tree is a visual image with greater impact in the film than in the novel. The fact that the bodies are merely straw men actually adds tension regarding the fate of the archaeologists, since this is only a threat and does not deter them from continuing their investigations.

Mercero also adds several incidents to build greater dramatic tension in the confrontation between the villagers and the outsiders. When Jero, Marga (Ana Alvarez), and the other students arrive in the small town where the treasure was

A fight against greed and ignorance: Antonio Mercero's *El tesoro*, starring José Coronado and Ana Alvarez. *Courtesy Escorpio Films, S.A.*

discovered, an excavator symbolically blocks the road, and the montage of the low-angle shots of the operator, the gigantic shovel, and Jero, who honks repeatedly to have the operator clear the way, is a foreboding entrance into the provincial atmosphere that foreshadows the denouement. Later, as the archaeologists walk down the street, a woman throws her bucket of cleaning water in front of them, again symbolically blocking their progress.

The rejection of the archaeologists grows as the film narrative progresses: when Marga first enters the bar to use the telephone, she is met with sudden silence, but on the second occasion, the men in the bar bang their glasses against their tables. The most antagonistic townsperson is Papo (Alvaro de Luna); his physical condition as a cripple who uses a crutch is also symbolic of his mental attitude toward the scholars. Although Mercero deletes the obscene gesture with which Papo greets the archaeologists in the novel (37), the film version accentuates his antagonistic actions against them. During a night sequence, Papo kills a pigeon and throws it through Jero's window. The breaking glass is less disturbing, however, than the message tied to the dead bird's body: "Largo, cabrones, que venís a robar el oro" (Get out, you bastards, who have come to rob the gold). After the shepherd threatens to hang Lino and his female companion, Pelaya, Papo also leads a group of men to Lino's house, where he carries a container of gasoline and sets fire to Lino's tractor.

The change in narrative from telling (124) to showing visually heightens the climate of violence. Mercero likewise shifts the narrative style in the episode regarding Escolástico, the mayor of the village. Although in the novel the disorderly conduct of the townspeople is blamed on his unjustified disappearance (106), in the film Papo visits Escolástico while the latter is skinning rabbits, and the mayor decides to turn a blind eye to the cripple's activities—"De lo vuestro no sé nada. No puedo enterarme de nada. ¿Lo entiendes?" (I don't know a thing about what you are doing. I can't find out anything. Do you understand?) The blood on Escolástico's hands is symbolic of the violent denouement, and the Pilate-like washing of his hands cuts to a low-angle shot of buzzards circling the group of archaeologists to further connote impending death.

After an ominous ringing of the town bell, a repetition of the low-angle shot of the buzzards precedes a montage sequence that heightens the tension as the level of confrontation increases: the townspeople, armed with shovels and hoes, approach on foot and by tractor as Jero admonishes the students to keep working and avoid violence. Papo's lack of respect for authority —"Decir en Madrid que aquí no escarba nadie aunque venga la Reina" (Tell them in Madrid that even if the Queen comes, nobody is going to dig here)—the shepherd's renewed threat of hanging, and the townspeople's chorus of "Thieves" are too much for the archaeologists, who must withdraw.

Jero's appeal to provincial authorities in Segovia seems to resolve the issue, as the director general visits Ganomes in his Mercedes, which he sees as a symbol of power with regard to these country bumpkins. Mercero wisely condenses his meeting with town officials at the schoolhouse in which they come to an accord; in the novel, this dialogue occupies a full twelve percent of the narrative (97-111). In contrast, the film adaptation shifts the vandalization of the archaeological site from an after the fact description (122) to showing the destruction, taking the confrontation between Jero and Papo to a violent conclusion. Mercero tries to milk the fight scene between the archaeologist and the cripple by using five slow-motion segments, but this overkills the scene and diminishes the value of the denouement. In this machista confrontation, it is ironically Marga who saves Jero by hitting Papo with a shovel as the villain is about to strangle the archaeologist with his crutch; in a bit of double irony, the swinging shovel from the excavator gives Papo the deathblow. The final crane down to an abandoned earthen vessel as the rain washes more soil away symbolizes the lack of winners in this struggle between greed and scholarship, sophisticated urbanites and close-minded provincials.

The expansion of Marga's role throughout the film is one of the most important departures from the original text. In the novel, Jero merely speaks to her on the phone, and she only appears on the very last page of the narrative. The girlfriend's expanded role is meant to appeal to younger audiences who can relate to the accomplishments and problems of the modern Spanish woman: her mysterious phone calls to Madrid turn out to be inquiries about a pregnancy test, and when she discovers that she is indeed pregnant, she and Jero discuss a possible abortion and whether or not to marry. At the end of the novel, Jero's tender whisper of "How much I need you" contrasts with her more forthcoming role at the end of the film, where she consoles the archaeologist, "Jero, olvídate de esto. Piensa en nuestro hijo. Voy a tenerlo" (Jero, forget about this. Think about our son. I'm going to have him). Likewise, the students' use of slang, which does faithfully capture the linguistic element of the novel, and which brings to mind the similar linguistic element in *El diputado voto del Señor Cayo* would also appeal to younger audiences.

Mercero (207) notes that the lack of commercial distribution of the film may have been due to its poor reception at its the 1988 Valladolid Film Festival, which he blames on "provocateurs" who disrupted the showing, and García Domínguez (195-196) suspects that there may have been a plot to abort the film's success.

In 1990, Luis Alcoriza adapted Delibes' novel *La sombra del ciprés es alargada* (*The Cypress's Shadow Is Elongated*, 1947) to the screen. As in the original novel, the narrative is divided into two basic temporal components: Pedro's life as a child at a *pensión* and boarding school in Avila, and his adult life as a ship captain. As an orphan, Pedro lives with his mentor, Señor Lesmes (Emilio Gutiérrez Caba) and family—wife Gregoria (Fiorella Faltoyano), daughter Martina, and their dog Bonnie, described by Pedro as "lo mejor de la casa" (the best part of the house). Lemes, an austere teacher who reads Seneca and often quotes stoic aphorisms to his young pupil, leaves an important spiritual imprint on Pedro.

Avila, a city of medieval ramparts in the Castilian tableland that is known for being the home of Saint Teresa, also has a spiritual impact on the boy. In a sense, Avila becomes another character in the first half of the film, with the initial sequence of the carriage travelling through the streets of the city, the interior shots of its gothic cathedral, and the touristy long shot of the city from the "Four Posts" to its west, where Alfredo compares the walled city to a ship, thus initiating the maritime theme.

This sea metaphor is only one of the elements that Alcoriza adds to the film text in order to provide a smooth transition from one half of the narrative to the other. Young Alberto's fascination with the sea, an element not contained in the original novel, provides an element of narrative unity to the film version. As Pedro's roommate and best friend, Alberto shares his viewing device with its scenes of the sea, and his conch shell in which Pedro can "hear" the waves. These objects, together with the sailor's suit that Alfredo wears in the pharmacy scene, metaphorically underscore Alfredo's fascination with the sea. He later gives Pedro a ship in a bottle, an object that becomes one of the central metaphors of the narrative. His dream of them both becoming sailors is truncated, however, by his early death when the sickly youngster becomes ill after a midwinter nocturnal escapade.

The family's visit to the cemetery allows Alcoriza to explicate the novel's title, which in turn underscores the death theme in the narrative. Alfredo complains that he does not like cypress trees—a ubiquitous element of Spanish cemeteries and symbol of death—since they cast a very long shadow which is like "una manecilla del reloj de los muertos" (a hand on the clock of the dead).

The director opts to finish the first section of the narrative in a poetic tone. After receiving extreme unction, Alfredo asks his friend to be near him, and as he listens to the seashell, we hear the wind—another nondiegetic symbol of death, and Alcoriza cuts to a long shot of the bed on the beach. Alfredo's final words, "El mar era de los dos; ahora es solo tuyo" (The sea belonged to us both; now it is just yours), precede a long pan of the waves and a tracking shot of the ocean from a ship. However, the poetic import of the visual image of the bed on the beach does not seem to mesh with the visual discourse of the rest of the film, which is dominated by the aesthetics of realism, and this lack of congruity diminishes what is otherwise an adept transition to the second half of the narrative.

In the novel, the adult Pedro goes to sea and visits the United States, where he meets Jane. The transition of Jane's character to the screen presented certain obstacles. What language would this American girl speak on screen? What about the budgetary considerations of filming in Rhode Island? Alcoriza skirted these obstacles by transforming the setting to Vera Cruz, Mexico, where Jane is an American anthropologist who speaks Spanish fluently because of the many years that she lived in Spain. (García Domínguez [217] speculates that this change may have been at the behest of the Mexican co-producers.) In many ways, Alcoriza seems to modernize Jane's character, imposing a liberated career woman of the 1990s onto the 1940s.

When Pedro (Juanjo Guerenabarrena) meets Jane (Dany Prius) ashore at a cafe, it is evident that both Lesmes's philosophy and Avila's atmosphere have molded the sea captain's character. Recalling Alfredo's burial—the only flashback in an otherwise lineal film narrative—Pedro comments that "La vida es un perder mucho para ganar un poco. Quien se entrega a amores intensos mucho va a sufrir cuando se le vayan" (Life means losing a lot in order to gain a little. Whoever gives in to intense love is going to suffer a lot when it goes away). Jane's comment that Pedro keeps his emotions under lock and key synthesizes his character. Pedro also tells Jane that he prefers the snow and cold over the tropical heat of Vera Cruz because they are "pure." Jane, however, retorts, "Por eso eres tan frio" (That is why you are so cold), underscoring how Pedro's character was shaped by the city of his youth.

Meeting Jane gives rise to an inner conflict in Pedro of passion versus reason. However, Alcoriza's treatment of the sexual relationship between Pedro and Jane represents an important change in tone from the original narrative, where its elliptical obliqueness lends it a platonic quality. The film version has several scenes charged with sexual insinuations, culminating with the scene of them in bed making love, which represents Alcoriza's attempt to update the original narrative to interest contemporary Spanish film audiences who have become accustomed to or even expect *destape* in their films.

The ship in the bottle that Alfredo gave Pedro becomes a central metaphor for his character. When he first shows it to Jane, he explains, "Alli estoy yo, o mejor dicho, soy yo mismo" (I'm in there, or better put, that is me). He is shut up in a glass bottle, unable to reach out. Jane's decision in the film narrative to terminate her relationship with Pedro corresponds to the more contemporary characterization and represents an important change in tone from the original narrative, as Jane's accidental death loses some of its tragic dimensions. In the novel, Jane was the happy and faithful wife awaiting her husband's return, and her loss represents a greater tragedy for the sea captain. In the film version, Pedro was about to lose her anyway, since she was going to terminate the relationship, and this mitigates the viewer's sense of loss.

Alcoriza visually exploits the accident scene that Delibes narrates so concisely. He uses a montage sequence of Jane driving her car around the corner with screeching tires, the shots of Pedro observing the tragic scene from the deck of the ship, the long shot of the truck that cuts her off and causes the crash, and the medium shots of Jane slumping over the steering wheel before the car plunges into the water, and the final cut to Pedro covering his tragedy-stricken face with his hands.

The final temporal segment of the film narrative occurs in Avila. Pedro's destiny was to accede to the magnetic pull of the city of his youth. With a study filled with ships in bottles that provide the visual and spiritual continuity to the earlier segments of the film, Pedro has literally become another Señor Lesmes, occupying his position both professionally—taking his place as teacher—and in his home, having married his daughter. The final still of Pedro in the plaza embracing the new dog to the accompaniment of Beethoven's "Für Elise" that the young Martina attempted to master in the early segment of the film completes the narrative circle. This represents an important departure from the original narrative, where Pedro's obstinate, almost antisocial character would inexorably lead him to loneliness, as the shadow of death would rob him of his few loved ones.

Another departure from the original narrative consists of a sequence that alludes to the Spanish civil war. When he visits her apartment, Pedro asks Jane why she has a Republican flag. Jane responds that her father fought for the Republic in the Abraham Lincoln Brigade, and he is still obsessed with the Spanish civil war. Pedro, who studied at the naval academy in Barcelona, regrets that he was in Galicia when the war broke out, and therefore did not fight for the Republican cause: "Algunas veces pensé en escaparme, quedarme en algún puerto y pasarme al otro lado, pero nos tenían muy vigilados" (Sometimes I thought about escaping, about staying in some port and going over to the other side, but they really kept watch on us). The scene immediately cuts to a dinner party the next day at Jane's house in which Alfonso (Julián Pastor), a Republican exile living in Mexico, irately exclaims, "Eso son leches. Miles del otro bando se pasaron a nuestro lado, y muchos se quedaron en el camino" (That's bullshit. Thousands from the other faction came over to our side, and many of them were left on the road). The excuses offered by Jane's "capitancito de mierda" (fucking little captain), as Alfonso calls him, are inadmissible.

The component of *cainismo* in the film may seem superfluous, since it has nothing to do with the rest of the plot development of the film and does not appear at all in the original novel; it seems that the civil war is not just an obsession for Jane's fictional father, but for director Alcoriza and millions of other Spaniards.

The main difficulty with adapting this novel for the screen is the problem of adequately capturing the interior world of the protagonist—the meditations, doubts, and feelings manifested in the first-person narrative. The film version eschews any voice-overs that would have captured Pedro's interior monologues that occur throughout the novel, and which often helped underscore his predestination. Alcoriza is not as successful in capturing the spirit of this, Delibes's first novel, as one would like, and the result was a relative lack of both critical and commercial success.

Fernando Fernán Gómez

Fernando Fernán Gómez (b. 1921) is a multifaceted talent in contemporary Spanish culture whose work in cinema, theater, literature, and journalism garnered him the Príncipe de Asturias Prize for the Arts in 1995. Fernán Gómez's career as an actor spans his entire life (he was even born while his mother, an actress with the María Guerrero company, was touring in Peru and Argentina). American audiences are most familiar with him for his role as Manolo in Fernando Trueba's *Belle epoque*, the 1993 Oscar-winning best foreign film. He is also a film director, novelist, and playwright—his *Las bicicletas son para el verano* (*Bicycles Are for Summer*) not only won the prestigious Lope de Vega Award, but was also adapted for the screen by Jaime Chávarri in 1984.

In 1986, Fernán Gómez successfully directed the cinemato-graphic adaptation of his own novel from 1985, *El viaje a ninguna parte* (*The Trip to Nowhere*). It was the winner of several prestigious awards, including Goyas for best picture, best director, and best script. The film portrays a company of itinerant actors during the 1940s and 1950s, and stars Fernán Gómez, José Sacristán, and Gabino Diego as three generations of comedians: Don Arturo, Carlos, and Carlitos Galván. The structure of the film consists of a series of twelve flashbacks following the opening close-up of an elderly Carlos saying, "Hay que recordar" (One must remember). The shadowing space of this preliminary shot turns out to be an old folks home in 1973 where Carlos undergoes sessions with a psychiatrist about his memories—or about his memory, since the very act of remembering is called into question.

After Carlos rediscovers his long lost seventeen-year-old son and incorporates him into the troupe (a process that contains some of the most humorous sequences of the film), the actors travel from town to town, fighting for their survival. Their enemies include other troupes of actors as well as rival entertainment such as soccer ("our worst enemy"—even Carlitos momentarily abandons the troupe), and cinema, which evokes anger on the part of the clan elder. Don Arturo's outbursts, with typical Spanish billingsgate, humorously counterbalances the tragedy of their situation: he threatens the movie entrepreneur, Solís, saying, "Me cago en el jodido peliculero. Le mato. Voy a estrangularlo con sus jodidas películas" (Fuck the fucking movie man. I'll kill him. I'm going to strangle him with his fucking movies). Nevertheless, Juanita (Laura del Sol), Carlos's lover and a member of the troupe, succinctly captures their misery with the lament, "Tengo hambre, Carlos" (I'm hungry, Carlos). She later complains, "Esto no es un oficio, Carlos. Somos vagabundos" (This is not an occupation, Carlos. We're bums), and says that people prefer the movies, and she does, too. Ironically, she abandons Carlos "with somebody from the movies" in order to work at a bar in Rota (where there are American sailors with money), and this is the first in a series of death blows to both the troupe and Carlos. Eventually even Carlos capitulates, and he decides to go to Madrid to work as an extra in the movies, to which his die-hard father-actor exclaims, "Me cago en el padre de los hermanos Lumière" (Fuck the father of the Lumière brothers). The inherent humor in this billingsgate helps mitigate the pathetic situation of the actors. Don Arturo himself had attempted to work in the movies, but much to the consternation of the film director, the old man was unable to accommodate his dramatic declamation to the cinema. The director's exacerbation grows until he shouts, "Corte o me corto yo los huevos" (Cut, or I'll cut my balls off), and Don Arturo must retire from the scene crying, a defeated man.

The sociopolitical element of the film appears very subtly. One of the initial reasons for the economic hardships that the actors face is a satirical comment about the social life of the Caudillo, and how his personal mores were imposed on the nation: the theaters had to close early—"cosas de Franco, como no salía" (it was one of Franco's things, since he never went out at night). The moral climate is intertwined with political ramifications when Don Arturo expresses his surprise and chagrin at seeing a rival theatrical troupe in town. The setting is during mass, and his use of more curse words ("¡Coño, son los Calleja Ruiz!" [Shit, it's the Calleja Ruiz family]) offends a local matron, Doña Florentina. Although Don Arturo, with hat in hand, contritely apologizes in the plaza after mass, Doña

Florentina will have none of it: "Hay que apedrearlos. Son rojos, rojos, rojos" (We should stone them. They are reds, reds, reds). The repetition of the term underscores the political divisions that culminated in the fratricidal conflict of almost twenty years before.

The political component continues as Don Arturo angrily informs us that another competing theatrical company was a student group sponsored by the *Falange*. Nevertheless, the relationship between these itinerant dramatists and the government also brings them favor; this is due to the fact that one actor, Juan Maldonado (Juan Diego) fought in the "Blue Division" in Russia and therefore had "inside influence." Indeed, it is through Juan's contacts that Carlos, as an old man, is able to obtain a place in the old folks home. Maldonado's fascist past, however, leads to what is the weakest segment of the film, a drunk scene in which the script, especially Carlitos's dialogue, is marred by ill attempts at humor.

Maldonado's privileged place as "ex-combatiente" (veteran) helps to get him housing at a *pensión* in Madrid, and Galván also subtly refers to it when his psychiatrist questions what would have been normally unacceptable behavior during the Franco regime. The interrogative refers to the episode when Solís offers the troupe work as actors in a film. The local men who want the work threaten the itinerant actors, "Ningún forastero nos quita el pan" (No outsider is going to take our bread and butter away), and after the shot that culminates the threatening posture—an extreme close-up of the local mayor—Carlos responds with an eloquent verbal rebuff in which he extols the locals' hard work, justifies his mission in life ("la gente necesita reírse y nosotros les llevamos la risa" [people need to laugh, and we bring laughter to them]) and appeals to their sense of solidarity: "somos vuestros hermanos en el trabajo, o la falta de trabajo y la falta de pan" (we are your brothers in labor, or lack of labor and lack of bread). A cut to the present shows an incredulous psychiatrist: "¿Y usted, Galván, dijo todo esto en un pueblo de España en los años 50?" (And you, Galván, said all this in a town in Spain in the 1950s?) The retired actor's response is two-fold: that is the way that he remembers it, and that Juan Maldonado also spoke. The second half of the response indicates Maldonado's privileged place as a veteran; he would be allowed to speak words that would have been prohibited of others; the first half reflects the problem of the mechanism of remembering. Indeed, the scenes in the present with the psychiatrist often refute Carlos's memory. When the actor remembers Kennedy's visit to Spain (the visual image of the plaza festively decorated and Spaniards waving American flags as the cars pass by is an homage to García Berlanga's 1952 *Bienvenido, Mr. Marshall*), a cut to the psychiatrist not only rectifies Carlos's faulty memory, but also subtly criticizes the Franco regime: "Kennedy nunca visitó España. Ni el Caudillo quitó la censura" (Kennedy never visited Spain. Nor did the Leader remove censorship). Carlos's flawed memories of his successful screen acting career (festivals in Venice, Cannes; his photograph on the cover of *Primer plano* film magazine) are ironically counterbalanced by the arrival at the old folks home of the famous actor Daniel Otero, who has a trunk full of newspaper clippings that attest to his brilliant career. Why does Carlos confuse reality? As the elderly Maldonado (now a bookseller) observes to his friend, "Tu oficio es mentir" (Your occupation is lying).

In *El viaje a ninguna parte*, the function of memory has both a political/historical dimension and a personal dimension that addresses the question of the fine line between fiction (drama) and fact, memory and imagination. The multiple fade-outs at the end of the film formally underscore the fusion of these opposites: the images of a young Carlos dancing with Marilyn Monroe, the troupe walking through the Spanish countryside, the cars from the Kennedy entourage stopping to pick them up, and the final long shot of the bus on the country road constitute the dreams and reality of an itinerant actor in the Spain of the 1950s. Pérez de León (99) notes that the jazz on the soundtrack that accompanies both the opening credits as well as these images underscores the spontaneous sentiments of an artist. The final shot of the bus on the empty road graphically captures the title of the film; reality, in the end, outweighs fantasy.

El mar y el tiempo is another film directed by Fernando Fernán Gómez that is based on his own work; it had its debut in

October of 1989. The film stars José Soriano as a Republican who returns to Madrid in 1968 from Buenos Aires after twenty-nine years of exile, Fernán Gómez as his brother Eusebio, and Rafaela Aparicio as their aging mother—a role which immediately brings to mind an intertextual relationship between this film and her role as mother-figure in Saura's *Ana y los lobos* and *Mamá cumple cien años*. The first dialogue between the reunited brothers addresses the political question, and delineates a marked difference between the two: Jesús inquires what Eusebio thinks of the work of the exiles, and the latter's cynical response is, "¿Qué labor?" (What work?) Generally, however, the political dimension in the film is displaced from the exile question to that of the younger generation of Eusebio's daughters and their friends. The latter live in an apartment adorned with a poster of Ché Guevara, sing "Al vent" ("To the Wind," the protest song by the Valencian singer-songwriter Raimon that was popular at the time), name their daughter "Libertad," and participate in student demonstrations in both Madrid and Paris. The only intersection of the two political components occurs when the young Mariano meets Jesús and expresses his political solidarity with the older generation: "Estamos con todos los que se fueron como usted" (We are with everyone that left like you did). The action is set in 1968, and the official news from Spanish radio and television differentiate the sociopolitical situation in Spain from that of the rest of the world: the assassination of Martin Luther King, the war in Vietnam, and student rebellions in Paris manifest a turbulent world that contrasts with the news that manifests thirty years of "peace": the Franco regime's "Birth Prize" for a family with nineteen children.

Jesús experiences the normal reactions of the exile: he is unable to relate to his changed homeland. He expresses his lack of reintegration throughout the film narrative with statements such as "No reconozco nada" (I don't recognize anything), "Yo lo recuerdo de otra manera" (I remember it in another way), "No es lo que yo dejé" (It's not the same as I left it). Eusebio takes his brother to see a statue that he remembers from his youth as one in which they could see its sexual organ

Brothers reunited: Fernando Fernán Gómez's *El mar y el tiempo*, starring Fernando Fernán Gómez and Pepe Soriano. *Courtesy Ión Producciones, S.A.*

protruding from the side. A low-angle circular tracking shot reflects the brothers' vain attempt to confirm the boyhood memory; the close-up of the statue shows no protruding organ, and the sudden appearance of green leaves in front of the camera causes Jesús to remark, "Lo taparon con el arbolito" (They covered it up with the little tree). More than a veiled barb at censorship during the Franco regime, this statement functions as a safety valve so that Jesús can avoid admitting his faulty memory.

Unlike in Jaime de Armiñán's *El amor del Capitán Brando*, where the linguistic element is a cause of alienation (as Fernando complains that he does not even seem to speak Spanish), in this film the linguistic element manifests the reintegration theme. During a card game in the restaurant, the players insult each other with expressions of typical Spanish billingsgate ("Tonto del culo" [Asshole], "Vete a hacer puñetas" [Fuck off], etc.), and this strikes a real chord in Jesús, who exclaims, "Sentí por primera vez que había vuelto" (For the first time, I felt that I had returned).

Jesús's inability to achieve reintegration into Spanish society is manifest in allusions to visits to old friends in Vallecas. Since this community forms part of the "red belt" around Madrid, the narrative connotes an attempt to reformulate the friendship with old leftist companions from the pre-war days. This attempt is unsuccessful, however, as Jesús notes on two occasions that he found them "different" and that "No me entendí con ellos" (I didn't get along with them).

The greatest breach, however, is between the brothers themselves. Both reminisce about the hard times that they went through after the war. Jesús became a pimp in Buenos Aires; Eusebio was a black-marketeer in Madrid, and only later was able to find work in the restaurant where he is currently employed. His admission that a member of the Opus Dei backed him in the restaurant draws protest from his brother and provides a glimpse into how Eusebio betrayed his prior intellectual and political point of view. The change in Eusebio is confirmed during the most poignant scene in the film, when Jesús visits his brother's ex-wife, Marcela (María Asquerino). As in many Saura films, music functions here as a Proustian device to trigger memories of the past: with songs such as "La canastera" ("The Basket Maker") and "En el barranco del lobo" ("In the Wolf's Ravine") from the 1930s, Jesús comments to Marcela that he can see her skipping rope. But times have changed: Marcela is now an alcoholic, and her tragedy stems from the war, since her husband was a different man before the war, one with ideals who wanted to change the world, not the "desecho que es ahora" (wreck that he is now). Indeed, the relationship between Eusebio and Lupe, his young "compañera," confirms Marcela's opinion of him: steeped in cynicism, Eusebio seems happy to have as his female companion a woman who deals in a world of drugs, bribery, and influence peddling.

Doña Eusebia cannot accept the fact that her son has returned. She has a fossilized image of her son, that shown in the close-up of the young Jesús in a soldier's uniform that Eusebia wears in a locket. After a close-up of a tin box of "dulce de membrillo" (quince preserves) that she has prepared for him, she complains that although he loved it as a boy, he did not even look at it during their reunion, proof for her that this

Ontological questions: *El mar y el tiempo*, with Rafaela Aparicio, Fernando Fernán Gómez, Aitana Sánchez Gijón Iñaki Miramón, and Cristina Marsillach. *Courtesy Ión Producciones, S.A.*

man is not Jesús. For Eusebia, this man is an impostor; her son drowned in the sea trying to escape after the war. When Jesús decides to return to Argentina, he expresses to his mother yet another statement reflecting his lack of integration: "Esta España no es la que yo conocía" (This Spain is not the one that I knew); her response, "Ni usted es usted" (And you are not you), represents the ontological underpinning of the dilemma faced by all exiles. The relationship between exiles and the motherland is one of fossilization: while both the individual and the society change, the act of separation freezes the dynamics of the interrelationship between the two and makes the possibility of successful repatriation ever more difficult with the passage of time. The final shot of the film, the superimposed image of the sea and phonograph speakers, manifests a circularity in the narrative, since the opening shot was of the sea and a radio; it thus underscores both in visual imagery as well as the accompanying soundtrack of the tango, "Mi Buenos Aires querido" ("My Dear Buenos Aires"), the inevitable failure of repatriation, and the ineluctable departure from Spain of the exiled Republican to return to his adopted land.

Wenceslao Fernández Flórez

Wenceslao Fernández Flórez was a very popular novelist in Spain in the 1940s and 1950s, and no fewer than twelve of his works were made into movies between 1935 and 1962. In addition, Fernández Flórez was scriptwriter for several movies. Since 1965, two of his novels went from page to screen: *El hombre que se quiso matar* (*The Man Who Wanted to Kill Himself*) and *El bosque animado* (*The Animated Forest*).

Rafael Gil's 1970 version of *El hombre que se quiso matar* is in fact a remake, since this same director had made a screen version of this narrative in 1942. In this newer version, Gil makes some changes from both the original and the earlier versions: the protagonist, Federico (Tony Leblanc), is a teacher instead of an architect. In either case, both his professional life and his personal life are failures. When he gives a speech, the little applause and the laughter when he trips and falls contrasts with his dream sequence in which he is greeted with great applause and a beautiful woman presents him with a rose. The school director refuses to give him a raise, and he is the object of laughter when he drinks a glass of milk at a bar. His life changes, however, when he announces that he will commit suicide next Friday, since he will now have the will to do whatever he pleases, a "luxury" that no one else in his audience has ever really had. His complete freedom now allows him to court Irene (Elisa Ramírez) even in front of her boyfriend. He decides to visit the school director and political boss, Evaristo Argüelles, and threatens to kill him just before committing suicide, since he says he needs a conversational companion for the long "journey" that awaits him. Argüelles, however, convinces him not to kill anyone, in exchange for a cushy job with a huge salary.

The film is in comic tone with vaudeville music on the soundtrack to make Federico seem even more ridiculous, and sight gags, such as when Argüelles convinces Federico that he is not the cultured conversationalist that he wants for the journey, since everything about him is false—and he lifts up his wig. Likewise, when Federico takes revenge on a bully by making him drink an enormous glass of milk at the bar, the camera zooms in to a close-up as the bully burps at the end. Finally, a new episode at the end adds a bit of irony. As Federico and Irene escape in a car, it goes off the road, and Federico exclaims, "Qué horror, por poco me mato" (Oh, my God, I almost killed myself). Equally ironic, however, is the fact that the townsfolk declare themselves democratic and decide to vote on whether or not he should kill himself, with the result that everyone is against him. Aside from Spaniards traditional penchant for black humor, this was, after all, 1970, with five more years before the Franco regime would end.

In 1987, Spaniards founded a national academy of motion pictures in order to foment their motion picture industry and to recognize their best films with awards (Goyas). In the second year of the competition, *El bosque animado* (*The Animated Forest*), the screen adaptation of Fernández Flórez's 1943 novel, received five Goyas, including those for best picture, best actor (Alfredo Landa), best script (Rafael Azcona), best costume design (Javier Artiñano), and best music (José Nieto). The film was directed by José Luis Cuerda.

El bosque animado provides a pantheistic vision of a forest in Galicia, in northwestern Spain. The adjective of the title not only means "alive," but also connotes "having a soul," thus conjuring up images of spirits in this misty region of Spain inhabited by Celts. The novel begins by describing the forest as a "being made up of many beings;" indeed, the characters in the novel include both flora and fauna, ranging from pine trees that converse with their neighbor, the eucalyptus, to a mole named Furacroyos, and from a mountain bandit nicknamed "Fende-testas" to the wandering spirit of Fiz Cotavelo. Many of the animal characters in the novel lend a Kiplingesque air to the narrative, and animal characters often serve an allegorical function in the narrative to underscore the inexorable laws of the forest: each individual being is mortal, but the forest transcends their individual existences; all beings must struggle to survive, and they must all conform to a natural order of things. Thus, when the trout realize that they have been tricked by artificial bait, they affix a rusty tin can to the fisherman's hook: metal bait deserves a metal catch. The band of stray cats that attacks an ox inevitably fails because their enterprise is unnatural, and the episode also serves as an anti-militaristic allegory. The flies that band together to cause havoc among the folks that inhabit the forest serve as an anti-communistic allegory. Director Cuerda eliminates animals from the narrative and concentrates on the relationships among the human characters. Cuerda (63) admits that the allegorical narratives of the novel that are based on the personification of plants and animals pertain to another cinematography. Nevertheless, he does include close-ups of the mole (Furacroyos's wife in the novel) that the young Fuco kills in order to sell its pelt; and Esmoris's dog appears in the film as the guard dog for the cottage rented by the Roade sisters.

Alfredo Landa, in the role of the bumbling robber "Fendetestas," shows his superb acting range and confirms that talent of the actor who moved from many inferior comic roles in the 1960s and early 1970s to his best acting performance in Camus's *The Holy Innocents*. Director Cuerda accentuates the humor of this character in the novel. At times this is the result of cuts that juxtapose characters' questions or comments with the image of the bandit: in the opening sequence, he declares that he is tired of being unemployed, and he will be come "Fendetestas the bandit," but he later accompanies Gerardo on a well-digging job. The visit to the aristocrats' house provides him with the opportunity to furtively steal an old pistol, and when the job falls through and Gerardo asks his friend what he plans on doing without work, the humorous response to the well digger's question appears in the cut to Fendetestas in a cave practicing his "battle" cry with his pistol—"Alto, que me caso en Soria" (Halt, I'm getting married in Soria). As an obvious euphemism ("me caso" substitutes for "me cago" [I shit]), this expression has comic overtones throughout the narrative.

Later, when the Roade sisters arrive for a summer respite from the city, their hostess Juanita calms their apprehensions about the forest, saying "Pues más tranquilo que esto . . ." (There's nothing more tranquil than this . . .), which is immediately followed by a cut to a tracking shot of the bandit about to rob a farmer—a foreshadowing of the disturbance that will later drive the sisters out. The accentuation of the humor

From well digger to bandit: José Luis Cuerda's *El bosque animado*, starring Alfredo Landa and Fernando Valverde. *Courtesy Classic Films Producción, S.A.*

of Fendetestas's character is particularly noted regarding his desire for tobacco, which becomes a real obsession in the film. His justification for becoming a robber is "Estoy harto de no tener ni para tabaco" (I'm tired of not having enough money to even buy tobacco). After robbing his first victim, the bandit politely inquires, "¿Tiene usted un cigarrillo?" (Do you have a cigarette?) He also asks for tobacco of Gerardo, and then has him go to town to buy for him. When the civil guard informs Gerardo that his friend should come down himself for tobacco, Fendetestas's humorous response is "You mean to say that thieves aren't allowed to smoke?" Fendetestas then tries to rob tobacco from a nocturnal wanderer in the forest, whose head is wrapped in a bandage; he is unable to oblige the bandit since, he says, they did not put tobacco in his pockets when they shrouded him. Although devoid of the white sheet and chains of the original narrative, this wandering soul of Fiz Cotovelo has the same dry humor and irony in the film. Fiz breaks the monotony of Fendetestas's solitude, (in the novel, instead of trying to rob him, the bandit simply complains that the worst thing about being the forest bandit is that he cannot go into town for tobacco [39]), but the spirit is bad for business, since no one wants to travel through the forest anymore, knowing that there is a lost soul wandering there (41). The bandit excuses his harsh reprimand, "Vete a penar en otra parte" (Go grieve somewhere else), with his nicotine addiction: "De no tener tabaco, me pone de mala leche" (Not having tobacco, I get in a pissy mood). A solution to his dilemma comes when he identifies a string of torch lights in the distance as the "Holy Assembly," a group of lost spirits who wander the countryside and add victims to their number. Since they are heading toward the ocean, Fendetestas convinces Fiz to join them and continue on to Cuba, where he had always desired to travel when alive. Fendetestas's dream of robbing the priest's house (36, 108) is also related to tobacco. The novel tells of his agony: "He would give anything for a packet of cigarettes"(159). When the occasion arises and he is able to fulfill his dream, he ironically becomes a benefactor, helping the incompetent housekeeper and priest's brother to deliver a heifer. Nevertheless, the difference between his rewards in the novel and the film—a mere cigarette (165), and a handful of cigars—visually manifests the emphasis on tobacco as a comic element in the film.

In the episode in which Fendetestas finds young Pilara's lost *duro*, which equals an entire month's wages (104), the film narrative adds humor to make up for the lost lyrical qualities of the original. When the bandit is unable to lie to the child about having seen the coin, he evokes a bit of Spanish folklore, saying that he saw a magpie with it; Pilara pursues him, and the novel's lyrical dimension stems from the repetition of diminutives as well as personification of the forest (110). The transformation to humor in the film comes from the bandit's excuse for not returning the coin to its rightful owner: "La gente me perdería respeto" (People wouldn't respect me anymore). Both the novel and the film contain the ironic and humorous use of his "war" cry, "me caso en Soria," to signal defeat in the face of young Pilara's persistence. Aside from this euphemism, another humorous linguistic element of the film is Fendetestas's use of Sancho-like proverbs. Visually, Fendetestas' bandit disguise—simply rubbing charcoal on his face—is also a source of humor, since it leads to the instant recognition of him not only by his friend Gerardo (with the humor intensified by Fendetestas's ingenuous question, "¿Cómo me has conocido?" [How did you recognize me?]), but also by his first victim, the affluent farmer Roque Freire. The first encounter does not appear in the novel; it serves not only to foreshadow the second encounter, but also serves to further develop the friendship between the bandit and Gerardo, the solitary well digger. The second encounter faithfully captures the humor of the original, as the farmer haggles with his former employee over how much he could rob of him (106-108).

The solitude of Gerardo stems from the theme of unrequited love. Gerardo's loss of a leg at sea seems to cause a certain shyness with women; scriptwriter Azcona accentuates this characteristic in the film through Gerardo's stammering each time that he attempts to talk to Hermelinda. In the novel, we read, "En las fiestas y romerías, su cojera le mantenía apartado del baile y de las mozas, y bebía entonces con exceso"(28). Fendetestas advises Gerardo that he should someday get a wooden leg of the proper size: the constant squeaking of the knee section is an auditory symbol of Gerardo's awkwardness and failure with women. After hiding behind a tree when he sees Hermelinda coming, he ventures out to ask her if she is going to the dance: "Vas . . . vas al baile?" (Are you . . . are you going to the dance?) When she admonishes him to oil his leg, he excuses himself, and after she leaves him behind, he hits his wooden leg in a gesture of frustration. At the dance, we see a visual expansion on the curt description of the novel: the band plays, Hermelinda dances with another man, a medium shot shows Gerardo drinking, and we see him purchase oil, and apply it to his leg in a close-up; he calls to Hermelinda, thinking that he has fulfilled her wishes, but her curt response while in the arms of another, "Qué bien" (Great), leaves Gerardo dejected, and he turns and asks for another glass of wine.

The film also expands on the moment when Hermelinda decides to leave for the city. Tired of being exploited by her aunt, the young girl packs her bags to seek out a new life. In the film, Cuerda shifts the narrative from telling to showing, expanding on the brief description in the novel as he constructs a poignant departure scene, as Gerardo sees her with suitcase in hand and pursues her to the train platform. Although Gerardo cannot initially respond to Hermelinda's inquiry about why he is there—stammering the lie that he is waiting for a tool that is being shipped—as the moment of departure comes near, he confronts his shyness, admonishing Hermelinda not to suffer the same fate of other women that have left for the city, becoming women of easy virtue; after she climbs aboard, the cross-cut low- and high-angle shots poignantly capture the lack of communication between the two as Gerardo, running alongside the train, shouts, "Que tú y yo . . . Que podríamos . . . Que si quieres . . ." ("You and I . . . We could . . . If you want . . ."), as Hermelinda gestures that she cannot hear. Gerardo's stumble as he tries to run alongside the moving train visually underscores his amorous rejection, and the shift from close-ups to long shots of Hermelinda as the train recedes connotes the unbreachable distance between the two. Gerardo, in his dejection, is interrupted by the Roade sisters, who have just arrived from the city and are asking directions.

The most significant transformation in the narrative has to do with Gerardo and Hermelinda. In the novel, the last chapter is entitled, "The Marvelous Subterranean World," and represents the culmination of the supernatural element in the novel. The depiction of the world of a strange and marvelous creature that lives underground stems from a cave-in suffered by Gerardo while digging a well, and from the concept that "an entire century of dreams fit in one second." In a narrative device similar to that used by Ambrose Bierce in "The Occurrence at Owl Creek Bridge," or by Jorge Luis Borges in "El milagro secreto" ("The Secret Miracle"), Gerardo, in the last second of his life, is able to live the way he had always desired: strange creatures serve him foods that he had seen displayed in restaurant windows in the city, he is offered unimaginable riches, and most importantly, he is reunited with Hermelinda, who exclaims, "Look at me; I am pure and simple, just as you want me to be, just as you have dreamed me to be." This reunion provides momentary happiness before darkness settles over Gerardo and he must exclaim, "I cannot see you, Hermelinda." In the film narrative, Gerardo's reunion with Hermelinda also brings momentary happiness, indeed ecstasy, and it interweaves the magic, the country/city dichotomy, the superstition, and the humor found throughout the original narrative. Magic is represented by Moucha, the town witch, whose secret *Book of Saint Ciprian*—actually the book of Caesar's *Gallic Wars* in Latin—gives her special powers. Gerardo swings from illusion to disillusion and back again as Moucha reads her cards: when she sees a young woman and a young man, a close-up of Gerardo shows great hope, only to be dashed as Moucha's vision of a young man becomes the vision of young men. However, the amulet that the witch provides works its magical charms, and soon Hermelinda returns from the city. Dressed in red, we must surmise that Gerardo's admonition that she not become a prostitute was in vain.

The matronly Roade sisters manifest the city/country dichotomy: they come from the provincial capital to rent a summer cottage in search of peace and tranquility. In the novel, they praise the healthy life of the country: the fruit tastes better, their physical appearance is improved. But unaccustomed to the noises of a forest, they must acquire a dog to protect them at night. The wind in the trees, the clamor of a metal pot knocked over outside by a prowling dog keep them continuously on edge. In the novel, loud noises in their attic lead them to hysterically exclaim, "A man! There's a man up there!", but the real cause turns out to be only a marten. In the ilm, the sisters have been even more frightened by tales of the "Holy Assembly," and script writer Azcona transforms their fears of a man upstairs into reality. After attending young Pilara's funeral, Gerardo and Hermelinda get caught in a rainstorm and take refuge in the attic, where their reunion culminates in ecstasy, much to the chagrin of the Roade sisters, who confuse the moans of orgasm with those of moaning souls. There is a certain irony in that these same Roade sisters who interrupted his attempt to convince Hermelinda to stay are now

Returning home: José Luis Cuerda's *El bosque animado*, with Alejandra Grepi. *Courtesy Classic Films Producción, S.A.*

driven out after hearing the spirits/lovers.

The death of Gerardo in the novel is followed by an epilogue that affirms the transcendent nature of the existence of the forest: life goes on. The film narrative successfully conveys the sense of ongoingness in the life of the forest as well: the young Fuco becomes the apprentice of Fendetestas, thus assuring a forest bandit for the next generation; Gerardo greets a milkmaid carrying her milk can on her head, thus repeating the opening sequence of the film, where Fendetestas also greets a milkmaid; now, however, the milkmaid is Pilara, and since the young girl died in an accident involving the train, this is another spirit who will wander the forest; the soul of Fiz Cotovelo reappears (spirits can travel to Cuba and back in the blink of an eye!) and disappears behind Fendetestas and Fuco into the mist of the trees as another permanent component of this animated forest. Nevertheless, the epilogue with which the film ends, "Esto ocurrió en aquellos años en que una gallina costaba dos pesetas y el bosque de Cecebre era más extenso y más frondoso," hints at a consciousness of ecological problems that confront shrinking ecosystems in the 1980s, but which were not a factor at the time when the novel was written.

The denomination of each chapter of the novel as a "Stanza" immediately connotes a lyrical aspect to the narrative that appears throughout the novel in Fernández Flórez's use of poetic language. Cuerda captures this poetic quality of the forest from the opening frames of the film— low-angle shots of the trees and pathways in the woods—to the final image of the spirit of Fiz Cotovelo as it fades into the mist of the woods. Director José Luis Cuerda has created a film narrative that is different from the original, but which captures the poetic spirit of the novel. The greater interweaving of plot components related to the human inhabitants of the forest creates a tighter narrative than the original, and in many ways, Cuerda's *El bosque animado* is superior to the original by Fernández Flórez.

Jesús Fernández Santos

Jesús Fernández Santos (b. 1926) is a novelist who studied cinematography in Madrid and who earned his living as a director of short films. His 1977 novel, *Extramuros*, won the National Prize for Literature, and was adapted to the screen in 1985 by Miguel Picazo. It is a historical novel that deals with Spain's Golden Age, the period of its greatest political and military hegemony, as well as religious fervor.

The end of the fifteenth century saw the successful completion of a crusade in Spain, as King Fernando and Queen Isabel ended the Reconquest of the Muslims in Spain with the defeat of the kingdom of Granada. Spain's discovery and conquest of lands in the New World provided new opportunities for evangelization. In Europe, Spain saw itself as protector of the faith against the rising tide of Protestantism and the threat of the Turks. The Inquisition, established in Spain in 1478, ferreted out heretics and maintained the purity of the faith. Publication of religious books—hagiographies, confessional manuals, etcetera—reached unprecedented levels, and Spain's two greatest mystics, Saint Teresa of Avila and Saint John of the Cross, wrote their masterpieces. They also labored in founding convents and reforming their order of Discalced Carmelites, but some convents disdained the austerity of the monastic vow of poverty and served as homes for the daughters of wealthy aristocrats. There was a fine line between mysticism and heresy, however, and groups such as the illuminati caused great controversy in cities such as Toledo and Llerena. This period also saw great hardships in Spain because of frequent wars, droughts, and pestilence.

Against this historical background, Fernández Santos weaves a tale that seems to continuously echo Spanish Golden Age narratives. Concha Alborg ("El lenguaje") has shown how his use of archaic expressions, proverbs, and antithesis echo Saint Teresa's style. The first-person confessional brings the picaresque novel *Lazarillo de Tormes* to mind, and the being /seeming dichotomy (what is true?) and the importance of faith strike Cervantine resonances. The film version eliminates the intercalated story of the nun's trip to see her dying father

141

and simplifies the multiple narrative points of view in the novel, which shift throughout the original narrative.

The opening shot of the film shows the silhouette of a convent in the darkness. As we hear the voices of nuns singing, the camera slowly zooms in to focus on the light emanating from a window. The chiaroscuro aspect of the lighting symbolizes the divisions that ravage the convent underneath the façade of holiness (symbolized by the nuns' singing), divisions that will eventually engulf the convent in darkness and destruction.

In *Extramuros*, the themes of love, power, faith, and truth are inexorably intertwined. The love is between the nun/narrator and her sister, both unnamed in the original narrative, but called Sor Ana de la Cruz and Sor Angela de la Consolación in the screen adaptation. With drought and famine decimating the convent, Sor Angela (Mercedes Sampietro) decides to save her sisters by fabricating stigmata in her hands and thus stimulate people's faith and generosity. To carry out such an enterprise, she needs the assistance and compliance of her lover. The domination of the sister over the narrator is accentuated in the film when Sor Angela fetches Sor Ana (Carmen Maura) at night to her cell. During a long shot of them crossing the cloister, the church bell rings, and Sor Ana freezes with fear; her sister grabs her and drags her along, giving greater intensity to the original description: "its sound left me motionless and upset, looking for shelter in the shadow of the arches" (33). When Sor Angela inquires about her devotion, Picazo transforms the narrator's thoughts of being her "slave" (34) or her "love serf" into concrete dialogue: "Mi aliento y mi voz os pertenecen. Todo yo soy vuestro" (My breath and my voice pertain to you. I am all yours).

This domination by Sor Angela also appears in other elements of the mise-en-scène. When the suspicious prioress (Aurora Bautista) suddenly opens the door to Sor Angela's cell and discovers the nuns embracing in bed, Sor Ana cowers in fear in the background as Sor Angela confronts the prioress with accusations of mismanagement. When the doctor comes and examines Sor Angela's hands, Sor Ana appears in the background in the hallway, and suddenly retires. Later, when the Duke (Conrado San Martín) kneels to kiss Sor Angela's hands,

Sor Ana is also in the background: her twisted body, with her back toward the figures of importance as she twists her head to observe the scene, manifests the inner torment suffered by Sor Ana because of her self-doubt regarding her complicity in the perpetration of deceit, thus reflecting the tone of the constant rhetorical questions on the part of the narrator in the novel.

The illicit sexual union between the two nuns is handled stylishly and discreetly in both narratives, imbuing their relationship with an extraordinary dimension of spirituality. After Sor Angela faints during choir, Sor Ana tends to her in her cell, and a medium close-up of their faces together as the ill nun drinks her soup is the first image connotative of their relationship. Later, Sor Angela offers Sor Ana her hands, and a close-up as they kiss each other's cheeks beautifully captures the original prose: "Her hot breath, her trembling hands, her eyes at the level of my mouth . . . the soft rubbing of her flesh on my flesh" (41). Both narratives allude to their "so many nights, the two of us together, consoled, united" (34-35) and "so many days and nights together in the shadows of her cell until the break of day" (40).

The title, *Extramuros*, implies a division between the life within the convent walls and life in the outside world. The object that best signifies this division is the lattice of the convent windows (8, 11, 120), and which at times in the film visually functions as a prison-like element in the background of the nuns' cells. Another element of the mise-en-scène that connotes imprisonment is the wrought iron screen or grille in the convent. In particular, the scene in which the priest gives a sermon against the lascivious behavior of lost souls is shot looking through the screen, giving the connotation of imprisonment for sexual deviance. When a noisy and agitated group of "lost souls" (men and women who have fallen into evil ways) passes by the convent, the agitation seems to contaminate the nuns, and they scuffle to reach the upper windows where they break open the lattices in order to view the tumultuous parade: penitents carrying crosses, women cursing the sun for causing droughts, men masturbating. The priest condemns this group in a sermon, and the masturbation condenses the theme of lust that appears in the novel on several occasions (40, 62-63, 69-69, 73) and which contrasts with the spirituality of the relationship between the two nuns.

During Sor Angela's illness, Sor Ana reads the life of a nun/saint on whose hands appeared the wounds of Christ. A significant reaction shot in close-up of her sister plants the seeds of their subsequent actions. When they meet to carry out their plan, a zoom in to close-up of Sor Angela's hands captures the description of the original narrative, as Sor Ana kisses them before making the incision (43-44). The repetitions of this visual image—a zoom-in to close-up when the duke kisses them, and the final shot of the film, in which we see a close-up of the lovers' hands together create an analogous poetic impact to that of the description in the novel—"Those hands, sweet in love, wounding, fierce when that love arrived in the dark hours of the night, wise when stretched out, dead, proud, recognized at the first touch, eternally cold, dignified, aching" (132).

The nature of her wounds, together with the sacrificial element of Sor Angela's physical suffering for the good of her order, make the nun a Christ-figure, and the composition of the still shot used for the cover of the 1986 edition of the novel brings the Pietà to mind: the wounded and suffering Sor Angela is inclined across the lap of Sor Ana.

The belief in the miraculous nature of the stigmata on the part of the other nuns—desperate for divine intervention to relieve them of their miseries—as well as that faith engendered among the townspeople who seek her out for miraculous cures, brings into question the themes of seeming/being and the nature of faith. Although this theme is more fully developed in the novel, the belief of others even affects the perpetrator of the hoax, and transforms Sor Angela's false divine signs into a true mystical experience: she confides in a close-up shot, "For some time now, there are moments in which my soul shakes in sweet raptures. I am unaware of everything, I can hardly distinguish anything that surrounds me except my own hands" (cf. the indirect dialogue, 110). The devotion and fame that the stigmata bring her result in her election as prioress, financial support from the duke , and the arrival at the convent of the duke's daughter (played by Assumpta Serna and referred to as the "Guest" in the novel). However, this also leads to a power struggle between the sister and the prioress, and the sister and the Guest.

Picazo manifests the power struggle between Sor Angela and the prioress beginning with their confrontation in the former's cell. Aside from accusing the prioress of mismanagement, Sor Angela knocks the candle from her hand. This gesture has the symbolic connotation of Sor Angela not wanting her illicit love affair to come to light. The physical confrontation continues when Sor Angela encounters the prioress searching through her room for the knife with which she caused her wounds. They struggle as Sor Ana enters the room, in contrast with the prioress's vituperation that changed to humiliation in the novel (108-109). Both physical confrontations represent the transposition and condensation of the original narrative in which the nuns, divided into two bands, come to blows (101) or "war" (191, 215). Picazo also captures this thematic element with an added scene of the nun who throws a rock through the Guest's window.

Picazo's use of montage underscores the antithesis between the Guest and the rest of the nuns. The reverse angle shots in the scene in which the Guest and Sor Angela meet each other symbolize the gulf between them. The same technique is used during interviews between the Guest and male visitors, and further underscores the *extramuros* theme manifested by their separation by lattices. Picazo also uses reverse angle shots during the dinner scene between the former prioress and the duke's daughter. In addition to fulfilling the normal function of transcending the frame of the screen and signifying a conversation between the two, it also connotes the same theme of separation: in spite of what seem to be machinations in common, the two are in reality rivals, since both want to be prioress.

A cut from the simple meal of the sisters to the unloading of the Guest's many trunks of possessions manifests the vast difference in material goods between them, and reveals the Guest's hypocrisy. Likewise, the juxtaposition of the sumptuous dinner for the former prioress and the Guest in the latter's cell with the humble repast of the other sisters in the dining room shows the gulf between the powerful and the humble. When Sor Angela questions the Guest's adhesion to the vows of the order, the noble woman's ostentatious garb and the services of her handmaiden (putting perfume in her mouth in order to spray it on her lady), and the close-up of the Guest applying make-up before a mirror, all attest to the utter disdain that the duke's daughter has for monastic life. The mirror as an element of the mise-en-scène to signify hypocrisy and vanity appears at other points in the film narrative, as well. When the Guest speaks of the deceit of the false stigmata, the shot shows her standing in front of a mirror. This aristocratic woman also craves power, proclaiming to Sor Angela that some day she will be prioress, as well as to the former prioress that she desires power or glory or both. In her power struggle with Sor Angela, the Guest threatens to write to her father to close the convent (161), and clearly favors a guilty verdict by the Inquisition (206). The rich and powerful in society use the mechanisms of authority to their advantage. The film connotes this manipulation through the cut from (1) the scene in which the duke, with his daughter by his side, is unable to convince the community to elect the Guest as the new prioress to (2) the Inquisition's reading of the guilty sentence of the two nuns.

In the film, Picazo manifests the motives and actions of the former prioress by switching the emphasis from telling to showing, as he depicts her listening to Sor Angela's delirium. In both narratives, the former prioress confesses to the duke's daughter that she wrote the accusing letter to the Inquisition.

As the protagonists are summoned by the Inquisition, the power of the Holy Tribunal over the nuns' lives becomes apparent in the mise-en-scène. When the two sisters arrive at the tribunal's palace, an inquisitorial guard appears above them on the stairway. A high-angle shot of the tribunal through bars on a window gives a sense of powerlessness to the nuns, as well as connoting imprisonment. However, the cross-cutting between the inquisitorial prison and the convent (6 times) does not fully convey the duration of the trial in the original narrative, as the months and seasons change. In addition, Sor Ana's lament in the dark cell, "They forgot about me" does not fully capture the sense of solitude, silence, and darkness conveyed in the original narrative.

At the end of the film, after Sor Angela and Sor Ana have returned from their inquisitorial imprisonment during their trial, the former leaves her sickbed; Sor Ana searches for her throughout the convent and finds her in the Guest's former cell, sitting in front of a mirror and wearing the courtly dress that the duke 's daughter left behind. With her back to the camera, she falls dead from the chair: "she only wanted to slide, to fall to the ground more dried up than dead" (cf. 251). The earlier scene when the Guest is applying make-up before the mirror relates this object to vanity, and the satin dress of the noble woman is a symbol of worldly desires, as well as of wealth and power. Putting the dress on symbolizes the breaking of her final vow: first chastity, then obedience, and now poverty. This final succumbing to vanity represents the ambiguity in Sor Angela: did she sacrifice her life for her community of sisters, or was she a vain woman intent upon achieving power and fame?

The final scene of the film version achieves a high emotional charge, while subtle transformations that Picazo takes with the novelistic text imbue it with a slightly more erotic tone than the original. After Sor Ana drags Sor Angela's dead body to bed, her very emotive speech (a condensation of the last page and a-half of the novel) manifests Navajas's contention (242, 248) that the novel constitutes a confession by the narrator to her sister (Sor Angela), a confession that examines the nature of sexuality and of power. The film version of the speech makes some subtle but important lexical transformations that emphasize the amorous relationship of the two nuns. (The original wording appears here within brackets.)

Aquí, a mis pies, está toda mi vida, mis sentidos, mi placer, mi compañera y madre. . . Nadie toque mi amor, nadie se acerque a nuestro lecho y nido . . . ¿Cuándo vendrá, Señor, nuestro tiempo de gloria, por tanto tiempo prometido? Aquí estamos, las dos pendientes de ese amor tuyo capaz de salvarnos, de trocar en dicha la pena miserable, y recorrer juntas [de mostrarnos] ese camino que lleva hasta ti . . . Las dos, lejos de hermanas y prioras, viviremos por siempre pidiendo al Señor [pidiéndote] que . . . nadie vuelva a separarnos [despertarnos], nadie venga a sacarnos de este lecho de amor [tranquilo] donde las dos a solas amamos y esperamos. (Here, at my feet, is my whole life, my senses, my pleasure, my companion and mother . . . Let no one touch my love, let no one approach our bed, our nest . . . When,

Lord, will our time of glory come that has been promised for so long? We are both here, waiting for that love of Yours that is capable of saving us, of changing our miserable sorrow into happiness, and to travel together [to show us] that road that goes to You . . . The two of us, far from sisters and prioresses, will live forever asking the Lord [asking You] . . . to not let anyone separate [awaken] us again, that no one come to take us from this bed of love [tranquil bed] where the two of us, alone, loved and hoped.)

Changes in the lexicon are not the only elements that place further emphasis on the sexual relationship between the two; the mise-en-scène also underscores the erotic element of the text. The final image of the narrator in the novel is of her praying: "getting down on my knees, I began to pray." In the film version, however, a medium shot shows Sor Ana crying as she embraces and kisses the dead body of her sister. A close-up of their enjoined hands is perhaps the perfect image with which to end the film before the final fade-out.

The excellent photography by Teo Escamilla and the haunting music by José Nieto add substantially to the quality of the film version of *Extramuros*. In particular, the constant use of chiaroscuro (not only in the convent cells, but also during the inquisitorial tribunal) adds to the beauty of the film and, as we have mentioned, underscores the thematic thrust of the narrative. Nieto's music is for period instruments: recorder, organ, harpsichord. The music for recorder, in particular, provides a tender and emotive background for the intimate scenes between Sor Angela and Sor Ana, culminating in the final scene of the film. The strong percussion parts during the procession of heretics and the crowd's protests of the arrest of the nuns add to the tumultuous feelings in those scenes. The superb acting by Mercedes Sampietro in the role of Sor Angela won her the best actress award at the 1985 San Sebastián Film Festival, and Carmen Maura's portrayal of Sor Ana is equally praiseworthy. Both the original novel and the superb cinematographic version of *Extramuros* capture the multiple dimensions of the religious atmosphere in sixteenth-century Spain, as well as the struggle of women who loved too much.

Antonio Gala

Vicente Aranda adapted Antonio Gala's best-selling novel *La pasión turca* (*The Turkish Passion*, 1993) for the screen in 1994. As the title implies, the narrative deals with passion that is imbued with an exotic element. The geographical displacement connotes an emotive displacement that takes this passion beyond normal boundaries. The opening sequence, however, manifests a deflation of the exotic element and foreshadows exactly where the passion will lead us. The narrative begins with the gaze, the close-up of eyes looking out a jalousie; this, together with the close-up of a hand with Turkish prayer beads, immediately places us in the geography of the title. But the reverse-angle shot shows the object of the gaze—a cemetery—and the voice-over by Desideria (Ana Belén) manifests her disillusion: "¿Quién iba a pensar que mi paisaje cotidiano en esta ciudad tan soñada iba a ser un cementerio?" (Who would have thought that my daily landscape in this city that I dreamed of so was going to be a cemetery?)

The flashback to the preparations for Desi's wedding to Ramiro (Ramón Madaula), the sexual patter of her friends, foreshadows the element of desire that in Desi will become a force that dominates her very being. Ramón, on the other hand, appears inadequate from the very beginning, as he declares on his wedding night, "Te quiero tanto que no sé si voy a ser capaz de mostrártelo" (I love you so much that I don't know if I will be able to show you). When Desi later declares, "No puedo tener hijos" (I cannot have children), Ramón tries to console her: "No te desanimes. Basta de estar contigo para ser feliz" (Don't get discouraged. Being with you is enough to make me happy). Nevertheless, the cut to the photograph of Desi in her wedding gown connotes disillusionment and a deflation of the hopes and happiness in the beginning of their relationship.

A trip to Turkey by several couples changes Desi's unfulfilled existence when she meets Yamam (Georges Corraface), a handsome tour guide. The first mirror shot in the film constructs desire through the gaze, but here it is the female gaze and the construction of female sexual desire. The close-up point of view shot of the back of his neck and of his

Insatiable desire: Ana Belén and Silvia Munt in Vicente Aranda's *La pasión turca. Courtesy Iberoamericana, S.A.*

mouth reflected in the rearview mirror of the bus and the cut to the close-up of Desi gazing at him begin a montage sequence that fades out to show the effect of this newborn desire: Desi is literally dizzy. Yamam helps revive her and declares, "Estoy dispuesto a hacer todo lo que haga falta para que se enamore usted de este país" (I am willing to do anything necessary so that you fall in love with this country). The phrase seems charged with double meaning, as we almost anticipate that the final words will be "so that you will fall in love with me." Indeed, after he explains how when Europe was in the Dark Ages, Turkey maintained "pleasures and voluptuousness," Desi puts make-up on as if to anticipate such pleasures for herself.

When Yamam appears behind Desi in the shadows of a mosque and the montage of close-ups heightens the sexual tension, there is a sense that Yamam may have a dark side to his character.

Their first sexual encounter occurs at Desi's initiative, when she gives the excuse of having left something on the bus. Yamam lifts her dress over her face, and her moans of ecstasy with her face covered over implies a sexual fulfillment that also covers something more profound. The following sequences also contain sexual encounters between guide and tourist—on a ship, in a rug store—and imply Desi's sexual insatiability. At the same time, their mutual declarations of love contrast with the seemingly ephemeral nature of their relationship. When Desi and Ramiro return to Spain, she is pregnant, and as she stands before the bathroom mirror, the reflected image manifests a moment of self-exploration, and she decides to tell her husband the truth.

In spite of Ramiro's initial jealousy, the birth of her son seems to open the possibility of rapprochement with her husband, but the sudden death of the infant throws Desi into a crisis that can only be resolved with her return to Istanbul. The shot of her walking the streets with suitcases in hand foreshadows the final shot of the film. When she finally encounters Yamam, her declaration, "Soy yo" (It is me), which she repeats three times, implies not only the confirmation of an unimagined reality (the reuniting of distant lovers), but also the affirmation of a new identity for Desi. Their lovemaking after this reencounter significantly occurs in the shadows, with Desi verbally enunciating her sexual passion.

Verbal repetition becomes a pattern with Desi and ironically underscores her empty reality. In their next sexual encounter, Desi repeats "Ya no estoy sola" (I am no longer alone) three times, as if by repeating this "incantation," it makes it so. As Yamam kisses her belly, we hear the chant of an imam in the background, thus underscoring the cultural differences between the two. Indeed, these differences grow in a long crescendo, as Paulina (Loles León) at the Spanish embassy tells her that she should learn Turkish, even though it would require a tremendous effort. Nevertheless, Desi seems willing to make the effort at cultural assimilation, as the next mirror shot shows her looking at herself dressed in Turkish garb: Desi is making a conscious attempt to become the "other." As she looks in the mirror, she addresses not her own image, but the

The exotic object of feminine desire: Georges Corraface in *La pasión turca*. *Courtesy Iberoamericana Films, S.A.*

skeptical and critical Spanish embassy representative, verbally affirming her own willingness to accept Turkish culture. Yamam's reaction, however, is negative, telling her that she has gone crazy. It is clear, however, that Desi equates the exotic element of Turkish culture with the erotic, as she says, "Quiero que mi amo entre en mí" (I want my master to enter into me), but the shot of Desi saying this is out of focus, underscoring how their very relationship is unclear and equivocal.

The following sequence echoes the shot that opened the film: the cemetery that is now her daily landscape. When Desi now discovers that Yamam has children by an earlier relationship, her world begins to crumble. It is easy to don Turkish garb, but it is not the same as communicating with Yamam's mother in Turkish. When one of her greatest illusions—to have a child—is about to be fulfilled, she serves

Yamam champagne to celebrate the good news, but this causes another process of disillusionment. When he responds, "Ni lo sueñes" (Not even in your dreams), she lets the champagne glass drop. It breaks, symbolizing the shattering of Desi's illusion. After an abortion that leaves her sterile, her response is to verbally confirm her happiness, but the chant of "Soy feliz" (I am happy) gives way to "Quiero ser feliz" (I want to be happy), implicitly recognizing the chasm between desire and reality.

Her world takes another slide downward when she realizes that Yamam's instructions to be friendly with an Egyptian client interested in purchasing rugs means that she has to prostitute herself. A return trip home causes her to confront her true nature: "soy una guarra; grito como una bestia cuando me folla" (I am a pig; I shout like a beast when he fucks me). But her friend Laura (Silvia Munt) believes that she is now crazy. Desi's sexual desire takes control of her, as she picks up a man in the park for a tryst. When she returns to Yamam, he hits her, and an overhead shot that shows the blood on her hands like stigmata foreshadows that Desi's martyrdom is to begin in earnest now, as she becomes the whore to a gigolo who uses her to foment business. When she delivers an envelope with money to a mobster, she reaches her lowest depth. Since Yamam owes much more than he has paid, Desi is at the mercy of the mobster. He masturbates in front of her, and his ejaculation onto her face is a symbolic discharge that foreshadows the shooting of the denouement. When Desi returns home to find Yamam having sex, his cigarette that she snuffs out also foreshadows the denouement. Sitting next to Yamam at a party, she is humiliated when he kisses other women. Desi takes out a pistol and shoots him in the crotch, an act of vengeance that metes out just deserts. Freixas (37) points out that this constitutes a symbolic castration, which is a recurring theme in Aranda's filmography.

One of the interesting controversies regarding Aranda's screen adaptation of La pasión turca is the fact that the director filmed two endings: in the first, Desi commits suicide, and this represents an ending that is faithful to the original narrative. In the other, Desi shoots Yamam and leaves Turkey.

The final decision of which ending to use was left up to producer Andrés Vicente Gómez, who believed that the suicide ending offered less commercial viability. This is one of the most salient examples of how extratextual factors shape the final form of the film text. (After the film appeared on video, a second version was released that contained both endings.)

Several recent Spanish films construct female sexual desire through the female gaze, and they are by both female directors such as Pilar Miró and Iciar Bollain as well as male directors such as Bigas Luna. Given the sexual content of Aranda's other films, it is not surprising that he would undertake such a construct, as well. The erotization of the exotic Other, and in particular, the Eastern, has a long tradition (manifested in nineteenth-century European paintings such as Ingres's *Odalisque with a Slave* and *The Turkish Bath* or Renoir's *Woman from Algiers*). Contextualizing it within the female heterosexual desire in contemporary Spanish cinema is the result of both a recent liberation of female sexuality in Spanish society as well as a possible discontent on the part of women toward male sexuality in contemporary Spain. Hooper notes that whereas in 1975, the year of Franco's death, 42 percent of Spanish women lost their virginity by the age of twenty, by 1987, 56 percent had sexual relations by the age of 18, whereas studies from the mid-1980s show that "there was less love-making in the land of Don Juan than in any other EC country" (*New Spaniards* 161). The symbolic castration of the male in the film would also manifest this discontent.

Freixas (34) is of the opinion that "the film only resembles the novel in its skeleton" and that Aranda's reading of the original "has considerably and felicitously modified the meaning, the structure, and the language" of the novel. As with all of the novels that he has adapted for the screen, Aranda has again made an original reading, which in this case has been coupled with the pressures of the market.

José Antonio García Blázquez

No encontré rosas para mi madre (*I Didn't Find Roses for My Mother*) is Rovira Beleta's 1972 adaptation of the novel by José Antonio García Blázquez (1968). This film is a good example of the attempt during that time period to broaden the base of Spanish cinema and transcend national borders by making the movie a coproduction (Spain-France-Italy) and using an international cast. In addition to Spanish star Conchita Velasco, who appears as "Africa," Gina Lollobrigida appears as Naty, Danielle Darrieux is Teresa, Susan Hampshire is Helia, and Renaurd Verley is Jaci. In spite of these rather grandiose intentions, the film is not stellar quality.

The title implies a futile attempt to please one's mother, and it seems to connote a possible frustrated Oedipus complex. This is indeed the case, as Jaci, a young delinquent, overtly has strong feelings toward his mother but is ultimately rejected by her. In the opening sequence, Jaci and a friend steal an old man's wallet, and he uses the money to buy flowers that he says are for his girlfriend. However, it turns out that they are for his mother, Teresa, and he gives her this present of love while she is bathing. The latent sexuality of the relationship continues in one of the next sequences, when Jaci serves his mother breakfast in bed while he is wearing an apron over his bare torso. When mother and son go to the park, she comments that someday he will find a girl and marry, to which he retorts, "La muchacha eres tú y la esposa también eres tú. Fuera de ti no hay nada" (You are the girl, and you are also the wife. Outside of you, there is nothing). Although she disapproves of this statement, a voice-over indicating her thoughts manifests another problem in the relationship. Teresa remembers how she brought Jaci to that same park when he was young, and her desire that he would never stop being a kid, that nothing would change. Teresa is unable to accept her son's passage into adulthood.

Although Teresa tells her son that they are broke, Jaci is determined not only to get enough money so that they can survive, but to acquire a mansion that his mother has admired. His work as an artist's model in Ibiza and with a group who sell fake Picassos does not provide the desired money, so he and his friends develop a scheme to rob the artist and his wife of their jewelry. The real money, however, comes from a more elaborate scheme. The appearance in the early park sequence of a mentally retarded young woman of wealthy American parents finally acquires its significance, as Jaci marries the mentally retarded woman only to get her money. Jaci's moral turpitude is accentuated in the postnuptial party, when he and his friends get drunk and trash the mansion, even smashing a grand piano. Jaci has to interrupt the sexual activity that he initiates with Elia in order to kick his two drunk friends out of his new wife's bedroom.

Now that Jaci has money, he goes to get roses for his mother. As the title has anticipated, there are none, and when he arrives home, the roses that are in Teresa's house are dried up. Teresa's voice-over reads her final letter to him in which she blames her own misguided affection as dragging him toward evil, and she recognizes the need to end it in order to save him. Her marriage abroad to her English boarder is her way of finally separating from her son, since "sólo lejos de mí serás por fin capaz de vivir tu propia vida" (only far from me will you be able to live your own life).

The main problem with this film is the script. The ill-conceived plot goes in too many directions and is at times quite implausible (the marriage to the rich Marianne, and the lawyer handing over a huge check after seeing how the house has been trashed). The excessively overt flower symbolism from the film's title and final sequence, together with the overly didactic message in the final voice-over make this a - film with great expectations that were not fulfilled.

Pedro García Montalvo

José Luis Cuerda's *La viuda del Capitán Estrada* (*Captain Estrada's Widow*, 1991) is the screen adaptation of Pedro García Montalvo's *Una historia madrileña* (*A Story from Madrid*). Like many other contemporary Spanish movies, the setting of the narrative is the post-civil war era. The film incorporates motifs common to narratives about that era—the ideological split within the family caused by the civil war, the Republican soldier in hiding, the economic contrasts between victors and vanquished, and the repressive security forces. In this narrative, however, the portrait of Spanish society in the 1940s is merely a backdrop for a story of a femme fatale and passions gone awry.

Although being the son of a Republican military officer in exile is a black mark, Captain Javier Zaldívar (Sergi Mateu) proved his loyalty to the Nationalist cause by fighting in the Blue Division against the Russians and serving for three years in the Spanish Sahara. His asking his friend Baltasar (Nacho Martínez) upon his return to Madrid, "Cuéntame de Luisa" (Tell me about Luisa), indicates the passionate obsession for the woman that he left four years ago. Although she had married Mariano, Javier's companion in arms, she is now a widow, and again the object of Javier's desire. The first sequence with Luisa (Anna Galiena) indicates her involvement with another man, however, and the web of multiple triangles begins to form. Luisa gets out of her chauffeur-driven car in a poor neighborhood and furtively leaves a package in a receptacle, and the close-up of a man's hand withdrawing the package further underscores the secret nature of the encounter. Luisa is hiding—and feeding Juan (Chema Mazo), a former Republican soldier who escaped from a Nationalist prison, in her parents' house. But Luisa's guile is not limited to Juan. The cross-cut shots between Luisa, clad in a pink bathrobe that is quite revealing with her legs crossed, and Tomás (Gabino Diego), the impoverished librarian who puts her collection in order, connote a erotic charge between the two. She admits to the elderly Marcos (Germán Cobos) that he was the first man toward whom she felt physical attraction, but she rejects his

157

advances. Both Tomás and Marcos become her suitors, as they both appear at later moments in the film with flowers for the widow. Baltasar likewise brings flowers to Luisa, but after being rejected, he says that they are from Javier. The fact that Baltasar brazenly confesses to her face that he wants to have sex with her connotes a loose reputation on her part, a reputation that he later concretely states to Javier, calling Luisa "puta de rojos" (a whore for reds). Javier adamantly rejects these accusations; his passionate obsession for Luisa blinds him regarding her real character. Javier's obsession reveals his contradictory nature when he admits to Luisa that he left her four years ago because he lacked courage. Javier is thus a combination of soldierly machismo and childlike debility that wavers back and forth throughout the film.

Luisa is an independent spirit who does not fit well within society's constraints and stereotypical images. Her conversation with the priest who wants to control her behavior ends with remarks that the priest considers insolent. Javier takes her to a luxurious restaurant that contrasts with other locales of relative squalor portrayed in the film—Luisa's old neighborhood, Marcos's humble abode, the streets with young beggars and pickpockets—and thus connotes his power. Luisa shows her independent spirit by not submissively following Javier's suggestions for her order. Although Javier confesses his desire to marry her, Luisa inquires, "¿Crees que hace falta que nos casemos?" (Do you think that we need to marry each other?), implying that she would be just as happy being lovers. The scene when Javier presents her with a brooch that belonged to his mother captures the basic aspects of both characters. Luisa is aloof in her acceptance of the gift, and Javier switches from macho—pushing her—to childlike, placing his head on her lap.

Javier's desire is to possess Luisa totally. Following the elliptical fade-out of their first amorous encounter, he begs her, "Júrame que no vuelves a abandonarme" (Swear to me that you will never abandon me again), and "Júrame que sólo me querrás a mí" (Swear to me that you will love only me). This desire for total possession is apparent in their next amorous encounter. While making love, Javier grabs Luisa's wrists and pins them

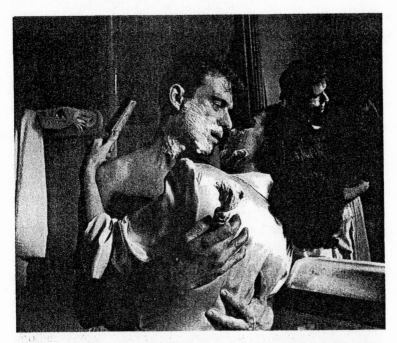

Passion and an unbridled spirit: José Luis Cuerda's *La viuda del Capi-tán Estrada*, starring Anna Galiena and Sergi Mateu. *Courtesy Classic Films Producción, S.A.*

down, and the point-of-view shot clearly shows Javier on top of Luisa, as if dominating and subjugating her. But Luisa is too independent to lose her freedom. In a later scene, Luisa turns the tables; not only is she on top of him, but she grabs his wrists and pins him down.

The juxtaposition of two scenes—when Javier performs target practice with his pistol and Baltasar talks about the difficulty of administering the coup de grâce, and when the latter makes accusations against Luisa—serves as a foreshad-owing of the denouement. Javier arrives at Luisa's house just as she is catching a taxi. He pursues her to Marcos's house, and jealously misinterprets their embraced silhouettes on the shade. (Luisa does embrace Marcos, but only as a friendly good-bye). After a night of whoring and drinking, Javier waits for Luisa after mass. As she leaves church, the shot of Javier through the bars of the grating connotes the prison that will await him for his crime. The juxtaposition of the smiling Luisa and the close-up of the pistol that Javier extracts from his holster can only lead to his final act of jealousy: as Luisa approaches Javier and kisses him, he shoots her. The point-of-view shot showing Javier from the ground echoes the low-angle shot during their lovemaking: Javier's domination is indeed total; no one else will have her anymore.

Two important images of Luisa recur throughout the film: those in a mirror, and those of a photograph. The mirror image of Luisa occurs in her bedroom. In the sequence in which Luisa appears after her amorous encounter with Juan, she takes off her dress and sits in front of the mirror, contemplating her own image. The wheelchair located to the right of the mirror only acquires full meaning later in the narrative, when the priest laments her late husband Mariano's paralysis. Since only her own image is reflected, the mirror image is also an expression of her solitude. Indeed, when Javier romantically claims that he spent the past four years "with her" (by remembering her always), she retorts that she was "sola delante de un espejo" (alone in front of a mirror). After her date with Javier, which terminates with his rejection of her suggestion that they could become lovers rather than man and wife, she contemplates her double image in the twin mirror of her wardrobe. The duplication of the reflected image underscores her inherent duplicity, as she takes one lover after another. The cross-cuts between Luisa and the wheelchair give the latter a metonymic importance, and she angrily pushes the wheelchair down the hall, thus lashing out at her husband Mariano, whose paralysis and death left her both sexually frustrated and alone. Following her amorous encounter with Marcos (which she initiates, by embracing him, and taking off his sweater and shirt), Luisa returns home. Her mirror image now serves as the voice of conscience, as she contemplates herself and exclaims, "Tienes pinta de puta" (You look like a whore).

The photograph from about five years before in Luisa's study captures the triangle that constitutes the thematic structure of the narrative. It depicts a picnic in which Luisa is seated among her military friends—Javier, Mariano, and

Baltasar. She is significantly placed between her future husband and her future lover. Both Tomás and Javier contemplate the photograph in the study. For the former, his exclusion from this image connotes his effective exclusion from becoming Luisa's lover. Javier had lost his copy of the photograph, but confesses to Luisa that he always remembered it, since the photo represents, as Casas notes, the "memory of an idealized past" (63) for Zaldívar. Contemplating the photograph now, the absence of his rival in the image (because of the death of Luisa's husband) confirms that she will be his. After her murder, Baltasar searches Javier's desk and finds a copy of the photograph. He takes it with him, but as he is getting into his car during a heavy rainstorm, the photo falls from among his papers, and floats along the inundated street: both the potential happiness and the web of relationships that the photograph depicts have been washed away.

The change in title from novel to screen was undoubtedly an attempt to arouse interest in a movie-going public that might catch the possible erotic connotations in the name of the film adaptation, as opposed to the rather anodyne title of the novel. The passions portrayed on screen never burst into flames, however; the opposing nature of the protagonists dooms the relationship to its tragic end from the very beginning.

Adelaida García Morales

Adelaida García Morales's first publication consisted of two novellas: El sur (*The South*) and *Bene* (*Bene*, 1985), for which she won the Icaro Prize, awarded by the Spanish newspaper *Diario 16*. She also garnished the Herralde Prize for her novel *Silencio de las sirenas* (*Silence of the Sirens*, 1987). Both these early works and her more recent novels make her one of the most important feminine voices in contemporary Spanish literature.

Víctor Erice's film adaptation of *El sur* (1983) is the only example of a film that was released before the publication of the original novel. Novelist García Morales, director Erice's wife, undoubtedly shared the manuscript with him before its publication. Erice changes the names of the characters in the film adaptation: Adriana becomes Estrella, Rafael is Agustín, and Teresa is Julia. This gives Erice as screenwriter and director more control over them and certain autonomy regarding the original characters, obviating the familiar complaint that the screen protagonist is not the "Adriana" of the novel.

The novel's epigraph, "¿Qué podemos amar que no sea una sombra?"(What can we love that is not a shadow?, 5) could have been used by Víctor Erice as the epigraph for his film adaptation, since it connotes both the psychological and visual qualities of both narratives. A shadow is darkness surrounded by light, and this translates visually into the chiaroscuro that dominates the visual aesthetic of the film. At the same time it can connote malevolence, or a lack of corporeality, and as a visual motif in film, it often connotes a divided self or inner conflict. Agustín's anguish and the guilt felt by the adult Estrella are the two fundamental yet intangible components of *El sur*'s shadowy world.

As in Erice's first film, *El espíritu de la colmena* (*The Spirit of the Beehive*, 1973), the narrative of *El sur* deals with a young girl's passage from innocence to knowledge, from childhood to adulthood. Just as Erice obtained a masterful performance from child actress Ana Torrent in *El espíritu de la colmena*, he also receives stunning interpretations from Sonsoles Aranguren and Iciar Bollain, the two young actresses who portray Estrella. Also like the earlier film, it portrays a father who is unable to communicate with his wife, all set in an atmosphere of post–civil war Spain that is marked by a society that is divided into victors and vanquished.

The initial caption places the action in the fall of 1957, and the opening shot of the dark room with a window at the right side through which a bluish light penetrates serves as a foreshadowing of the chiaroscuro vision of the soul of the father, Agustín (Omero Antonutti). The barking of a dog provides an ominous signal, and we learn through Julia's anguished phone call (heard off screen) that Agustín is missing. The close-up of a fifteen-year-old Estrella opening a box that she has found under her pillow and taking out a pendulum on a chain is accompanied by the voice-over of the adult Estrella: "Aquel amanecer cuando encontré su péndulo debajo de mi almohada, sentí que todo era diferente, que él nunca volvería a casa" (That dawn when I found your pendulum under my pillow, I felt that everything was different, that he would never come back home).

The voice-over narration of Estrella is one of the most important technical elements in the film, and it attempts to capture the first-person narrative of the novel. Kazloff (41) comments that "first-person narration is the more common form of voice-over in fiction films . . . such narration can serve a variety of functions, including recreating/referring to a novel's narrative voice, conveying expository information, and aiding in the presentation of complex chronologies." Nevertheless, a first-person narration in film is bound to include omniscient narration as well. Attempts to find a purely visual equivalent to the literary first-person narrator, such as in Robert Montgomery's *Lady in the Lake*, have been failures. Lotman (351-52) notes that "many experiments have proved that shooting long sequences of film from the viewpoint of one of the characters results in a loss in the sense of subjective focus rather than a gain, since the audience starts to interpret the shots as normal scenic filming. In order to present a sequence of film text as embodying the point of view of a particular character, it is necessary (through montage) to alternate the shots taken from his space with shots which fix his position from somewhere

outside him, from the audience's (i.e. nobody's') point of view
or that of other characters." Rubio Gribble (177-78, 181) notes
that the first-person narrator (Estrella's voice-over) is present
throughout the film, sometimes prompting images, sometimes
commenting on them, making the action advance or going back
to an earlier past in order to explain something, and that "all
this seems to establish a link or identity between the act of
narrating in voice 'off' and the narration of the camera." In
addition, this creates a spatial dimension for the narrator
which helps explain what Rubio Gribble (182-83) refers to as
the "frequent static planes" that appear throughout the film:
the house seen in both long and medium shot, the garden, the
close-up of the weather vane, the façade of the movie theater,
and the shot of the dead father. According to Rubio Gribble
(171), "the recreation of the memory of the father is the central
theme" of both the novel and the film, but that there is an
important difference in the process of reading both texts, since
the film narrative is not directed to a "you" (i.e., her father).
This is evident in the contrast in the opening words of each
narrative. In the novel, the narrator speaks to her father in the
second person ("tu tumba"), whereas in the film, she refers to
him in the third person ("su péndulo").

Just as in the original novel, there is a temporal dichotomy
between the act of narration and the acts narrated. The voice-
over often represents the act of remembering her youth, as she
says: "Nunca olvidaré la cara que se puso mi padre" (I will
never forget the face my father made)—an act that is based on
a reading of her childhood diary—and"Hoy cuando vuelvo a
leer las páginas que dan cuenta de aquellos días" (Today when I
reread the pages that tell about those days). However, we must
question the reliability of Estrella as a narrator, since
sometimes these memories are imprecise—"No lo recuerdo
ahora con exactitud" (I don't remember precisely)—or pertain
to events that she did not witness—her father in the movie
theater or in the boarding house—or that are mere fantasy—
such as when she examines the postcards from Andalusia.

Unlike the original novel, which opens with information
concerning the death of her father—"Mañana . . . iré a visitar
tu tumba, papá (Tomorrow . . . I'll go visit your grave, Papá, 5)

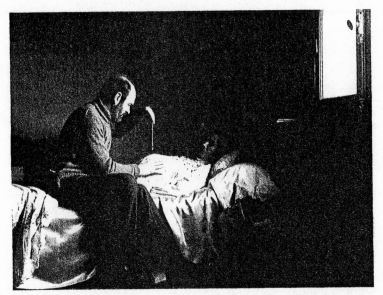

A chiaroscuro vision of the soul: Omero Antonutti and Lola Cardona in
Víctor Erice's *El sur. Courtesy Elías Querejeta, P.C.*

and immediately identifies it as a suicide, calling it "tu muerte
elegida" (the death you chose, 6), the film narrative
withholds the exact nature of Agustín's absence—his
death—until the end of the movie. Nevertheless, Glenn notes
that absence is a fundamental theme in the narrative, and Erice
captures it through the use of photographs, which "function as
a sign of an absence," as well as "shots of the empty road beside
which the house is set [that] heighten the impression of
loneliness and remoteness" (243, 245).

Erice uses fade-outs throughout the film, thus adding to its
dark tone. The first one occurs in the opening sequence: an
extreme close-up shows Estrella's cupped hands, which slowly
open to reveal their magical contents—the box with the
pendulum—and a close-up of Estrella holding the pendulum
and crying precedes a fade-out that underscores the emptiness
that constitutes the tragedy of her loss, and also serves as a
temporal transition the moment before her birth when her
father Agustín uses his pendulum with her pregnant mother

Julia to foretell the birth of a girl (7). The pendulum, then, is an object that links father and daughter even before the latter's birth. The close-up chiaroscuro image of Agustín and Estrella in which he shows her how to use the pendulum captures the unity of the father and daughter as they share this mysterious force, but also subtly underscores the division that is both within them and between them. (As is the case in many novels that are made into films, the cover of El sur contains an image from the film; in this case, it is this haunting close-up shot.) García Morales manifests this chiaroscuro division in the early portrayal of the father in the novel as being luminous but sad and characterized by a horrible shadow (6, 9).

The division between father and daughter exists in part because Estrella never really comprehends her father, and this is mainly because she does not understand his past. Estrella comments, "Los orígenes de mi padre siempre fueron para mí un auténtico misterio" (My father's origins were always an authentic mystery for me) as the camera shows close-up shots of the old photographs and postcards of Sevilla that evoke his past in the south while the soundtrack plays music by Andalusian composer Enrique Granados. The sea gull on the weather vane of the house also symbolically connotes Agustín's irretrievable past, since it "points south to a distant region of mystery and miracles, but is frozen in flight" (Evans and Fiddian 129). The elliptic dissolve of the weather vane has temporal, spatial, and symbolic connotations: we move not only from winter to spring, but the southward pointing sea gull also foreshadows the arrival, from the south, of Agustín's Aunt Milagros (Rafaela Aparicio) who comes for Estrella's first communion; the thawing sea gull thus also represents a thaw in strained familial relationships and a relinking with that lost geographical and temporal plane. The first words spoken by Milagros to Agustín, "Cuántos años, y cuánta desgracia por todas partes" (So many years, and so much misfortune everywhere) allude to this temporal division, but also link Agustín to a broader historical and social context and a theme that Erice foregrounds in this film version of the narrative: the Spanish civil war.

Although it is only mentioned once in the original narrative (8), the war dramatically shapes the destiny of Estrella's family in the film adaptation; her mother was a "maestra represaliada después de la guerra civil" (a teacher who was blacklisted after the civil war) who could not find work and who therefore taught the young girl at home. The impact of the war is especially acute in the case of her father, Agustín. Although never explicit, this could also be the root of his employment problems. The film version has a brief scene with the family travelling in a train as Estrella's voice-over declares, "Fui creciendo mientras nos trasladábamos de un lado para otro. El buscaba un trabajo fijo" (I was growing up as we moved around from place to place. He was looking for a steady job). Milagros provides Estrella with information about her father's past: in a clear reference to the civil war, she talks of "la cantidad de muertos que han [sic] habido; todo por las ideas" (so many dead; all because of ideas). She later explains that Agustín and his father quarreled over political ideas, and that it was never clear if her father left home or if her grandfather kicked him out. To make clear Agustín's political persuasion, Milagros states that before the war, Grandfather was a "bad guy" and Agustín was a "good guy," but when Franco triumphed, Grandfather became a "saint," and Agustín, a "devil" who went to jail. Erice has admitted that Agustín represents "many men who have a split personality—the civil war exemplifies that split—and who cannot find themselves" (Hidalgo, "El espíritu" 2).

Evans and Fiddian (130) note that Estrella's first communion ceremony has the character of an initiation. The night before the ceremony, Milagros tells Estrella how beautiful she will be in her white gown, dressed as if it were for her wedding, "igualita a una novia" (just like a bride). Although Estrella protests that she will not marry when she grows up and that all brides have stupid faces, Milagros repeats the phrase the next day as they dress Estrella in her gown. Estrella's attitude captures that of the advice against domestication and conventionality given by Rafael to Adriana in the novel: "Cuando seas mayor, no te cases ni tengas hijos, si es que quieres hacer algo de interés en la vida" (When you are older, don't marry nor have children, that is if you want to do something of any interest in your life, 28). The wedding analogy manifests that "those around her are already conspiring to make her conform to a conventional role and a conventional image" (Evans and Fiddian 130), and sets the context for one of the most poignant sequences of the film—the first communion dance between Estrella and her father. The gunshots coming from outside during the preparations, however, are a discordant note of protest by Agustín against these activities, and also serve as a foreshadowing of his suicide.

Although Agustín does not go to the church with the women, he appears from the shadows at the ceremony, and the voice-over of the young Estrella captures her thoughts that affirm the special relationship between father and daughter: "Lo ha hecho por mí" (He did it for me). The following sequence beautifully portrays Agustín dancing with Estrella in her first communion gown. The low-angle shots of the father magnify his stature in the eyes of the young girl, capturing her admiration for him, and the approving "olés" of the guests precede a zoom-in to the white cape and crown that lay on the chair, which could well be those of a bride. Although it constitutes a change in content, this sequence perfectly captures the tone of the original narrative in which Adriana dreams of being rescued by her father during a flood, with her only desire being to marry him (34). And this sequence represents—just as does the original narrative—a clear "illustration of the post-Oedipal attraction to the father as described by Freud" (Evans and Fiddian 130). These same critics also point out that this ceremony as a loss of innocence is further emphasized by the fact that we later learn (during the scene in the Gran Hotel when we hear the same music again) that the dance tune is entitled "En el mundo" ("In the World"), thus subtly underscoring the transition from childhood to adulthood (130).

In the sequence following the dance, Estrella finds out that there was another woman in her father's life: Irene Ríos. Estrella discovers that this woman is an actress—a blonde movie star in a film noir who is killed by her boyfriend. The name of her fictitious film, *Flor en la sombra* (*Flower in the Shadow*) echoes both the epigraph by Hölderlin and the coming attraction that later appears in the movie theater and which Evans and Fiddian (133-34) consider as a major influence on *El sur*: Hitchcock's *Shadow of a Doubt*. Compitello (77, 85) notes that this metafilmic sequence when Agustín goes to the movies at the Cine Arcadia "represents Erice's major structural change in García Morales' narrative," and he believes that the intertextual reference to the Hitchcock film "harbours the uncertainty that actually characterizes *El sur* 's narrational flow." Irene's shooting death as the result of unrequited love again foreshadows Agustín's later suicide. Estrella burns the movie program with Irene's photograph "because she sees in her a rival for her father's love" (Evans and Fiddian 132). When the actress—Laura—responds to Agustín's letter, her comment that everything in the movies is a lie echoes the comments that Isabel makes to her sister Ana in a bedroom conversation in Erice's earlier film, *El espíritu de la colmena*. The transformation from Gloria in the novel to actress Laura/Irene in the film adaptation constitutes the metafilmic irony of this statement. Both Agustín's emotional reactions while viewing the film and his resulting epistolary correspondence and suicide all show the powerful impact of the seventh art. It is impossible to relive the past, however, and as Agustín reads Laura's response in a café, the discordant notes of the piano being tuned interferes with her voice-over reading of her response to him and symbolizes the impossibility for harmony in the relationship.

The reaction of both mother and daughter toward this woman capture the tone of the original: Julia feels jealous, and Estrella feels that she is her father's secret accomplice. (Estrella's mother is more sympathetic—less hysterical, and more loving—in the film version in this sequence and throughout. She, too, suffers [9, 49, etc.] and in the film version her emotional suffering appears in her physical illness.) Erice makes other important transformations in the screen adaptation of *El sur*, including the elimination of certain episodes—Adriana's mischievous interaction with Mari Nieves —and of characters—Mari Nieves, Josefa—in spite of the fact that this type of condensation is normally associated with adaptations of longer works. Estrella's complicity in the novel comes from secretly delivering Gloria's letters to her father (26); in the film, she lies to her mother about the identity of Irene Ríos. The mother's jealous fit in the novel, when she rips up Gloria's letter (25), becomes a heated conversation off screen which terminates in Julia slamming a door shut. The barking of the dog heard off screen, when taken in syntagmatic relationship with that of the initial sequence, means that this is a decisive moment in their relationship—a break that inexorably leads to the tragic end.

Estrella is caught up in this web of suffering, and Evans and Fiddian point out that Estrella's throwing some red wool on the floor was "borrowed conspicuously from the final 'cuadro' of Lorca's *Bodas de sangre*, [and] is both an omen of the family's fate and a symbol of their tangled emotions" (131). Estrella's inner torment leads to her desire to escape, and she does so by hiding under her bed all day. This sequence synthesizes different scenes in the novel: Adriana's fits of crying, the escape under the bed, and the subsequent encounter with her father at the supper table in which she realizes that her suffering, in comparison with his, is "banal and ridiculous" (30). The film version condenses these and accentuates the sense of suffering and lack of communication through their physical separation (they do not meet at the supper table) as well as through the nonverbal communication of the father, tapping his cane against the floor.

Estrella's suffering also causes her to express her desire to suddenly become older and flee; Erice beautifully captures the first of these wishes through an elliptical dissolve that manifests the transition from youth to adolescence: young Estrella (Sonsoles Aranguren) goes down her country road lined with bare trees on a white bicycle accompanied by a puppy in late fall, and following the dissolve, the older Estrella (Iciar Bollain) returns on a red bicycle with a grown dog as leaves now cover the ground in early fall of a later year.

Although Evans and Fiddian (131) contend that her photograph in a store window manifests a threat to her independence, because it is "set among those of conscripts (men as warrior stereotypes) and brides-to-be (domesticated victims with 'caras de tontas,')" her attitude toward the boy who is

courting her—El Carioco—indicates a degree of independence
and unconventionality that comes from being her father's
daughter: a telephone conversation reveals that she stood him
up, and she tells him that she is tired of him. She later
attempts to erase his graffiti from the wall. Furthermore,
elimination of the scene with her father's violent reaction at
seeing her with the boy (35) imbues the father with a greater
dimension of pathos, since his violence in the novel detracts
from our empathy toward him.

Agustín's initial nocturnal departure—with Julia's
anguished voice calling his name, and the barking of the dog
both heard off screen—foreshadows his definitive departure on
the night of his suicide. His initial attempt to return to the
south is unsuccessful when the train departs without him. Lying
in the bed of the boarding house, he covers his face with his
hands. This image of desperation must be taken in syntagmatic
relationship with a later image in the film, and in associative
relationship with two moments in the novel. Later in the film,
when Agustín invites Estrella to lunch in the Gran Hotel, she
attempts to establish better communication with him, but at
the same time, she lays bare his suffering. Why does he drink
so much? Who is Irene Ríos, and why did he write her name so
many times? The anguished look on Agustín's face relates
syntagmatically to the episode in which Estrella recalls when
she saw him writing a letter in the Café Oriental, which was
like catching him red-handed in an act of infidelity. Estrella
has caught him again, but this time it is as a young adult.
Agustín's reaction is to excuse himself from the table and go to
the lavatory, where he washes his face, and in a close-up shot
in which the camera functions as a mirror, he contemplates the
reflection of his face, almost as if he were trying to recognize
himself. This reflects the face motif that is important in
García Morales's narrative: Rafael's reaction to his daughter's
question about the reason for his suffering is that the worst kind
of suffering doesn't come from anywhere in particular, as if it
didn't have a face (37). A bit of information that is not
revealed until late in the plot of the novel has to do with
Rafael's lack of a "face" from the very beginning—the only
photograph that his son Miguel has of him does not show his

face, since it is covered with a mask (44) that Adriana has already determined to have belonged to her father (37). The film version beautifully captures the tone of these passages without slavish imitation.

The wedding festivity that takes place in the adjoining room of the Gran Hotel serves as a counterbalance to the luncheon meeting between father and daughter. The band plays the same *pasodoble* as during the first communion festivity, but the now adolescent Estrella cannot play the role of *novia*, and Agustín's shattered relationship with both Laura and Julia leaves him with the nothingness that leads to suicide. Alborg states that the *pasodoble* of the bride and groom also suggests the loss of his daughter, since someday she, too, will also dance it with another man, and that his suicide can be interpreted as a reaction to the loss of his daughter (16). All that is left is Estrella's sense of guilt. As Estrella leaves the restaurant, Agustín is left sitting alone, and her voice-over proclaims, "Le dejé allí, solo, abandonado a su suerte. ¿Pude hacer por él más de lo que en ese momento le hice? Eso es lo que siempre me he preguntado porque esa fue la última vez que hablé con él" (I left him there, sitting next to the window, listening to that old song, alone, abandoned to his luck. Could I have done anything more for him in that moment than what I did? That is what I have always asked myself, because that was the last time that I spoke with him).

The temporal dichotomy between the act of narrating (the voice of the adult Estrella) and the events narrated (Estrella's youth) constitutes a narrative frame (through flashback) that comprises the entire narration. According to Pipolo (167), framing represents "a sentimental gimmick for placing the action in the past and having it represent the former, rich, active life of the protagonist who, in the frame narrative is revealed as older and wiser, remorseful or nostalgic, etc." This expression of the adult Estrella's remorse reinforces the meaning of the narrative structure to the point that Rubio Gribble (173) believes that the purpose of the narrative discourse has changed from page to screen, from a tone of reproach in the novel to one of guilt in the movie version. After the panning shot that shows the river, the bicycle, and

Agustín's dead body, the initial close-up of Estrella holding the pendulum in her bedroom repeats itself, thus capturing the circular form of the original narrative.

After her father's death, Estrella is at first despondent, but she finally decides that in order to understand her father, she must go to the mysterious place of his origin. The final scene shows Estrella packing her suitcase as the voice-over proclaims, "Por fin, iba a conocer el sur" (At last, I was going to get to know the south). The closing of her suitcase represents the closing of one phase of her life. This ending constitutes the most radical narrative change from the novel to the film, since the film narrative terminates when Estrella is about to leave home, going to Sevilla to search out her father's past. In the novel, she makes the trip, meets with Gloria and her son Miguel, Adriana's half brother, and there is a brief romantic attraction between the two. Erice's original plans included filming a final segment of the movie in Sevilla; indeed, he considered that a vital aspect of the theme of searching for the past would be the confrontation of "two types of landscape, two worlds" (Cristóbal 7). Nevertheless, producer Elías Querejeta must have been anxious to enter the film at the Cannes Film Festival, where it was exhibited on the final day, and this created a rush to bring the production to a conclusion. The presentation of an "unfinished" film caused considerable controversy. Erice admits to presenting the film even though he was unable to complete his initial concept of the work because of financial reasons: "I'm conscious of the need of the company that has financed the preparation and the filming of the movie to recover its investment" (Rubio 129-30). Nevertheless, I believe that the ending of the film imbues the work with an even greater mysterious and poetic quality and certainly cannot be considered a defect. Indeed, it perfectly captures the sentiment expressed by Adriana in the novel: "siempre era mejor lo que se queda en el espacio de lo posible, lo que no llega a existir" (whatever is left in the realm of the possible, whatever does not come to exist, is always better, 41). The screen adaptation of El sur epitomizes, then, the question of viewer response regarding the question of fidelity, in that reading the novel first invariably creates certain expectations—in this case, disappointment at what might seem a truncated narration. Viewing the film first, however, obviates this problem, and the fact that the film was released before publication of the novel makes an even stronger case for accepting the film narrative as an autonomous entity. *El sur* won the Golden Hugo at the Chicago Film Festival, as well as a gold medal from the Centro de Investigaciones Cinematográficas for its testimonial character regarding recent Spanish history, and Manuel Fernández calls *El sur* "an authentic allegory about the maturity of thousands of Spaniards who, like the young Estrella, were born after the civil war and tried to know about the past in order to link their lives with the earlier tradition" (40).

Compitello (76) notes that both the "thematics and structural disposition" of *El sur* pertain to postmodern literary discourse: "these texts tend to be highly metafictional and self-reflexive, and to blur the border between fiction and history by subsuming them into the category of narration. Often they give primacy to the subjective and the personal rather than inscribe the validity of narrative in a historical context." In this regard, screen adaptation truly captures the tone and spirit of the original. Even though director Erice has said that for him, it is a "painful fact that *El sur*, although distributed as a finished product, is not at all complete from a narrative point of view" (Besas 248), *El sur* is a magnificent film and one of the best screen adaptations in Spanish cinema.

Rafael García Serrano

Rafael García Serrano fought in the Spanish civil war, and according to Soldevila Durante (123), he manifests a "permanent nostalgia for combat and for the absent brother-enemy without whom the ambiguous mechanism of scorn and exaltation of the bellicose impulse ceases to function." He is the author of the novel *La fiel infantería* (*The Loyal Infantry*, 1943), which was adapted for the screen by Pedro Lazaga in 1959, and he both wrote (in 1958) and directed (in 1966) *Los ojos perdidos* (*Lost Eyes*).

The main stylistic element of the narrative is the flashback: at the beginning of the film, a soldier gives Margarita Sanz a letter from second lieutenant Luis Valle that contains his insignia, a metonymical device to symbolize Luis's death. The chronology of the rest of the film is straightforward, narrating the brief hours that Luis and Margarita have after they meet and fall in love in San Sebastián before the lieutenant has to report to the front.

García Serrano underscores the theme of religion in the film from the moment the protagonist appears on screen. In his first scene, Luis enters a church to pray for courage, for his comrades, for chastity, less of a desire to drink, a just victory and peace for all—an almost incredible wish list, even for the Nationalist hero that the director wishes to portray. His prayer, intercut with views of the crucifix in church, manifests a combination of religion and the theme of reconciliation between the two sides as he prays "por todos los milicianos en la guerra bajo cualquier bandera y a los de las Brigadas Internacionales. Esos tipos también son tus hijos y mis hermanos" (for all the soldiers in the war under any flag and for the International Brigades. Those guys are also your sons and my brothers). Nevertheless, these "conciliatory" words seem to mask a condescending tone, especially toward the International Brigades ("esos tipos" [those guys]), which is a common element in many films by pro-Nationalist directors. The heroic aspect of the protagonist is echoed in his statement to Margarita: "Yo lucho para que todo lo que suceda mañana sea más bello de lo que sucede hoy" (I fight so that everything that happens tomorrow will be more beautiful than what is happening today). The religion theme later reappears in the comment, "Tú ya sabes que los muertos en campaña van derechos al cielo" (You already must know that those who die during the campaign go right to heaven), a comment that underscores the crusade ideal of the Nationalist side. A more important attempt in the dialogue to put forth the theme of reconciliation between the two sides of the fratricidal conflict occurs in Luis's words in the barbershop: "Mi padre está tan a gusto en el otro lado como yo en éste. Y con la misma lealtad. El cree que estoy equivocado; creo que el equivocado es él. Esto se llama guerra civil" (My father is as happy on the other side as I am on this one. And with the same loyalty. He thinks that I'm wrong, and I think that he is. This is what they call a civil war). This speech represents the theme of *cainismo* that appears in many Spanish films in an almost literal sense—the division and fighting within the family, but here with a sense of respect for each other.

All of the action of the film takes place in San Sebastián. Repeated long shots of the city and the beach give the film a "touristy" look at times. The film also includes icons of Nationalist leaders—there is a clearly displayed photograph of the young General Franco in a bar, and one of José Antonio in a jewelry store. We only see the war through offical documentary footage when Luis and Margarita go to the movies. Otherwise, the director seems to take a two-fold approach to the fighting itself. On the one hand, there is an attempt at humor, with references to it as "un jaleo" (an uproar) and "las cataratas del Niágara" (Niagara Falls) or the joke in the dialogue that accompanies the shot through the window of a convoy of trucks carrying soldiers to the front: "'Van al fregado.' '¿Tú crees?' 'A menos que se trate de una excursión de fin de semana'" ("They're going to where the action is." "Do you think so?" "Unless it might be a weekend excursion"). On the other hand, the fighting is portrayed as so horrendous that the civilian population cannot comprehend it. When the Nationalist soldier Pablo gives a short story that he has written to a newspaper man, the latter complains that it is a cruel story, and that "la guerra que pinta es feroz" (the war that you portray is ferocious). Nevertheless, the war is never seen, as the film limits its portrayal of a day in the life of the rear guard. Although the title and the opening scene in which Margarita receives the announcement of the death of the soldier portend the theme of the loss, García Serrano does not delve into its consequences.

Almudena Grandes

Almudena Grandes is an author who catapulted to fame overnight with her *Las edades de Lulú* (*Lulú's Ages*, 1989), which won the "Premio Sonrisa Vertical" for erotic fiction in the series edited by Luis G. Berlanga. The cover of the novel displays the portrait of a young girl and the erotic emblem of the series—labia behind a keyhole—so the reader has no doubts about the intent of the narrative. Is it a mere coincidence that the title of Almudena Grandes's work and its film adaptation parallels the titles of the two of Spain's most famous pornographic movies—*El chupete de Lulú* (*Lulu's Pacifier*) and *El ojete de Lulú* (*Lulu's Asshole*)—starring Lina Romay, "Spain's only genuine sex film star" (Slade 5)? However, Morris and Charnon-Deutsch contend that the publication of the novel by Tusquests gives it "institutional and intellectual authority of high literary value," which places the work "beyond the bounds of pornography" (303). The novel became a best-seller, and by 1996 it had been translated to six languages and had sold over one million copies. Producer Andrés Vicente Gómez undoubtedly wanted to capitalize on the novel's popularity, and he got J. J. Bigas Luna, known for his previous films *Bilbao* and *Caniche*, to direct the screen version of the novel.

The opening sequence of the film may have had the intent of capturing the emblem of the "vertical smile" series, but the close-up of a baby girl's genitalia is, in the words of Casàs, simply "obscene" (31). This is due not only to its syntagmatic relationship with the rest of the film, but also because of its exploitative nature.

Las edades de Lulú narrates the descent into the hellish world of hard sex of the protagonist, played by Francesca Neri. (Angela Molina was originally cast in the role, but she abandoned the project, scandalized by the depraved nature of the sexual scenes. Molina has shown in her previous films that she is certainly no prude, so this decision certainly says something about this movie.) Lulú's husband Pablo (Oscar Ladoire) imagines a ménage-à-trois with Lulú's own brother Marcelo (Fernando Guillén Cuervo), who has always felt incestuously attracted to his sister. Pablo convinces Lulú to take part in this sexual experiment without revealing the identity of the other man, and she has sex with her own brother while blindfolded. Lulú then abandons Pablo, saying "No quiero ser más una niña" (I don't want to be a little girl any more). The main problem with the protagonist, however, is precisely her lack of self-esteem and the domination of her by male characters. Although she really is a young girl when she has her first date with Pablo, his comments about the conduct of well-behaved *señoritas* are more appropriate of a controlling father. Lulú seems to have little will of her own, since she is constantly dominated by men who make her do things that she finds objectionable: Pablo shaves her pubis against her wishes (an act that reduces her to a dominated prepubescent), has anal intercourse over her protests, and gags and ties her up for the ménage-à-trois; in the final sexual scene, Jimmy (Javier Bardem) drags her into the room in spite of her screaming resistance and constrains her with forced bondage.

Her sexual odyssey in the night world of hard sex for hire begins with her husband when they meet the transvestite Ely (María Barranco). It ends in a private orgy with various sexual paraphernalia appropriate to porno films in which Lulú is being raped while tied to the ceiling. She has become nothing more than the cold cuts shown in close-up that a rich client selects. The rescue of Lulú by her husband and the police gives the movie what Casas (31) calls an overly clear moral concerning the hell that will result from leaving one's husband and tasting the forbidden fruit. Nevertheless, Casas believes that *Las edades de Lulú* is indeed pornographic, except for the fact that it escaped the official classification as such—shots of penises are flaccid, not erect, for example.

The novel's success is undoubtedly due more to its scandalous reputation than for its literary merits, and the same can be said of the movie. Although both represent the relative freedom in terms of sexuality that Spanish society currently enjoys, it can also be argued that like Bigas Luna's earlier *Bilbao*, this film demonstrates that "the post-Franco era is not really so free" and that "Spaniards still retain an internalized repression that cultivates a taste for perverse sexuality" (Kinder 262).

Perhaps true freedom will come when characters like Lulú truly stop being little girls and become independent women.

Alfonso Grosso

Los invitados (*The Guests*, 1987) is Víctor Barrera's screen adaptation of the novel from 1978 by Andalusian novelist Alfonso Grosso (1928-1995). The novel is a hybrid narrative combining fiction with journalism that relates an unresolved crime that occurred on an Andalusian ranch called Los Galindos in 1975. Grosso's attempt to create a hybrid narrative combining fiction with documentary is a weak point of the work, since as Vásquez (235) points out, the journalistic and classic crime modes of narration come into conflict with each other. The narrator's attempts to reconcile the two, as when he says that "the colloquial version" of the conversation between characters Tony and Georgina "must inevitably be approximate" (67) proves bothersome. Director Barrera eliminates this weak point of the novel and instead emphasizes the story itself, which is a "classic crime tale, with an emphasis on action, suspense and surprise" (Vásquez 233). Although the film claims that the characters and locales are imaginary, there is such a similarity between what is portrayed on screen and the actual events, the claim can only be viewed as a protection against the lawsuits that director Barrera perhaps anticipated.

Life for workers on a ranch in Andalucia is difficult, and complaints of unemployment, low salaries (especially in contrast with the wealth of the aristocratic landlords), the lack of solidarity among workers, and the need for agrarian reform constitute the thread of a social theme that is evident in many of Grosso's narratives. But the arrival at the ranch of Tony Mackenzie (Pablo Carbonell), an English smalltime criminal, changes the lives of the workers forever, since he makes the proposition to the grandfather (called Manuel Zapata Villanueva in the novel, played by Raúl Fraire in the film) that they plant marijuana on a remote site of the ranch. The common bond between the two men is that they were both ex-Spanish Legionnaires, and this, together with the enticing promise of millions, convinces the grandfather to accept the proposition.

The film adaptation makes several transformations of the original work. It decreases the element of chance found in the original narrative: whereas in the novel, Tony's car breaks down (94), in the film, he deliberately cuts a belt in the motor after a long shot shows him checking the quality of the soil. This greater causality occurs because Barrera eliminates the character of Georgina Leighton from the original narrative. The initial sequence, set in England, immediately introduces the idea of planting marijuana in Spain because of problems that the crime organization had with the Moroccan crop. Tony's plans are more premeditated in the film, although the choice of the ranch itself has a certain element of chance. Of course, things do not go as planned. However, director Barrera slightly changes the fortuitous and fatal discovery of the illegal crop; instead of legionnaires on maneuvers (145-47), it is simply unnamed outsiders who rob some plants, which when taken in syntagmatic relationship with the earlier threat that manifested the mob's insistence on accountability—"hasta la última hoja, no lo olvide" (down to the last leaf, don't forget it)—augers danger for the grandfather and the other workers who have entered the web of organized crime.

The film adaptation adds motives to the grandfather's decision to burn the entire crop. His wife (after a long hiatus, Lola Flores returned to the screen for this role) is against the whole business, and her fears even bring her to threaten leaving him. Repeated television footage on the problems and dangers of drug abuse (with tearful mothers relating the terrible effects of addiction on their children) underscores the motivation to terminate the crop and somewhat echoes the journalistic narrative mode of the original work.

Barrera also adds sequences that increase the suspense of the narrative. The dream sequence related to the grandfather manifests his fears of scandal and possible prison as a result of his involvement. Although he sleeps in the field to defend the crop, the arrival of a truck bringing outsiders causes him to run, since he knows that he is doomed, and he decides to burn the entire field. Although he accepts the responsibility for his decision to eliminate the crop, this does not appease the mafiosi who counted on huge profits. The shoot-out at the end of the film is the reenactment of the actual crime: the Mafia kills five members of the ranch personnel—but the latter do not die without a fight, as the grandfather wounds Tony with his shotgun before the latter can escape with his female accomplice. The mafiosi, meanwhile, escape on a waiting Piper Cub.

Using a suspense narrative, *Los invitados* is one of a growing number of contemporary Spanish films that deals with the problem of drugs in Spanish society. However, the film does not include what for me was one of the most hair-raising aspects of the original work and which corresponds to the journalistic narrative: two years after the homicides at the ranch, Tony and Georgina were murdered in London. Organized crime has the memory of an elephant and the tentacles of an octopus; perhaps Barrera's early disclaimer is also a way to avoid incurring its wrath.

Eduardo de Guzmán

Mi hija Hildegart (*My Daughter Hildegart*), the 1977 film directed by Fernando Fernán Gómez, stars Amparo Soler Leal as Aurora Rodríguez Caballeira, and Carmen Roldán as her daughter, Hildegart. The movie is based on a novel by Eduardo de Guzmán entitled *Aurora de sangre* (*Bloody Aurora*), which is in turn based on a series of historical events: the notorious homicide and resulting trial that occurred in 1934. Although the majority of the narrative is concerned with the turbulent years preceding the civil war, the actual chronological limits of the film are expanded through the use of flashbacks. Indeed, the main portion of the narrative is in itself a flashback, since the story is narrated in the present by Aurora's lawyer for the case, Eduardo, who, now an old man, is telling the story at a bar. Fernán Gómez uses Aurora's trial as the vehicle for the narrative, and events prior to the main narrative include Aurora as a child with a doll; the night of Hildegart's conception, when Aurora mechanically performs the sexual act with a man in order to be able to have a child; Hildegart as a young girl; and the declaration of the Republic. Director Fernán Gómez handles these flashbacks in a rather primitive fashion, using tinted frames to signify a chronological change in the narrative: red for Eduardo's narrative in the bar, and brown for the flashbacks to the earlier events.

Pistol shots heard off screen return the narrative from the initial bar scene to the past as Aurora leaves her apartment building to inform her lawyer that she has killed Hildegart. The flashbacks thus function to explain how this woman came to commit such a heinous crime. The return to Aurora's childhood brings on the earliest events of the narrative: as a young girl, she clutches a doll and asks her father, "Papá, cuando sea mayor, tendré una muñeca de verdad y nadie me la va a quitar?" (Daddy, when I am older, will I have a real doll that no one will take away from me?) Of course, her daughter Hildegart later becomes the doll, and Aurora cannot stand to see her/it reach maturity and become independent. Indeed, Hildegart was a mere object to be manipulated from the moment of her conception, as Aurora explains to the jury during her trial that Hildegart had to consecrate herself to women's liberation. This liberation, in Aurora's mind, was both sexual and political. It is clear that Aurora views sexual relations with great disdain. After the scene in which she confesses that her daughter was certainly not the fruit of a passionate encounter, since the presence of the male procreator did not represent gratification, but was simply a mere biological necessity, Aurora tries to organize women in prison against the "exploitation of the body" and in favor of the prohibition of prostitution. Another example of Aurora's attitude toward sexual exploitation occurs in a later scene when Hildegart is in her late teens: Aurora accompanies her daughter and a friend, Antonio Villena, to a fair and they witness a midway game in which boys throw balls at a target in order to make women fall out of their beds. Aurora becomes furious, calling the game "barbarous" and "filthy." (Footage of this scene also appears during the opening credits, further reinforcing the sexual theme.)

The themes of possessiveness and sexual inhibition culminate in the scene in which Hildegart is about to leave on a date with her friend Antonio: the mother takes her into the bathroom and writes "Aurora" on the girl's stomach, chest, and back, telling her that if the signatures are erased when she returns, she is "lost." Aurora's exclamation during the trial, "Hildegart solo era mía. Aquel hombre no tenía ningun derecho sobre ella" (Hildegart was mine alone. That man had no right to her), further underscores the possessiveness theme. As Hildegart tearfully leaves, she strikes the keyboard of the piano, and the discord of the notes symbolizes the irreconcilable discord that has arisen between herself and her mother. Of course, such divisions did not always exist between mother and daughter. Aurora tells the jury that Hildegart was a precocious child; she wrote her first article in the *Socialista* at the age of fourteen, and her first book appeared two years later. Hildegart's request that her mother sign a copy of the book symbolized their unity at that time.

As vice president of the Young Socialists, the daughter echoed her mother's ideological convictions, stating in speeches that matrimony represented sexual enslavement, and that solving women's problems solved social problems in the interest of humanity. Hildegart came under attack for her views, and both mother and daughter become disenchanted with the party to the point that Hildegart turned in her membership card. Aurora justified this act, commenting, "quien se ha alejado del socialismo es el partido" (the party itself has grown away from socialism). This loyalty theme is also fundamental to the relationship between mother and daughter. Just before the day of the murder, Hildegart tells her mother that she is leaving to go to Mallorca alone. When Aurora threatens to call the police, we see a close-up of Hildegart telling her that she (Hildegart) has sacrificed herself and done everything for her mother. Aurora's reply is, "¿Estás segura? ¿No será al revés?" (Are you sure? Isn't the opposite true?)

The day of the crime, Aurora tries to justify her attempt to maintain her dream and prevent Hildegart from leaving her. Aurora waits at night for Hildegart to return home, and as she loads a pistol, the camera pans the wall with its testimonials to Hildegart's achievements and their former unity: diplomas, photos of mother and daughter together. Aurora sees a book written by her daughter entitled *Sexo y amor* (*Sex and Love*), and she reads (with Hildegart's voice off screen) the section on "Cain y Abel" in which she provides a political interpretation of the myth by saying that Cain is the symbol of progress, the first anarchist in Hebrew legend, and that his act constituted legitimate, just conduct. This reading provides Aurora with a justification for her crime. As she tells the jury, however, "No es fácil a una madre quitar la vida a su hija" (It's not easy for a mother to take away her daughter's life), and Aurora's sobs wake her sleeping daughter for a final confrontation, as the mother holds a pistol to the daughter's temple. Aurora tells her daughter that she only wants to save her—from herself and from her own weakness, and she again accuses Hildegart of a lack of loyalty: "No serás la primera en traicionar el proletariado" (You won't be the first one to betray the proletariat). The flowers that fall from Aurora's hands to the floor of the courtroom symbolize the end of her internal conflict, and the death of Hildegart as the narrative weaves back from the trial to the final moments of the daughter's life. Hildegart, at only nineteen and still very much under the influence of her mother, tells her to kill her, and Aurora's ironic shouts, "No estoy loca" (I'm not crazy), accompany the homicide.

The abolition of capital punishment during the Republic meant that Aurora's sentence consisted of incarceration. In July of 1936, however, prison doors were opened (a truck marked "CNT," which stands for the anarchist group called Confederación Nacional del Trabajo [NationalConfederation of Work] appears in the street to the tune of "A las barricadas" ["To the Barricades"]), and women prisoners, including Aurora Rodríguez Caballeira, were set free. The film ends as it begins, with a caption regarding the historical events: "Pero desapareció para siempre. Se ignora si está viva todavía o si ha muerto. No se ha vuelto a saber de ella" (But she disappeared forever. We do not know if she is still alive or if she is dead. No one knows anything about her). Nevertheless, recent investigations have discovered that Aurora Rodríguez died in 1955 at the insane asylum of Ciempozuelos in the province of Madrid (Fajardo 130).

Mi hija Hildegart suffers from an overly ambitious story, with overly crude markers to denote transformations in the narrative. The scene in which we see Hildegart's bare breasts as Aurora paints her name over her daughter's torso corresponds to the *destape* phenomenon, whereby, after the death of Franco, Spain seemed to suddenly discover sexual freedom. There is a sad irony in the film, however, in that this rather gratuitous display, which seems geared toward better box office receipts, goes completely against Hildegart's beliefs regarding sexual exploitation.

Manuel Hidalgo

The opening scene of Augusto M. Torres's *El pecador impecable* (*The Sinless Sinner*, 1987), based on the novel of the previous year by film critic Manuel Hidalgo, sets the tone for the rest of the film: the old mother (Rafaela Aparicio) complains about the sardines that she ate the night before, and her huge fart connects to a scatological humor that has been present in Spanish culture since the Infantes de Carrión soil their garments in the *Poem of the Cid*. Here, however, it contributes to the vaudevillesque tone that dominates the film and that represents a shift in tone from the original novel, which was published in the "Sonrisa vertical" series of erotic literature edited by Luis G. Berlanga. The combination of eros and humor is probably due to the protagonist of the film, Alfredo Landa. Indeed, this film is a continuation of the "landismo" phenomenon, the sex comedies that made Landa famous in the 1960s and 1970s.

The film portrays the sexual awakening of the fifty-year-old Honorio Siguenza (Landa), who has his affairs in his deceased mother's bed. The sudden death of his mother is a blow to Honorio, and the narrative shifts from pathos to humor: as he lies in bed, his neighbor says that she only wants to console his grief, and she takes off her dress and throws herself on him, to which he responds that she is "the Good Samaritan." Throughout the film, this role reversal in which women are the sexual aggressors provides much of the humor. As if it were a fairy tale, the narrative has a three-part episodic structure, with the sexual advances of his neighbor (Alicia Sánchez) followed by those of a widowed hairdresser Mercedes (Queta Claver), and those of a female lottery seller (Julita Serrano). The hairdresser turns out to be almost more than Honorio can handle, however, as after a romantic evening of dancing, her sexual tastes turn out to be of the "S & M" variety. Of course, this is also the basis of humor, as the scene of whipping Honorio's buttocks cuts to the young Valeria witnessing Honorio limp as he gets out of a taxi, and blames his altered gait on his sciatica.

Humor often results from an inversion of expectations, and

this is the case when Honorio consummates his affair with the lottery seller in the bathroom. One expects condemnation of this licentiousness from the woman's sister who listens to their moans of ecstacy from behind the bathroom door, so her comment, "¿por qué no lo hacen en la cama como gente normal?" (Why don't they just do it in bed like normal people?) provides one of the more comic moments of the film.

As if his three female suitors were not enough, Honorio really pines after Valeria, the fifteen-year-old girl who goes around on roller skates. (The image on the poster that advertised the movie shows a close-up of Honorio surrounded in the background by the three mature suitors, and his gaze longingly follows the young girl.)   To further complicate matters, the woman who pursues him the most is undesirable to Honorio: his cousin Veni (Chus Lampreave), who constantly complains that she is merely his cousin, and reminds Honorio that his mother's last wish was that they marry.

The combination of the unexpected and hyperbole contributes to the humor in the scene in which Honorio, whose health is affected by his recent activity, is examined by his physician. When the doctor assumes that being sexually very active means two to three times "per month," Honorio retorts that it is "per day." While in bed on Epiphany day recuperating from these excessive activities, Sabina, Mercedes, and Marta all come to visit him. Their presents, however, are not exactly those of the three Magi, as they all get in bed with him at once.

The film version is a free adaptation of the original novel, with changes in the names of the female characters, the addition of cousin Veni's character, and the elimination of Honorio's death at the end of the narrative. Most importantly, the film eliminates some of the overtly sexual scenes (the anal intercourse with María, the phallic shoehorn episode with Magdalena, the fondling of young Valeria) in order to provide a "light" version of the erotic component (unlike the film adaptation of *Las edades de Lulú*, another "Sonrisa vertical" novel), with much greater emphasis on the comic.

Although Landa proved, beginning with *El puente* in 1976 and culminating with *Los santos inocentes* in 1984, that he was capable of a wider range of acting, it has proven difficult for him to break out of the mold. However, the same year that he starred in *El pecador impecable*, Landa was able to show greater integrity in comic roles, such as that of Fendetestas in *El bosque animado*. Nevertheless, Spanish audiences perennially love comedies of this type, and the box office is not to be ignored.

Fernando Lalana

Pedro Olea's 1995 adapation of Fernando Lalana's novel, *Morirás en Chafarinas* (*You Will Die in Chafarinas*, 1989), is a well-crafted detective story. The Chafarinas of the title is a small group of islands off the coast of Africa where Spain maintains a military presence, as it does in the main location of the narrative, the Spanish city of Melilla in northern Africa. The screen adaptation stands well on its own, but pales in comparison with the original narrative because of a fundamental transformation of the ending of the narrative.

This narrative is similar to other contemporary manifestations of the postmodern detective genre in that there is a displacement of the traditional sleuth in favor of a more marginal character. Just as in Isasi's adaptation of Benet's *El aire de un crimen*, the sleuth is a soldier—in this case, Alvaro Cidraque (Javier Alabalá), a serviceman of questionable background (the film narrative accentuates this trait by giving him a criminal file) who is forced into this role due to circumstances somewhat beyond his control: Captain Contreras (Oscar Ladoire) assigns him the task of investigating the heroin death of a soldier not only because he is smart, but because he was in the military jail for insubordinate actions when the other soldier died of an overdose. Cidraque's companion Jaime (Jorge Sanz) is the unnamed first-person narrator of the novel. Lalana's work thus manifests Todorov's observation that the detective story "is often told by a friend of the detective, who explicitly acknowledges that he is writing a book" (45). Although screen adaptations can never fully capture a first-person narrative, Jaime's role as protagonist in the film captures this point of view fairly well, but it does not represent this narrative element in the original work, in which the narrator refers to the tale as his "memoirs" (186). Cidraque explicitly states to Jaime that the murders of soldiers are crimes that they will solve by themselves. Jaime, however, later becomes exasperated with Cidraque and claims that his friend has used him. Cidraque, however, counters that he is solving the puzzle ("rompecabezas") out of love for Victoria, the sister of one of the victims.

191

The opening sequence sets the tone for the rest of the film in terms of pacing and camera work. A soldier who is a crazed junkie has entered a mosque with a weapon and Jaime and Cidraque have to apprehend him. The beautiful low-angle shot looking straight up at the candelabra that falls from the ceiling almost killing Jaime is a symbolic foreshadowing of the death of the pursued soldier who likewise falls from the roof, with an overhead shot of the dead body in the street echoing the earlier low angle shot. When they search the dead soldier's locker, they discover a number of uniforms, and the question "¿Para qué los quería?" (What did he want them for?) is the first piece of the puzzle that must be solved.

As is often the case in detective stories, sheer chance is a key element in the ability of the sleuth to solve the crime. While crossing a plaza, Jaime happens to grab a young Arab who has just committed a purse snatching. When he convinces the victim, Elisa (María Barranco), not to press charges because the thief is just a child, the young Arab becomes indebted to the Spanish soldier, and this debt will naturally be repaid later in the narrative. This chance encounter also establishes a relationship that will later become important between Jaime and Elisa, who turns out to be the captain's wife.

As the soldier-detectives enter the maze of alley ways in Melilla, Olea artfully uses camera work to create suspense. A point-of-view tracking shot that follows Cidraque through the bazaar suddenly closes in on him rapidly, thus making us falsely believe that he is about to be attacked. The alleys are later the locale of a suspenseful chase scene that ends happily for Jaime, since he escapes into Elisa's house. There is an ironic twist to his escape, however, when she orders him at gunpoint, "Desnúdate, cabo" (Undress, Corporal). Olea also creates a beautiful montage sequence in which Cidraque explains one of the murders by recreating the crime as Gayarre stood in front of a spotlight but then moved to blind Villalba before killing him. With Elisa's confession that she has not slept with her husband in over a year and a half, knowledge that drugs were sewn into the linings of uniforms at a local laundry, and the fact that long-time friends Captain Gayarre (Ramón Langa)—a known homosexual—and Captain Contreras are owners of the laundry, the pieces of the puzzle begin to come together.

When both Captain Contreras and Cidraque are shipped to the Chafarinas, the soldier is able to confront his superior and bluff about how much he knows. One of the final pieces of the puzzle is how Contreras would be able to leave the island with the drug money. The answer supplied to Cidraque—that only the death of a family member would allow such an extraordinary event—syntagmatically relates to the chance encounter early in the narrative: the obvious victim is Elisa. There is a spatial shift in the narrative back to the mainland, and a close-up of the lock on her door opening creates suspense, since we know that the assassin is closing in on his victim. Jaime, however, was able to enlist his Arab friends to thwart her homicide, as the assassin shoots at pillows placed in her bed to trick him and then they subdue him.

The arrest of Contreras begins the final suspenseful sequence of the film with a confrontation between Cidraque and the drug dealer. The captain's macho taunt as Cidraque aims his rifle at him—"No tienes cojones" (You don't have the balls)—causes the soldier to hestitate enough for Contreras to escape to a speedboat, but justice prevails as a montage of close-ups of Cidraque and the trigger of his rifle together with long shots of the escaping drug dealer culminate in the slow motion sequence that manifests the sleuth's marksmanship, as Cidraque shoots Contreras in the forehead.

Olea's transformation of the ending provides the screen adaptation with a sense of closure that radically changes the tone of the original. In the film, after Captain Contrera's death, the briefcase with the drug money is returned to his widow, and at his funeral, Cidraque proposes a deal with Luisa. In the final scene, as the two soldiers wait in civilian clothes for their boat to depart for Málaga, it becomes clear that Luisa has deceived them and will not appear. Cidraque, who thought she would come because he believed she was in love with Jaime, laments about how close he was to becoming a rich man. Jaime chides the sleuth, saying, "Parece mentira, y con lo listo que eres para otras cosas" (It's unbelievable, with how smart you are for other things). This outsmarting of the smart character ends the film narrative on an ironic note, tempered by the comic final comment that things could have been worse—they could have had a war with Morocco.

Olea originally planned a different ending to the film. In the published script, the final sequence has Elisa on board at last, with Jaime kissing her while Cidraque triumphantly grabs the briefcase (Olea 131). Nevertheless, Captain Gayarre is also on board and is observing them, as he symbolically throws his cigarette into the sea. Following the technique that Olea used earlier when Cidraque proved one of the murders using the blinding spotlight, Gayarre is unrecognizable to Cidraque because he is in the sun—connoting that Cidraque, just as Villalba before him, will be the next victim. The director did not include this ending because he believed that it did not fit well with the tone of the rest of the film narrative (Olea 14). However, it corresponds much better to the tone of the ending of the original.

In the novel, the narrator tells us that Elisa is indeed assassinated, thus precluding any future relationship with the narrator-protagonist. The confrontation with Captain Contreras occurs at night, with Jaime and Cidraque and two other soldiers discovering a subterranean passageway to another island where Contreras receives his drug shipments. Filming this as a night scene may have proven difficult: the explosion of the tunnel and escape from the rushing sea water also would have been costly to create—director Olea (14) comments that he would have needed a budget like that needed for *Cleopatra* in order to film an ending that was faithful to the original novel—whereas the day scene in the film offered no technical difficulties. The final confrontation in the novel is not between Cidraque and Contreras, however, but—in a marvellous plot twist— between Cidraque and the narrator. As the narrator confronts his companion and friend who is carrying the briefcase with heroin, the question becomes, Is Cidraque a "good guy" or a "bad guy"? Did Cidraque really figure out the crime and was he overcome by a moment of greed, or did he plan everything so as to get the drugs for himself? If the novel had ended there, it would have constituted a wonderful open ending, but Lalana went one step further in the epilogue, which takes place seven years after the earlier events. The appearance of a Ferrari (202)—the car Cidraque had earlier said that Jaime could buy if he took his share of the drugs (194)— outside the protagonist's door, and his fear as he awaits Cidraque, constitute a final plot twist that makes this such a good thriller. Olea, however, eliminates this open ending that is filled with both doubt and fear in favor of one that is much more generically conventional.

Porter states (85) that a detective story "moves from mystery to solution and from crime to punishment" and that "works in the genre always take a stand in defense of the established societal order . . . The deep ideological constant, therefore, is built into the action of investigation. The classic structuring question is always 'Whodunit' and secondarily, how will justice be done" (125). The ending of the film narrative gives us this more traditional sense of closure. The bad guy (Contreras) has gotten his just deserts. The fact that Luisa has gotten his money is, in a sense, recompense for her victimization at the hands of her husband. However, the original novel, and to an extent the original script, transcend the conventional generic structure and constitute a postmodern or even anti-detective narrative. Compitello believes that "the postmodern detective story undermines the most fundamental assumption of the model: the ability to order the world" ("Spain's" 183). The resolution of the crime in the traditional detective novel implies a (temporary) restoration of order to society based on the triumph of good over evil, but this is not the case in the novel. Lalana's *Morirás en Chafarinas* is then an "anti-detective novel" in which the solution "is ambiguous and partially unfulfilling" (Tani 24). Spanos calls the "anti-detective novel" "the paradigmatic archetype of the post-modernist literary imagination . . . the formal purpose of which is to evoke the impulse to 'detect' and/or to psychoanalyze in order to violently frustrate it by refusing to solve the crime" (154).

Wood ("El maestro" 117) notes that Olea's previous film, *El maestro de esgrima*—also a detective narrative—conforms to the Hollywood canon, and the same can be said of *Morirás en Chafarinas*. Conformity often implies less risk, and in a relatively weak industry like Spanish cinema, taking risks can be very difficult.

Julio Llamazares

In 1987, Julio Sánchez Valdés directed *Luna de lobos* (*Wolves' Moon*), based on the novel of the same name by Julio Llamazares. The movie stars Antonio Resines in a dramatic role (rather than his normal comic role), together with Santiago Ramos, Alvaro de Luna, and Kiti Manver. The narrative takes place over a nine-year period, from 1937 until 1946, and traces the gradual attrition and disappearance of a group of *maquis* or guerrilla fighters in the mountains of León and Asturias who continue the resistance against Franco. The opening line of the film, "Bueno, parece que esto se acaba" (Well, it looks like it's all over), is a prelude to the inexorable elimination of these *maquis*. Indeed, in the opening scene, as six men sit around a campfire, shots ring out, and two of the group are killed. Throughout the rest of the film, the remaining *maquis*—Angel, Gildo, Ramiro, and Juanín—struggle to survive as the Civil Guard hunts them down one by one.

Although these guerrilla fighters live in the mountain forest, contact with villagers who support their cause seems essential to their survival. Quite often, however, townspeople, such as the miller, want to have nothing to do with them, since it puts their own lives in danger. This is particularly the case of the priest, Don Manuel, whom the *maquis* kidnap (but later release) because he refused to aid Angel's brother. The guerrillas often attempt to contact family members, who provide them with food or boots, and one of the most important villagers to provide shelter and support for the *maquis* is María, whose love for Ramiro helps him survive. Although María finds her situation to be almost unbearable, and when Angel receives a stomach wound from another ambush, Ramiro seeks María's help only to find her in bed with Sergeant Argüello, from the Civil Guard who is hunting the *maquis*. When María later meets again with Ramiro, she explains, "Yo también estaba acorralada, Ramiro. Yo también sabía lo que es el miedo y la soledad" (I was also surrounded, Ramiro. I, too, knew what fear and loneliness are).

The first exchange between María and Ramiro clarifies the title of the film. When she exclaims, "Hueles a monte, Ramiro.

The *maquis* continue the armed struggle: Sánchez Valdés's *Luna de lobos*, starring Antonio Resines, Alvaro de Luna, and Santiago Ramos. *Courtesy Anola Films, S.A.*

Hueles como los lobos" (You smell like the woods, Ramiro. You smell like the wolves), he replies, "¿Y qué soy, María? ¿Qué soy ya más que un lobo?" (And what am I, María? What am I other than a wolf?) Sergeant Argüello also adds to the metaphor as he explains his strategy for capturing the guerrillas: "A un lobo no se le sigue, hay que esperarlo" (You don't follow a wolf, you wait for it). There are frequent night scenes with a full moon, and Ramiro comments, "La luna es el sol de los muertos" (The moon is the sun of the dead). Although this adds to the inexorable fate of these "wolves," a close-up of a wanted poster for Ramiro Luna Robles reveals that the title of the film refers not only to the metaphor and the visual imagery, but also to a play on words with one of the protagonist's surnames.

At the beginning of the film narrative, the *maquis* show a certain generosity and altruism: although they must steal to survive, they pay farmers for their losses, and even decline to take a sheep that is pregnant. In the next temporal segment, corresponding to 1940, they have become more criminal, robbing a bus of passengers, and killing a man in a store who calls them "hijos de puta" (sons of bitches) and reaches for a gun. In an attempt to acquire money with which to bribe their way across the border, they resort to kidnapping Don José, a mine owner. The Civil Guard attempts to ambush the *maquis*, and the slow-motion shots that Sánchez Valdés uses for both this scene and the previously mentioned shooting seem superfluous. After the death of Angel and when the Civil Guard begins to close in on Ramiro, finding his cave and nearly discovering him hidden in a stable, his only recourse is to flee. Transformed by a shave, haircut, and suit, Ramiro is able to board the train, and a long shot of the train's departure ends the film. Wood (88) notes that this open ending of the film leaves the spectator up in the air regarding the fate of the protagonist, whereas in the novel, the reader intuits that he survived to write his "autobiography."

At the beginning of the film, the narrator's voice-over gives us words from the prologue of the novel that describe the guerrilla fighters: "Dejaron los mejores años de sus vidas y una estela imborrable y legendaria en la memoria popular" (They left the best years of their lives, and an indelible and legendary imprint on popular memory). The novel itself, however, is narrated in the first person, and first-person narratives have always proven problematic in terms of their screen adaptations. The use of the present tense in the original narrative gives it a cinematographic quality, and the author recognizes that these two technical elements convert the protagonist into a virtual film camera (Marco 28). Although the use of voice-over by the protagonist is a technique often used to assimilate the first-person narrative, Sánchez Valdés did not choose to use it in this way. Wood (82, 88) believes that the change in the protagonist from Angel to Ramiro is a response to this difficulty of capturing the first-person narrative in cinema, but that this shift in point of view

A doomed struggle: Sánchez Valdés's *Luna de lobos*, starring Antonio Resines, Alvaro de Luna, and Santiago Ramos. *Courtesy Anola Films, S.A.*

weakens the identification between the reader and the protagonist that existed in the novel. To what extent, then, does the identification between the viewer and the film's protagonist, Ramiro, correspond to that analogous process in the novel?

In spite of the fact that the initial voice-over refers to the *maquis* as legendary, they are never treated as heroes in the film. When Ramiro sneaks into the village to visit his father's deathbed, the women there reject his presence. Don José sums up the opinion of the townspeople regarding the *maquis*, saying, "Para unos sois unos simples ladrones y asesinos, y para otros, aunque no lo digan, unos pobres desgraciados que lo único que hacéis es tratar de salvar la vida" (For some folks, you are simply thieves and assassins, and for others, although they might not come out and say it, you are a bunch of poor devils

who are only trying to save your skins). When Ramiro decides
to leave, his own self-exile is a recognition that he is an outcast
among his own people in his own land: "Esta tierra no tiene
perdón; esta tierra es maldita para mí" (This land has no
pardon; this land is accursed for me). The exceptional
photography by Juan Molina Temboury, with numerous long
shots of the beautiful countryside of León and Asturias, which
beautifully capture Llamazares's prose descriptions, and the
thematic counterpoint in the music by Luis Mendo and Bernardo
Fuster (the drum motif of the Civil Guard contrasts with the
accordion motif of the *maquis*) add to the quality of the *Luna de
lobos*. As we have shown (Deveny *Cain* 95-122), many
contemporary Spanish films examine the role of the *maquis* in
the years following the civil war, and *Luna de lobos* is one of
the best.

Torcuato Luca de Tena

Rafael Gil's screen adaptation of *La mujer de otro* (*Another Man's Wife*, 1967) is based on Torcuato Luca de Tena's novel from 1961, which won the Planeta literary prize for that year. As the title suggests, the film deals with a sexual affair, and both Luca de Tena and Gil manifest the dominant moral tone of the Franco regime. The affair is a tale of youthful romance that was cast aside and found anew, but at a time when present circumstances that reflect other paths taken—marriages and children—preclude a simple renewal of their former relationship. Ana María (Marty Hyer) and Andrés (John Romane) loved each other when they were young, but Andrés, a budding artist, abandoned Ana María to go to Paris to seek fame and fortune as a painter. They meet at an exhibition and discover that their feelings for each other have persisted over the years, as Andrés confesses that her memory is in every corner, and Ana María admits that she saw all of his exhibits and cut out all the reviews of his work. The renewed relationship begins with dinner in his studio—including music from yesteryear—and progresses to a tryst on the island resort of Mallorca.

The moral condemnation of the affair begins to enter the narrative when Ana María repeatedly mentions her sense of guilt. This guilt is based not only on the cheating on her husband, but on the idea of abandonment, as Ana María plans to leave her husband Enrique and the children in favor of a new life with her lover. The abandonment theme occurs both in the brief flashback to the anguish felt by Ana María in reaction to the curt letter that Andrés left her as his only farewell, and also in a later flashback to her childhood when Ana María is abandoned by another man—her father. The poignant plea, "Papá, no te vayas" (Daddy, don't leave), is meant to underscore the emotional import of this theme.

The narrative resolves the moral dilemma in a overly facile manner with the characters of Pepa (Analía Gadé) and Commander Montero (Fosco Giachetti). Pepa is a friend of Ana María, but in contrast with the adulteress, Pepa is a saintly figure who not only does community service in an old folks home, but puts up with the irrational and uncivilized behavior of some of the old folks with such great patience. Pepa takes interest in the well-being of an elderly gentleman who takes his meals at the facility; she follows him home, only to discover his real identity. Photographs on his desk show him in his military uniform in Africa, and also show his young daughter: Pepa then realizes that he is the former Comandante Montero (Moscoso in the original narrative)—Ana María's father. Montero functions as a dramatic deus ex machina to resolve the moral dilemma—with a little help from the "angel" of the narrative—as Pepa recruits him to intervene on behalf of his long lost daughter so that Ana María's husband and children will not suffer the same ill effects caused by abandonment. The ending of the film superficially manipulates the concept of "good guy" and "bad guy" with the adulterer Andrés obviously falling into the latter category. When Montero confronts him, Andrés does not resort to violence, saying that he does not hit old men, to which the former commander retorts, "Me sorprende. Quien es capaz de cometer una vileza es capaz de cometerlos todos" (That surprises me.Whoever is capable of committing one vile deed is capable of committing them all). Pepa is able to thus thwart Ana María's abandonment of her family, and unite them all in an idyllic scene in which the children happily recognize their long lost grandfather.

Both the novelistic and the filmic versions of this tale are products of their time, when the Franco regime and the Catholic church held sway over Spanish society.The appearance of the film adaptation in the late 1960s may indeed be a response to the changing mores—the so-called "Revolución de la sueca" (Revolution of the Swedish Woman)— caused by the influx of foreign tourists into Spain.

Juan Madrid

Juan Madrid (b. 1947) is an author who is known for his crime fiction. Two of his works have cinematographic versions: *Nada que hacer* (*Nothing to Do,* 1984), and *Días Contados* (*Running Out of Time,* 1993).

Gerardo Herrero's adaption of *Nada que hacer* has a change in title to *Al acecho* (*Lying in Wait,* 1988). The film tells the tale of a hoodlum's vengeance. When the blind friend Doroteo gives Roca (Giulano Gemma) a pistol, he tells him that he thought that Roca was a has-been ("Tu época ha terminado"), and a flashback gives us the motive for this statement as well as for the latter's desire for revenge. After Roca makes a drug delivery for el Chino (Joaquín Hinojosa), the latter's thugs shoot Roca, but do not kill him. The return to the present is signalled by Roca's question to the blind man, "¿Crees que puedo olvidar así como así? (Do you think I can forget just like that?) More than mere vengeance, however, Roca seeks the money that is owed him. Using force to get information on more than one occasion, Roca tracks el Chino down and gets his money.

In the corrupt world depicted here, no one can be trusted. The police state that they owe Roca a favor, since thanks to him, they discovered what was happening in their own "house." However, when they later apprehend Roca while seeking a stolen briefcase with compromising documents, they beat him. Only Roca's threat that the documents will go to the press if he does not appear tomorrow seems to save him, and they later dump him from a car. The conversation of two former cops also manifests the corruption in the police, and we see the proof of this when the police finish off the gangster Chakor and dispose of his body in a dump. In the final sequence, the police pursue Roca, but he is able to escape on a train to Lisbon.

The official summary of the film states that Roca "enters a tangle of deceits and treachery . . . where nothing and no one are what they seem (*Cine español* 13). For the screen version, unfortunately, this translates as a film narrative that is very confusing at times.

Imanol Uribe's screen adaptation of Juan Madrid's novel, *Días contados* (*Running Out of Time*, 1994), won the Golden Shell award for best film at the 1994 San Sebastián Film Festival. It also garnered the Silver Shell award for best actor for the performance by Javier Bardem. It later received the Goya award for best Spanish film of the year. *Días contados* is a thriller that portrays characters who live at the margins of contemporary Spanish society. Director Uribe ("*Días contados*" 2) notes that what attracted him to the novel was the female protagonist, Charo (played in the film by a newcomer to Spanish cinema, Ruth Gabriel). Charo is a junkie who lives in a world of addicts, pushers, and pimps. The other character on the edge of society is Antonio (Carmelo Gómez), a member of the Basque terrorist organization ETA who has come to Madrid to plan a bombing. (The fictitious events of the film reflect all too keenly this unfortunate facet of reality in contemporary Spain, as this threat continues to plague Spanish society. Only seven months after the film's debut, ETA commandos set off a car bomb in an assassination attempt of the leader of the opposition party, José María Aznar, and after Aznar was elected president, ETA has killed members of his party.)

The opening sequence of the film presents two important and intertwined features of Antonio's character: his sexual appetite and his lack of the strict discipline usually needed by a terrorist. The fact that he picks up a prostitute who offers to perform fellatio in his car causes him to run the risk of ruining the whole operation, and draws the ire of fellow terrorist Lourdes (Elvira Mínguez). This renegade aspect of Antonio surfaces later when he complains about the inept leadership of the organization, and when he shoots a policeman in the head at point blank range because of his frustration that their initial car bombing did not go exactly as planned.

Antonio's encounter with his neighbor Charo continues the sexual motif and also introduces the drug motif: when he allows her to use his bathroom, she first shoots up, and then decides to take a bath. Since Antonio's cover is that of photographer, he takes pictures of the nude Charo as she poses provocatively, and cannot resist grabbing her crotch as he leaves. This sexual attraction to the junkie will prove to be fatal, and Uribe uses

The dark world of prostitutes and junkies: Imanol Uribe's *Días contados*, starring Candela Peña and Ruth Gabriel. *Courtesy Aiete Films, S.A.*

close-ups of syringes to underscore Charo's drug addiction at two key moments of sexual attraction: in the initial bathroom scene, and in the later bathroom in a hotel in Granada where they have gone to consummate their relationship. In the latter sequence, the images of Antonio in the bathroom mirror reflect the duality of the character and prepares us for the following moment of anagnorisis: he is at once the photographer Antonio who has fallen in love with Charo, and the terrorist José, as he is identified when Charo sees his image on television as a wanted criminal, thus learning the truth about him. The pan down of the bathroom to the close-up of water running in the sink symbolically captures the fact that their relationship has now gone down the tubes. (A previous scene in which there is a televised alert concerning an ETA commando in Madrid does not sufficiently apprise her of his true identity. It does, however, manifest Antonio's irascibility, as he angrily turns off the television set, and it sets up Lisardo, played by Javier Bardem, as an antagonist, since the latter refers to Basque terrorists as "sons of bitches.")

The development of the relationship between Antonio and Charo is paralleled by a growing estrangement between Antonio and his fellow terrorist, Lourdes. Her initial anger at him for endangering the mission with the prostitute that he picks up displays itself at their next meeting, as she slaps Antonio and says, "No estoy dispuesta que nos la juguemos por un coño" (I'm not willing to risk losing everything on account of a cunt). Later, when Lourdes enters Antonio's bedroom, he rejects her, and the shots of Lourdes sitting against the wall crying manifests the emotional rift that grows between the two. Finally, when Antonio meets with the other terrorists to go over the final plans (he will have twenty seconds to escape after he triggers the car bomb), he tells Lourdes, who wants to accompany him after the operation is over, "Ya no puedes venir conmigo" (You can no longer come with me).

Drugs and sex permeate the segment of society portrayed on screen. One of the strongest images in the film is that of Lisardo shooting himself up in the neck. Both Charo and her roommate Vanesa (Candela Peña) obtain money for drugs through sex. Licentiousness results in punishment even in this open and marginalized society, however. When Charo opens her apartment door in anticipation of Antonio, the unexpected return of her husband from prison results in his anal rape of his wife as an implicit chastisement (a fact that is later underscored in the film narrative in the bathroom scene at the party). Other characters also live with the threat of punishment or violence constantly over their heads. The police take the local drug dealer, el Portugués (Chacho Carreras), to a deserted spot in the countryside and feign assassinating him: his breakdown before what he believes to be his imminent death shows the fear that all of the characters live with, as the policeman comments, "Todos tenemos miedo" (We're all afraid). All of the characters are "running out of time."

This pressure is most acute in Antonio, however, since he must carry out his objectives and escape before being caught by the police. The two television announcements about the Basque terrorists increase the tension, as the second gives more specific information regarding his identity. (The driving drums heard

Passion overcomes discipline: Imanol Uribe's *Días contados*, starring Ruth Gabriel and Carmelo Gómez. *Courtesy Aiete Films, S.A.*

on the soundtrack serve to underscore the tension.) The scenes that show the intervention by the police in the lives of both Charo and Lisardo also tighten the circle around Antonio. When Rafa (Karra Elejalde), the police inspector, barges in on Charo and Vanesa, it is clear that he knows about their drug dealings with el Portugués. The inspector even goes so far as to declare, "Sé todo lo que pasa en el barrio" (I know everything that goes on in the neighborhood). Some of his statements cause Antonio to surmise, "Tiene un chota (He has an informant). (Here, as throughout the film, the characters use the same contemporary urban slang that is found in the novel.) We later learn that the informant is Lisardo, as a long shot shows Inspector Rafa and Lisardo talking in a cafe. The medium shot of the junkie informant and the policeman sitting across the table from each other, both dressed in black leather jackets, equates the unscrupulous and corrupt nature of the two characters. When the latter learns of Antonio's true identity, he tries to contact the policeman, but his inability to make

Informant and unscrupulous police: Imanol Uribe's *Días contados,* starring Javier Bardem and Karra Elejalde. *Courtesy Aiete Films, S.A.*

direct contact (which would have led to Antonio's arrest) leads to the denouement. Inspector Rafa does pick up Vanesa and Charo and take them to the station. Antonio sees them arrive at the very moment that he has set the car bomb in motion. Uribe presents the final images of the film in slow motion: Antonio running after the car as it enters the police station is intercut with Lourdes's reaction—lowering her head in a combination of sadness and rejection.

The strong sexual component throughout the film ranges from the romantic (the lovemaking between Charo and Antonio in the hotel in Granada, with numerous shots through a translucent glass panel with a soft focus) to the sordid (as prostitutes, Charo erotically dances wearing only a red turtleneck while Vanesa performs fellatio on a shopkeeper; the aforementioned anal rape of Charo by her husband is an element not contained in the original narrative). Although the sexual motif contributes to the sordid atmosphere of the film, and Uribe's adaptation even eliminates the numerous descriptions of male genitalia in the original narrative, the graphic nature of the sex scenes precludes the film from entering the international marketplace as fully as it could. (Just the "crotch shot" of Charo in the bathtub would prevent widespread distribution of the film in the United States.)

Although *Días contados* is a quality film overall, it does have some weak moments—scenes that appear implausible in nature. When the police visit Charo and Vanesa, Antonio also happens to be in their apartment, and he argues with the inspector about his right to interrogate the women. It seems that the last thing that a terrorist would do is confront a policeman and risk being discovered. Indeed, for critic Antonio Castro, the transformation of Antonio into the Basque terrorist is a basic defect in the film, since "in the novel it was probable that the protagonist would approach Charo and her world of junkies and prostitution, [but] in the film it is highly improbable" ("Un 'thriller'" 43).

Director Uribe indicates that he saw material in Madrid's novel that would allow him to tell his own story, using the material as a point of departure, while going off in a different direction (Castro, "Un 'thriller'" 43). What attracted Uribe most to the novel was Charo's character, because "it seemed to me that she was a very strong and very attractive character, very much in the tradition of Mérimée's Carmen, and I needed to look for a character who was different from Juan's character in the novel in order to tell a story of *amour fou*, of love at the limit, which was what I wanted to do" (Castro, "Un 'thriller'" 43-44). (Uribe's admiration of Carmen appears in the street mime's representation of scenes from *Carmen*, which allows Antonio to surreptitiously take photographs of the police station where he is planning to set off a bomb.) Consequently, the most important change from page to screen is in the male protagonist. In the novel, he is Juan, a photographer who is trying to record the *movida madrileña*, a cultural movement that flourished in Madrid during the 1980s. In the film, he is Antonio, a Basque terrorist. This transformation allows Uribe to confront Charo's character with one who also exists at the margins of Spanish society, but who counterbalances her hedonism with someone who lives and kills in the name of an ideology (Castro, "Un 'thriller'" 44). It also allows this Basque director to attempt to come to grips with some of the fundamental problems facing Basque and Spanish society—terrorism and violence. [1]

---

[1]Gabilondo's analysis of the film conflates Basque terrorism, masculine masochism, and Oedipal structures, as he states that the film "simultaneously signifies the Spanish public sphere as cinematic object and the Basque terrorist position as cinematic point of view" (60) and that "a Basque masculine masochist position is articulated in order to legitimize a hegemonic postnational Spanish subject position" (67).

José Angel Mañas

Montxo Armendáriz's screen adaptation of José Angel Mañas's *Historias del Kronen* (*Stories from the Kronen Bar*, 1994) appeared just one year after the publication of the novel. It is a film that portrays the life of Spanish teenagers in the 1990s as consisting of three elements: sex, drugs, and rock and roll. The title comes from a bar where teenagers drink, get high, and pick up members of the opposite sex. Carlos (Juan Diego Botto) is the protagonist who epitomizes this vacuous generation. His abuse of alcohol is evident from the opening sequence when he asks for another beer and the barman quips, "Chupáis como verdaderas esponjas" (You drink like sponges). This leads to a crescendo of problems, as we see the results of his early consumption when a girl that he is "hitting on" in a disco pushes him away, and when he hits a shopper in a market and gets thrown out by the guard.

Cocaine is the drug of choice, and to support his habit, Carlos resorts to stealing. He robs money from his mother's bedroom, and this makes especially ironic the earlier comment by his mother that she has been robbed three times and that one has to be careful because there are a lot of drug addicts out on the streets. When his mother fires the maid because she has discovered that she is missing money, Carlos receives the news with absolutely no moral qualms. A compelling mirror shot presents an image of Carlos that even makes his friends realize that perhaps he has gone too far: a close-up shows him looking at his nose that is bleeding from over-sniffing. This vacuous character contains no capacity for self-recognition and assessment, however, and Carlos simply wipes off the blood, helps his friend vomit, and they leave the bathroom to continue dancing.

Carlos's sexual appetite seems voracious, and his lack of scruples in this regard becomes more and more evident throughout the film narrative. He tells the older family maid that she would still be a good lay, has sex with a girl on a table, makes love to Amalia (Nuria Prims) in a borrowed car, tells his friend Roberto (Jordi Mollà) that he thinks of laying his younger sister, tries to have sex with Amalia in her

212

Sex, drugs, and rock and roll: Montxo Armendáriz's *Historias del Kronan*, starring Juan Diego Botto. *Courtesy Alta Films.*

bedroom in spite of the fact that her mother is in the living room, tells his sister that he masturbates thinking of her, and has sex with prostitutes in a car. After the sequence in which Carlos and Roberto run around the swimming pool naked and end up rolling around the ground on top of each other, there seems to be a questioning of sexuality. However, this construction of sexuality is strictly machista, and hints of anything otherwise are firmly rejected. When Carlos calls Roberto a queer while the latter is driving his car, his reaction is decisive: he drives into a tunnel on the wrong lane, going against traffic in a kamikaze-like gesture to show that he is indeed macho.   When in the bar, someone pushes his friend Pedro (Aitor Merino), Carlos defends him, but he tells Pedro, "Tienes que ser fuerte, si no, te comen" (You have to be strong; if not, they will eat you alive). The aggressor's challenge, "A ver si tienes cojones. Vamos al puente" (Let's see if you've got balls. Let's go to the bridge) puts the teenager's machismo on the line. The following sequence is the most famous of the film, as the two boys hang from the bridge over the busy highway in a battle of both strength and will to determine who is more macho.

Although Armendáriz tones down the stronger homosexual overtones of the novel, where Carlos and Roberto mutually masturbate each other (218), the fact that he masturbates his friend at the party seems to cross the heterosexual/machismo line. Nevertheless, when Roberto tries to kiss him, Carlos's reaction is negative, pushing him away. The machista attitude is most prominent in the videos that Carlos and his friends watch that objectify and denigrate women, such as "Henry, retrato de un asesino" (Henry, portrait of a killer) in which the victims are prostitutes, and in Carlos's interest in obtaining snuff films.

The music of the film is a driving rock and roll that reflects the nihilistic attitude of the protagonists, as we hear in a band's rendition of "No hay sitio para ti" ("There is No Room for You"), a song that expresses the teenager's conception of society's attitude toward them, as well as "Cargados de alcohol" ("Loaded with Alcohol"), which underscores the constant condition of the protagonists. Anything "lighter" is considered "música de mierda" (shitty music) which is immediately changed in favor of hard, driving rock.

Carlos's attitude and lifestyle cause conflicts that are often generational, yet the subtext of the film points a blaming finger at the older generation for a lack of moral leadership. They seem only capable of asking empty rhetorical questions. Carlos asks his parents for the keys to the car, but they refuse, asking "¿Sabes cuánto costó arreglarlo?" (Do you know how much it cost to fix it?) When Carlos mentions that studying French in the summer is a "coñazo," his father reacts, "Hay algo para ti que no sea un coñazo" (Is there anything that is not a pain in the ass for you?) and his mother simply sighs, "¿En qué nos hemos equivocado?" (Where did we go wrong?) And after being arrested for the bridge incident, his father rhetorically asks, "¿Qué se puede esperar de vosotros?" (What can we expect from you?)

Even the earlier generation is critical, but without moral leadership. When Carlos visits his ill grandfather, the latter also poses the rhetorical question, "¿Qué va a ser de vosotros?

Machismo run rampant: Montxo Armendáriz's *Historias del Kronan*, with Aitor Merino. *Courtesy Alta Films.*

Gente sin principios" (What is going to become of you? People without principles).   Carlos shows his disdain for the older generation's rules when, in spite of his aunt's orders, he gives his grandfather the cigarette that he craves. This causes the infirm old man to cough, and his dismissal of his cancer—"La edad me mata" (It's old age that is killing me)—indicates that the older generation is also not as honest as it could be.

Carlos's friends sometimes provide the moral counterpoint to the vacuous protagonist. When Carlos tries to have sex with Amalia in her bedroom, she calls him a pig and throws him out. Roberto becomes incensed when Carlos mentions his sexual desires toward his friend's younger sister, and he asks Carlos about respecting social norms, but the protagonist quips, "Las normas son para los borregos" (Norms are for donkeys). When Roberto later complains that he wants something more out of life, like friendship and affection, Carlos retorts, "La amistad es para los débiles. Los fuertes no necesitamos nadie" (Friendship is for weaklings. We strong folks don't need

Friendship, but only for weaklings: Montxo Armendáriz's *Historias del Kronan*, with Jordi Molla, Aitor Merino, and Juan Diego Botto. *Courtesy Alta Films.*

anybody). This developing antagonism between the two characters culminates in the final sequence, which represents a significant change from the original narrative. At a party at Fierro's house when his parents are not there, things get out of hand when, with Carlos in the lead, they tie the host up and force alcohol down the throat of this young man who has earlier been identified as not able to drink. From the party, we cut to the hospital, where the unscrupulous Carlos blames the victim for getting drunk. However, Roberto cannot stand the situation anymore; he calls Carlos a coward, and he shouts, "No sabes más que mentir" (You don't know how to do anything except lie). The videotaping of the party transcends a metafilmic glimpse at a generation's vacuousness—although Carlos would have it so, desiring to show it to friends—since the videotape documents a crime. (Taken in syntagmatic relationship with the earlier videos, perhaps it is precisely this "snuff" aspect of the video that attracts Carlos.)

Unlike the novel, in which the two-part epilogue that follows the crime consists of a vacuous Carlos on vacation in Santander, and a guilt-ridden Roberto visiting a psychiatrist, the film develops a clash between the two friends. Roberto wants to take the videotape away from Carlos in order to erase it, and the final confrontation again comes down to a question of machismo. Carlos tells Roberto that he doesn't have the balls to take it, and that he should admit that he likes guys. Roberto throws an object into the mirror on the wall, breaking it. Although we saw in the earlier scene that the mirror does not provide any insight or self-recognition, the shattering of the mirror here connotes the end of this superficial and vacuous existence. In the ensuing struggle, the two antagonists move off-screen, and one of the boys is strangled before the final fade-out. In our desire for just deserts, we can only hope that Roberto is the winner of the struggle.

The popularity of the novel and the film adaptation prompted articles in the Spanish press (such as the one that appeared in the Madrid daily newspaper, *El país*, " Ser padre de Kronen) in which psychiatrists and sociologists discussed the Kronen phenomenon that is manifested in the movie. The frequent use of long shots of Madrid underscore the message that the characters portrayed in this film represent an entire generation in Spain today.

Juan Marsé

Juan Marsé (b. 1933), a novelist from Barcelona, is one of the most important authors of post-civil war fiction. His novels portray life in his native Catalonia with a critical eye, and as a person who lived through the civil war and the difficult postwar period, Marsé often writes of those events. Five of his novels have been adapted for the screen: *La oscura historia de la prima Montse, La muchacha de las bragas de oro, Ultimas tardes con Teresa, Si te dicen que caí,* and *El amante bilingüe.*

Jordi Cadena's *La oscura historia de la prima Montse (The Dark Story of Cousin Montse,* 1978) is the screen adaptation of Marsé's novel from 1970. The title connotes a historical record of past events that are tragic or sordid in nature, and of a story that is recorded or remembered by family members. In effect, the original narrative is a complex interweaving of present and past, which Marsé initially accomplishes by changing the narrative point of view as well as the spatial and temporal frame in alternating chapters, and even within chapters. The narrative thus explores the nature of memory together with the sense of the characters' guilt over the tragic events of the past. In the present, Paco Bodegas (Ovidi Montllor) has returned to Barcelona from Paris and is visiting his cousin and former lover Nuria Claramunt (Christa Lem), who is thinking of abandoning her husband Salvador (Xavier Elgorriaga) to go to Paris with Paco. These two characters remember the past and talk about Monste (Nuria's sister), a very religious young woman who serves the poor by visiting prisons. As in other Marsé novels, this narrative world is divided between Catalan bourgeois society and outsiders who bring a critical view of it. In this case, the outsiders are Paco, an Andalusian character who is typical of many of Marsé's novels, and Manuel, who is finishing a jail sentence.

Cadena's film debuted shortly after the death of Franco, and he took advantage of the new freedom of the film industry. Indeed, the most salient feature of the movie is the *destape,* especially with one of Spain's most beautiful screen stars, Ana Belén, who plays the role of Montse. The nudity in the scenes with Nuria and Paco comes from the original text (41, 98), but

Montse's lovemaking scene with Manolo (Gabriel Renom) does not. Although implied in the original, Cadena emphasizes the "showing" aspect for commercial exploitation.

When Montse becomes pregnant, the option of abortion was not legally allowed by Spanish society, and this leads to a crisis for her. The true motivation for her suicide, however, is revealed in the final flashback of the film. Although Montse had already witnessed Manuel in bed with another woman, when she runs into her sister Nuria in the place where Manuel lives, she learns the terrible truth that her own sister is cheating on her with her boyfriend. (In the novel, Nuria's black stockings reveal this more poetically.)

The film attempts to follow the complicated narrative structure of the original. Quesada (442) notes that Cadena uses blue and pink filters to delineate different moments in the past. However, the film narrative is very confusing unless you have recently read the novel by Marsé. One aspect that adds to the confusion in the film is that we do not learn some of the characters' names until well into the movie. Although Cadena uses close-ups of photographs to evoke the past, the film does not do justice to Marsé's poetic evocation of the complicated nature of memory, such as when he compares it to ocean minerals that have been transformed over the years (150). Cadena's film version of Marsé's novel does not do justice to the original.

A statement by Ramón del Valle-Inclán regarding the complex mechanism of memory and the relationship between the present and the past, "Things are not as we see them, but as we remember them," is the nexus of the 1979 film directed by Vicente Aranda, *La muchacha de las bragas de oro* (*The Girl with the Golden Panties*), which is based on Marsé's novel of the same name and winner of the 1978 Planeta Prize. Critic Ramón Freixas states that "with the excuse of remembering a past life, *La muchacha de las bragas de oro* . . . acquires a magnificent dimension regarding the political tergiversation sustained by the Franco regime" (62). In this case, the aging Falangist Luys Forest (Lautaro Murúa) decides to write his autobiography in order to understand himself. In his own words, "Me voy enterando de mi vida en la medida en que la escribo" (I'm finding out about my life as I write about it). The film begins with the voice-over of this character as he walks along the beach: "Los trágicos sucesos de aquellos años que me conviertieron en nómada. Era un extraño en mi propio pueblo. Habían de trastornar para siempre el curso de mi vida, convirtiéndome en ese buscador furtivo de una segunda identidad, abandonada en algún recodo del pasado, quizás basada en el cenegoso entusiasmo de aquellos años arrogantes obligatoriamente calificados como victoriosos" (The tragic events of those years made a nomad out of me. I was a stranger in my own town. Those events were to change the course of my life forever, making me a furtive seeker of a second identity that was abandoned in some corner of the past, perhaps based on the muddy enthusiasm of those arrogant years that were obligatorily certified as victorious). This opening statement reveals some important characteristics of the protagonist as well as major themes of the work. Luys is Catalan but was a Falangist, unlike the majority of his compatriots who supported the Republic, including his own father. Although Luys was "cronista oficial de la victoria" (an official chronicler of victory), he would have us believe that he slowly began to doubt his ideological stance; hence the search for his real self. Luys writes, "No era posible para mí tras la celebración de la eufórica victoria ignorar más tiempo una serie de pequeños acontecimientos que golpeaban mi conciencia778 (After the celebration of the euphoric victory, it was no longer possible for me to ignore a series of little incidents that knocked at my conscience).

A flashback takes us to a key scene in the development of a new political consciousness: as we see workers who speak Catalan being detained as they leave a factory, the camera recedes to behind a window in a bar where the young Luys (Pep Munné) and a friend view the scene and complain that, in the words in Luys's memoirs, "Se están pisoteando una lengua y una cultura" (A language and a culture are being trampled on). In the next scene, the young mustachioed Luys paces up and down in his blue Falangist uniform while a friend reads Luys's resignation from the party.

These flashbacks constitute Luys's memories of the past, and he tells his niece Mariana (Victoria Abril), "Nada es como es, sino como se recuerda, dijo Valle-Inclán" (Nothing is as it is, but rather, as it is remembered, Valle-Inclán said); Aranda intentionally contrasted the styles of the scenes representing present and past. Alvares and Frías note that the flashbacks are short and contain only one shot each (122). Aranda uses the visual image of an old painting that is mentioned in the novel to develop this theme. After a disagreement about the identity of a woman in the painting—Luys thinks that it is Mariana's mother, and Mariana believes that it is her Aunt Sole, Luys's estranged wife—he begins the same line of thought, saying, "Las cosas no son como son . . ." (Things are not as they are . . .), but his niece quickly corrects him, saying, "Pues tampoco son como se recuerdan" (They are not as they are remembered, either). The visual imagery of the film creates a greater sense of irony in the process of negation of Luys's false memories. A tracking shot toward a small mirror hanging from a tree privileges it as the locus of an important act of self-recognition and self-realization, and the extreme close-up point of view shot shows the young Luys shaving his "bigotito cursi y simbólico" (pretentious and symbolic little mustache), a physical attribute that linked him to the Fascist ideology. However, his niece later calls this memory into question, saying, "Sin embargo, yo de niña te recuerdo con bigote, y no hace tanto tiempo" (Nevertheless, as a little girl I remember you as having a mustache, and that wasn't long ago). All of the subsequent flashbacks show the young Luys with the mustache, belying his claims.Indeed, Luys admits, "No lo hice, pero lo pensé infinidad de veces" (I didn't do it, but I thought about it an infinite number of times).

The mustache is just one example of Luys's duplicity. Although at the beginning of his memoirs, he states that he was able to gain his father's freedom from Fascist prison, Luys later admits that his father died in jail. His resignation from the Falange is likewise false, as Luys admits to his niece, "Esa carta no la escribí nunca, pero me la sabía de memoria" (I never wrote that letter, but I knew it by heart). Luys also confuses and falsifies his relationship with his wife, Sole, her sister

Mariana, and the latter's husband, José María Tey. While writing his memories, he says, "Habrá que reinventar fielmente aquel piso" (That apartment will have to be faithfully reinvented), but the dissolves linking the image of the elder Mariana in a gray shawl and Sole in a pink shawl and then both in the same image while playing the piano, indicate either an inability to faithfully reconstruct the past or a conscious effort to falsify it. A flashback to a lovemaking scene at the piano is the justification for Luys's marriage to Sole, since he says that he later realized that it was she, and not Mariana, who had been playing.

Although Aranda does not include in his film narrative the episode in which the drunken Luys has sex with Mariana while sheltering a prostitute elsewhere in his house, he nevertheless includes similar flashbacks that show that other encounters between Mariana and Luys were charged with eroticism. Even though Luys negates any wrongdoing to his niece, he must finally face the truth that Mariana is not his niece, but his daughter. In the film version, when Forest learns of his incest, he goes to his bedroom to get his pistol. While we see an exterior shot of his window, we hear a shot, and can only guess that he has committed suicide. Forest, however, has merely shot himself in the hand. In the novel, the old pistol does not go off and the two Marianas find Luys crying on the floor; this transformation of the ending provides a greater sense of irony and a heightened sense of poetic justice regarding his repugnant act in the 1930s of shooting a young man in the hand who was urinating while leaning against an exterior wall of his house where the symbol of the Falangist party was displayed. In the novel, this irony occurs when a showerhead installed by the young man falls on Luys's head (250). In the final scene of the film, Forest tells Mariana that she is his daughter. Her flippant response, "Bueno, ¿y qué?" (Well, so what?) represents the final manifestation of her rejection of his moral and ideological code.

Critic Ramón Freixas points out that the role of the young Mariana in the film represents the dichotomy of provocation and destruction by the female, but that in this narration, the dichotomy transcends a merely sexual context and acquires a political meaning as "settling of accounts" (62). Sobejano-Morán (n.p.) believes that Mariana's erotic role in the film—exhibitionism, bisexuality, and incest—all subvert the patriarchal order of the Franco regime as embodied in the character of Luys.

Aranda explains that the visual nature of film sometimes necessitates creative solutions for capturing the metaphors of literary language. Such is the case of the golden panties of the title. "In the book this was all literary tropes or imaginings of the characters . . . but in the movies . . . you have to make it more specific, and we changed it, so they painted the panties [on her]" (Alvares and Frías 120-21). Other times, Aranda creates new metaphors, as Sobejano-Morán (n.p.) points out that whereas the sea along the beach where Luys strolls is turbulent in the novel (symbolically representing his tormented conscience), the sea in the opening sequence of the film is calm, and his niece Mariana's disrobing and entering the water metaphorically represents her entering his life and his writing.

While the nudity and sexual scenes caused some Spanish critics to object to the film as being pornographic, novelist Juan Marsé has defended his narrative, stating, "This is the convulsive story of two characters who strip in public with very different moral spirit. One does it on the outside, the other on the inside . . . the truth is that the nudity of Forest-Lautaro Murúa . . . is the only exhaustive, shameless, and immoral nudity that the film offers. Contrary to what is often believed, interior 'nudity' can often be more scandalous—and in this case it is, as well as being more pathetic" ("Vicente Aranda" 23).

Vicente Aranda's *La muchacha de las bragas de oro* is the first screen adaptation for this director from Barcelona, who will make bringing contemporary Spanish novels to the screen a fundamental aspect of his career. It also marks the continued collaboration between Aranda and Victoria Abril, which began in 1976 in *Cambio de sexo* (*Sex Change*)and would last through many films. Most importantly, it is a significant reexamination of the nature of personal and historical memory regarding Spain's recent past, and its commercial success showed that the nation shared in this process.

The opening words of Marsé's *Ultimas tardes con Teresa* (*The Last Afternoons with Teresa*, 1966), stress the importance of the protagonist's nickname: "There are nicknames that illustrate not only a way of living, but also the social nature of the world that one lives in. The night of June 23rd, 1956, with Saint John's Day festivities, so-called Pijoaparte emerged from the shadows of his neighborhood in a brand-new cinnamon-colored summer suit . . ." (13). The first half of the nickname is a slang term that refers to the male sexual organ; the second half might connote "in a class by itself," thus giving the nickname an overall connotation of "supermacho." (The author also has explained that the nickname refers to "an individual whose erotic activity tries to be outside the neighborhood" [Hart 187].) It is important to note that in the film version, directed by Gonzalo Herralde, the protagonist is called Manuel or Manolo, and he is not referred to as Pijoaparte. This represents a substantive change in the tone of the narrative, given the symbolic importance of the nickname—a symbolism that transcends the merely sexual and includes important social connotations as well. Like the protagonists of many of Marsés's novels, Pijoaparte is a *charnego* (a condescending term that refers to an Andalusian residing in Catalonia), who dreams of leaving his lower-class working neighborhood behind and moving up the social ladder. Pijoaparte, however, is not a blue-collar worker, but a picaro, a thief who specializes in stealing motorcycles; he steals them and races toward Montjuich (12). This conveys a certain daredevil element in Pijoaparte's character, and gives us the geographical setting for the action of the novel: Barcelona. More importantly, he goes from the lower-class neighborhood of Monte Carmelo to the upper-class area of San Gervasio, thus establishing one of the many dichotomies in the narrative, this one based on two novelistic spaces (Sherzer 74). Herralde establishes this dichotomy early in the film with the point-of-view long shot in which Manolo overlooks the city lights from his lower-class hilltop neighborhood.

Another important dichotomy in the narrative is the difference between the *charnego* Manolo (Angel Alcázar) and

Teresa (Maribel Martín), daughter of a rich Catalan industrialist; this dichotomy is based on skin color as a reflection of class distinctions. Manolo is a swarthy Andalusian; Teresa is a blond, fair-skinned Catalan girl. When Manolo sees her at the party, she is with Maruja (Patricia Adriani), and Teresa's premature departure leaves Manolo with the latter. Manolo believes that he is picking up an upper-class girl, and he does not fully comprehend her denial that her dark complexion comes from spending a lot of time on the beach (thereby conflating racial and class distinctions). After spending the night with her, his discovery of her true identity—as revealed in the point-of-view shots of her maid's uniform and the photograph in which she appears in her domestic attire with the "señorita Teresa"—indicates that he is not very astute, after all, and is ultimately a loser.

The sexual dichotomy in the novel is related to the north/south, blond/dark-skinned contrasts. The swarthy Andalusians—both Maruja and Manolo—are passionate and sexy; the Catalans—Teresa and Luis (Juanjo Puigcorbe)—are repressed and impotent. Herralde captures this division in the montage sequence in which Manolo and Maruja's love-making is intercut with the conversation and subsequent unsuccessful amorous encounter between the Catalan protagonists. Herralde transforms the sexual impotence implied in the original narrative by changing the literary trope ("as if someone had vomited") into reality: Luis vomits in Teresa's bedroom, thus ending their romantic episode. The cross-cuts contrast the impotence and frustration of the upper-class Catalans with the sensuality of the lower-class Andalusians.

Manolo is at one apex of the novel's three important love triangles: Manolo-Teresa-Luis, Manolo-Maruja-Teresa, Manolo-Teresa-Hortensia. Although in the novel, Hortensia (Cristina Marsillach) never appears in a scene with the other two characters together,the film version beautifully captures the latter love triangle with a tracking shot in which Manolo and Teresa walk down a street in the Monte Carmelo neighborhood, and Hortensia appears in the background in her yard and follows them. Her higher physical position constitutes a triangular composition in the frame that visually captures this thematic component.

Herralde's screen version simplifies the highly intricate temporal pattern that Marsé weaves in the original narrative, which includes numerous foreshadowings that point to the narrative's denouement. The film version presents a chronological narrative of a more condensed nature: the sixteen months of the main narrative in the novel are reduced to a mere three. This makes the change in Hortensia, from a young girl in braids to a miniskirted nymphomaniac, seem somewhat abrupt.

One problem with the film is the casting of the protagonists. Although the common complaint regarding film adaptations that a particular actor does not fit our image of a particular character may be fallacious, it seems that there should be an attempt in casting to capture certain essential or characteristic physical qualities. Angel Alcázar, who plays Manolo, is handsome—indeed, handsome enough to fit the description that he is "alarmingly handsome" (114). Nevertheless, he does not correspond to the image of Pijoaparte. To begin with, Alcázar and Maribel Martín (age twenty-nine), are too old for the roles. In the novel, Teresa is around nineteen (161) and Manolo is nineteen or twenty (207). In addition, his perfect haircut contrasts with an important image from the original narrative. In the novel, Teresa fusses over and defends his long hair (283), and this physical attribute becomes one of the many dichotomies in the original narrative: when Luis, the student leader, recognizes Manolo in a bar after the latter has been released from prison, he thinks that "what stood out the most was the brutal and ignominious haircut" (327). Herralde, however, does capture the 1950s atmosphere with various elements that work well in cinematographic language: popular music from the period plays at the party, we see a television broadcast of the news in which Franco dedicates a dam, Teresa listens to a clandestine radio broadcast (which helps to form a dichotomy between the rebellious, albeit politically ingenuous, Teresa and her bourgeois parents), and she reads an Hola magazine of the period. The director also attempts to capture a period look in his use of occasional wipes for transitions between scenes.

Although much of the dialogue is faithful to the novel, the subjectivity of the novelistic narrative is lost. The inner thought processes of both protagonists—especially Manolo's fantasies that equate sex with power or with social importance—disappear in the screen version. Herralde does capture some of Teresa's fantasy (based on her ingenuousness) in which she makes false assumptions about Manolo's political involvement. This occurs in the scenes when she and Maruja converse on the beach (Teresa takes the maid's tears as a confirmation of her assumptions; cf. 128), and when she converses with Luis on the patio, in which her student friend finally retorts, "Eres una mitómana" (You're a myth maker). In the novel, Manolo, wanting to win her affection, never contradicts this false image that Teresa has (158), but the absolute contrast between illusion and reality point to the fundamental irony that the narrator shows toward the characters. Unfortunately, the cinematographic adaptation does not capture this important stylistic component.

Likewise, the process of Teresa's disillusionment does not appear as fully developed in the film version. The dance hall scene does not capture her confrontation with the reality of the lower class. The image of Teresa pushing away her dance partner and leaving the dance floor does not capture the disillusionment of the original narrative: Teresa initially thinks that it is "marvelous," but when an electrician asks her to dance, he suddenly becomes "a desperate octopus with fifty hands" (250). Her next disillusion is when she discovers that "the great Bernardo" of whom Manolo had so often spoken turns out to be a drunkard who exposes himself in dark alleys (259-61). Her reaction is one of nausea, disillusion, and depression. On screen, her anger over Bernardo is mitigated by Manolo's explanation in the film, "Bernardo será un desgraciado en su vida personal, pero es más comunista que todos tus amigos de la universidad" (Bernardo might be a miserable swine in his personal life, but he is more of a Communist than all of your friends at the university). This statement goes against the spirit of the original narrative, since it justifies Teresa's ingenuous view of the residents of Monte Carmelo.

Throughout the novel, Manolo wavers between confidence and self-doubt, and Marsé portrays this tension at the beginning of the narrative when Manolo crashes an upper-class party. Herralde visually captures Manolo's status as an outsider in his beige suit, which contrasts with the dark suits worn by all the other men at the party. Ultimately, however, Manolo's inability to enter into Teresa's social sphere is due to the cultural abyss between the two of them (184). The original narrative manifests his lack of understanding on numerous occasions, and is specifically related to the lexicon used by Teresa and her university friends. In an attempt at one-upsmanship against his rival Luis, when the latter mentions that Mauricio is in Barcelona, Manolo retorts, "He spoke to me about you" (241). The film changes "Mauricio" to "Federico" in a clear allusion to the underground pseudonym of former Communist activist Jorge Semprún. Although the film does not stress Manolo's lack of cultural sophistication and lack of comprehension with regard to certain vocabulary or concepts— even the word "ciclostil" is used for "dittomachine" in the movie version, thus eliminating his confusion about "linotipia"—the creation of an episode in which Manolo is shown counterfeit bills and is given the opportunity to make money by passing them actually creates a better sense of motivation for his visit to Paco and the beating that Manolo receives there (266-71).

In an example of the condensation that is often necessary in the transformation from novel to script, Herralde changes several details of the denouement of the novel. In the original narrative, Manolo receives a love letter from Teresa and wants to go to Blanes to see her. When Cardenal refuses to lend him a motorcycle, he commits his last robbery and speeds toward the beach resort, and he is stopped by the police. The final chapter occurs two years later, when Luis recognizes Manolo in a bar after he has been in prison. When the student asks the thief what he plans on doing, Manolo responds, "You'll see" (330) and walks out of the bar with his hands in his pockets—body language that connotes Manolo's defeat and future without hope. In the film, Manolo agrees to give Cardenal's niece, Hortensia, the motorcycle ride that she has always wanted, but tricks her and escapes on the vehicle, an act that captures Manolo's deceptive nature. When she runs after Manolo and picks up the love letter that he has dropped, a close-up of Hortensia biting her finger is an image that connotes her anger and motivation for revenge. During a tracking shot of Manolo on his motorcycle, we hear Teresa's voice off screen read the letter, and Herralde dissolves to a low-angle shot of Teresa coming out on the balcony at Blanes. Manolo's fall from the motorcycle as the police stop him is as much metaphorical as it is physical. Manolo walks directly toward the camera, a movement that seems very stilted, as Teresa's voice-over continues: "Sé orgulloso y atrevido hasta la muerte . . . (Be proud and daring right up to your death . . .). A cut to a long shot of the dark outline of the house at Blanes is accompanied by Teresa's final words, ". . . porque así es como me gusta recordarte" (. . . because that is the way that I like to remember you). A freeze frame of a long shot of waves crashing against the rocks and the house ends the film. The low-angle shot of Teresa on the balcony corresponds to earlier shots of this type, such as the low-angle shot of Teresa and her student friends at a party when Manolo and Maruja go to pick up the blond student. These shots underscore the social hierarchy and the impossibility for Manolo to realize his dream and become a part of bourgeois society. The final shot likewise freezes the symbol of that society—the beach house—at a distance beyond the reach of the picaro. Nevertheless, by changing the narrative order—in the novel, Teresa's love letter is the motive for his risking one "final" robbery, but in the film, the voice-over of the letter occurs at the very end—we are left with a rather sweet, romantic image of the protagonists. In the novel, the ironic demythification of them prevails: Teresa laughs when she discovers Manolo's incarceration; Manolo returns from jail to a life that has no possibility of moving up in society.

Herralde's *Ultimas tardes con Teresa* is a film with certain merits, but will hardly satisfy readers of Marsé's novel mainly due to its inability to capture the tone of the original narrative. Some of the problems here are inherent in any adaptation: the loss of interior thought processes, the difficulty in capturing the ironic stance of the narrator, or in transferring tropes of novelistic language, such as the animal metaphors that Marsé uses throughout. Ultimately, however, the main problem is that Pijoaparte is missing.

Si te dicen que caí (*If They Tell You I've Fallen*) directed by Vicente Aranda in 1989 is the cinematographic version of the novel that was first published in Mexico in 1973, and then in Spain in 1976, after the disappearance of censorship by the Franco regime. The novelist from Barcelona admits that he "wanted to reflect in the hardest, most sordid, and most sinister way possible what had been my childhood in those years" after the war (Amell, *Literatura* 110). The film takes its title from the Falangist hymn, and therefore ironically subverts the sociopolitical discourse of the regime as it offers multiple images of the misery and oppression of postwar Barcelona.

Two sequences at the Roxy movie theater manifest the everyday oppression of the regime. The first sequence begins with an excellent example of visual synecdoche: a long shot of two *maquis* entering the movies is disrupted by the torso of a policeman crossing directly in front of the camera, and he stops so that only his right side (his arm bent at the elbow with his hand on his hip above his pistol) appears in the foreground on the left side of the frame. This ominously foreshadows the violence of the next scene—the interior of the movie house, when the policeman asks the *maquis* for their identif ication—and the *maquis* gun him down. In a second movie house scene, Java (Jorge Sanz) sits next to the prostitute Ramona (Victoria Abril), and she charges him two pesetas for a feel. When the lights come on and the Nationalist hymn is played, with an image of the *caudillo* on the screen, their chatter results in a Fascist shouting "Silence" and slapping Java several times. Both scenes contain a montage of film from the 1940s, first from the official newsreels that show images of the Führer and announce General Franco's imminent meeting with Hitler, and later, scenes from *Sin novedad en el alcázar* (*No News From the Alcazar*), a film that glorifies the Nationalists troops resistance during the siege of the alcazar in Toledo and therefore contributes to the regime's official discourse regarding the civil war.

The film portrays the fear and misery of these "years of hunger" in postwar Spain on many levels. Origami birds and an empty plate with a spoon are the telltale signs of a m ole—someone who lived clandestinely, hiding in fear of the Franco regime after the war. In this case, Java's brother Marcos (Antonio Banderas) is hiding from both the Fascists and the Communists. Java's threat to denounce a girl to the authorities for past crimes if she does not assist him in his search for Aurora Nin serves as a foreshadowing of his denouncement of his own brother to the authorities, which we can surmise from a conversation on a park bench between Java and the one-eyed Fascist. When a woman opens the door to a bar in order to raffle a chicken, the mere sight of the one-eyed Fascist causes her to retreat in fear. The *maquis* refer to beatings of civilians by blue-shirted Fascists, and the shooting of prisoners of war, and when one of the children suggests that they sell firearms that they have found to the *maquis*, another retorts that they would be put in front of a firing squad for doing so. The reappearance of Luis Lage, a Republican who has been released from jail, represents a note of joy and happiness, as well as the opportunity to undermine Nationalist propaganda, when Luis tells his son to note that his hands are not stained with blood. Joy turns to shame, however, when Luis later confronts his wife who prostituted herself in his absence. She tearfully defends herself, saying that she wanted to put some meat on their children's table, and did nothing wrong.

Sexual degradation is most significant in the character of Java, the young rag collector. Conrado Galán (Javier Gurruchaga), a Nationalist lieutenant who was wounded in the war and is now confined to a wheelchair, pays prostitutes to perform as he voyeuristically observes them from behind a curtain, showing his displeasure or impatience by pounding his walking stick on the floor. Java announces to Ramona that the show must last one hour, and the montage of the sexual activities and extreme close-ups of Conrado's voyeuristic eye as the sex becomes ever more degrading and brutal—Java sodomizing her, beating her, and finally urinating on her—makes for an extremely harsh sequence. This is even more the case because of director Vicente Aranda's desire to cast his favorite actress, Victoria Abril, in this role, in spite of the fact that she was six months pregnant at the time. Author Juan Marsé comments that this resulted in scenes that were brutal in and of themselves being even more brutal, and that the film version was overly sadistic (Abad 101). The close-ups of Conrado's voyeuristic gaze are accompanied by chilling violin chords that bring the shower scene from Hitchcock's *Psycho* to mind, and which, together with an eerie, ominous squeaking of his wheelchair, become Conrado's motif on the soundtrack.

Sex and violence are also linked in two later sequences in which Java and the other boys interrogate Juanita and Fueguiña about Aurora Nin. In the second of these, the children are in a costume shop and are play-acting. Java's role is that of Conrado: he order the actors to be silent and to continue and strokes a hammer, analogous to Conrado's walking stick. (The close-up wide-angle shot of Java produces an expressionist distortion that recalls the early sequence preceding the initial sexual scene between Java and Ramona in which Java enters an elevator as Conrado in his wheelchair enters the lobby: shots of both Java and Conrado through the old elevator glass create a distorting effect that foreshadows their moral warping as male prostitute and voyeur.) Dressed in a cardinal's costume, Java raises his hands and the cape is transformed into curtains. An extreme close-up of Java peering between them, accompanied by the chilling violin chords associated with Conrado, complete the transformation of victim into victimizer. Fueguiña is tied to a crucifix, and when Java approaches her to interrogate her, the shot of him from the back, in which he draws his cape over his head, transforms him into a vampire figure, and he draws blood as he kisses her through the knife blade that cuts her lip.

Combining sex and religious imagery occurs at other moments as well and serves as part of the overall social criticism of the film: in the early sex scene, Ramona at one point also wears a cardinal's cape and cap; when Conrado directs a school play, Lucifer (Java) at first attacks, then seduces Saint Michael, who is played by a girl, as the paralyzed lieutenant voyeuristically observes in close-up as he strokes his phallic walking stick; and on two occasions, prostitutes are said to be friends of the bishop. The only characters in the film that escape the devastatingly negative portrayal of postwar Spanish society are the young boys who constitute Sarnita's gang of friends. The boys survive these difficult times partly by escaping into the fantasy world of their "aventis" or tales invented by Sarnita.

Both novel and film portray the lives of the *maquis* or guerrillas who continue to fight after the end of the civil war. However, in contrast to other Spanish films that portray *maquis* as doomed heroes fighting against fascism, the maquis here are hardly heroic. Unlike their rural counterparts portrayed in Spanish films such as *Los días del pasado* (*Bygone Days*), *El corazón del bosque* (*The Heart of the Forest*), or *Luna de lobos* (*Wolves' Moon*), they do not suffer many privations. They eat sumptuous paellas at home or enjoy cognac and cigars at a bar. A close-up of the wife of a *maquis* cutting a melon in half, followed by the wife and her husband smelling how good it is, indicates the companionship and plenty that these guerrilla fighters enjoy. The squabbling among the *maquis* over ideological issues leads one to question whether they are motivated by ideology, or if they are simply common criminals. Palau (Lluis Homar) says, "No me canso de repetirlo. Nuestra primera obligación es vaciarles el bolsillo" (I don't get tired of repeating it. Our first obligation is to empty their pockets). Indeed he doesn't tire of it, since in a later scene in a bar, he tells the other *maquis*, "Si quieres acabar con los fachas, quítales la cartera" (If you want to get rid of the Fascists, take their wallets away from them). In the final sequence, which takes place in the present (the movie theater in the background is showing Martin Scorsese's *Last Temptation of Christ*, from 1989), the elderly Palau exclaims, "Mientras los ricos tengan dinero, yo me dedicaré a quitárselo" (As long as the rich have money, I will dedicate myself to taking it away from them).

Although during the first meeting of the *maquis*, one of them responds, "Que no somos atracadores, tú" (We're not robbers), it appears that they truly are little more than that, and the main activity of the *maquis* is to rob Fascists in brothels. Their bursting into rooms to interrupt the activities of the Fascists with their whores contributes to the portrayal of moral decadence of the period. When one of the clients turns out to be merely a plumber, the *maquis* give him money back so that no one will say that they abandon workers, but it seems to be a weak attempt at solidarity. It is especially ironic that kidnapping and killing Menchu because she is the lover of a rich black marketeer contradicts earlier convictions regarding prostitutes as expressed in street banners of the Republic that proclaim "Libertario de la prostitución" (Defender of the freedom of prostitution). Unlike other Spanish films that deal with the subject, *Si te dicen que caí* demythifies the *maquis*, and portrays them as one of the many negative elements of postwar Spain.

William Sherzer points out that from the opening line of the novel, the reader will have to depend on something that has been told, and that "telling" connotes a potential relationship with what is not real, with fiction (93). The definitions of "aventis" given in the novel could well apply to the narrative itself: "the tale became impetuous and abrupt, fleeting, leaving here and there small puddles of incongruities and loose ends" (82). Aranda's *Si te dicen que caí* interweaves different layers of fiction on several different temporal planes, thus following the labyrinthine structure of the original narrative. At the beginning of the film, a caption indicates that the action begins in 1970. An ambulance delivers a dead body to a hospital, and as Ñito prepares the cadaver, he sees a large ring on its left hand and recognizes the drowning victim. He asks Sor Paulina "¿Se acuerda usted de Java, verdad?" (You remember Java, don't you?) Ñito then evokes events of the past: a second caption identifies the temporal plane as 1940 as the shabbily dressed Ñito (or Sarnita) as a boy tells "aventis" or tales that constitute a "handy and cheap way of dreaming" to the other boys in his gang of friends. A close-up of Sarnita saying "I'm going to tell you . . ." cuts to the ragman Java on the way to his first sexual encounter with Ramona. The line between history and fiction blurs and becomes murkier as the film progresses.

One of the principal causes for confusion is the prostitute character(s). There are three whores: Ramona, with whom Java has sex in front of the voyeuristic eye of Conrado, and with whom he later falls in love; Aurora Nin, the "red" whore who had worked as a housekeeper for Conrado, and whom Conrado and the other Fascists are looking for as responsible for the death of Conrado's father; and Menchu, the platinum blonde lover of the rich black marketeer. The narrative itself creates confusion among these three characters as others give information that links them together: that Aurora probably changed her name and dyed her hair (is she now Menchu?), that Menchu's name could not be mentioned at a girls' home because of something terrible that she had done (did she, and not Aurora, cause the death of Conrado's father?), or that when Java finds Ramona in a bar he calls her Aurora. The film thus reflects the confusion that exists in the novel surrounding these three characters, as when in chapter 10, Sarnita tells an aventi based on the life of Menchu, and not that of Ramona/Aurora, or in chapter 15 when Ramona's past seems confused with that of Menchu. To add another layer of ambiguity, the description of homicide of the blonde prostitute by the *maquis* who kill her in a Ford refers to "la rubia Carmen" (not Menchu), which further confuses fiction and reality, since, as Sherzer points out in his edition of the novel, the whole scene is based on a real crime, the assassination of the famous prostitute Carmen Broto (338). Director Aranda underscores the confusion in the narrative by casting Victoria Abril in the roles of all three prostitutes. The most distinguishing physical characteristic of the whore(s) is a scarred breast. Java's brother Marcos tells him that the Fascist Conrado caused the scar with a champagne bottle, but Java replies that it was a wound from a bomb. Jumping back in time to the beginning of the war, Marcos confronts Conrado's mother about the incident, saying that her son caused it with a corkscrew, but Aurora says that it was an accident. Sarnita tells the other boys that the "red" whore has a microfilmed document implanted in her breast. These multiple and contradictory versions of the cause of the scar create an atmosphere of total ambiguity in the narrative.

The blurring of reality and fiction also occurs in dramatic representations. The children rehearse for a religious play directed by the former Fascist lieutenant, Conrado. Java has the part of Lucifer, and Saint Michael is played by a girl. As

Java's representation switches from confrontation to seduction, Conrado voyeuristically observes them as if they were the paid prostitutes in his bedroom. The children also practice another drama, a surprise for Conrado, during which Java interrogates Fueguiña. The costumes of the other children, (especially the use of skulls, which underscores the sex /violence/death motif) manifest the play-acting qualities of the scene. When Java interrogates Fueguiña about the prostitute, he assigns her the role of Aurora, and the girl's declamatory style emphasizes the dramatic, unreal quality of the narrative in this scene.

Sarnita often has the role as unreliable narrator in the film. As an adult in the morgue, he even admits to his dead friend that his sordid tale is better than what occurred in reality: "Deberías darme las gracias, Java, por lo bien que quedas en mis aventis" (You should thank me, Java, for how well you come out in my tales). When the boys see Java sitting on a park bench with Justiano, the one-eyed Fascist, Sarnita says that he can read lips even at that distance, and he tells what they are saying. His narrative, however, is transformed into the dialogue of a western: "Yo buscarte, Flecha Negra. Yo fumar contigo la pipa de la paz. Yo decirte toda la verdad" (I look for you, Black Arrow. I smoke peace pipe with you. I tell you whole truth). This scene cuts to a scene in which Java, arriving at Conrado's house, learns that he will earn triple pay for today's performance, only to enter the bedroom and discover a young man waiting for him in bed. We then return to Java and Justiano on the bench, and the young ragman tells the Fascist, "Oiga, camarada, tengo que abrirme camino como sea. Quiero quitarme el mugre y los piojos de la trapería. El quiere volver a la sarna y el odio, a la sangre y a las barricadas. Quiere quemar las iglesias otra vez y saquear a los ricos. Ese no es mi hermano, no. Nunca pensé que pudiera ser mi hermano ese sucio guiñapo. Les quitarán el miedo. Podrán descansar al fin" (Listen, comrade, I have to get out no matter what. I want to be rid of the crud and the lice of the old clothes shop. He wants to go back to the rage and the hate, the blood and the barricades. He wants to burn churches again and sack the rich. That's not my brother. I never thought that dirty bum could be my brother.

They'll take their fear away from them. They will be able to rest at last). Juxtaposed with the scene in which the level of Java's prostitution reaches its greatest degradation (as indicated by the face that Java makes when he discovers his new assignment), the dialogue manifests Java's willingness to climb the social ladder at any cost. The switch to an unidentified third person singular (he) in Java's dialogue causes momentary confusion, but we realize that the mention of his brother means that Java has sunk down so low as to betray him. (A later scene in which the one-eyed Justiano arrives at the old clothes shop with a carload of armed Fascists confirms the betrayal.) Java's further shift to third person plural (they) adds another layer of confusion. Is Sarnita not reading Java's lips correctly? Does "they" refer to Marcos and Aurora? The couple escapes just before the armed Fascists arrive, but the blast from a bomb or buried mine in the empty lot that they were crossing causes the irate Justiano to shout, "Ya nos han jodido otra vez estos cabrones" (Those bastards have screwed us again). Has their escape frustrated the Fascists again, or is it their death that has done so? The camera pans vertically through the dust and smoke, and we see a low-angle long shot of the couple running in slow motion. Are they now amidst the clouds of a celestial sphere for lovers? Sarnita and the boys comment on the victim that lies in the empty lot. Was she the whore who gave handjobs in the movies? Only the lover of a black marketeer could afford the coat that she was wearing. Did the *maquis* dump Menchu's body in the lot so as to have it appear to be the victim of the mine, or was her appearance there a mere coincidence? The epilogue adds to the confusion. In the present (1989) when the elderly Luis asks Palau what ever became of that blonde, the former *maquis* dismisses him, but from the back seat of a taxi he sees the old whore and an elderly man begging at an outdoor café. Dressed in shabby clothes with a hat that has what looks like small pieces of paper on it—bringing to mind Marcos' origami birds—the brief glimpse of the couple underscores the fact that all of the characters in the film are losers.

Aranda's use of the soundtrack adds to the ambiguity of the film with regard to the multiple temporal planes of the narrative. As we jump from 1970 to 1940, or to 1936 (at the beginning of the war, in the army headquarters) or to the single episode before the war when Conrado can walk and begins his voyeuristic activities as he spies Marcos and Aurora having sex in his bedroom, Aranda often marks the transition from one moment to another with a sound bridge, such as music, or the moaning of lovemaking. Since these sounds occur on both sides of the cut from one scene to another (on two temporal planes) the result is a fusion—or confusion— of time.

Si te dicen que caí is a harsh, brutal, negative, ambiguous film that reflects a reality of equal qualities. Certainly Marsé intended to capture the ambiguous and confusing aspect of postwar reality: Sherzer notes that "according to the author, 'One day they would tell you one thing, and the next day they would tell you the opposite.' There was an official truth and a real truth, and no one could ever distinguish between the two" (175).

Critic Ramón Freixas ("Si te dicen" 42) calls it "one of the key films of recent Spanish cinema" and the critics from the Spanish film journal Dirigido voted it one of the best Spanish films of the decade. Yet the controversial brutality of the film, together with its decidedly confusing narrative, detract from the film's positive qualities. This may in part result in differences in expectations regarding the reception or consumption of novels and films. Both Mangini (278) and Amell (Literatura 122-23) believe that Marsé's novel is representative of what Baquero Goyanes calls a "perspectivist structure." The perspectivist structure of a novel often functions as the expression of a world—that of today—in which nothing appears certain and solid, threatened as it is everywhere by ruptures, changes, suspicions. As opposed to the order and linearity of classical novelistic structures, the current broken, zigzagging narrative structures offer reiterations, displacements, silences, ambiguities, and double, triple, quadruple, and even multipliable versions of events (Baquero Goyanes 171-72). Marsé's novel presents the reader with a series of enigmas, both in plot and in style, that the reader can and should decipher, although he may need a second reading to do so (Sherzer 174). The purchase of a novel may allow the consumer/reader who has the time and the patience the opportunity to do so, but normal expectations of the filmgoer are of a different nature. When even film critics (that is, a spectator who supposedly has a certain sophistication regarding film texts) leave the theater totally confused about what they have just seen (Llopis 126), then one must consider the words of Ignacio Soldevila Durante that apply to both the novel and the film versions of *Si te dicen que caí*: "when a work has to be re-read a second time for an exact understanding of its first level of significance, one must ask if the border between complexity and confusion has been breached" (261).

Vicente Aranda's cinematographic adaption in 1992 of Juan Marsé's *El amante bilingüe* (*The Bilingual Lover*, 1991) artfully uses the mirror and the mask in the mise-en-scène to manifest the theme of the double, or as Keppler terms it, the "second self" in the narrative. At the same time, the mask points to a carnivalesque logic that permeates the narrative. This allows the theme of the double to transcend the individual, and contributes to a parody of certain aspects of contemporary Spanish society.

The opening sequence takes place during the childhood of the protagonist, Juan Marés (Imanol Arias), and the adult Juan declares in a voice-over, "De niño soñaba con irme lejos, lejos del barrio, lejos de la miseria familiar. Con Norma lo había conseguido" (As a child, I dreamed of going far away, far from the neighborhood, far from the misery of the family. With Norma I had achieved it). This brief allusion to the 1950s resonates throughout the rest of the film, since it immediately postulates a series of dichotomies: past/present, the childhood *barrio*/adult abode, childhood misery/adult affluence, and solitude/companionship. Nevertheless, the following sequence, which occurs after five years of matrimony, reveals Norma's true personality and complicates the nature of these dichotomies. Juan returns home one day to find his wife in bed with a *charnego*, an Andalusian bootblack. The true personality of Norma (Ornella Muti) is that of a rich Catalan nymphomaniac who has a penchant for *charnegos*, a fetish for shoes, and a disregard for her husband's feelings, as she blames the irate Juan for returning home early and discovering her in bed with another man. This crisis in Juan's life leads to a flashback to when the two first met at a political protest. When Juan inquires during their honeymoon, "¿Quién eres? ¿Por qué estás enamorada de mí?" (Who are you? Why are you in love with me?), Norma's answer, "Una filla ben follada" (A really fucked gal), should have given Juan a hint that his matrimonial bliss was not to last. The low-angle shot from behind Juan that shows a shoe hanging from his erect penis humorously complements the earlier shot of the bootblack, and signals the return to the present, as the *charnego* offers Juan the advice to look for his wife in order to get her back.

The two shots of Juan reflected in a mirror as the bootblack departs constitute the first manifestation of this important visual motif in the narrative, and hint at the subsequent change in his character. Juan must now fend for himself, and the montage of his street musician acts—he is dressed successively as a bullfighter, a Mexican, an Englishman, and a Tex an—likewise serves as a foreshadowing of Juan's split personality, as well as humorous counterpoint to the tragedy that follows: as Juan plays his accordion, skinheads throw a Molotov cocktail at him. The shot of his accordion in flames constitutes a visual metonymy for Juan's suffering; he is now both emotionally and physically maimed.

The crux of the doubling theme occurs when Juan returns home, and laughter seems to emanate from his dirty toilet and sink while he hears his name being called. As Juan falls asleep watching a television program with advice about love, his second self appears: Juan Faneca, whose cinematographic persona perfectly fits the description in the novel as "un charnego fino y peludo, elegante y primario, con guantes y mucha guasa" (a *charnego* who is thin and hairy, elegant and primary, with gloves and a lot of charm, 47) and "exactamente el tipo que necesitaba: embustero y camaleónico, atrevido y rufianesco" (exactly the type that I needed: deceitful and chameleon-like, daring and scoundrel-like, 83). Faneca tells him to wake up, because he will help Juan get Norma back: "Tú, déjame hacer a mí . . . iré yo en tu lugar" (Let me do it . . . I'll go in your place).

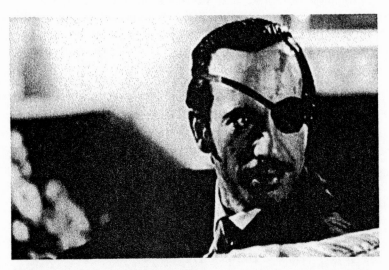

The mask and the second self: Vicente Aranda's *El amante bilingüe*, starring Imanol Arias. *Courtesy Iberoamericana Films, S.A.*

For Faneca's second visit, director Aranda artfully combines the mirror and the doubles, as Faneca appears to come out of the mirror on Juan's dresser as the latter is sleeping. His exhortation to Juan, "sal de tu sueño y entra en el mío" (Leave your dream and enter mine), also underscores the dream motif in the narrative. In the novel, the dream motif appears throughout: "Era difícil saber si entraba o salía del sueño" (It was difficult to know if he was coming out of or going into the dream, 46); "Primero se introdujo en el sueño un furioso olor a brillantina y poco después le vio sentado al borde de la cama" (First a violent odor of hair cream introduced itself into the dream, and shortly afterward, he saw him sitting on the edge of the bed, 81-82); "Vivo en un sueño que se cae en pedazos" (I live in a dream that is falling apart, 90).

Two intertextual references in the film text to the *Phantom of the Opera* underscore both his disfigurement and the mask as a basis for the theme of the double, just as does the novel's epigraph by Antonio Machado: "Lo esencial carnavalesco no es ponerse careta, sino quitarse la cara" (The essentially carnivalesque is not to put on a mask, but to take off your face).

He dons the leather mask in front of a mirror, thus intensifying the theme of the double due to what Rogers (7) points out as the widespread belief that reflections are the same as the soul. This doubling of Juan's personality intensifies when he makes a phone call to the Department of Linguistic Normalization of the Generalitat (Catalan parliament) where Norma works, just so he can hear her voice. The doubling here is vocal: Juan's voice now acquires an Andalusian accent as he pretends to be an immigrant store owner who wants to know the names in Catalan for certain intimate garments. The theme of the double, then, transcends the individual, and acquires here a broader social significance for contemporary Catalonia through the linguistic dimension that is alluded to in the narrative's title.

Marsé treats this sociolinguistic situation with great irony, and this irony is augmented in the film version of the narrative because of what Metz terms film's inherent multiple "channels of information." These include: "1. images which are photographic, moving, and multiple; 2. graphic traces which include all written material which we read off the screen; 3. recorded speech; 4. recorded music; 5. recorded noise or sound effects" (Andrew, *The Major Film Theories*, 218). The inclusion in the film text of spoken Catalan, standard Castilian, and Castilian with a marked Andalusian accent manifest what Bakhtin calls heteroglossia, or intralanguage differences, and polyglossia, or interlanguage differences (Clark and Holquist 289); each utterance constitutes a rung on the sociolinguistic ladder of power, which the narrative undercuts. Polyglossia, in and of itself, is a demythifying element: "Two myths perish simultaneously: the myth of a language that presumes to be the only language, and the myth of a language that presumes to be unified" (Stam 58). According to Clark and Holquist (69), Bakhtin sees heteroglossia as "the larger polyphony of social and discursive forces" and "a way of conceiving the world as made up of a roiling mass of languages, each of which has its own distinct formal markers."

The fact that Juan stumps the Catalan linguist with the question of how to say "exhaust pipe," and ends his telephone call with the ironic statement in "andaluz," "No sabe cuánto le agradezco la atención que ha tenío con este pobre charnego ignorante que está tan agradecío a esta Cataluña tan rica y tan plena" (You don't know much I thank you for the attention that you have given to this poor ignorant *charnego* who is so thankful to this Catalonia that is so rich and so full; cf. Marsé 65) is a manifestation of ironic discourse that parodies "catalanismo." Hooper (*Spaniards* 241, 243) notes that "about half the population of Catalonia today is of immigrant stock" and that "the repressive measures taken by Franco's government and the influx of this new wave of immigrants presented a dual threat to the Catalan language which, by the time the dictatorship ended, was facing a crisis." Consequently, the policy of the Catalan government has been to "impose" the Catalan language and culture on immigrants. An additional element in the film of the demythification of catalanismo is, as Freixas notes, the "presence/metaphor of the Walden 7 building, work and art of [Catalan architect] Ricardo Bofill, residence of Juan Marés, which is falling apart" (40-41).

Juan explains to fellow street artist Cuxot (Arnau Vilardeso) that his ex-wife likes a guy named Faneca, whom Juan describes as "Uno que soy yo pero que es otro" (One that is me but is another). This is a perfect example of the second self, since as Keppler (10) notes, the second self is a "contradictory being, a paradox of simultaneous outwardness and inwardness, of difference from and identity with the first self." Juan /Faneca represents a combination of disassociation—the dual or multiple personality (Jekyll/Hyde)—and autoscopy, or the visual hallucination of the physical self; multiple personality involves behavioral dissociation in time, whereas autoscopy involves visual "dissociation in space" (Rogers 15). Rogers notes that "decomposition in literature and the related phenomena of dissociation and autoscopy in clinical practice always reflect psychosexual conflict" (15), and the latter is often related to wish fulfillment (Rogers 30). Juan's frustrated desire to sexually possess his ex-wife results in the manifestation of these psychological phenomena, that is, Juan/Faneca.

When Juan returns home, he bumps into his neighbor Griselda (Loles León), and causes her to lose a contact lens. This accident further underscores the theme of the mask and the double, since Juan later discovers the missing lens in the cuff of his trousers, and realizes that Griselda's blue eyes are not really that color. Faneca reminds him how his father would disguise himself to become Fu-Ching, the Chinese magician, and he advises Juan, "Abre la caja de los milagros" (Open up the box of miracles). Juan's opening of his father's make-up box as he sits before his dresser mirror proves miraculous, indeed. The disfigured Juan now dons wig, mustache, eye patch, and blue contact lens to become someone else. The extreme close-up of Juan's eye underscores the importance of seeing and perception—or the lack thereof. The man that both the reader/spectator and other characters now see is truly an "other." The down-and-out Juan has become the debonair Faneca. The linguistic register in the film marvelously underscores this transformation, as Imanol Arias delightfully portrays this character with a thick Andalusian accent.   Faneca tells Juan/Faneca to get to work and try out "unas maniobras que demuestran que no hay tía que se detenga delante de un servidor" (some maneuvers that demonstrate that there is not a gal who will hold back with yours truly). His neighbor Griselda will provide the trial run for his attempt to regain Norma.

Juan/Faneca becomes a vehicle for Marsé's irony, as he pretends to be a public pollster who asks Griselda's opinion as to whether or not the Generalitat should promote opera star José Carreras as a "universal Catalan." Griselda's affirmative response to this question represents her desire to assimilate into the dominant culture; elements of the mise-en-scène such as the Barça soccer club pillow on her sofa, together with her confession of being an immigrant from Sevilla who is studying Catalan so that she can get a job at the Corte Inglés department store all humorously underscore the bicultural, bilingual theme. The new Juan/Faneca successfully woos Griselda, but Juan later suffers from remorse about his role as "burlador" or Don Juanesque trickster, calling Faneca a "charnego de mierda" (fucking *charnego*). When Juan complains, "Mi amiga es sólo una pobre solitaria" (My gal friend is only a poor lonely soul), Faneca retorts, "Todos somos unos pobres solitarios. Tu Norma también" (We're all poor solitary souls. Your Norma is, too).

The film's carnival scene further manifests the mask motif, as the disguised Juan hears Norma and her Catalan friends talk about him. This humiliating encounter with his ex-wife causes him to later declare as he sits in front of his dresser mirror, "No llorarás nunca más, ¿me oyes?" (You won't cry any more, do you hear me?) Juan does cry again, however, when his accordion rendition of the "Vals de las velas" ("Auld Lang Syne") next to the cathedral for a young girl's birthday brings him memories of Norma. Consequently, a more complete transformation from Juan to Faneca is necessary for Juan to successfully win back his ex-wife. Juan then writes in his notebook, "Esta es la última página de mi vida. . . . Dejo de ser Juan Marés y me incorporo a la eternidad en sacrificio y homenaje a una sola deidad, a un sentimiento inmenso, océanico, universal: mi vida eres tú, Norma" (This is the last page of my life. . . . I stop being Juan Marés and I incorporate myself into eternity in sacrifice and homage to only one deity, only one immense, oceanic, universal feeling: you are my life, Norma). Juan's second self, Faneca, calls Norma at her home in order to see her, under the guise of being an old friend of her husband's who wants to give her his notebooks. Norma is skeptical, however, and her sense that this must be a trick on Juan's part (she uses the words "truco" [trick], "montaje" [montage], and "estratagema" [strategem]) adds another layer of irony to the narrative. Norma reads the notebook (in a voice-over by Juan) about the episode when she tossed a coin to the itinerant musician/street beggar who followed her and succeeded in arousing her with his salacious comments ("coño loco, niña pija, mala puta . . ." [crazy cunt, high-class gal, bad whore]), and his hopes that she would someday realize that this outcast was her ex-husband. Faneca's "mask" is so convincing that Norma notes that he is younger than Juan, and in spite of the fact that she says he has the same tastes as her ex-husband—and the fact that he dares to place his hand on her rear end shortly after Norma notes that Juan was obsessed with her ass—she is unable to see through the disguise.

Juan/Faneca's success also depends upon a change in locale, since he cannot give Norma their old telephone number. His new spatial reference is actually an old one, as Juan/Faneca

Antagonism between the first and second selves: Vicente Aranda's *El amante bilingüe*, starring Imanol Arias. *Courtesy Iberoamericana Films, S.A.*

goes to the Pensión Ynés on the Calle Verdi in his childhood neighborhood. The return to the *barrio* constitutes a confirmation of identity that Juan had lost along the way. The letter that Faneca subsequently writes to "ese guarro de Marés" (that pig Marés) repudiates the very being of the latter—his closing is "Ojalá revientes. Faneca" (I hope you die. Faneca)—and manifests the antagonism that Keppler (11) notes as normally existing between the first and second selves. Ironically, Faneca reports to Norma that the Juan Marés she knew "era un cuento chino, un personaje inventado" (was a fairy tale, an invented personage). ("Cuento chino" literally means "Chinese story," an ironic term, since in order to become Faneca, Juan uses the make-up box of his father, who performed as Fu-Ching the Magician.) The reality of the dream character subsumes that of the real character.

When Norma arranges to meet Faneca at a bar near the pensión in order to see his neighborhood and return Juan's notebooks, she brings along her current lover, Jordi Valls Verdú, another member of the Catalan bourgeoisie. Jordi's condescending remarks about the *charnego* Faneca cause Norma to quarrel with him, and Faneca then takes Norma back to the pensión alone. Their ardent lovemaking scene, with numerous segments in slow motion, is faithful to the tone of the description in the novel:

> Norma cogió la ardiente cabeza del charnego con ambas manos mientras se dejaba dulcemente separar los muslos, con sus frotamientos desasosegados a punto estuvo de desbaratar la peluca, el disfraz y la falacia . . . Se le despegó una patilla y no la pudo recuperar hasta pasado un buen rato, camuflada en el pubis impetuoso de Norma (Norma grabbed the *charnego*'s ardent head with both hands as she sweetly separated her thighs, and her anxious rubbing was about to ruin his wig, his costume, and deceit. A sideburn came off, and he couldn't recover it for some time, as it was camouflaged in Norma's impetuous pubes, 210).

In the film, however, what Norma discovers in her pubic hair as she puts on her panties is not Juan's fake sideburns, but rather, his false mustache, and the deep shot of Faneca in the background worriedly touching his bare upper lip constitutes the humorous near unmasking of the *charnego*.

As they leave the pensión, her inquiry, "¿Está usted satisfecho de haberle puesto cuernos a su amigo Marés?" (Are you satisfied of having made your friend Marés a cuckold?), implies a radical separation of the two male characters based on rivalry. Faneca's response, "No . . . yo de lo que estoy contento es de haber conocido a la mujer que follaba a Juan Marés" (No . . . what I'm happy about is having known the woman who used to fuck Juan Marés), not only eschews this adversarial relationship, but also connotes the beginning of the release from an obsession.

When Norma leaves, Faneca sees a drunk vomit on the sidewalk: it is Juan, and Faneca initially rejects him, even referring to Norma's concept of the relationship, saying, "Anda por ahí, cornúo, ya se ha acabao todo" (Get along there, you cuckold, it's all over now). However, there is a reconciliation between the two: "Espera hombre . . . Vamos a ir a ver a mi Griselda, que tiene un culo estupendo, sabes, y un corazón que no le cabe en el pecho" (Wait up, man . . . Let's go see my Griselda, who's got a wonderful ass, you know, and a heart so big that it doesn't even fit in her chest). The two go off, riding the exterior

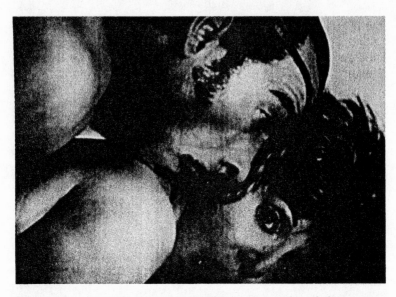

"In Catalan please": even orgasm has a sociopolitical dimension. Vicente Aranda's *El amante bilingüe*, starring Imanol Arias and Loles León. *Courtesy Iberoamericana Films, S.A.*

escalator that provides the link between the two spatial components of the narrative, which are also symbolic of the two components of the protagonist's identity. Juan and Faneca truly become fused only after this return to the barrio of his/their youth, only after recovering a part of himself that had been lost. The novel's author notes, "the final transmutation of Juan-Faneca fits the intention of recovering a type of lost identity, which in this case was the childhood of his past"(Rodríguez-Fischer 23). Film director Aranda comments, "I wanted to show that at the end they achieved an agreement. There was a schizophrenic situation in an individual who, in his desire to transform himself into another almost kills the one that he was first, but that's all there was. Schizophrenia is only cured by coming to an agreement. . . . Although it appears that he finds Juan Faneca outside himself, the truth is that he is within him" (Freixas and Bassa 46). The return to the barrio empowered Juan-Faneca to sexually reconquer Norma, but after having done so, he can finally leave his obsession with Norma behind. Consequently, Faneca's presence in the narrative fulfills a fundamental role of the second self, which "compels self-awareness, and in the agony of the process, brings self-enlargement" (Keppler 195). In this regard, Costas Goberna (26) notes the tension in the novel between the reality of the lost paradise and the crazy desire to recover the impossible, as well as the fact that paradises don't exist, but have to be built, and that Juan Marés did not know how to do so. Only the fusion of Juan with Faneca allows him to begin the building process.

Parody, the double, and carnival are all connected in this novel. The notion of parody is intrinsically linked to that of the double, even in its etymology, since as J. Hillis Miller notes, the pronoun *para* is "a double antithetical prefix, signifying at once proximity and distance, similarity and difference, interiority and exteriority . . . something simultaneously this side of a boundary line, threshold or margin, and also beyond it" (Miller 219). Bakhtin notes that "in antiquity, parody was inseparably linked to a carnival sense of the world. Parodying is the creation of the *decrowning double*; it is that same 'world turned inside out'" (Bakhtin, *Problems* 127). This narrative incorporates many elements of what Bakhtin (*Rabelais* 5ff) considers the culture of folk carnival, including ritual spectacles (carnival pageants), various genres of billingsgate (the vulgar, salacious language both directed at Norma and used by her), emphasis on the "lower body stratum" (copulation), the theme of the mask, and comic verbal compositions (parodies of both written and oral speech—the Andalusian accent, the linguistic incompetence of the Catalan specialists, the relative bilingualism of the Andalusian immigrants) (Bakhtin, *Rabelais* 40). This latter element is the most important feature of carnivalesque logic in *El amante bilingüe*. The film's multiple "channels of information" provide opportunities for greater doses of irony than in the original novel. Norma and her friends speak in Catalan while Spanish subtitles appear on the screen. Although Norma's speech utterances represent an official discourse of hierarchical importance, the bilingual Andalusian immigrants ironically undermine it. This irony appears most significantly in Faneca's interview with Norma at her home when he admits that he cannot speak much Catalan in spite of having lived in Barcelona for so many years. When Norma insists that he surely must know something, he says that he is embarrassed. Since Norma works at the office of Catalan Linguistic Normalization, she comments that it is natural for him to have an accent. However, when Faneca leans forward and says, "Fesme un francès, reina" (Give me a blowjob, babe; cf. Marsé 184), it is the signified not the (correct Catalan pronunciation of the) signifiers, that provides the sense of shame—and the irony. The irony culminates in the lovemaking scene between Juan/Faneca and Griselda, when the former exclaims in Spanish, "Que me corro" (I'm going to come) and Griselda retorts in Catalan, "En català si us plau" (In Catalan, please). Even orgasm has a sociopolitical dimension.

Carnival also celebrated "the temporary liberation from the prevailing truth and from the established order" (Bakhtin, *Rabelais* 10), and there is a peculiar carnivalesque logic of the "inside out" (Bakhtin, *Rabelais* 10), or as Orloff (15) would say, everything in carnival is reversed, inverted. Consequently, Norma rejects her normal Catalan bourgeois companion in favor of the *charnego*, the lower-class Andalusian. Although this sexual liberation is only temporary, it provides a far greater liberation for Juan, since he is now freed from his obsession. The reconciliation with his second self will allow him to achieve happiness in a relationship with Griselda. The movie ending represents a change from the original narrative, in which Faneca's happiness comes from his relationship with Carmen, the blind girl who works at the boarding house and for whom he interprets (and invents) television narratives: "Trastornado, indocumentado, acharne-gado y feliz, se quedaría allí iluminando el corazón solitario de una ciega, descifrando para ella y para sí mismo un mundo de luces y sombras más amable que éste" (Mad, undocumented, made into a *charnego*, and happy, he would remain there, illuminating the solitary heart of a blind girl, deciphering for her and for himself a world of lights and shadows that is happier than this one, 218). Director Aranda eschews the somewhat bitter irony of the novel here, eliminating a final scene that is contained in the published script of the film (Aranda 144). Since Griselda is also an Andalusian immigrant, and one who is becoming "successfully incorporated" into Catalan society, the displacement of the novel's Carmen by the film's Griselda allows for a greater thematic synthesis on many levels (Juan-Faneca, childhood *barrio*-adult abode, past-present).

The carnivalesque logic of *El amante bilingüe* is an essential component of the parody of *catalanismo*. The mirror and mask not only manifest this carnivalesque logic, but also point to the theme of the double, which has both a psychological and a sociopolitical dimension in the narrative. In addition, the ambiguity provided by the dream motif, together with the importance of sociolinguistic parody, allow both the novel and the film the ability to overcome what Rogers (32) calls the "limitations inherent in the use of the overt double." Consequently, Aranda's cinematographic version of Marsé's *El amante bilingüe* is one of the most successful screen adaptations of novels in recent Spanish cinema.

Andreu Martín

In 1984, Vicente Aranda adapted Andreu Martín's novel *Prótesis (Prosthesis)* for the screen with the title *Fanny Pelopaja (Fanny with the Straw-colored Hair)*. The close-up of false teeth during the credits manifests the element of prosthesis that gave the original narrative its title and it will serve as a fundamental symbolic element throughout the film. Aranda opens and closes the film with a narrative frame that was not in the novel: the voice-over narrative of Paca, a female social worker. Aranda says that the addition of the social worker/narrator Paca was a concession to his associate producers in order to give the film a better reception (Vera 148). The link between the narrator and the protagonist appears in the opening sequences in which Fanny (Fanny Cottençon) robs her at knife point.

A series of flashbacks lead us to the raison d'être of the false teeth and the symbolism that they hold. A policeman called Andrés, "el Gallego" (the Galician, played by Bruno Cremer) follows Fanny into a store and then takes her aside for questioning. His initial comment to her, "Sigo tus pasos, paloma" (I've been following you, babe), indicates more than a professional interest in Fanny. Indeed, his unprofessional character grows in repugnance throughout the film narrative. This begins when he violently grabs Fanny's hair when she refuses to give him information about her hoodlum boyfriend called Manuel "el Gato" (the Cat) and later when she makes fun of him, he obliges her to sleep with him.

Just as Aranda would later be motivated by an article that he read in the press to film *Amantes*, the scene here in which Fanny smuggles the pistol into the prison hospital by inserting it in her vagina—a scene not in the novel—was inspired by a press article (Vera 146). After Fanny helps Manuel escape, Andrés hunts them down and kills the boyfriend in what appears to be an act of jealousy that has nothing to do with his professional duties. Aranda underscores the scene with the close-up of the pistol, the reverse-angle shot of the shooting, and the blood covering Manuel's head before he falls to the ground in slow motion. The violence with which Aranda

252

portrays this scene is accentuated because the killing follows a loving embrace between Fanny and Manuel, therefore emphasizing Andrés's jealousy. Although Andrés offers to let Fanny off easily so that they can be lovers, she is repulsed by him: "Antes me acostaría con una culebra" (I would sleep with a snake first). Her repetition of the phrase "Me das asco" (You make me sick) leads to a violent reaction on Andrés's part that finally reveals the importance of her false teeth: he repeatedly beats her in the mouth with his pistol. The story thus becomes a tale of vengeance, with Fanny seeking revenge for the loss of both her teeth and her boyfriend. A temporal jump following the three years that she spends in jail finds her plotting with her friends Julián (Francisco Algora) and his wife la Nena (Berta Cabré) who is also the sister of the dead Manuel el Gato. She naturally wants to know the whereabouts of Manuel, who was dismissed from the police force following the beating incident and now works as a guard for an armored truck company.

Fanny's revenge takes the shape of one of the most spectacular crime scenes in Spanish film. She and her team of criminals masquerade as a moving company with a large van, a construction crew, and a traffic cop, and they cut off traffic and use a fork lift to place the entire armored car into the moving van and steal it. After they force the guards out by using a gas canister, Fanny's desire for individual vengeance overcomes her, and she smashes his mouth with her pistol. Even though she is wearing a mask, this symbolic gesture of vengeance is enough to let Andrés know who his assailant is. The tale now becomes one of multiple revenge, and Andrés's repugnance grows with each act of vengeance. He goes to the house of Julio and Nena and brutally beats the husband, and brutally sodomizes the wife with his pistol before he kills them both. His next victim would be Fanny, but earlier narrative information that functioned as foreshadowing—the close-ups of her knife, her threat after Andrés makes her go to bed with him that some day she would stab him, and her later threat when taken into custody that she would wait until after getting out of prison to kill him—leads us to the denouement: the police find them in bed together, with a knife sticking out of Andrés's back. The film ends with a slow zoom into the psychiatric center where Fanny is now confined, and with the voice-over of the social worker that completes the narrative frame as she explains (with a note of irony) that Fanny, who now only contemplates the passage of time with indifference, is in the same institution that had previously held Andrés.

There are important differences bertween the two versions of this tale. In spite of the fact that the film has some violent scenes (especially the violation of la Nena with the pistol, followed by her cold-blooded murder), Aranda notes that one of his worries in adapting this text was to reduce the violent cruelty found in the original, and he believes that not only did he reduce it considerably, but he also tried to add a justification for the violence in the character, which was not in the novel (Vera 140). Another of the major transformations from novel to screen is the change from a male protagonist to a female. Aranda explains that he accepted this film project proposed by Carlos Durán, but had difficulty writing the script; he did not want to deal with the homosexual theme, and he finally realized that the love-hate relationship between protagonists would work better if they were a man and a woman (Vera 140-41). Contractual obligations with his French coproducer caused him to include French actors, and it was simply the selection of the blonde Fanny Cottençon as the leading actress that led to the new title.

Aranda insists that he told the main actors that this was a love story (Vera 143), and both Vera (146) and Alvares and Frías (148) believe that the scene at the end when Fanny and Andrés meet and point their pistols at each other without firing is evidence of the combination of love and hate that they felt toward each other. These opposing sentiments, together with the desire for revenge, dominate the emotions of this rivetting film adaptation.

Carmen Martín Gaite

A major factor in the transformation of a narrative from page to screen is often the condensation or selection of narrative material. The longer the novel, the more narrative that must be eliminated in order to fit into the standard movie format. The opposite is the case in Angelino Fons's *Emilia, parada y fonda* (*Emilia, a Stop and an Inn*, 1966), which is based on Carmen Martín Gaite's short story "Un alto en el camino" ("A Stop Along the Road" from her *Ataduras* (*Ties*, 1960) collection. The brevity of the original narrative makes it only the germ of this free filmic adaptation, as Fons builds on some elements of the short story, freely invents other narrative elements, and radically changes the structure of the narrative.

Martín Gaite's short story is framed by the stop of a train at the station in Marseilles as the widower Gino, his son Esteban, and second wife Emilia travel from Spain to Milan to visit Gino's family. During the stop, Emilia leaves the train to have a furtive encounter with her sister Patri, who lives in Marseilles. Although Emilia states that she loves Gino, and that he is a good man, Patri believes that he treats her sister badly, since she has it written all over her face (95-96). Small details confirm Patri's opinion about Emilia's unhappy marriage: Gino does not allow Emilia to write letters to her sister, Emilia states that happiness is not of this world, Gino's snoring on the train trip reflects five years of martyrdom for Emilia as her sleepless nights lead her to thoughts of homicide, and Gino angrily greets her when she returns from the encounter with her sister, and there is even the hint of a threat of physical violence, as he clenches his fist as he calls her "crazy." In contrast, Patri has found freedom in France: she has her own apartment and a French boyfriend.

Fons's film narrative begins with the same train stop (although here the station is in Calsot). The adaptation's radical transformation of the narrative structure is based on a series of flashbacks to when Emilia (Ana Belén) and Patri (Lina Canaleja) were young, to Emilia's amorous relationship with Jaime (Juan Diego)—a character added by Fons and scriptwriter Juan Tebar, who had author Carmen Martín Gaite's collaboration—the meeting of Emilia and her future husband, named Joaquín (Francisco Rabal) in the movie, scenes of their domestic life, Joaquín's extramarital affair, visits by Emilia to her Aunt Ignacia (Pilar Muñoz), and a trip by Emilia to France.

The flashbacks manifest the girls' incipient desire for freedom, and they are sometimes triggered by the dialogue, as Patri asks, "mirábamos mapas, ¿te acuerdas?" (we used to look at maps, do you remember?) and we jump back to their youth, with Emilia looking at a map and Patri contemplating her image in a mirror while they listen to a radio broadcast about a castle in Marseilles. Geographic relocation thus not only carries the connotations of freedom but also the romantic and the sensual. The adolescent mirror image constitutes an act of self-recognition and taking consciousness. Patri, who has declared that she is "up to here with this place," does indeed escape, as does Jaime, Emilia's first love.

The addition of this character provides the film narrative with the lost love theme. Although this loss initially constitutes the justification for Emilia's acceptance of an elderly widower as her husband, it is difficult to overcome her feelings. Even after going to France and not writing anymore to Emilia, Jaime retains a presence in her life. A flashback from Jaime and Emilia kissing in the hallway cuts to the married couple's bedroom, where Joaquín's bald head is meant to connote his unattractiveness. Emilia takes out a photograph of Jaime, remembering his conversation (in voice-over); she then takes her wedding photo on her dresser and places it face down, a gesture that symbolizes her rejection of her husband, in contrast with the warm memories of her lost love.

Emilia wonders about her own attractiveness, and Fons captures this preoccupation in two mirror shots. The first one is in her bedroom. While Joaquín snores (a motif taken from the short story) she looks at herself in the bedroom mirror, touching her own face and breasts—the body parts that are important for being sexually attractive—while the snoring continues. In the second sequence, Emilia tries on a black slip in a clothing store. The reflection of Emilia in this sexy garb affirms her attractiveness. Joaquín enters and confirms it by both telling her how sexy she looks and by touching her. Emilia, however, will have none of it, and she complains about his mistress, Maruja. A flashback to Joaquín in bed with Maruja complaining about his wife ends on a comic note, with the mistress defending Emilia, with the ensuing dispute ending with Maruja throwing Joaquín's toupee at him from her balcony. This episode, which was not in the original narrative, emphasizes the double sexual standard in Spain at that time. The repression is such that a store clerk even notes that the police consider a nude female mannequin in the window to constitute a "provocation."

Although still under the Franco regime, Spain was also changing in the 1960s. The Beatles poster in the girls' bedroom manifests how new music and new lifestyles from outside Spain influence the country. There is thus an inversion of the traditional religious values in the original narrative (happiness is not of this world) when Emilia expresses her unhappiness by hoping to die, since then, at least, she would meet the devil, whom she imagines to be handsome and sexy.

Emilia is emotionally and sexually unfulfilled by her snoring, bald husband. (Although this is mutually the case, since Joaquín complains that she always waits until he goes to sleep to come to bed, his extramarital affair makes Emilia the victim.) Emilia looks to satisfy her needs with Jaime, who has returned from France for a visit. Her reflection appears in a mirror shot just before she departs from her home to wait for Jaime in the hopes of having an affair with him, and once she is in the street, we see her reflection in a store window just before Jaime crosses the street; both of these shots underscore her duplicity. This encounter does not work out, so Emilia goes to France. The advertisements for sex shops with bare-breasted women underscores the freedom that Jaime had mentioned, and their incorporation into the film—together with the shots of Ana Belén's naked breasts during her affair—also manifests the new freedom allowed in Spanish cinema and the beginning of the *destape* phenomenon. After she discovers that Jaime has left Perpignan, she meets Claude, and they end up in a hotel together. The fact that they do not speak each other's language does not matter, since Claude represents the Count of Monte Cristo to Emilia, thus tying into the romantic dreams of her youth. As she stands before the bathroom mirror before going out to her waiting lover, she has a dialogue with her "other" self in which she not only queries the relationship between visual image and eroticism ("Are you going to go out to him with something on?"), but she also questions her relationship with Jaime. Her symbolic gesture of throwing the ring that Jaime had given her into the trash can represents a break with the past. Nevertheless, this lost love is deeply embedded in her subconscious, and during their love-making, she calls out Jaime's name.

The film ends with a curious sequence that again subverts the religious element of the original narrative. In the short story, Emilia would like to confess her thoughts of murdering her snoring husband. In the film, the final sequence is precisely a confession, but its subversion begins with location of the protagonist. Emilia, shot in profile, is in front of the confessional, the normal location for a male confessant. (Women do not face the priest directly, but rather confess from the side of the confessional.) What Emilia says is not a traditional confession—a recounting of one's sins with a desire for forgiveness. She "confesses" her longings for emotional and sexual fulfillment (a kiss, a hidden caress) and expresses how her affair in France was with a "real man." Although it may not have resolved her problems, it made her happy. Sexuality—even adultery—appears in this changing Spain not as a source of shame, but as a source of pleasure. The "priest"—who turns out to be Aunt Ignacia!—advises her not to tell her husband, since he just would not understand. Having a woman in the role of the priest as well as the advice that she gives completely turns the traditional religious component on its head. Emilia's physical location during the confessional syntagmatically relates to her earlier activities. The double sexual standard has been erased: women, just as men, can take the sexual initiative and find pleasure in it.

All of the mirror shots throughout the film are underscored by the soundtrack, which features Luis Eduardo Aute's composition, "Así sea," sung by Ana Belén. The lyrics state, "Cada mañana veo en el espejo la víctima eterna . . . que es mi sonrisa" (Each morning I see in the mirror the eternal victim . . . that is my smile). The lyrics manifest a taking of consciousness of a state of unhappiness. The film narrative, however, ends on a positive note: there is no condemnation or guilt, but rather understanding and a sense of happiness, albeit temporary. *Emilia parada y fonda* is thus an important manifestation of the cultural changes in Spain in the mid-1960s.

Luis Martín Santos

The novel *Tiempo de silencio* (*Time of Silence*), published by Luis Martín Santos in 1961, is one of the most important narratives in twentieth-century Spanish letters. The tragic death of Martín Santos (1924-1964) in an automobile accident truncated what might have been a brilliant literary career. This work revolutionized the aesthetics of the post–civil war novel. The novel's most important contribution was stylistic: as opposed to novels of social realism that were prevalent at the time, *Tiempo de silencio* incorporated new narrative techniques, especially the use of interior monologues, changes in point of view (with predominance of the first-person narrative), a mixture of narrative discourses, and a neo-baroque use of language. Following Chatman's distinction (23) that "story is the content of the narrative expression, while discourse is the form of that expression," it is clear that in *Tiempo de silencio*, there is an important foregrounding of discourse. Consequently, this novel, more than any other of those contemporary Spanish narratives that have been adapted for the screen, presents the dilemma that is inherent in any page-to-screen project: how do you adequately move from one language to another? Many thought that cinematographic adaptation of the novel would be impossible, but in 1986, Vicente Aranda released his screen version of *Tiempo de silencio*. Aranda wanted to film the novel from the moment of its publication in the early sixties, but he had to wait twenty years to do so because no producer considered the project a viable one, given the technical complexity of the original novel (Alvares and Frías 170). Contrary to the common opinion that the work was unfilmable, Aranda believed that the story was indeed important to Martín Santos: "Everybody kept saying that what the author was really interested in was the discursive part of the work, that is to say, the monologues and the digressions, with the anecdotal part [the story] being less important. But I didn't share that opinion" (Alvares and Frías 170).

The title of the novel critically points to a difficult period in post–civil war Spain: the late 1940s, when dictatorship and its concomitant censorship created a stifling intellectual atmosphere. This portrait of postwar years appears on screen in Aranda's 1986 adaptation. Pedro (Imanol Arias), a researcher who studies cancer, has run out of mice in his laboratory, and he has no funds to purchase more of these expensive laboratory animals from the United States. Nevertheless, his assistant Amador (Francisco Algora) informs him that he gave some of the mice to his cousin Muecas (Francisco Rabal) who lives in a shanty town outside of Madrid, and that this poor man has successfully bred them with the help of the "natural heat" of his daughters, Florita and Conchi. The incredulous scientist goes to the shanty town to obtain the mice. The shot of the old woman scraping the ground, searching for a bit of food, together with the long shot of the shanty town, underscore the atmosphere of misery that existed in Madrid during those "years of hunger." This setting contrasts markedly with the living room of the house of Matías (Juan Echanove), whose wealthy family can import the latest records from England, and can maintain a lazy son as a "señorito." Indeed, Matías's lifestyle draws Pedro into two other important settings in the film that portray life in Madrid: the café, in which intellectuals drink and discuss literature and the arts, and the bordello.

Pedro's boarding house is another important setting, since it is the locus of desire in the film: the grandmother who runs the boarding house desires to catch the physician for her nineteen-year-old granddaughter, Dorita (Victoria Abril). Her erotic aspect is clear from the very first shot of her, a medium profile shot in which she is bent over with her curved back in a horizontal position as she adjusts the radio. The rhythmic squeaking of her rocking chair in the living room foreshadows the squeaking of her bed when the drunken physician makes love to her: this noise awakens the grandmother, who ironically rejoices that the doctor has finally taken the bait. Likewise, the scene in which the grandmother speaks to the photograph of her dead husband foreshadows the doctor's fall to temptation, not only in her speech "Creo que picará" (I think he'll nibble [the bait]), but in the symbolism of the phallic sword that she thrusts under the mattress. Although Pedro emanates a certain coldness throughout the film, Aranda manifests the physician's subconscious desire for Dorita by also casting Victoria Abril in the roles of the existentialist intellectual "girl in glasses" (Martín Santos 69) in the café, and as one of the prostitutes in the bordello. In case the dark wig, glasses, and beret of the existentialist are too much of a disguise, her loud laugh syntagmatically relates to Dorita's earlier laugh in the rocking chair when she ironically undercuts the grandmother's characterization of Pedro as a "gentleman." Victoria Abril is not the only actress cast in more than one role. Alvares and Frías (173) note that Charo López's two roles as Matías's mother and as a prostitute is an attempt to underscore the Oedipus complex that is already present in the original narrative.

Pedro's coldness distances the spectator from him; Freixas (32) points out that Aranda suppresses the sympathy toward Pedro that is found in the original narrative, and accentuates his cowardice. A key scene in that regard that manifests this lack of courage occurs when the drunken Pedro buys cigarettes in the Plaza Mayor, telling the vendor, "Soy un cobarde, un pobre hombre. Nunca voy a llegar a nada" (I'm a coward, a poor guy. I'm never going to amount to anything). This foreshadows the cowardice that he manifests the following morning. Muecas summons him to his shack to help his dying daughter Florita, who is bleeding to death after a botched abortion. The scene of the screaming girl tied to a table next to a bloodied fetus and needle is the most gripping of the film. However, for Aranda—and for the spectator—the most upsetting element of the abortion scene is not the visual image of the nude and bloodied Florita (Diana Peñalver) tied to the table: it is the sound of the instrument as it scrapes her uterus (Alvares and Frías 180). However, Aranda justifies the brutal nature of the scene, saying,"There had to be a criticism of brutal back-alley abortions, and that is what I did" (Vera 166). Pedro's cowardliness occurs afterwards, as he leaves the scene; it is underscored when the lawyer interrogates Matías concerning Pedro's behavior, asking repeatedly about when Pedro reported the news of Florita's death to the police. Of course, he was too afraid to do so. The comments by the policeman who arrests

Pedro in the bordello constitute some of the sharpest social criticism of the film, as hypocrisy of postwar Spanish society is laid bare: "Comprendo que un médico haga abortar a una duquesa o a una hija de estraperlista, eso lo entiendo. Pero que un médico aborte en unas chabolas y venga a esconderse en una casa de putas, eso no lo he visto. No se puede caer más bajo" (I understand that a doctor would perform an abortion on a duchess or the daughter of a black marketeer, I understand that. But a doctor performing an abortion in some shacks and then hiding out in a whorehouse, that's something that I've never seen before. You can't get any lower than that).

Interior monologues are fundamental to the original narrative, and the best scenes in which the film enters into Pedro's subconscious occur at the reception and in jail. Following the philosophical lecture, Matías's mother throws a party for those who attend, but tracking shots of Pedro walking among the guests connote his alienation. The mirror in front of which he sits symbolically functions as a window to his soul, and Pedro's guilt and cowardice conjure up a terrible image: as the soundtrack shifts from the loud murmurs of party conversation to a tinkling of chimes, Pedro "sees" Florita's dead naked body on the floor among the guests, a vision that is broken by the return of the murmurs and Matías's mother asking, "¿Qué hace allí solito?" (What are you doing there all alone?) Aranda emphasizes the sense of confinement and isolation in the scene that depicts Pedro's incarceration not only by shooting through the bars of the cell, but by shooting through the small barred window on the cell door. Rubio-Gribble (73) notes the frequent scenes throughout the film that are shot through glass (in the bar, at the reception hosted by Matías's mother) or through bars (the caged dogs, Pedro in jail) "give the spectator the sense of limited, enclosed spaces, and the lack of freedom of movement." In this jail scene, Pedro, seen through this small opening pacing in circles, seems like a caged animal. The voice-over in this scene represents the first incorporation of the many interior monologues from the novel, and the echoing of Pedro's voice as his very thoughts seem to bounce off of the cell walls accompanies the close-up shot of him drawing on the wall in frustration: "No pienses. No pensar. No pensar. Tranquilo. . . .

Eres un ser libre para pensar o para dibujar en la pared con la uña o con lo que sea . . . eres libre de hacer las rayas tan largas como quieras" (Don't think. No thinking. No thinking. Calm. . . .You are a free being to think or to draw on the wall with your fingernail or with whatever . . . you are free to make the lines as long as you want). His thoughts on freedom underscore the irony of the whole narrative. The interrogation scene that occurs in the darkened room, with Pedro shot in chiaroscuro lighting, marvelously symbolizes how the regime controlled and manipulated official discourse, as the police officer provides the authoritative version of events, with the doctor's words not counting for anything. Although freed through the intervention of Dorita, their happiness is short-lived because of Cartucho's intervention.

Cartucho (Joaquín Hinojosa) maintains an ominous presence throughout the film. The anger of this shantytown thug and beau of Florita grows with each visit by outsiders to Muecas's shack. The low-angle shot of Cartucho standing over Amador gives him as much power as the knife that he then holds to the lab worker's throat, as he extracts the false confession from the fearful Amador that the doctor was responsible for Florita's pregnancy. His omnipresent knife foreshadows the ending of the film, especially when he angrily stabs the earth after his mother denigrates his manhood by calling him a cuckold. Her statement that Muecas is causing him to be so is not totally clear until taken in syntagmatic relationship with the abortion scene: the close-up of the two women in the shadows at the back of the shack who blame Muecas for incestuously impregnating Florita functions like the chorus from a Lorca tragedy. The silent presence of the thug as he shadows Pedro and Dorita increases in its ominous nature as the rhythm of appearances increases: he appears on the street outside of the bordello where Pedro hides, in the door of Muecas's shack to block Dorita's exit, on the stairway of their boarding house; he then appears three times in the background of the fair sequence—in back of the organ grinder, in front of the carousel, and as seen through the hanging candies that connote his criminality as if they were bars on a cell—before he suddenly appears and stabs Dorita—not in her side, as in the original narrative (232), but lower down, in the womb, bringing full meaning to the earlier stabbing of the earth, as well as providing a symmetry with Florita's death, for which Cartucho has now taken vengeance, "hembra por hembra" (woman for woman).

The final voice-over again incorporates one of the novel's interior monologues, and again underscores the irony of the original narrative. Pedro is in his laboratory—a change from the novel, where Pedro is on his way to "exile," to a small town to become a rural doctor. His prior coldness is now pure emptiness: "Estoy como vacío porque me han pasado una gamuza y me han limpiado las vísceras por dentro . . . Es agradable, a pesar de estar castrado, tomar el aire y el sol mientras uno se amojama en silencio. Estamos en el tiempo de anestesia" (I'm empty because they've wiped me with a chamois and they've cleaned my viscera from the inside . . . It is pleasant, in spite of being castrated, to take some fresh air and sun while you dry up in silence. We are in the time of anesthesia).

On the soundtrack, numerous radio broadcasts help capture the atmosphere of the 1940s in which radio served to present the official discourse of the Franco regime, and sirens ominously fill the background with frequency. The silence of the title is imposed during a key scene at a bar when Matías and Pedro attempt to join in on singing "En los pueblos de mi Andalucía" ("In the Towns of My Andalusia") with the verse about the birds in the countryside who enjoy love and freedom repeated again and again, and symbolizing their own song for freedom, but it is silenced by the night watchman.

Aranda has commented on the process of adapting this seminal novel for the screen: "like always, the problem [of adapting the novel] was one of synthesis, of reduction. It was less of a problem here precisely because the expository part was so extensive; the simple fact of doing away with it simplified the material a lot" (Vera 163). Aranda notes that the "music" of the original narrative was in his head during production: "We went around with the novel in our hands during almost every day of the shooting . . . we were doing things immersed in the spirit of the novel, not with the desire to respect it, but with the idea letting that music come into us and then to transfer it to the film" (Alvares and Frías 172).

One change from the novel is that Dorita in the film is a more active character than in the original narrative, perhaps due to the director's relationship with Victoria Abril, but Aranda maintains that her change in character corresponds to the idea that Matías has of her in the novel (Vera 164). The increased appearances of Dorita can sometimes be inferred from the original text, and they all serve to make the film narrative tighter. Aranda transforms the "someone" (Martín Santos 141) who interrupts the party with something important to tell Pedro into Dorita with the news that the police are looking for him. Dorita's visit to Muecas's shack, though not in the novel, provides excellent motivation for both the confession by Muecas's wife, and the suspense caused by the stalking by Cartucho, who is able to visually identify her at that time. Her additional presence in the bordello, at the interview with the lawyer, and when Pedro is released from jail, all serve to tighten the emotional bonds between her and the doctor. Rubio Gribble (65) also notes that the act of Dorita's throwing the lawyer's glasses onto the floor is a social criticism, since it emphasizes "his blindness regarding the facts."

Aranda's version of the absurd world in which Pedro lives does not depend on the subtle ironies of the literary text, however; the humor of many scenes even elicits overt laughter. Some of the jokes are taken directly from the novel, however. Thus, when there is a blackout in the bordello due to postwar electrical restrictions, the poetic Matías tells the prostitute, "Electra, come to me" and she ingenuously responds, "Even though you call her, she won't be here until 6 o'clock," (Martín Santos 91). The scene that best reflects the subtle irony of the novel is that of the philosophical lecture in which a professor, holding an apple out to his audience, explains that the apple they see is different from the apple that he sees because they see it from a different perspective. Aranda ironically undercuts the tone of discourse by including a cat in the scene, with a montage sequence that includes a low-angle point of view shot of the cat. He continues to play with this concept throughout the film with additions or modifications to the original narrative: the madam of the bordello, Luisa, holds a tomato with the same stance as the apple, Dorita dumps a basket of apples on the bed of the bordello, and Dorita and her mother eat candied apples at the fair, thereby substituting for the coconut of the novel (226).

Naturally, screen adaption of such an important work was bound to result in diverse opinions about its success. Whereas Vera calls Aranda's version of *Tiempo de silencio* "an intelligent and creative reading of a key novel of contemporary Spanish literature" (9), Angel A. Pérez Gómez calls it a very "uneven" and "unsuccessful" film ("Tiempo" 295, 296). Rubio Gribble believes that "the most interesting thing about this adaptation is the strategy of perspectivism that the implicit narrator adopts in the film text" (68) and that director Aranda is able to "transmit the ironic and desolating tone of the narrator" (45). Both versions of *Tiempo de silencio* are seminal contemporary Spanish narratives.

Carlos Martínez-Barbeito

El bosque del lobo (*Wolf Forest*, 1971), directed by Pedro Olea, is the film adaptation of Carlos Martínez-Barbeito's 1947 novel, *El bosque de Ancines* (*Ancines Forest*). The Galician novelist based his work on the historical case of Manuel Blanco Romasanta, "The Wolf-Man," who was executed in La Coruña in 1854. Olea frames his narrative with the voice off screen of a minstrel who sings a ballad that places the narrative within the context of the poetic oral tradition in Spain: "Atención pido señores / para contar este caso. / Aquí en Galicia ha ocurrido / con el siglo comenzado. / Benito Freire, su nombre / por las ferias, buhonero / guiaba a los caminantes /de un pueblo a otro pueblo" (I ask your attention, gentlemen / in order to tell of this case. / It occurred here in Galicia / at the beginning of the century. / Benito Freire was his name / a peddler at fairs / who guided travellers / from one town to another). This voice-over narrative accompanies a long shot of a man—Benito (José Luis López Vázquez)—walking through the Galician wood, and provides the frame for the film adaptation of the narrative.

Olea uses nondiegetic elements throughout the narrative to signal that Benito is about to become transformed into a crazed murderer. As he guides Avelina through the forest, the camera movement suddenly becomes very jerky, and a close-up of Benito's face is accompanied by the twangy music of a *birimbao* (Galician jew's-harp). He then strangles the woman to death. The visual image that closes each attack is a close-up of his hand clawing at the earth. Before he leaves the scene of the crime, Benito puts the clothing of his victim in his pack, since this represents a source of income for the peddler.

When Benito arrives at the next village, he enters a tavern, but leaves momentarily to meet with Doña Pacucha, as Olea introduces the secondary plot of the narrative. Benito serves as a messenger between Pacucha and Don Nicolás, who, in spite of being married, carries on an amorous correspondence with this lady friend. When Benito returns to the tavern, he sees a young woman dancing on a table with Avelina's shawl, and a strong reaction shot of Benito underscores his culpability as he runs to recover the shawl that he had taken from his first

victim. His explanation that it is not for sale causes an
incredulous reaction on the woman's part: how can a poor
peddler have an article of woman's clothing that is not for
sale? He makes a gift of the shawl to her to buy her silence, but
in the end, this action will cause his undoing.

Cross-cuts between a man in the tavern who tells the story
of a wolf-man and Benito, with the final shot of the sequence
that of Benito as he covers his face with his hands, establish
the connection between the man's tale and the protagonist's
predicament: Benito himself is a wolf-man. The presence in the
tavern of Don Roberto, an English Protestant missionary,
provides the rational explanation for the phenomenon. As the
two walk through the forest together, the Englishman talks of
classic tales of wolf-men, but says, "No creo en estas fantasías"
(I don't believe in these fantasies). More importantly, he
provides the explanation that so-called wolf-men are probably
epileptics.

Two flashbacks in the film tie these narrative strings
together. The first flashback occurs after Benito complains of
suffering from fever, and Don Nicolás arranges for him to enter
the hospital. A medium shot of Benito in his hospital bed
with a nurse/nun at his bedside praying triggers the first
flashback to a religious procession. Close-ups of the altar boy
indicate that this is indeed Benito as a child. He seems to have
difficulty carrying the cross in the procession, and the brief
montage sequence of the altar boy overcome by the sun conveys a
sense of cause and effect in the narrative. The second flashback
occurs when Benito falls asleep at the lodging house run by the
mother of Minguillos. His panting, another signal of an attack,
together with the sound off screen of a wolf howling, and the
zoom in to a wolf skin hanging in his room all trigger the
flashback to his childhood as someone in a group of hunters
proclaims, "Hemos cazado al lobishome" (We have captured
the wolf-man). As in the previous flashback, close-ups of a
young boy in a night-shirt indicate that he is the sickly young
Benito. We now see a procession of a different nature: the
hunters and townsfolk accompany an ox-drawn cage. The
contents of the cage are purposely hidden from view until the
cage passes before the child. Here the sequence changes to slow

motion to further emphasize the dramatic impact of the image of the wolf-man—another poor epileptic?—on the young boy. These two flashbacks capture the spirit of comments made by Benito in the novel about his past: when a tinker asks him what he suffers from, he replies, "Cómo se nombra no sé, pero viene de una maldición que me echaron siendo menino" (I don't know what it's called, but it comes from a curse that they put on me when I was a lad, 43).

Olea's film version portrays several Galician cultural elements in the narrative: the funeral ceremony of circling the dead body (cf. 12), the bagpipes that are played on festive occasions, the *queimada* (wine with brandy that is set on fire), and superstition or magic in the episode with the *sabiador* —the Gallician term *meigo* (witch) is used in the novel (106)—who is able to detect the wrongdoing through both acute observation—the camera zooms in to show the telltale sign of blood on the shawl of one of Benitos victims—as well as through reading tarot cards.

The priest who leads the search for Benito also finds proof of the peddler's crime. The film version sanitizes the original narrative somewhat: instead of finding the gruesome burned remains of Teresa (124), he merely finds a rosary that belonged to her. Olea uses visual metonymy to connote the beginning of the community effort to capture the criminal, as we see close-ups of a shotgun and farm instruments such as a pitchfork being taken from their shelves. After his capture in a hunting trap (in the novel, they smoke him out of a cave) a close-up of Benito shows him crying and giving thanks to his captors/liberators. A final long shot of the procession of men on horseback who have taken him prisioner parallels the earlier procession scene, and the narrator's voice off screen closes the framing device with which the film began: ". . . por una mala fada once muertos le culparon. La paz volvió a la comarca, gracias al Señor que os damos" (he was guilty of eleven deaths because of his bad fairy. Peace returned to the region, we give thanks to the Lord).

Olea eliminates the final eight chapters of the novel and gives greater narrative concentration to his screen adaptation. The motivation of the protagonist changes slightly from novel to film, and in the screen adaptation, he is a somewhat more sympathetic figure. The novel makes him out more as a wolf-man: Benito rips off his clothing, howls, and joins the wolves before killing Avelina and her baby (19).The film version also portrays a sense of Benito's remorse on several occasions: as mentioned, he buries his face in his hands when he hears the story of the wolf-man at the tavern; after he kills Teresa and Riquitina, a close-up of the peddler shows him crying, and the low-angle shot of the sun that follows parallels the same shot during the flashback; thus implying that Benito is a victim of his sickness. After strangling Pacucha, Benito sees his reflection in a pool of water, and a close-up of his hand tapping his reflected image indicates that he cannot stand himself. Likewise, this close-up of his hand parallels the numerous shots of his hand grasping the earth at the end of each crime, as if he were trying to grab ahold of—and return to—reality and normality. The final image of Benito—when he is discovered, caught in the hunting trap—shows an appreciative attitude on his part, as if he were relieved at being apprehended; this contrasts with the final image of the peddler in the novel as he shouts, wails, and roars as they lead him to be executed.

This film by Pedro Olea shows the promise that the filmmaker had in making screen adaptations, which was more fully realized in later film versions of novels such as *El maestro de esgrima* (*The Fencing Master*) and *Morirás en Chafarinas* (*You Will Die in Chafarinas*).

Eduardo Mendicutti

Veteran filmmaker Jaime de Armiñán brought Andalusian novelist Eduardo Mendicutti's novel *El palomo cojo* (*The Lame Dove*, 1991) to the screen in 1995. Armiñán not only filmed this autobiographical narrative in Mendicutti's hometown of Sanlúcar de Barrameda, but the interiors were mainly shot in the house that belonged to the author's grandparents. The film is a period piece set in the 1950s, as Guillermo (Valeriano Andrés) asks if President Eisenhower is going to visit Spain.[1]

The narrative tells of a young boy's summer visit to his grandparents' home. Diagnosed as sickly and confined to bed, Felipe (Miguel Angel Muñoz) soon discovers a world of eccentric and fascinating characters who ensure that his summer will be memorable. The foremost of these is Mary (María Barranco), the talkative and foul-mouthed maid with a strong Andalusian accent; Uncle Ricardo (Francisco Rabal), who, like Felipe, mostly appears in pajamas, but who quixotically plans to discover a sunken treasure, and whose pet doves both furnish a contact with the young boy and provide the title to the narrative; and Aunt Victoria (Carmen Maura), the opera singer who symbolically dresses in red and pink and whose recitations of erotic and anti-Franco poetry constitute an attack on the Franco regime that censored director Armiñán on more than one occasion. Other eccentric characters include the elderly Caridad, who believes that parts of her body are missing —"No tengo perfil derecho . . . Me falta una pierna . . ." (I don't have a right profile . . . I'm missing a leg . . .), and Doña Carmen, the senile great-grandmother who constantly repeats the erotic memories from her youth—"Eran cuatro bandoleros y estaban locos por mí . . . (There were four bandits and they were crazy for me . . .). Carmen's repetitive verbalization as well as Victoria's recitation of verses seem to underscore the literari-

---

[1]Although it is a small detail, it is bothersome that the car that brings young Felipe to his grandparents' home is an anachronistic 1963 Cadillac (and not the Hispano of the novel).

ness of the source, but only ironically so, since neither is explicit in the original and therefore both constitute a transformation from telling to showing in the two versions of the narrative. The most significant part of the narrative is the search for sexual identity on the part of the child protagonist. The theme of latent homosexuality first occurs when the maid shows Felipe some "secret documents" pertaining to his Uncle Ramón: a postcard from 1936 signed by someone named Federico contains a dog looking at a dove with what Mary terms a lovesick face. The allusion to homosexuality (both animals, *perro* and *palomo*, are masculine) and to homosexual poet García Lorca in particular is confirmed at later points in the film narrative: in a conversation with Uncle Ricardo, Felipe tells of Mary's belief that "los palomos cojos son mariquitas" (lame doves are queers) and then inquires, "¿Yo soy rarito?" (Am I "strange"?) Although Ricardo denies it, he does not do so when the boy asks the same question regarding Uncle Ramón, evasively responding, "Ya no me acuerdo del tío Ramón" (I no longer remember Uncle Ramón). When the latter arrives, the sexually disoriented youth inquires, "¿Qué sabe mejor, un hombre, una señora o una gachí?" (Which tastes better, a man, a lady, or a young gal?), to which Uncle Ramón (Joaquín Kremel) responds, "Las señoras y las gachís saben a gloria y una vez conocí a un señor que sabía a queso manchego" (Ladies and young gals taste great, and I once met a man who tasted like Manchego cheese). Felipe immediately identifies this man as Federico. The boy's latent homosexuality manifests itself when he compliments Ramón on having gorgeous eyes. (*Piropos* traditionally are compliments that are expressed by men toward women.) Ramón's eyes are not his only physical attribute, as an earlier scene included a photograph of him in a bathing suit in which María and Felipe both notice that he is well endowed.

This fixation on the penis occurs throughout the narrative: when Felipe arrives, Mary believes that he is ashamed to undress in front of her, but Felipe says that other boys envy his penis size; when Mary asks him if a girl has ever touched his "bell ringer," he answers, "No seas guarra" (Don't be filthy— a response that might also have homosexual connotations). Armiñán emphasizes this motif by including two scenes that

response that might also have homosexual connotations). Armiñán emphasizes this motif by including two scenes that are not in the original narrative: when the maid removes the magazine that covers the sexual organ of the sleeping Luigi, she cries out in surprise at the size of his penis; and when Mary gives the gay magazine to Felipe, his response on seeing the nude male models is "vaya pollas" (what dicks). This motif continues as the maid then shows the photographs of the *Adonis* magazine to the aged and senile Doña Carmen, telling her, "Esto sí que levanta un muerto" (This would raise someone from the dead), and the latter's reaction is, "Ay, gloria bendita" (Oh, heavenly bliss). When Mary curses Felipe for turning her in after she stole Aunt Victoria's ring, many of the maledictions are directed at his penis and have homosexual or bisexual connotations.

This fixation with the penis also appears in a sequence with mirror shots. As Felipe stands in front of his wardrobe mirror, a long shot of his reflected image fades to that of his Uncle Ramón in his bathing suit; Felipe mimics the same pose, placing his hands on his hips. A medium shot of Felipe follows, as he looks down, presumably comparing his own "package" with that of his uncle, and he then directs his gaze toward the mirror image again. The juxtaposition of mirror images relates Felipe with his bisexual uncle and the young boy's gaze further underscores the phallic obsession in the narrative. Armiñán eschews the first-person narrator's thoughts that he would not mind if Uncle Ramón tried to corrupt him or pervert him (69, 193) or the dialogue in which the uncle implies that sexual relations with men is not that bad (236), thus treating the development of the boy's homosexuality in a more metaphorical fashion.

Aunt Victoria also appears in a mirror reflection. The tripartite mirror on the dresser in her bedroom only reflects her image in the right hand panel, however, connoting and foreshadowing a sense of incompleteness or lacking. She calls her secretary Luigi into the bedroom, and he approaches dressed in a pajama bottom and bare torso. She does not have sex with the handsome man, however, and tells him to sleep on the sofa. This constitutes a lacking that culminates the following day when Victoria discovers not only that Luigi is missing, but that he has run off in a homosexual relationship with a local fish seller (another motif added to the film adaptation).

Felipe's reflected image again appears in a scene that foreshadows the denouement. When Aunt Victoria plays the piano late at night, Felipe furtively enters the room. When Victoria discovers him, Felipe and his mirror image appear just before his aunt shows him her expensive ring. The double image connotes possible duplicity or hypocrisy on the young boy's part. After the ring is stolen, Felipe discovers the thief, but Armiñán changes the discovery scene considerably. Whereas in the novel, the boy sees the ring on Mary's finger when the sexually excited maid reaches for Uncle Ramón's crotch during Aunt Victoria's poetry recital (213), in the film adaptation, Mary dances naked for Felipe under the starlight, and a close-up of her hand shows that she is wearing it. This transformation undoubtedly reflects not only the attitude in Spain in the 1990s toward nudity in general, but toward (female) nudity on the screen: it helps sell tickets. Although their companionship has been one of the central elements of the narrative, Felipe tells his grandfather of Mary's crime, and her violent reaction toward him seems based on his betrayal (his duplicity toward her) more than anything else, and she calls him a "squealer." (Uncle Ricardo later reiterates this accusation when he justifies Ramón's departure, telling Felipe that he left because he did not want to sleep under the same room as a squealer.) Felipe betrayed his friend, but remained true to his family and social class.

Mendicutti has commented that "Armiñán changed things [in the screen version], since my novel is narrated in the first person and is based more on sensations than on actions" (Apaolaza 85). The Uncle Ricardo character has much more predominance in the film version of the narrative, undoubtedly due to the fact that the role is played by veteran film star Francisco Rabal, who has worked so closely with Armiñán over the years. (Rabal's star factor functions here in fleshing out the character in a similar way to his role as Ricardo Sorbedo in Mario Camus's version of *La colmena*.) The ending of the film contrasts starkly with that of the original narrative in both action and tone. Based on the mention in the original novel of Uncle Ricardo's visits to the beach (186), Armiñán invents an entire episode for this character in which, together with Victoria and Felipe, he sets out to sea on a treasure-seeking adventure. This filmic "happy ending" contrasts with the subdued, melancholic ending of the novel in which Felipe, at his bedroom window, talks to the crippled dove of the title (which is earlier identified as homosexual), offering the bird solace when it feels lonely. However, the bird flies off, and the narrator feels that his pedigree is insulted, his own homosexuality is underscored, and his loneliness is accentuated. The spacial contrast between the two scenes—the vast exterior space of the open sea versus the interior of the bedroom—underscores the contrasting tones in the two endings. Did the director succumb to the idea that happy endings sell more tickets?

Based on David Harvey's comments on the "opening given in postmodernism to understanding differences and otherness, as well as the liberatory potential it offers for a whole host of new social movements (women, gays, blacks, ecologists, regional autonomists, etc.)" (48), Molina-Gavilán believes that Mendicutti's novel El palomo cojo gives voice to the marginal on two of these counts—homosexuality and regionalism (112). Within the context of contemporary Spanish cinema, however, this "voice" is rather weak: films by Imanol Uribe (La muerte de Mikel [The Death of Mikel]) or Pedro Almodóvar (¿Qué he hecho yo para merecer esto? [What Have I done to Deserve This?], La ley del deseo [The Law of Desire],etc.) deal much more directly with homoeroticism. In addition to the microregionalism manifested in Catalan and Basque cinema, Andalusian regionalism appears more strongly in Roberto Fandiño's screen version of Manuel Barrios's novel, La espuela, (The Spur) or in Víctor Barrera's film adaptation of Alfonso Grosso's Los invitados (The Guests). Part of the reason for this is that aside from Uncle Ricardo's excursions to the port and Mary's going out to the street or the market, almost the entire film is shot indoors. This corresponds to the claustrophobic point of view of the supposedly sickly protagonist. Linguistically, both Mary's vocabulary—often faithful to the original—and her Andalusian accent, together with Uncle Ricardo's constant repetition of "Ajú, qué lío" (Oy, what a mess—which becomes a comic motif, since he denies ever saying such a thing) constitute regional elements of the film narrative.

Eduardo Mendoza

In a poll of Spanish writers and critics in 1992, novelist Eduardo Mendoza (b. 1943) and his *La verdad sobre el caso Savolta (The Truth About the Savolta Case,* 1975) were voted the most important author and novel of the post-Franco era. Both this novel and his *El misterio de la cripta embrujada (The Mystery of the Bewitched Crypt)* have been adapted for the screen.

In 1980, Antonio Drove directed the cinematographic version of *La verdad sobre el caso Savolta,* for which he won the Premio Sant Jordi for best Spanish film of the year. This novel represents a type of narrative that is difficult to adapt successfully for the screen. It is a long novel (463 pages) with a richly textured plot constituted by shifts in narrative voice and a fragmentation of both space and time. The title of the novel indicates a search for the truth, and therefore places the narrative within the framework of detective fiction. The setting of the narrative is Barcelona and its environs from 1917 to 1919, and Amell is of the opinion that "in order to show the reader the socio-political problems in Catalonia in the first third of the century, Mendoza uses elements of the detective novel" ("Literatura" 195-96). Drove seems to have favored this type of "reading" of the original text, since he eliminated many of Mendoza's rich narrative strategies, and emphasized the social unrest of the period. Thus, the film begins with thugs beating a worker, and ends with an epilogue that states that 523 workers were assassinated between 1914 and 1921, with the final words of the film exclaiming that "the repression was directed principally against Catalonia."

This Spanish-French-Italian coproduction has a transnational cast that reflects the film's funding. Savolta (Omero Antonutti) is the wealthy head of an arms factory in Barcelona, and he is assisted both by long-time associates such as Nicolás Claudedeu (Ettore Manni) as well as the newcomer Paul-André Lepprince (Charles Denner), the Frenchman who is engaged to Savolta's daughter. Javier Miranda (Ovidi Montllor) provides the bridge between the world of the rich capitalists and the world of the workers, since he is Lepprince's friend and toady, and he is also the friend of Domingo Pajarito de Soto (José Luis López Vázquez), an anarchist newspaper writer.

The mise-en-scène underscores the importance of the bosses: symbols such as large cigars, Savolta's walking stick, Lepprince's new automobile, together with low-angle shots of the bosses (sometimes used excessively) connote their wealth and authority. Their hypocrisy toward the workers is evident from the early sequence: immediately after Savolta protects and supports a worker's widow, and Claudedeu exhorts the laborers to work together as one big family, the bosses meet behind closed doors where Savolta refers to the workers as animals, and his associate callously remarks, "Si muere alguno, que le vamos a hacer" (If one of them dies, what can you do?) It is clear that the thugs who beat or kill workers are paid by the bosses.

Drove uses silent news footage of strikes and newsreels captioned "Anarchy and Revolution in Russia" to underscore the sociopolitical element in a broader context and to provide the background for the strike that the workers call for in Soto's newspaper, La voz de la justicia (The Voice of Justice). Lepprince wants Soto to collaborate on a study of the company in order to identify problems and thereby help to avoid a violent confrontation with workers.

Sotos's exclamation that he knows more about Savolta constitutes part of the withheld information that is fundamental to mystery narratives. Director Drove reveals the information about halfway through the film when Soto confronts Savolta in a meeting in the director's office on New Year's Eve: not only is Savolta guilty of tax fraud and breach of contract with the French government, but he has clandestinely been shipping arms to the Germans. Savolta denies the charges and ejects Soto from his office. Following an earlier clandestine payment by Lepprince to the lawyer Cortabanys, the former's offer to intervene on Soto's behalf in exchange for a forty-eight hour delay in the strike can only be met with suspicion. The subsequent massacre of anarchists by a group of hoodlums with Soto being removed from the group is another thread of mystery. When Lepprince tells Savolta that the deed must have been carried out by the rival Socialists, the factory owner's negative response, "No podemos creernos nuestras propias mentiras" (We can't even believe in our own lies), belies his own culpability.

The New Year's Eve party constitutes the moment of Savolta's anagnorisis: realizing that he himself has become the victim of treachery, he symbolically removes Lepprince's mask in the study but is interrupted by the entrance of his daughter, who takes both men into the party. Their respective costumes are symbolic: Lepprince's harlequin garb, with its black-and-white squares, connotes his hypocrisy, whereas Savolta's Julius Caesar costume foreshadows his imminent assassination, which occurs on the stairway of his palace. Savolta's dying word, "Lepprince," has a different meaning for the viewer as compared to the other characters, since the latter have no reason to suspect the Frenchman's motivations. Another component of the mise-en-scène—the image of Lepprince in front of the huge mirror—further underscores the two-faced quality of his hypocrisy.

The meeting between the Frenchman and Savolta's other associate clarifies the trail of culpability: Claudedeu asks, "¿Lo has planeado todo tú?" (Did you plan it all?), and the close-up of Lepprince smoking a cigar connotes how the upstart newcomer has appropriated the symbols of power of his former boss. Although Claudedeu is horrified by the death of his friend, saying that he does not want to get involved, the Frenchman defends his actions, and retorts, "Tú y yo estamos atados al mismo carro" (You and I are in the same boat).

In a clarification of motivations that does not occur in the original narrative, Lepprince adds that their interests coincide with those of the bank. And certainly these are also the interests of the government, since Lepprince's earlier meeting with a banker contained a request that the government intervene against subversives, which in turn led to the persecution of laborers, as depicted in the brief montage sequence of fleeing workers being shot. Laborers, however, blame Soto as a traitor, since he was the only one to survive the massacre of anarchist workers. After his arrest for a "libelous" newspaper article, he is freed, but he is then accosted by thugs, only to be "saved" by Lepprince. Since the viewer is privy to Lepprince's machinations, but Soto is not, we see him falling into the trap. When the anarchist newspaperman admits that his incriminating documents are in the custody of Javier Miranda, the trap shuts a bit tighter. Lepprince easily manipulates his toady friend, making him believe that Soto has already been killed, when indeed it is Miranda's compliance in destroying the documents that prompts Soto's death: as soon as the documents are burned, Lepprince signals his henchmen to carry out the "accident" in which Soto, who was forced to drink a large quantity of alcohol, is run over by a car. The anarchist's end does not come ignominiously, however, as he dies without fear, knowing the truth and denouncing Lepprince as "un monstruo parido por el capitalismo" (a monster born of capitalism), again underscoring Drove's sociopolitical emphasis in the film text.

The death of his friend Soto causes Miranda to reveal his true character. Although he confronts Lepprince with pistol in hand, the criminal is able to talk his way out of being killed by offering Miranda a better job, which he accepts after he admits being weak, ambitious, and easily manipulated. The final sequence, which shows Miranda making payoffs to different men, is accompanied by the voice-over epilogue that notes the number of historical deaths of both labor leaders and workers during the period. It is quite evident that Miranda has sold his soul. Miranda's earlier behavior foreshadowed this betrayal of his friend Soto's ideals, however, since Miranda had already betrayed him on a personal level. In the screen adaptation, his relationship with Soto's wife Teresa is anything but the platonic one of the novel. The mirror in Teresa's bedroom that reflects their images not only connotes their hypocritical and adulterous behavior, but also associatively links Javier with Lepprince and therefore serves as a foreshadowing of their common criminal endeavors at the end of the film narrative.

Miranda's affair with Teresa also functions as a type of condensation, since Drove eliminates in his film adaptation the character of María Coral, the gypsy girl who was Lepprince's mistress and Miranda's wife. Drove also diminishes the role of

Max, Lepprince's bodyguard who turns out to be a German spy, as well as the entire chase section of the novel when Max runs off with María Coral. Marco (48) points out that Miranda's condition as cuckold, with his admired employer having his wife as a mistress, is an important element of the narrative, because it manifests that he is the passive subject of events that he does not understand. The elimination of this kernel is substantial, and it is one of many important changes from Mendoza's original narrative.

The first-person narrative of the novel is constituted by flashbacks from New York in 1928. Miranda has emigrated from Spain, and as he awaits a judicial decision regarding the disposition of Lepprince's insurance money, he notes, "These memories have sprouted from the trial and my testimony" (459). Although this is the most important narrative thread of the novel, Marco notes that two other fundamental narrative strategies in the novel are the documental information relating to the trial, and the third-person narrative (48). Drove eliminates this spatial-temporal framework, as well as the interwoven narrative voices. The final zoom-in to Javier Miranda certainly underscores his importance throughout the film as a protagonist, but does not manifest the same level of narrative importance as in the novel.

Some narrative techniques and kernels that create a sense of mystery in the original work are not part of the screen adaptation. Self-referential comments and foreshadowings, together with a limited or partial divulging of information (in the character of Nemesio Cabra Gómez) are eliminated, thus causing a shift in narrative strategies between novel and film. In the novel, many of the threads of the mystery are left dangling until near the end of the narration, when Commissioner Vázquez puts the pieces of the puzzle together. However, not all the pieces are there: Miranda's discovery of Lepprince's death is accompanied by a rhetorical question (430) that does nothing to dissolve the mystery surrounding it. As Marco (49) notes, the story is incomplete, broken, and that is its essence; in this consummate example of Spanish postmodern fiction, the title rings of irony, because the complete truth is never—can never be—known. Mendoza's gripping narrative loses much interest in the film version.

The film also contains bothersome elements such as the multiple dissolves during the cemetery sequence and strange extradiegetic sound effects—boinging, whirring noises—ostensibly used to underscore certain dramatic moments. There are times when the film is too controlled (after the group of workers accuses the bosses of being assassins, their growing crescendo of voices is just too cold), and the montage of fleeing workers being gunned down is somehow not convincing. Even some of the most consummate actors of the Spanish screen provide less than stellar performances on this occasion; Antonutti seems too controlled, and López Vázquez—whose presence probably justifies the expanded role of Soto in the narrative—not controlled enough. Quesada notes that many difficulties arose during the production of *La verdad sobre el caso Savolta*, including a two-month hiatus in filming during which there were heated negotiations concerning its resumption, and the intervention of labor unions in three countries (the film was a Spanish-French-Italian coproduction); he concludes that the film was "obviously damaged by these confrontations" (459). Nevertheless, Drove's emphasis on the sociopolitical element of the original narrative is in keeping with many works in contemporary Spanish cinema. In addition, novelist Mendoza has expressed a positive evaluation of Drove's screen adaptation: "I like it to the extent that I believe it differs from the situations and even the characters in the novel, and on the other hand, maintains that same spirit which corresponds to a similarity of intention as well as the same attitude toward Spanish reality of that moment" (Mendoza, May 9, 1994).

La cripta (*The Crypt*, 1981), by director Cayetano del Real, is the adaptation of Mendoza's *El misterio de la cripta embrujada* (*The Mystery of the Bewitched Crypt*, 1979). The title of the original narrative sets forth aesthetic expectations based on generic conventions. Nevertheless, humor replaces suspense as the main component of the narrative as Mendoza subverts the generic conventions of the detective story. The author carries out this process of subversion on many 1 evels—language, characterization, structure, and story; the film version, although humorous at times, does not capture the subtlety of the original narrative, which Colmeiro calls "totally parodic" (412).

In the original narrative, there is scatological humor, sexual humor, and humor that serves as social satire. Humor often comes from the element of surprise or coincidence, deformation, inversion of the "normal." The offer of freedom to an insane criminal if he can solve the mystery of a missing girl represents the subversion of the traditional detective story.

Humor in the film, both visual and linguistic, has similar functions. However, one verbal exchange between Commissioner Flores and the unnamed protagonist (José Sacristán) is accompanied by Sacristán's reaction of a vaudeville straight-man that underscores the humor's relative flatness in the film version. Nevertheless, audiences tend to laugh throughout the film, with low humor, such as in repeated billingsgate, eliciting the most reaction. Numerous sight gags—the protagonist secretly drugs and then interrogates the school gardener—and Sacristán's rendition of the protagonist's numerous changes in identity during a telephone conversation in order to obtain information also elicit laughs.

The sexual humor in the novel becomes sexual consummation in the film, as Mercedes Negrer, for whom the novel's protagonist has strong feelings—ends up in bed with him on screen. Ironically, the *destape* that Mendoza parodies (55, 126) materializes on screen. The *esperpento* element of the original also disappears: the grotesque Cándida becomes the beautiful Nati, the protagonist's wife.[1]

In a more fundamental change, Cándida's Swedish customer becomes an Irish drug addict who forcefully enters Nati's apartment and proceeds to destroy it—as the protagonist helplessly watches—in search of heroin, and succumbs for lack of a timely fix. Although in both narratives the police come to the apartment, in the film they are clearly in pursuit of the

---

[1]The *esperpento* is a genre invented by Ramón del Valle-Inclán and represents the systematic distortion of characters and reality in order to make them seem grotesque, absurd, and ridiculous.

Irish drug addict/dealer and not the protagonist, which in the novel manifests the theme of the "pursuer pursued," an ironic inversion of the normal role of the detective that is lamentably absent from the screen version.

In the original narrative, humor appears on virtually every page and is often based on plays on words; as to be expected in the transformation from the language of the novel to the language of cinema, these constant word plays virtually disappear from the cinematographic version.

The presentation of misinformation causing plot twists occurs in both narratives as Mercedes Negrer tells the details of her role in the disappearance of Isabel Peraplana six years before: she stabbed and killed the man who was abducting her school friend. Director del Real transposes our discovery of this misinformation from the protagonist's bedtime ruminations (101) to an emotional after-dinner scene in which the sane/insane theme surfaces. The film transposes Mercedes's second (truthful) version of past events into a flashback by means of conjunctive fade-outs. When he asks Mercedes to show how she held the knife to kill him, he deduces that she could not have committed the murder—an example that parallels several deductions or astute decisions in the novel. These deductions and astute decisions in both narratives serve to tip the balance in the sane/insane equation, and underscore the protagonist's sanity. In the film, the ambiguity of his mental state surfaces in the opening sequence when Commissioner Flores's comments, "Loco, loco no se puede decir" (Crazy, you can't really say he's crazy). Nevertheless, when the protagonist appears and is introduced to the nuns, his first comment is a ridiculous one, "¿Quieren que les cante una copla?" (Do you want me to sing you a tune?), thus producing a quixotic-like tension in the narrative. The same is true of his criminality: when Dr. Sugrañes says he is a violent criminal, the protagonist exclaims, "Eso era antes. Ahora soy un hombre nuevo" (That was before. Now I am a new man). The protagonist is determined to prove his sanity, and in a close-up of him making a telephone call to the commissioner, he exclaims, "Voy a demostrar que no estoy tan loco y que no hace falta encerrarme en ningún manicomio" (I am going to demonstrate that I am not so crazy and that it is not necessary to lock me up in any insane asylum).

Del Real makes significant changes in the end of the narrative. In the novel, the protagonist solves the mystery, and explains, in true detective style, the involvement of Peraplana in a number of criminal dealings. Commissioner Flores, who represents the powers that be, stifles the protagonist by enumerating the "crimes" he committed during his investigation, and alludes to the harm that would be done to Mercedes if the case were pursued any further (174-76). His return to the asylum causes an initial sense of unfairness that is mitigated only by the protagonist's seeming resignation and his hope of having another opportunity to prove his sanity. In the film, there is an important transformation in the narrative with what initially seems a clever detective story plot twist based on the "lie becomes truth" motif: Mercedes accompanies the protagonist into the school, but is separated from him in the passageways leading to the crypt. The protagonist finds Peraplana, and just as the criminal is about to kill the protagonist, Mercedes stabs him in the back and kills him, thus transforming her earlier fabrication into fact. In a similar vein to the novel, the protagonist defends Mercedes, telling Commissioner Flores that she did not kill Peraplana. As Flores accompanies the protagonist to the asylum, the commissioner tells him in the police car, "No te inquietes. Es lo mejor que puedo hacer por ti" (Don't get upset. It's the best I can do for you). This comment gives the police representative an aura of goodness and justice, since he is looking out for the protagonist's best interests. His comment to Mercedes that she convince Isabel to tell everything she knows to a judge, and that she stay in contact with him, underscores the connotations of the comment to the protagonist, since it implies a carrying out of justice within the legal system.

These plot changes seriously damage the fidelity to the spirit of the original narrative. The "solution" of the case in the novel is, after all, a travesty of justice: the interests of the "powers that be"—including, of course, the rich and powerful (represented by Peraplana)—are protected at the expense of powerless (the protagonist). The resolution of the crime in the traditional detective novel implies a (temporary) restoration of order to society based on the triumph of good over evil, but this is not the case in the novel. *El misterio de la cripta embrujada* is, then, an "anti-detective novel" in which "the solution, although still present, is ambiguous and partially unfulfilling" (Tani 24). Spanos calls the "anti-detective novel" "the paradigmatic archetype of the post-modernist literary imagination . . . the formal purpose of which is to evoke the impulse to 'detect' and/or to psychoanalyze in order to violently frustrate it by refusing to solve the crime" (154). According to McHale, "the dominant of postmodernist fiction is *ontological*," and clearly this is the case in this novel, with its central insane/sane theme, and the constant change in identity on the part of the protagonist.

As to be expected, the adaptation for the screen implies a fundamental change in point of view: the loss of first-person narrative does not allow us to enter into the protagonist's inner mind. The final scene of the film, however, does utilize a voice-over to this end, but this is the only time that it is used. His thoughts, a synthesis of the final pages of the novel, express his resignation upon returning to the asylum and hope for the future: "Después de todo no me había ido tan mal . . . [y] habría otras oportunidades de demostrar mi cordura y que, si no las había, yo sabría buscármelas" (After all, it hadn't gone so badly for me . . . [and] there would be other opportunities to demonstrate my sanity, and if there weren't any, I would figure out how to create them). Director Del Real transforms the wish into action, as the protagonist turns and runs from the asylum door, with the film ending in a freeze frame. The open ending may serve to mitigate the initial feeling of unfairness, as it implies hope for the future. It also implies the possiblity of a sequel. This was the case with the novel, which Eduardo Mendoza realized in his publication in 1982 of *El laberinto de las aceitunas* (*The Labyrinth of the Olives*). Given the rather mediocre quality of the film version, no such sequel is in the offing.

Antonio Muñoz Molina

Antonio Muñoz Molina (b. 1956) is one of Spain's most important young novelists, having won the National Prize for Literature on two occasions: in 1987 for *Invierno en Lisboa* (*Winter in Lisbon*), and in 1991 for *El jinete polaco* (*The Polish Horseman*). While enjoying the success of his novel *Ardor guerrero* (*Fighting Fever*) in 1995, Muñoz Molina was surprised to have been elected to the Royal Spanish Academy, an honor usually reserved for more venerable writers. Director José Antonio Zorrilla adapted *Invierno en Lisboa* for the screen in 1990, with Dizzy Gillespie writing the score for the film as well as playing the role of the American jazz musician Billy Swann. Unfortunately, the film was shown only briefly in Spain to negative reviews, has never come out on video, and the Filmoteca Nacional in Madrid does not have a copy of the film (as Spanish law requires). Muñoz Molina was quite displeased by the film version of the text, especially with scenes of sadomasochism that he believed had nothing to do with the spirit of his narrative (Muñoz Molina n.p.).

The other Muñoz Molina novel transformed for the screen is Pilar Miró's film version of *Beltenebros* (*Beltenebros, Prince of Shadows*, 1990), which won the Silver Bear award at the Berlin Film Festival in 1991.[1] *Beltenebros* has Terence Stamp and Patsy Kensit as protagonists and was originally filmed in English.[2] Consequently, *Beltenebros* represents an attempt in

---

[1]*Beltenebros* is the name adopted by Don Quixote when he does penance in the mountains. The name originally was taken by the protagonist of the chivalric romance, *Amadís de Gaula*, and etymologically means "beautiful darkness." Novelist Muñoz Molina states that he chose this for the title of his novel simply because he liked the name (Muñoz Molina n.p.), and it is certainly appropriate for a narrative in the noir genre. In the novel, Muñoz Molina uses the name to refer to the villain Ugarte (223, 238). The subtitle of the English version, "Prince of Shadows," captures both the literal aspect of the character—Ugarte stays away from lights, and his torture victims never see his face—as well as the metaphorical aspect of this villain.

[2]I have seen only the dubbed Spanish version of the *Beltenebros*.

recent Spanish cinema to break through national boundaries and achieve better international recognition, entering what Kinder calls the cinematographic macroregionalism (14, 412 ff). *Beltenebros* is a movie in the tradition of film noir, not only in terms of its hard-boiled plot, but in its style, as the chiaroscuro lighting, camera angles, and setting that Miró uses all bring to mind some of the film classics of the 1940s and early 1950's. Indeed, Miró notes that *The Third Man* (1949) was a specific source of inspiration for *Beltenebros* (Pérez Millán 256).

The film opens with a tracking shot that follows Darman (Stamp) and Rebeca (Kensit) down the steps of the Atocha train station in Madrid. Rebeca nervously looks around and occasionally gazes at her immutable companion, and she expresses her fear of being followed before they board the train to Lisbon. Smith (39) calls this sequence "the first of a number of bravura Steadycam pieces which reveal an undeniable command of cinematic technique." Once on board, Rebeca's tears and the close-up of Darman's hand taking out his pistol add to the climate of mystery and suspense before a close-up of Darman and the accompanying voice-over: "Vine a Madrid a matar para un hombre que no había visto nunca. Todo lo que ocurrió después fue como el doloroso y agitado despertar de una conciencia y un cuerpo que durante años habían estado heridos, olvidados, o simplemente muertos" (I came to Madrid to kill a man I had never seen. Everything that occurred afterwards was like the painful and agitated awakening of a conscience and a body that for years had been wounded, forgotten, or simply dead). Although the first sentence of this voice-over closely corresponds to the opening words of the novel, the second sentence does not, and it synthesizes important thematic elements of the film version: the awakening implies a regaining of consciousness regarding earlier events that involve both the body (sexual desire) and the spirit (an awareness of guilt).

A dissolve at the end of this voice-over leads to the first flashback—a jump both in time and in place, as the caption identifies Scarborough, U.K., 1962, as the locus of the long shots of a seaside community. A gentleman enters Darman's bookstore to give him a coded message instructing him to travel to Poland.

Transnational casting: Terence Stamp in Pilar Miró's *Beltenebros*.
Courtesy Iberoamericana Films.

This is a change from Italy in the original narrative; the snowy urban landscapes of Warsaw and Cracow, with old trolley cars and horse-drawn carts do better justice to the tone of the film narrative than would have been possible to recreate in Florence. Indeed, Paul Julian Smith (39) goes so far as to say that "the true star of the film is the art design. Scarborough and Warsaw can rarely have been shot in such delicate shades of grey, and the mean streets of Madrid, dark and glistening, are interspersed with atmospheric locations which display the capital's architecture at its sombre best."

Darman's meeting with a young agent, Luque (Jorge de Juan) in his hotel clarifies the words of Darman's earlier voice-over, and also establishes the basic temporal structure of the narrative: Darman is to travel to Madrid to assassinate a traitor in the organization, just as he did back then ("como entonces"; the repetition of this phrase underscores the present/past dichotomy in the narrative). The fact that Darman has to correct Luque regarding his past exploits ("Nunca he matado a nadie con mis propias manos" [I never killed anybody with my bare hands]), indicates that Darman's reputation is mythic, but the aging captain insists that he is not the man he once was, and refuses to accept the mission. After Luque leaves, the close-up of Darman staring out his hotel window signals another flashback to a memory of how he did indeed kill in the past: he shoots a man three times as we hear a woman's voice off screen shout in anguish, "Es inocente. Mátame a mí, a mí, mátame a mí" (He's innocent. Kill me, me, kill me). This flashback constitutes a typical narrative strategy of detective fiction, providing information whose meaning is unclear until later in the narrative.

Bernal (Alexander Bardini), a leader in the organization, adds pieces to the narrative puzzle as he further explains the mission while showing slides of the traitor, Andrade. The fact that everyone who comes in contact with Andrade (Simón Andreu) ends up killed or apprehended by the police makes the organization suspicious, but two recent events seem to confirm his guilt: he miraculously escaped from a police van, and a large sum of money has appeared in his bank account. Bernal's instructions are adamant: "Debe morir sin más" (He should just be killed), and his comparison of Andrade to the earlier traitor, Walter, underscores his resoluteness. But is Andrade guilty? The anguished claim of innocence for the earlier victim raises the specter of doubt.

The locus of Darman's arrival in Madrid is the Atocha train station, and his actions connote the tacit presence of his resistance organization, since they have prepared for his mission: he furtively retrieves the key and goes to a locker, where he obtains his written instructions and the pistol with which he can carry out his assignment. The close-up of him hiding the key in his shoe reflects Darman's professional caution and connotes the probable significance of this action on later events, which is realized when he uses the hidden key to extricate himself.   When he arrives at the abandoned warehouse where he is to find Andrade, the close-up of the old novels by Rebeca Osorio that he discovers next to the lamp trigger a flashback (signalled by a dissolve) to Madrid, 1946. At a bar across the street from a movie theater, the young Darman has a copy of an Osorio novel, which functions as the visual bridge between the two time periods.

The meeting between Rebeca Osorio (Geraldine James) and Darman in the movie theater manifests the intertextuality that is so prominent in this film narrative. In this instance, the dialogue of the film on screen, *They Died with Their Boots On*, mirrors—or foreshadows—the action of the main characters, as Miró selected the courtship scene from Raoul Walsh's film in which Custer (Errol Flynn) tells Miss Bacon (Olivia de Havilland) that he would like to spend every day of his life with her. Rebeca Osorio, however, is married to Walter (John McHenry) who is the projectionist at the movie theater, and the man Darman believes to be the traitor to the organization. Walter himself expresses his belief that there is a traitor in the group, but when he asks Darman if the organization has lost confidence in him, the captain elusively responds that he is leaving in two days, thus heightening the suspense.

The other member of the clandestine organization who inhabits the movie theater is Valdivia (José Luis Gómez), an old companion of Darman who is recuperating from a bullet wound in the arm. The narrative constructs an ambiguous web around Walter's possible guilt. Valdivia's rhetorical question about how Walter was able to obtain penicillin casts suspicion on the projectionist, but when Darman presses him about details, saying that he wants to be certain, Valdivia confesses, "Sólo lo conozco de oídas" (I only know him through hearsay). Nevertheless, for Valdivia, the proof is his own wound, which was—he says—the result of a trap that Walter set for him. Rebeca later tells Darman that Walter is loyal to the cause, and she warns, "No te equivoques. Lo lamentarás toda la vida" (Don't make a mistake. You'll regret it all your life). The intertextual reference to another film whose soundtrack is heard in the background—talk of the death penalty in Frank Lloyd's *Mutiny on the Bounty*—foreshadows Walter's impending execution. Rebeca stops typing when she hears her door locked from the outside, and she rushes to the door to desperately shout "Darman, Darman . . . mátame a mí" (kill me), thus completing the meaning of the earlier flashback.

Darman's interest in Rebeca is evident from the image of her novels, which functions as a bridge between present and past. The books also function as a bridge between the two characters, as she brings a pile of reading material to Darman's bedroom, and a two-shot of Darman facing Rebeca, both in profile, connotes that there is more than the simple curiosity that the captain has expressed in her work. The visual image of the novel—and the act of writing it—again functions as a bridge in a later flashback: in Rebeca's apartment in 1962, Darman picks up a copy of a novel, and a zoom-in to the back of his head is accompanied by the sound of typing off screen, which precedes the dissolve as the sound bridge to the past. The long shot of Darman standing over Rebeca as she types again connotes the interest that the captain has in her. However, Rebeca's lovemaking with Valdivia, as Darman watches from the shadows in the hallway, complicates the relationship between these characters. Even with the elimination of Walter, a triangle remains. And the relationship becomes even more complicated through the theme of the double, which is made more interesting here because of the two-layered time framework.

In a sequence corresponding to 1962, Darman goes to the Boîte Tabú and discovers that the woman he saw in a warehouse while looking for Andrade is a stripper—Miró includes a sequence that pays homage to Rita Hayworth in Charles Vidor's *Gilda*—and she is called Rebeca Osorio. Vernon notes that while Rebeca thus "accrues to her role the attributes of the classic noir femme fatal, thus reinforcing her aura of unknowability, treacherousness, and heightened desirability," the intertextual reference to the Vidor film combines with both other elements of the narrative (the falsification of names and nationalities by the members of the resistance) and extra-diegetic elements (the transnational casting) in order to "elide the meaningfulness of ethnic or national identities"; in the end, however, Rebeca's assuming of Hayworth's star power appears "not to challenge conventional gender positioning but to proclaim the interchangeability of women, the woman as icon, as floating signifier but one that resists the imposition of meaning" ("Reading Hollywood" 51, 53-54).

Darman wryly notes that Rebeca Osorio was never a real name, and the filmic images underscore the theme of the double as we see the shot of the blonde woman in the dressing mirror when she confesses that Rebeca is not her real name. (Darman likewise often appears in mirrors—in the Atocha train station, at the Hotel Nacional—which reflect his divided self.) The doubling of Rebeca Osorio occurs within the framework of the triangle in the present, as well. As Darman enters the Boîte Tabú, a long shot of Police Commissioner Ugarte surrounded by the two officers who arrested Rebeca, later followed by an intercut shot of Ugarte during the striptease act, underscores the police commissioner's interest in Rebeca. Indeed, the commissioner summons her to his office, where he has her put on a tight gray dress, and as his heavy breathing increases throughout the scene, she sits on his lap as he fondles her. The close-up of her agonized face with her head hung in distress contrasts sharply with his cry of sexual ecstacy. After Rebeca later drugs Darman so that she can give Andrade the passport and money for his escape, the captain is ready to give up on this case, and he phones a call girl service from his hotel and asks

A doubling of identities: Terence Stamp and Patsy Kensit in Pilar Miró's *Beltenebros. Courtesy Iberoamericana Films.*

specifically for Rebeca. Is this request a sort of expiation of his sins from twenty years ago? The young Darman's mistake was two-fold: killing an innocent man, and losing the woman that he loved.

When Rebeca earlier gave the money and passport to Andrade so that he could escape, Ugarte's comment to his police officer, "Ahora me interesa más otro hombre. Darman. Si no está, no hemos hecho un buen trabajo" (Another man interests me more now. Darman. If he isn't there, we haven't done a good job), confirms the Machiavellian character of the police commissioner, who has made all the right moves to set the trap to catch his archenemy, thus confirming Bernal's earlier comment that Ugarte manipulates everything. The symbolism of the chessboard in Ugarte's office as he interviews Rebeca now becomes clear: in this match of intellect between the two rivals, Ugarte believes that he is nearing a checkmate.

The montage series of flashbacks that Darman has in the hotel bathtub subtly connotes the culpability of Valdivia, and it also foreshadows the ending of the film narrative. The series opens with Rebeca Osorio telling Darman that the traitor is not Walter, and it ends with a zoom-in to a photograph that Bernal shows Darman of Valdivia in his uniform, with his fist held high in salute, as Bernal explains that Valdivia was tortured so badly that he had to be tied to a chair when placed before the firing squad. Pérez Millán (253) notes that this photo was inspired by the iconography of Robert Capa, who often included a female soldier in his photos; the woman here is director Pilar Miró (in the lower right). This image is accompanied by a voice-over by Rebeca Osorio shouting, "Darman, Darman, mátame a mí" (kill me). This voice-over evokes the scene in which Darman kills Walter, and since Rebeca's explanation of her husband's innocence connotes Valdivia's guilt, the voice-over also foreshadows the shooting at the end of the narrative.

The film adaptation of the novel inevitably weakens the final manifestation of the theme of the double: that Valdivia and Ugarte are the same man. One of the surprises that is withheld until the end of the novel is this double, but the concrete physical presence of the same actor, José Luis Gómez, with the same important attribute—thick glasses—diminishes the surprise element in the film narrative. Nevertheless, these glasses take on a symbolic importance in the film narrative. When Darman first discusses Walter with Valdivia, the reasons that he gives as to why one becomes a traitor—fatigue, isolation, and the disappearance of ideals—ring with irony when taken in syntagmatic relation with his own later betrayal; he takes off his glasses—a self-incriminating gesture of fatigue—and Darman takes them, but ironically they do not help him to see the truth. Of course, Ugarte wears the same thick glasses, and he complains throughout that light bothers his eyes, thus the diminished lighting during his interrogation of Rebeca, or the fact that his torture victims never see him.

The seemingly illogical nature of events at the ending of the film can only be explained as occurring in Darman's imagination. (In the novel, there are references to "hallucinations" and "dreams" [202], and Darman's perhaps symbolic passage through the tunnel to the Universal Cinema includes a blow to his head that makes him feel he was swallowed by "the deepness of a well" [211].) Pérez Millán speaks of different "levels of reality" in the film, including these final sequences in which Darman "abandons the purely physical level" (253-54). When Rebeca arrives at Darman's hotel room as a call girl, her attitude of initial disdain seems to switch to affection too precipitously to be justifiable. Why the transformation from Rebeca as a victim (Darman hits her and she shouts, "No, no" and cries as he forces her to have sex) to the affectionate Rebeca kissing Darman's naked torso after a simple fade-out? Also, when Darman flees the police, he goes to the roof of the Hotel Nacional, where he not only encounters Andrade, but where Luque suddenly appears from nowhere and kills Andrade, but not before the latter confirms that the real traitor is the commissioner. The extreme low-angle shots of Andrade and Darman lend a tone of unreality to the scene. Pillado-Miller (26, 28) points out that the use of analepsis throughout *Beltenebros* produces a vertical development in the narration by putting an emphasis on the memories, desires, or dreams and other projections that give importance to the past, and that the camera work, with the abundance of high- and low-angle shots, underscores this vertical composition.

The climactic confrontation between Darman and Ugarte/Valdivia occurs in the abandoned Universal movie theater; the incongruous projection of *They Died with Their Boots On* can only correspond to Darman's subconscious, and it takes on symbolic importance at the end of the film narrative. Ugarte/Valdivia stands in front of the screen, and is dwarfed by the figures of Custer and his wife projected behind him. In almost every case of these giant figures appearing in a two-shot, Ugarte stands in front of the figure of Custer, thus identifying the two male characters with each other. Ugarte's admonition to Darman that arrogance blinds him is extremely ironic, since Ugarte himself is a victim of that sin, and he further manifests it in his justification for his treason: "Me cambié de bando para borrar el recuerdo de aquella vida de paria que me obligasteis a llevar mientras tú y los tuyos controlabais el partido desde vuestra cómoda Europa. Ahora soy yo quien controla cada uno de vuestros pasos" (I changed sides in order to erase the memory of that life of a pariah that you obliged me to live while you and the others controlled the party from your comfortable Europe. Now I am the one who controls every one of your steps). The intertextual reference to *They Died with Their Boots On* underscores the pride-before-the-fall theme in the larger than life action occurring on screen in back of Valdivia/Ugarte: in the final departure scene, Elizabeth Bacon Custer faints, as if foreseeing her husband's death. At that moment, a fire in the projector causes Valdivia/Ugarte to be blinded by the bright light, and a slight shift in camera angle together with Valdivia/Ugarte crouching somewhat under the blinding light echoes Mrs. Custer's faint. Just as Custer was an ambiguous hero, so is Valdivia. He tells Darman that he invented a glorious death for himself, a death that Darman admits caused him grief because he thought that Valdivia was "the best." The commissioner's response, "Qué héroe, Darman. Lamento haberte defraudado" (What a hero, Darman. I'm sorry to have disappointed you) is again ironic. Darman is the real hero of this narrative, as he is able to overpower one of the policemen and shoot Valdivia/Ugarte, which he must do three separate times. That is, Darman shoots at three "different" individuals located at three different spots in the movie theater, but who are all transformed into Ugarte through the object that metonymically symbolizes him: his thick glasses. This symbolically follows the triadic narrative pattern that is found in folk narratives involving heroes, and also can be associated with the Spanish verb *rematar* (to finish off), which etymologically means "to kill again." And when Darman shoots Valdivia/Ugarte, who stands in front of the movie screen, he uses three shots, thus echoing the three shots that he used to kill Walter. Significantly, the third is to his groin, and he howls like a wounded animal: the real rivalry between Valdivia and Darman was sexual, and here Darman takes vengeance for having lost Rebeca Osorio to him. (This represents a departure from the novel, where Ugarte falls through the railing on the theater balcony and plummets to his death; Miró's reading of the novel emphasizes the hero's guilt and expiation by transforming Darman's passivity in Ugarte's comeuppance to a level of activity that is overblown with the

In the shadows of noir: José Luis Gómez in Pilar Miró's *Beltenebros*.
Courtesy Iberoamericana Films.

triple shooting.) After the shootout, director Miró chooses a daring tracking shot in which the camera (not identifying witha point of view shot) rushes through the burning movie theater to focus on Ugarte's thick glasses that have fallen onto the steps. This visual metonymy for the Valdivia/Ugarte character symbolizes precisely his inablity to see.

One of the most visually striking shots of the entire film occurs during the early sequence in Poland. Bernardo complains to Darman of his life as an exile; his daughter is marrying, and the groom, as well as the music, is from Poland. Although they are playing a polka in the background, when Darman enters the room, it unexpectedly changes to an Argentine tango, "El día que me quieras" ("The Day When You Will Love Me"). A blonde woman in red grabs Darman and leads him onto the dance floor, and the overhead shot of the couple whirling around against the background of the multipointed star design on the floor is of great visual beauty. Perhaps it can be justified thematically if taken syntagmatically with later narrative information, since the blonde, Polish dancer, Magda Wojcik, looks remarkably like the Rebeca (without a wig) played by Patsy Kensit. Although it does not seem to fit in with the rest of the film narrative, Pillado-Miller (30-31) notes that the relationship between the two women is based on two references in the novel to sexual desire (51-53, 159). Rebeca, however, does not take an active role in pursuing Darman as she does in the dance scene; indeed, he pays for her as a prostitute. This overhead shot of the tango does relate syntagmatically with other overhead shots in the film—of the stairway at the hotel, and the stairway in the movie theater in which victim and pursuer circle. The whirling movement of the tango underscores the dizziness of the labyrinth connoted by the overhead stairwell shots that are worthy of Hitchcock's Vertigo. The doubling of Rebeca Osorio is also linked to the repetition of the overhead shot of the tango, which occurs during a montage of flashbacks when Darman is sitting in the bathtub of the Hotel Nacional: the overhead shot precisely follows, and is therefore linked to the shot of Rebeca Osorio saying that Walter is not a traitor.

As Rebeca and Darman finally comfort each other on the train to Lisbon as they escape, she asks him what they will do now, and Darman responds, "Seguir viviendo" (Go on living). If the final shot of the film, with the camera mounted on the front of the locomotive as the train enters a tunnel, is intended to give meaning to this expression, then it seems overly facile (that is, overly Freudian). It may be an homage to Hitchcock; his *North by Northwest* also ends with a train entering a tunnel, which Hitchcock called "one of the most impudent shots I ever made" (Truffaut 106).

Pilar Miró's *Beltenebros* is a splendid film that is aesthically daring; this quality can be a double-edged sword, since Pérez Millán notes that the jump from reality to imagination is "somewhat confusing," and for the spectator it may not be "so evident" (254). It is a film that is best understood and appreciated after a second viewing. For Pérez Millán (260), *Beltenebros* is "an impressive reflection about discipline and its capacity for engendering monsters" as well as on "the very meaning of History and its possible interpretations at the function of very diverse interests." Novelist Muñoz Molina was very pleased with this cinematographic adapta- tion, saying that this is happily a case in which the author not only admires the film that has been made of his book without reservation, but that he recognized the original work in the film (Pérez Millán 250).

Raúl Núñez

Sinatra (1988) is a film by Francesc Betriu that is based on the novel by Raúl Núñez. This portrait of marginalized urban society (in this case, in Barcelona) has its roots both in comedy and in melodrama: Alfredo Landa, who plays Antonio Castro, a.k.a. Sinatra, is a vaudeville singer who is down on his luck. After his wife abandons him, he ends up at a sleazy boarding house where he has to work as the night doorman in order to pay his rent. He befriends Begonia (Maribel Verdú), a waif whose "baby" is just a toy doll. After Antonio reads an advertisement in the newspaper for a friendship club, he begins to correspond with other lost souls who write him letters, telling him their dreams. Although this leads to further liaisons, the most important one is with Isabel (Mercedes Sampietro), a prostitute who takes him to a five-star hotel. Although he awakens alone, Isabel's companionship strikes an important nerve in Antonio, since their night together has given him hope to overcome his loneliness. He seeks her out, only to discover that she has been murdered by her former pimp. The single shot that best conveys Antonio's life shows his reflection in a shattered mirror. All of the characters in the film are indeed "Strangers in the Night" (appropriately heard on the soundtrack).

Francisco Moreno (242-43) notes that Betriu's films often deal with marginal characters, but that his treatment of them is often cruel, somewhat intellectual, and with roots in the *esperpento*, whereas Núñez treats marginal characters with more understanding and a sense of solidarity; for Moreno, the film (with a collaborative script written by the author and the director) seems to be an inconsistent hybrid of these two different approaches.

Angel Palomino

José María Forqué filmed Angel Palomino's novel *Madrid, Costa Fleming* in 1976, three years after its publication. The title refers to what at that time was a new neighborhood in northern Madrid that had a reputation for being the home of affluent executives, passing foreigners, and callgirls. Quesada calls the novel's style "semi-journalistic, semi-cinematographic" based on "flashes" projected on the various social groups of that urban nucleus, and he notes that Forqué's rendition of the novel emphasizes—and even augments—the erotic and comic elements of the original to the detriment of its social criticism (378-79).

The geographic locale of the neighborhood provides the unifying element to the many narrative threads in the film. The women who work in real estate agencies are obliged to do whatever it takes to make a sale (Maruja's striptease, and Chony's boss telling her that she should be willing to go to bed with a prospective client). The morality of one of the owners of a flat is exposed as hypocrisy when he turns out to be a voyeur. The picaresque element is present in Florencio, who sells false contraceptive pills and three prostitutes become pregnant and have to return to their hometowns, as well as in the defective construction of a building whose collapse leads to a miscarriage of justice when a foreman and an architect are bribed to take the rap for the speculators who are really responsible for the crime.

As is typical of other films that had their debut shortly after Franco's death, there is a good deal of *destape*, manifesting both the new freedom in Spanish cinema as well as the desire to increase the commercial success of the film. Of note is that the director's daughter, Verónica Forqué, who later went on to play leading roles in both Spanish cinema (Almodóvar's *Kika*) and Spanish television, began her acting career in this movie.

Carlos Pérez Merinero

José María Blanco both directed and starred as Miguel in *Bueno y tierno como un ángel* (*Good and Soft as an Angel*, 1988), the adaptation of Carlos Pérez Merinero's *El ángel triste* (*The Sad Angel*, 1983). This screen adaptation contains several intertextual filmic references, since protagonist Miguel is a film fanatic and spends his life drinking beer and watching videos in his apartment. This domestic tranquility is shattered, however, by the quarrels between his next door neighbors, Marcela (Amparo Moreno) and Braulio (José María Cañete). The corpulent wife's browbeating of Braulio causes Miguel to comment that his neighbor lacks balls, and that he would kill her. His wife's sarcastic comment, "Te dominaría igual que a ese" (She would dominate you just like him), is an affront to Miguel's machismo, and it drives him to drastic action: when Braulio is absent, Miguel carries out his threat and kills his contentious neighbor. Miguel first seduces Marcela, pouring the olive oil that he has come to borrow on her corpulent breasts; Blanco combines the erotic element with black humor as he uses extreme close-ups of his buxom victim.

Now that Miguel is a criminal, he continues his illegal activities by blackmailing Braulio with tape recordings of the quarrelling, and then he arranges to rob the automobile dealership where Braulio works. Since Miguel's world has been a quixotic immersion into fiction—in his case, cinema—the robbery manifests a pattern seen throughout the movie of intertextual references to other films. When Miguel sings, "Money makes the world go around," and asks for "Money, money, money," and the cashier doesn't respond, he quizzically inquires, "¿Usted no ha visto *Cabaret*?" (Haven't you seen *Cabaret*?) The murder of Marcela is likewise followed by a brief intertextual reference to *Dracula*. Miguel soon learns, however, that "reality" is not always like film, and when he decides to shoot Braulio, he (Miguel) is the one who ends up being shot. This disconformity with Miguel's (filmic) expectations does have its positive side, however, since it allows him to meet Maribel (Montse Bayó), a nurse with whom he falls in love. Maribel is as unscrupulous as Miguel: his confession to her

Intertextual references: José María Blanco's *Bueno y tierno como un angel*, with José María Blanco and Amparo Moreno. *Courtesy José María Blanco.*

that he robbed a car dealer elicits the flip response, "A mí qué más me da de donde sacas tu dinero" (What do I care where you get your money). They now become a criminal twosome, in ironic contrast to the "Mickey" and "Minnie" nicknames that they have given each other. They travel to Mallorca for a big job, but Miguel first visits his wealthy mother and attempts to scam money from her. His mother's ingenuous opinion that Miguel is "good and soft as an angel" gives the film its title, but the ironic context of the phrase is set by the movie poster even before the filmgoer enters the theater: the angel has devilish horns drawn over it in graffiti style. Since this scam does not have much success, they rob a gas station and a bank, where Maribel is captured by the police. At her trial, Miguel attempts to rescue her. The slow motion that Blanco uses to film this attempted rescue was undoubtedly meant to lend it an air of suspense. Like some of the other techniques in the film—the numerous dissolves during the lovemaking scene at the water's edge, or the flips that Blanco uses as transitions through out—the slow motion does not quite hit its mark. Finally, Miguel's reality does not conform to his quixotic/cinematographic world: instead of a happy ending, the shootout results in the death of both Maribel and Miguel. Undoubtedly, director Blanco wanted his spectators to ponder that lesson.

Arturo Pérez-Reverte

Pedro Olea's film adaptation of *El maestro de esgrima (The Fencing Master,* 1992) is based on the novel by Arturo Pérez-Reverte (1988). The book became a best-seller and by its third edition (1993) it had already sold 41,000 copies. Pérez-Reverte is not only the best-selling novelist in Spain today—over one million copies of his novels have been sold—he is the only Spanish author to have a novel made into a film in English directed by a non-Spaniard: his *La tabla de Flandes (The Flanders Panel)* was adapted for the screen in 1994 by Jim McBride as *Uncovered.* Pérez-Reverte's *El maestro de esgrima* is a historical novel with the structure of a thriller, and the screen adaptation contains superb performances by Omero Antonutti and Assumpta Serna in the roles of the protagonists Don Jaime Astarloa and Doña Adela de Otero, which make this one of the best Spanish films from 1992.

Tumultuous nineteenth-century Spanish politics provides the background for the narrative. Set in Madrid in 1868 when General Prim led a coup d'état against the dissolute Queen Isabel II, the honor and ideals of the fencing master are set against the corruption and treachery of much of society. The political background appears in both the streets of Madrid and in the Spanish custom of *tertulias*—gatherings in cafés to discuss political events (similar to the literary *tertulias* that we see in Camus's *La colmena,* the film version of Camilo José Cela's novel). The journalist Agapito Cárceles (Miguel Angel Rellán) is the political adversary of the monarchists in the *tertulias,* as the former rails against the sexual scandals and political ineptitude of Queen Isabel II, and advocates the use of the guillotine in the coming revolution. The streets echo the journalist's sentiments, and calls of "Down with the monarchy" resound among the cavalry charges that disperse the Republicans.

Don Jaime's early declaration that love and fencing are "dos floretes que no se cruzan" (two foils that never cross) sets up the opposite to occur in a test of the aging bachelor's convictions. The prominent statue of Don Quixote in the fencing master's apartment underscores the quixotic nature of Jaime, who clings to a form of self-defense that the pistol has relegated to the past, and to a code of honor that seems to also make him an anachronism. In the words of Don Luis de Ayala, Marquis de los Alumbres (Joaquim de Almeida), Jaime Astarloa is "el único hombre honrado que conozco" (the only honorable man that I know, cf. 149). The constant visual and auditory references to clocks in the fencing master's apartment provide an important dimension to the temporal theme: Don Jaime anachronistically lives in a world of values from a prior age, and as the mystery and suspense grow in the plot, the ticking seems to push us inexorably to the tragic ending.

A challenge to Jaime's values occurs when Adela asks to become his student so that she can learn a fencing thrust that Jaime has invented. The master refuses to accept her, because in Jaime's world, fencing is the reserve of men. Adela's wiles and persistence, however, are in her favor. When she asks to see Jaime's collection of arms, the camera pans his swords and daggers, and a close-up of a ring adorned with two crossed foils highlights the importance of this object as a bit of narrative information in the mystery that ensues, and serves as a foreshadowing of the denouement. Adela then selects a French foil and shows the master her impeccable position. Their short parry is, for Adela, an opportunity to show her fencing skills, and for Jaime, an examination that this mysterious woman passes in order to become Don Jaime's student. (Assumpta Serna and Omero Antonutti both took lessons and performed all of their own fencing in the film.) Wood ("El maestro" 121) believes that Jaime's unprecedented acceptance of Doña Adela as a pupil links her to the social rupture and transformation in society in 1868. After a later lesson, Adela asks to borrow the foiled ring in order to copy it, and the ring becomes an important identifying element later in the narrative. However, as Wood ("El maestro" 120) notes, of the many artifacts that function metonymically in the film, the foil is the key polysemic (professional, historical, and phallic) symbol of the narrative.

Jaime's inner emotional struggle regarding his pupil is evident from their first lesson at Adela's house. He sees her dressing through a crack in the door, and a close-up shows that he averts his gaze, but then looks in her direction again. Jaime will not only have to struggle with himself, however, as he soon has a rival for Adela's affections in the person of his other fencing student, Don Luis, the aristocratic lady's man who has political ambitions for a seat in congress. His fencing skills are not up to the master's; at the end of his lesson, he complains to Jaime, "Me has dejado hecho un nazareno" (You've made me look like a Holy Week penitent). The juxtaposition of a sequence in which the marquis, twisting his moustache and noting that Jaime must be involved in an affair of the heart, with the next sequence in which Jaime shows Adela his thrust to the opponent's throat, serves to connote the triangle of sentiments that will develop.

Jaime's emotional involvement dramatically increases during their next fencing lesson: when his face comes together with hers, Adela "faints"; after she opens the neck of her dress a bit, and in a scene charged with subtle erotic tension, Jaime gently applies cologne to her neck and forehead with a handkerchief to revive her. The reflection of Jaime's image in the mirror of his fencing studio at this precise moment underscores his inner conflict of scrupulous principles and amorous sentiments. Jaime admits to having loved once in Paris, a long time ago, but his newfound passions are slow to awaken. The amorous triangle soon solidifies: although Luis expresses a desire to meet the mysterious woman with such commensurate fencing skills, it is Adela who first looks at and waves to the marquis at a lecture by an Italian fencing expert. Jaime's look of chagrin when he sees Adela leave the lecture with Luis represents the first in a series of emotional setbacks for the fencing master. When Jaime next calls upon Adela, her maid Lucía says that she is out of town with friends, but following another exterior scene of street turmoil, Adela appears with the marquis at a casino. (Olea artfully captures nineteenth-century Madrid by carefully filming his exterior scenes in Aranjuez, La Granja, and Segovia). Luis appears to have displaced Jaime for Adela's affections. Nevertheless, a close-up shot conspicuously shows that she is wearing Jaime's ring with two foils. What two foils will cross to resolve the untenable triangle?

Affection and betrayal: Omero Antonutti and Assumpta Sernain Pedro Olea's *El maestro de esgrima*. *Courtesy Origen Producciones Cinematográficas, S.A.*

Having learned the secret of Jaime's thrust, Adela does not need to appear for any more lessons. When Jaime sees her at a distance in the street, she is holding the hand of a gentleman in a carriage whose identity is withheld. The pan down the door of the carriage provides a clue however, since it has a coat of arms containing a harpy, the same motif as in the silver boxes in Adela's apartment. Is there a third man in Adela's life? The next sequence further diminishes Jaime's possibilities: at the opera, a close-up shot pans members of the audience who have their opera glasses trained on the performance. When it arrives at Don Jaime, however, his glasses are pointed in a different direction: the box with Luis and Adela. The aria "Addio del passato" from *La Traviata* underscores Adela's character and the fencing master's predicament. Jaime's loss of control as he lashes out with his foil at the mannequin in his studio is an indication of his jealousy and anger.

The amorous and political threads of the narrative inter-twine ever more tightly in suspense when Luis gives Jaime secret letters for safekeeping (since Jaime is the only honorable man that the Marquis knows) and Luis is found dead the next morning. Was the one-eyed doll that Jaime found after leaving Luis's house last night merely a dream? Police Chief Jenaro Campillo (José Luis López Vázquez) is interested in Jaime's opinion of the crime, since death was caused by a slash to the neck, and the murder weapon was a foil. Could Adela de Otero have used Jaime's secret thrust to kill the marquis? The fencing teacher enlists Agapito to interpret the political significance of the papers that Luis entrusted him with, but the arrival of Adela's servant adds a double dose of suspense to the narrative: it both postpones the revelation of the secret letters' meaning, and it adds another murder victim to the story.

The narrative information regarding the latest mystery leads one to surmise that the latest victim is Adela. After seeing blood on the floor of Adela's apartment, Jaime unsheathes the sword from his walking stick, and proceeds to her bedroom. Olea adds a touch of irony to the film text, as a shot of her bloodstained bed is followed by the sudden appearance (in close-up) from behind the door of Police Chief Campillo. When the cadaver is discovered floating in the river, Campillo takes Jaime to make the positive identification. The woman's face has been sliced beyond recognition, but a close-up of the ring with two foils on the victim's hand allows Jaime—and the viewer—to identify her as Adela.

The narrative thread returns to the mystery of the papers, and suspense builds there as well: Agapito is no longer in Jaime's apartment, and the fencing master later finds him severely beaten in his own home, incoherently saying, "No tengo más documentos" (I don't have any more documents). Who wants the documents, and why are they so important? The knife that flies by Jaime's head and the ensuing fight continue to build the suspense. The next clue in the narrative is the coat of arms on the carriage in which Jaime's assailant escapes: a harpy. Wood ("El maestro" 123) points out that the harpy symbol on the coat of arms should be linked both to the sinister Doña Adela and to the greed that is preponderant in the Spanish society the narrative portrays. Jaime pays to discover the owner of this heraldic symbol, and he then visits Mr. Saranova (Alberto Closas), the banker whose grandsons are

Jaime's pupils. Tumultuous events are causing the banker to send them to Switzerland, and their carriage again contains the harpy coat of arms. The fencing master can now identify the criminal to Police Chief Campillo, but only the missing document alluded to by Agapito will provide definitive proof. Both Jaime and Campillo know that he will be the next target, but the fencing master's anachronistic sense of honor causes him to refuse the pistol that Campillo offers him for protection, since a pistol "es un recurso de criminales" (is resorted to by criminals). Campillo's retort, "O de policías" (Or by policemen), continues the ironic vein of this character.

The chessboard next to Jaime as he sits in his apartment late at night, waiting for the criminal to strike at him next, is an apt metaphor for the action of the narrative: like a chivalrous knight of yore, the fencing master patiently waits for his opponent's next move in a game that can have deadly consequences. The steps heard off screen and the opening of the door provide a moment of suspense before the next plot twist —Adela enters the room. Like an astute detective, however, Jaime's response to her question, "¿Me esperaba?" (Were you waiting for me?) is "Supongo que sí" (I suppose so). As in a classic detective narrative, the pieces of the puzzle finally come together. Adela now provides the withheld information that gives an explanation to the previous narrative elements: Saranova was playing a double game, currying the favor of both the queen and Prim; the marquis had secret documents to prove it, and was bribing Saranova. Since Adela loves Saranova and owes everything that she is to him, she is willing to do anything to obtain the documents. She says to Jaime, "Cada hombre tiene su precio y yo sé el suyo" (Every man has his price, and I know what yours is), and she takes off her mantilla and cape.

Throughout the film, and especially in this scene, Assumpta Serna imbues her character with a wonderfully charged—yet subdued—erotic tension. Whereas many contemporary Spanish film adaptations add some *destape* to the original narrative in the hopes of capturing the interest of Spanish audiences, *El maestro de esgrima* does just the oppo-

A historical detective story: José Luis Gómez and Omero Antonutti in
Pedro Olea's *El maestro de esgrima*. *Courtesy Origen Producciones
Cinematográficas, S.A.*

site, and with success. In this scene in the novel, Adela places
Jaime's hand on her bare breasts (266). The slight change in
dialogue, from Adela's original "Sé que usted me ama" (I know
that you love me) to "Sé que me desea" (I know that you want
me) followed by the close-up of their kiss is sufficient to create
a marvelous tone of passion. But appearances are deceptive
here: Adela's passionate declaration precedes a close-up of
their kiss, and the camera pans down, following her hand as it
caresses Jaime's arm and leg just before she retrieves a dagger.
The ensuing struggle leads to the final duel between master and
pupil. Adela grabs the sword from Jaime's walking stick, and
Jaime grabs a sword from the wall. As they cross swords, cross-
cut medium shots show the two opponents; director Olea then
shifts from deep to shallow focus in order to highlight the
crossed swords, thus underscoring Jaime's tactical disadvantage
in this duel: the inferiority of his weapon—the practice foil
with the button at its tip—seems to level the playing field and
make the outcome of the duel more unpredictable. The breaking
of the mirror behind them symbolizes that the game of deceit

between them is over; the single truth that they hold is the weapons with which they fight to the death. Adela wounds Don Jaime twice during the duel, and her brilliant swordsmanship heightens the level of suspense in these final moments of the film. (Assumpta Serna, who lives in Los Angeles, took her fencing classes in preparation for the film from the same fencing instructor as Dustin Hoffman had in preparing for *Hook*. Serna actually wounded Antonutti so seriously during the filming of this scene that it had to be completed with the Italian actor's double.) At the end of their animated duel, the meaning of Jaime's earlier dream now becomes apparent, as the fencing master stabs Adela in the eye, and the one-eyed "doll" falls to the floor. Ironically, when Jaime bends over to pick up her mantilla, he discovers that the letter that Adela had sought is lying underneath his desk. The subtle importance of two earlier scenes now becomes clear: during the first scene in Jaime's apartment, he shuts the window because of the breeze that is disordering the papers on his desk, and when Agapito later comes to examine the papers, he must pick some up from the floor, where the breeze coming through the window has deposited them. Mere chance—the breeze blowing one letter underneath his desk—caused the final chain of events.

A street scene in which the newspaper headline announces General Prim's arrival in Madrid brings the tumultuous sociopolitical events of the background to closure. In the final scene of the film, Jaime brings closure to part of his personal life as well: he throws his manuscript on fencing into the fire, and tells Police Chief Campillo that he is planning to sell his collection of weapons. The novel ends with the wounded master practicing his new thrust, and Wood (125) believes that the change in the ending of the movie makes the film narrative more suggestive than the original and that it links us to the beginning of the novel in which Don Jaime contemplates his tragic loss. His justification that he has lost his agility with age is clearly a ruse, however. As he examines the two-foiled ring, the close-up shot suggests the true reason for his abandoning fencing: his final crossing of swords cost him too dearly. The final shot of Jaime in front of the fire is accompanied by the aria from *La Traviata*, thereby underscoring the indelible imprint that Adela left on the fencing master. Pedro Olea's splendid *El maestro de esgrima* likewise leaves an indelible imprint on the viewer.

Pedro J. Ramírez

Director José Luis García Sánchez's *La noche más larga* (*The Longest Night*, 1991) is the screen adaptation of Pedro J. Ramírez's *El año que murió Franco* (*The Year Franco Died*, 1985). The film was the project of producer Andrés Vicente Gómez, who, according to critic Antonio Castro ("*La noche*" 34) is the Spanish producer who received the most protection, support, and subsidies from the Spanish Socialist party (PSOE), which was in power from 1982 to March of 1996. The film deals with the execution on September 27, 1975—two months before the death of Franco—of members of the FRAP (Frente Revolucionario Antifascista Patriótico [Patriotic Antifascist Revolutionary Front]) and ETA (Euskadi Ta Askatasuna [Basque Homeland and Freedom]) terrorist groups. For director García Sánchez, the film is a "reflection about what happened in those days, but also about how those characters have later evolved, and about the reasons for the kind of collective amnesia that exists which is especially worrying to me," and he adds that "it is more a film about the forgetting of some facts, rather than about the facts themselves" (Castro, "Entrevista" 37, 38). These comments reflect important structural as well as thematic components of the film.

The defense lawyer from the trial, Juan Tarna (Juan Echanove), meets the military prosecutor Menéndez (Juan Diego) on the train trip fifteen years later, and their conversation triggers the main narrative device in the film: a series of flashbacks to the events of 1975. The early sequence of black-and-white images from the NO-DO, the official newsreel of the Franco regime, attempts to evoke the historical period of the mid 1970s, and the song, "Mi querida España" ("My Dear Spain") sings of "esta España blanca, esta España negra" (this white Spain, this black Spain)—the Spain that is divided in two, with the light and darkness taking on important ideological symbolism.

The former prosecutor's asking about Gloria (Carmen Conesa) triggers the inital flashback, as she arrives by train to Madrid in search of her brother Fito (Gabino Diego), who had become a member of the FRAP terrorist group during this time of

Military justice: José Luis García Sánchez's *La noche más larga*, sta
Juan Echanove and Juan Diego. *Courtesy Iberoamericana Films.*

social disturbances and police repression that represents the
waning moments of the regime. The assassination of a
policeman by FRAP is the crime for which Fito and the other
terrorists are imprisoned. Juan, the defense lawyer, realizes
that he has a nearly impossible task in defending Fito against
execution, especially since Fito tells him from behind bars that
he was tortured into signing a confession. Although Juan's
quixotic nature makes him attempt to defend the indefensible,
he finds himself in jail for acts of solidarity or contempt of
court. Juan decides that Fito's only defense would be that he
did not shoot, and that it was his comrades who murdered the
policeman, but Fito's sense of solidarity causes him to respond
that he will not testify against his companions.

Juan's comment during the train conversation that during
that radical period, "Estábamos todos locos" (We were all
crazy), leads to a flashback of the criminal events, and a
confirmation of the lawyer's main line of defense: the firing pin
in Fito's shotgun did not function, and therefore only his
companions were indeed the material killers. However, the
atmosphere of the trial itself is also radicalized, as the cries of

"Asesinos" (Assassins) by the widow of the slain policeman, as well as "Viva Franco" (Long live Franco) and "Viva el ejército" (Long live the army) among the public, foreshadow the outcome of the trial. The climax of the trial, then, is not the verdict, but the confrontation between Juan and the military prosecutor in which the lawyer declares, "Entérese bien: usted es un verdugo" (You'd better understand: you are an executioner), and spits on Menéndez's uniform. In spite of demonstrations against the executions in Spain and around the world, there is no pardon from Franco, and the shots of the execution are heard off screen as Juan and Gloria join the crowd outside the prison. The voice-over of Fito's final letter to his sister declares that he did not kill anyone.

The final sequences of the film continue to intertwine past and present, and constitute what Antonio Castro ("La noche" 35) refers to as a "settling of accounts" between director García Sánchez and the Spanish Communist party, from which he was expelled in 1981. Following Gloria's disillusionment at Juan's inablity to keep his promise that Fito would not be killed, she strikes the lawyer and runs from him. The business suit that Menéndez wears in the present contrasts with the military uniform of the days of the trial, and visually underscores his declaration that he changed, a transformation that he says began in the moment that Juan spit at his uniform during the trial. The final flashback portrays the transition in Menéndez's character. In casual dress, Menéndez attends a Communist party rally, where he meets Gloria. In a gesture of reconciliation, she gives a sparkler to the former prosecutor. The music performed at the rally—a rendition of Violeta Parra's "Gracias a la vida" ("Thanks to Life") underscores the symbolism of the sparkler's light. Gloria's character is not well developed in the film, however.

Director García Sánchez calls La noche más larga a socially involved film that causes the spectator to arrive at a moral judgment, and that the moral component of the work affected the production at all levels—from the way actors asked him questions about how to best portray their characters to decisions regarding what type of lighting would underscore moral attributes of the characters (Castro, "Entrevista" 36, 37).

Spectators, however, will not find the film as engaging as others that treat the same historical period (Juan Antonio Bardem's *Siete días de enero [Seven Days in January]*), Gillo Pontecorvo's *Operación Ogro [Operation Ogre]*), or that deal with the theme of moral tergiversation (Vicente Aranda's *La muchacha de las bragas de oro [The Girl with the Golden Panties]*) that is not as fully developed here in the character of Menéndez. Nevertheless, *La noche más larga* helps to address the collective amnesia that so worries its director.

Carmen Rico Godoy

When Carmen Rico Godoy, a longtime columnist for Spain's premier weekly magazine, *Cambio 16*, decided to try her hand at writing popular literature, she had instant success with her *Cómo ser mujer y no morir en el intento (How to Be a Woman and Not Die Trying*, 1990). Actress and singer Ana Belén had her debut as director when she filmed its screen adaptation in 1991. Rico Godoy followed up on the venture with two other best-sellers, *Cómo ser infeliz y disfrutarlo (How to Be Unhappy and Enjoy It*, 1991), and *Cuernos de mujer (Cuckold Woman*, 1992), both of which were adapted for the screen by Eduardo Urbizu. Rico Godoy's novels follow the comic, colloquial style of writing that she developed as a journalist but include a tinge of melodrama. Since Carmen Rico Godoy is married to film producer Andrés Vicente Gómez, it is not surprising that all three of these works quickly had screen adaptations.

The film follows the novel's four-part structure by using captions to signal not only the changes of the seasons, but also the changes in her marital relationship during a year in the life of Carmen (Carmen Maura): The Truce; War; Life. Carmen is the prototypical modern Spanish woman: divorced, a journalist by profession, remarried to a businessman. She tries to juggle the needs of husband, family, and job while facing the potential crisis of middle age. Belén uses voice-overs to capture Carmen's inner frustrations, fears, schemes, and desires.

The first segment satirizes the illusion of enjoyment during summer vacation. As in previous summers, Carmen and her husband Antonio (Antonio Resines) follow millions of other Spaniards and foreigners to the beach, where Carmen's problematic relationship with men is first manifest. When Antonio falls asleep on the beach, this scene introduces one of the running gags of the film—Antonio's snoring, which, of course, he denies. The beautiful young blonde next to them on the beach gives rise to Carmen's inevitable jealousy, and her thoughts turn to accusations (in voice-over) when she wakes up to discover Antonio's absence: "Este se ha ido con la rubia" (He's gone off with the blonde). The after-beach shower manifests more male-female differences with the you-never-screw-the-top-on-the-shampoo problem. The evening restaurant date with another couple consists of a spat over proper diet, until Carmen's female friend Chela gets fed up with "el paternalismo gilipollas" (the fucking paternalism) of the men, and they decide to leave.

In the second segment, entitled "Fall: The Truce," the narrative portrays one day during which the problems in her relationship with Antonio continue to grow. Carmen has to carry out chores that show her to be an almost second-class citizen who ironically makes up for the incompetence of her husband: he asks her to bring his planner and keys to work (since he forgot them!) and pick up his son at the airport. This portrayal of the modern Spanish professional woman also includes dealing with the problem of machismo in male coworkers, such as Manolo. Carmen's main problem, however, is jealousy: when she arrives home at night, Antonio is not there, and she imagines that he is having an affair. Her tears are cathartic, but the arrival of Antonio does not assuage the situation, because there is no real communication between this couple. Antonio's excuse that he has to go to sleep in order to get up early gives the repetition of the snoring gag a poignant tone; in order to get to sleep herself, Carmen counts sheep—and, in a humorous note, a pig.

Her relationship with Antonio goes from bad to worse in the third segment of the film, "Winter: War." A Christmas visit and family reunion at the home of Antonio's mother shows both the stress of urban life in Spain—traffic jams that easily make one forget the spirit of the season—and the stress in other marriages. The scene of the women in the kitchen provides for a moment of feminine solidarity—they commiserate together, as Alfredo's wife complains about his haughtiness and asks Carmen how you separate from your husband—yet it subtly underscores the latent machismo in Spanish society. When they take the coffee out to the living room, Alfredo's remark, "Ya era hora" (It's about time) elicits a stormy response from his wife: "Me cago en Dios" (Fuck it) as she sends the tray crashing to the floor. Antonio's blaming of Carmen for the incident further worsens their relationship.

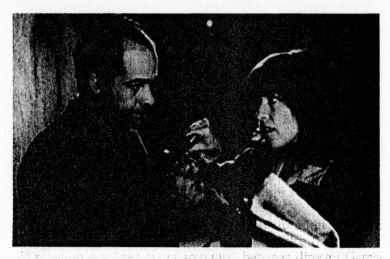

Modern marriage problems: Ana Belén's *Cómo ser mujer y no morir en el intento*, starring Antonio Resines and Carmen Maura. *Courtesy Iberoamericana Films.*

Carmen's professional life is fraught with difficulties, as well, and manifests the types of attitudes that a Spanish woman who is both married and a professional faces. When her boss offers her a position as coeditor of the Sunday supplement, Carmen rejects it because she thinks that she deserves better. Her boss's suggestion that she consult with her husband and then let him know elicits the funniest line of the film: "Quiero dirigir el Suplemento Dominical yo sola. Consulta con tu mujer y luego me lo dices, ¿eh?" (I want to direct the Sunday supplement all alone. Consult with your wife, and then let me know, OK?)

The last segment, "Spring: Life," brings further problems: worries about feeling old and fat, having to deal with a male gynecologist, dealing with Antonio's impertinence at a party. The final sequence is a lunch date between Antonio and Carmen that occurs in "neutral territory," since they have separated. This separation has caused changes in Antonio: in contrast with the earlier restaurant scene, his meager menu choice indicates a transformation. The separation has increased Antonio's self-awareness: "Reconozco que soy insoportable, a veces" (I recognize that I am unbearable at times). He wants—indeed, begs—Carmen to return home, but the ambiguity of her reaction transcends the facile "happy ending" and indicates that complicated domestic relations demand responses that are not clearly black or white: although she abruptly leaves the restaurant, she returns to the crestfallen Antonio to say, "que no pienso volver a casa . . . de momento" (I don't plan on returning home . . . for now).

Enrique Urbizu's adaptation of *Cómo ser infeliz y disfrutarlo* is a sequel to *Cómo ser mujer y no morir en el intento*, but now Carmen must face a midlife crisis of greater proportions: the unexpected death of her husband. (After the initial sequence, actor Antonio Resines appears in only one brief flashback.) Carmen must begin her new life by doing away with the old, and the close-up of Antonio's shaving utensils that Carmen puts into the garbage metonymically captures this break with the past. Carmen decides to get a new place to live, and her search for an apartment with a view of Madrid's Retiro Park is the basis for sight gags that border on the stupid—the clumsy real estate agent who bumps into things, or the delightful view from the balcony of hanging underwear.

As an attractive young widow, Carmen is the object of several men's desires. Felipe (Ferrán Rañé), who is looking for a woman to organize his life, is never really in the running. After a one-night stand with Diego (Francis Lorenzo), she rejects his advances; she then goes camping with the rich entrepreneur Romauldo (Ramón Madaula) who has his own ranch where he can be in contact with nature and where daily problems cease to exist. Romauldo proclaims that making money is not important, and although this is not meant to be ironic in the film, it certainly is, since Spanish yuppies like Romauldo are virtually the only ones in these works by Rico Godoy.

Carmen's problems multiply, as she discovers that her daughter Marta (Irene Blau) who lives in Paris is pregnant by her married lover. Carmen's initial reaction is incredulity—"Es imposible. Eres una cría" (It's impossible. You're just a kid) —but she soon confronts this difficult new situation with aplomb. The film ends with a shot of Marta with her new baby in front of the window, with the new grandmother Carmen in the background.

This film also contains Rico Godoy's penchant for humorous language, and this is especially evident in the use of billingsgate. Thus, after a shouting match with a taxi driver who is blocking her car, the former learns that she is newly widowed and expresses his condolences, and Carmen retorts, "Será gilipollas" (What an asshole).

Carmen is supposed to represent the feminist in modern Spain. However, the film sometimes hits the spectator over the head with this message. When Romualdo has an apartment tire, Carmen asks if he has a jack, saying, "Las mujeres tenemos que saber hacer todo hoy en día" (We women have to know how to do everything these days). While Freixas (78) praises Urbizu's intertextual references in homage to film classics by John Ford, he criticizes the stereotypical characters and themes as well as the lack of any real dramatic elements or conflict that would help the development of the plot.

In her third work, *Cuernos de mujer* (*Cuckold Woman*) Rico Godoy seems to have squeezed the narrative fruit dry. Based again on a four-part structure, this time a much more tenuous division of fire, earth, air, and water, the narrative—if it can be called that—is based on short vignettes that range from three to eight pages in length. Here Ana (played by María Barranco in Urbizu's film version) owns an interior decorating company and is married to a lawyer who is having an affair. When Ana wins the lottery, she can change her circumstances and begin a new life with her psychiatrist.

Carlos F. Heredero (40) calls *Cómo ser mujer y no morir en el intento* the "illustration of a best-seller," and the same is true of the other screen adaptations of Carmen Rico Godoy's works. The importance of both the original prose narratives and the movie adaptations is more social than artistic.

Emilio Romero

Casa manchada (*Stained House*, 1980) is José Antonio Nieves Conde's film adaptation of the novel *Todos morían en Casa manchada* (*Everyone Died in the Stained House*, 1969) by Emilio Romero. The initial sequence of assassinations based on tumultuous political events in Spanish history sets the fateful tone of the film adaptation: the deaths of the great-grandfather in 1867, the grandfather in 1905, and the father in 1936, all forebode the murder of the son, Alvaro (all played by the same actor, Stephen Boyd). The camera pans the portrait of these forebears to underscore the curse on the household.

Like many other Spanish films made in the years following Franco's death, this one has a narrative time frame of the period immediately following the end of the civil war. However, in contrast to many of these post-Franco productions that espoused a new point of view that is sympathetic to the Republican side of the conflict, *Casa manchada* does not take a strong ideological stand, but merely uses postwar violence as a type of divine punishment for the adulterous protagonist.

Alvaro, a Nationalist officer in the Spanish civil war, returns home to his sickly wife, Elvira, but soon abandons her in favor of a woman that he has found lying on the grounds of his ranch, and whom he takes into his home to bring back to good health. Since the affair between Alvaro and Laura occurs under their own roof, Elvira finally discovers the truth, fainting in disbelief. Alvaro's response, "Esto se va a arreglar" (This is going to be set right), prompts the possessive and jealous Laura to disappear. After Elvira's death, Alvaro marries Rosa, who studies in Madrid but was born on the Casa Manchada ranch. Finally, the fate hanging over Alvaro materializes in the form of *maquis*, the Republican guerrilla fighters who continue the battle against Franco after the end of the war. Although the local doctor warned Alvaro near the beginning of the film of the presence of the *maquis* in their area, the ex-Nationalist officer claimed to be retired from any political involvement, adding that he wanted to forget the past. It seems, however, that the past would not forget him, and the *maquis* take him for ransom. The film falls into the thematic rapprochement seen in other movies about the Spanish civil war, particularly those done by directors with Nationalist leanings, in which two ideological enemies like each other and offer the possibility of becoming friends instead of killing each other. The cigarette offered by the *maquis* to the prisoner underscores this rapprochement. As in other films, however, this is not meant to be, and the attempted rescue of the ransom victim backfires and results in his death. The film ends as his distraught young widow attempts to end the curse of Casa Manchada by setting fire to the ranch.

Quesada (370) notes that the novel is a complex narrative with crossing plot threads, and an ending that includes the next generation. Nieves Conde's film version attempts to simplify the original version, but the result is a loss in character development, and a plot that is at times disjointed.

José Luis Sampedro

Antonio del Real's *El río que nos lleva* (*The River that Carries Us*, 1989) is based on the 1961 novel by José Luis Sampedro. In some ways, the narrative constitutes a return to nineteenth-century *costumbrismo* in that it portrays a particular segment of Castilian life that has now disappeared: the *gancheros*, timbermen who use long hooks to guide trees down the Tagus River to the mill. Sampedro's novel has a third-person narration that shifts in the final chapter to first person, in which the narrator queries, "Haven't you understood yet that I am Shannon?" (355), referring to the Irishman who joins the Spaniards on their trip down the river.

Del Real's film version uses the voice-over from the opening sequence to establish Shannon as the narrator, as well as to establish the temporal context that is later confirmed in the titles "Upper Tagus 1946." Roy Shannon's voice-overs also reflect the four-part division of the novel that is based on the seasons, as he refers to the sudden arrival of spring and the heat of summer. More importantly, the voice-overs confirm what Sampedro considers a constant theme in his work, human dignity (Cristóbal 68): "Había llegado como un extraño y ahora me sentía parte de aquel mundo, de aquellos hombres, los gancheros, que me habían enseñado el sentido de la dignidad y de la solidaridad humana" (I had arrived as a stranger, and now I felt a part of that world, of those men, the timbermen, who had shown me the meaning of dignity and human solidarity). And yet, the film does not include the section from the novel that perhaps best exemplifies Shannon's sense of dignity and solidarity: the episode from chapter 15 in which he jumps into the river to save the drowning Galerilla, and suffers a broken leg when a log smashes it. Nevertheless, Shannon (Tony Peck) does provide one *ganchero*, Lucas, with greater human dignity when he teaches him how to read. The screen adaptation provides a treatment of this motif that is both poetic and political, as the text chosen by Shannon that Lucas can finally read is *Romancero gitano* (*Gypsy Ballads*) by Federico García Lorca, who was tragically assassinated by Nationalist troops in 1936.

The film admirably captures the local customs and folklore of the region of Castile through which the *gancheros* travel: the burning of Judas during Holy Week, the fireworks for Saint John's Night. The most important manifestation of local folklore occurs in the town of Sotondo. As they approach the town, a figure dressed in a devil's costume greets them with a rattle, and this is followed by a choreographed greeting by children who appear from behind the trees with their rattles. This is not just because Shannon is a type of "prodigal son" (in the film version, his maternal grandparents are made to be Spaniards from that village), but because, as one *ganchero* explains, the villagers greet them that way every year.

The visit to Sotondo also manifests a folkloric tradition— a "bullfight" in which a man dresses as a bull—that has an important social theme: the exploitation of the townsfolk by the *cacique* (political boss). Del Real emphasizes this exploitation by adding an episode that is not in the original narrative. Benigno (Carlos Mendy), the cacique, takes Shannon and Paula (Eulalia Ramón) to city hall, where portraits of Franco and Falangist leader José Antonio Primo de Rivera are prominently displayed on the wall, thus underscoring Benigno's dictatorial tendencies. When one of the "bullfighters" laughs at the *cacique*, Benigno slaps him, insults him, and fires him.

Del Real continues the political reading of this character when Benigno tells Shannon "Ganamos una guerra, ¿no?" (We won one war, didn't we?)—referring to the Spanish civil war—and remarks that the Irishman's great-uncle, a Republican, was "un rojillo" (a little red). These new scenes provide a better sense of just deserts to the following scene, which comes directly from the novel: as the rambunctious "bull" triumphs, the intercut shots of the barking dog lead up to the unleashing of the animal, but again the bull is victorious, killing the dog. When the "bull" turns out to be a *ganchero*, Benigno orders the crowd to kill him. The *gancheros* called "el Americano" and "el Negro" intervene, however, and the latter's invocation to the townsfolk not to obey the orders of the "bloodsucker" and "miserable exploiter" constitute the most important message of the narrative.

Both novel and film contain this type of social element throughout. Of the many songs in the original narrative, the film version utilizes one that contains social commentary: Lo que pasa en España / tiene salero / el hombre que no se apaña / se muere de hambre / aunque obrero (What's happening in Spain / is funny / the man who isn't clever / dies of hunger / even if he's a worker). Although the *ganchero*'s comment, "No teniendo tierra, no eres nada" (Without land, you are nothing) is not as strong as the novel's denunciation of latifundia whereby large land holdings are concentrated among few families (114), when taken in syntagmatic relation with the sarcastic comment, "En este país se toleran a los pobres mientras vayan a misa" (In this country, poor people are tolerated as long as they go to mass), it manifests a definite pattern of social criticism that is greater in the film.

The role of religion in Spanish society is stronger in the novel than in the film. This is most notable in the scene in which a confrontation between "el Americano" and some dam workers is avoided when a monk mysteriously arrives to open a rusted valve, an event that the timbermen deem a miracle. The Spain of 1989, when the movie had its debut, was much less Catholic than the Spain of 1946, when the novel's events occur, or even of 1961, when the novel appeared. In 1987, just two years before this film was released, only 49 percent of Spaniards considered themselves practicing Catholics ("Encuesta" 80). (Luis García Berlanga wanted to make a movie of it shortly after the book came out, but the project was blocked by censors.) The change in attitude toward religion also appears in the scene in which the priest, Don Angel (Fernando Fernán Gómez), gives a sermon with a tone of religious skepticism more in line with the times of the film production.

The sexual component is likewise more contemporary. There is a condensation of the episodes regarding the tavern (chapter 9) and Nieves (chapter 13), so that the sexual adventure of "el Rubio" in the film is with the tavern owner's wife, and this scene captures the raucous behavior of the timbermen from the novel. Also, the presence of a woman, Paula, among the timbermen gives rise to an amorous rivalry between Shannon and "el Encontrao" (Mikel Insua). The Irishman's feelings toward Paula are almost platonic, as he queries, "¿Podrías aceptarme a tu lado?" (Could you accept me by your side?); her negative response is followed by a low-angle shot of "el Encontrao" looking down on them from a bridge, thus visually underscoring the romantic triangle and the superiority of "el Encontrao" over the Irishman. Although their relationship is not consummated in the novel, the lovemaking scene between Paula and "el Encontrao" in the film creates a context brimming with irony, since it takes place as Benigno, thinking that he has Paula trapped, awaits her in frustration.

Benigno's attempt to blackmail Paula into becoming his mistress meets with the same just deserts in both narratives. Dámaso kills him with his logger's hook in the novel and with his umbrella in the film, a switch that coincides well with the spatial context of the end of the film: the urban scenes of Aranjuez, where the logging adventure concludes. Shannon's final voice-over captures the poetic tone found in parts of the novel: although loggers no longer exist (truck transport superseded the river), he learned that "La vida y la muerte son dos labios de una misma herida" (Life and death are two lips of the same wound).

El río que nos lleva won an award from UNESCO for its defense of natural habitats, and it is a faithful version of the novel, but it is a film that never grabs hold of the spectator. The long sequences of the logging on the river seem to drag, and the music that accompanies them, although composed by the admirable Catalan songwriter Lluis Llach, borders on the annoying. Nevertheless, it admirably captures this lost slice of life from Castile in the 1940s.

Ramón Sender

Ramón Sender (1902-1982) was a prolific writer whose career began in the 1930s and who, like many other Spanish intellectuals, left Spain for exile during the Franco regime. His works have served not only as the basis for feature-length films, but for made-for-television movies, as well. Spanish filmmakers have adapted two of the nine books that make up Ramón Sender's *Crónica del alba* (*Chronicle of Dawn*). The first is Antonio J. Betancor's *Valentina* (1982), based on the first book, which has the same title as the series. Betancor's *1919, Crónica del alba,* which was released the following year, represents the adaptation of the fourth book (*El mancebo y los héroes* [*The Young Man and the Heroes*]). Sender's most famous novel, *Requiem por un campesino español* (*Requiem for a Spanish Peasant*) made its way to the screen in 1985. Both *Valentina* and *1919, Crónica del alba* are films that were subsidized by Televisión Española (Spanish Television) in a competition that called for the screen adaptation of important works of Spanish literature.

The temporal framing of the narrative in *Valentina* provides a bittersweet tone to this story of the indomitable spirit of youth, and of the protagonist, Pepe Garcés. The initial voice-over of the film refers to the time long ago in 1939 when the narrator and other members of the Republican army had to seek refuge in France. He met Garcés while imprisoned there, and the latter's dignity, faith, and memories provided a special sustenance that helped him survive. In the opening sequence, this narrator visits Valentina Ventura to inform her that Pepe died in a concentration camp, and to give her his memoirs. The flashback to 1911 constitutes the rest of the narration until a final epilogue that ties this past to the event that fatally marks Pepe's adult life: the Spanish civil war.

Pepe (Jorge Sanz) is a mischievous and free-spirited youth who is constantly reprimanded and chastised by his strict father, Don José (Saturno Cerra). The opening sequences of the flashback capture the clash of these two diametrically opposed temperaments: Pepe shoots at cats with a slingshot from his rooftop, and after reviewing his academic work, his father

331

announces at the dinner table that Pepe's behavior will bring the family shame and vilification, and that he must be punished with twenty lashes. The visual metonymy of the close-ups of a girl's braids, shoes, and hair ribbon that are intercut while the punishment is being administered introduces the emotional bond between the victim, Pepe, and the girl he loves, Valentina (Paloma Gómez). A series of subsequent images confirms this amorous bond between them: Pepe encounters Valentina in the street and they go running off holding hands; he kisses Valentina in the street; Pepe communicates from his rooftop to Valentina in her bedroom by using hand signals, and a close-up shows the girls's deciphered message that "Pepe loves Valentina"; a close-up of Valentina reading a liturgical text about love clearly takes on the second meaning regarding their own relationship; and the reverse angle shot near the end of the film of Pepe and Valentina sitting embracing on the rooftop with the town in the background completes the bond between the two youths.

The idyllic nature of this tale of adolescent love is constantly threatened by the undercurrent of fratricidal conflict. Pepe views Valentina's cousin Julián (Damián Jareño) as a rival mainly because he identifies him on more than one occasion as "el hijo de un político nefasto" (the son of a stinking politician), connoting an ideological division in society, since Pepe is echoing the opinion of his father. Pepe attempts to eliminate this rival in a show of machismo, as he puts his finger at the end of the barrel of Julián's gun and tells him to shoot. Although Pepe stoically declares that the resulting wound is merely like a mosquito bite, the physician who later attends him states that if he had waited one more day, he would have had to amputate his finger. The physician calls Pepe a hero, but the reaction of Pepe's father, "Aquí estamos todos locos" (We are all crazy here) not only contradicts it, but must be read in the broader context of Spanish society and the wounds that its members will inflict upon each other. A river battle between two bands of young boys must also be read metaphorically as representing the future fratricidal conflict, as the two groups of boys line up on either bank of the river to attack each other. The battle gets out of hand when a group of adults in a rowboat attacks the boys, and Pepe responds by shooting a pistol, again showing his fearless character. What was merely a joke for the men (shooting at the boys with salt to scare them) gets out of hand and transcends both the adolescent rivalry and the ill-conceived prank that began the incident.

Although Pepe escapes punishment for his involvement in the river battle, he cannot do so when he kills several pigeons that Valentina's father had purchased in Zaragoza for breeding purposes. In contrast with his tyrannical father, Pepe befriends a father figure in the village priest, Mosén Joaquín (Anthony Quinn), who becomes Pepe's teacher and friend. Román (262) notes that the heightened duality in the film version between the intransigence of Pepe's father and the understanding nature of the priest adds a new dimension to the film narrative. Mosén Joaquín's principal lesson for Pepe does not involve Pythagoras's theorem or the fossils that they discover together, however, but rather the theory that the priest reads from an ancient family manuscript: there are three types of men—saints, poets, and heroes—and that Pepe must consider what type of man he will be. Pepe's father thinks that the boy is a poet, since he discovers rhymes by Bécquer in Pepe's room, but the fearlessness that Pepe shows throughout the narrative points to his heroism, and the final episode in the tunnels under the castle confirms the boy's bravery. The multiple images of a ghost in armor who wants to take Pepe away are the manifestations of a dream sequence that might scare a normal youth, but not Pepe. He calls the name of his beloved—true love provides empowerment. His escape with Valentina, however, is the straw that breaks the camel's back; the Civil Guard has to be called in to search for them, and his father announces that tomorrow Pepe will begin life at boarding school. The intercut close-ups of Pepe and Valentina when his father sends the boy to his room indicate that their love for each other will transcend any spatial separation. Nevertheless, the final scene of Pepe running after the automobile that takes Valentina and her family away, as she leans out the window to wave good-bye, represents a poignant separation that seems all too definitive.

Pepe's friendship with the priest also transcends time. As he departs, Mosén Millán eschews a simple handshake in favor of a warm embrace. However, the response to Pepe's final question to the priest, "¿Por qué matan a los héroes?" (Why do they kill heroes?), is a foreshadowing of his death in the war: "Desgraciadamente, cuando seas hombre ya lo vas a entender" (Unfortunately, when you are a man, you will understand). Although the temporal framework provided us with the information regarding Pepe's fate from the very beginning, the epilogue poignantly links Pepe's tragic adult experiences with these days of innocence: "José Garcés spent many years at a boarding school in Reus, and went a long time without seeing Valentina. One day, he woke up under the frost of dawn, worried that Valentina might have known the horrors of war."

Valentina is a delightful movie. The haunting score by Riz Ortolani contains Valentina's theme (which is repeated in harpsichord, piano, and orchestral versions), and the many long shots of the picturesque town and castle add to the visual beauty of the film. Much of the charm of this film adaptation stems from the excellent performances by two ten-year-old actors, Paloma Gómez and Jorge Sanz, as well as that of Anthony Quinn. Sanz would later go on to become one of the most important actors in contemporary Spanish cinema. Quesada (288) points out that the casting of Quinn in the role of Mosén Joaquín is undoubtedly a reason for the greater development of this character in the film version. Román (264) notes that Sender was able to capture many manifestations of child psychology in his original narrative, and that Betancor aptly uses them to add life to the film adaptation. Betancor follows the story of the original novel faithfully, with some condensation of the final episodes, such as when Pepe's father sends him to boarding school for fighting.

The year after *Valentina*, Betancor continued with Pepe's saga in *1919, Crónica del alba* (*1919, Chronicle of Dawn*, 1983). This film—at least in video format—exists in two versions, one with a frame of documentary footage from the Spanish civil war, and one without it. The initial voice-over narrative, which accompanies images of Spaniards fleeing across the border into France or leaving Spain by train, introduces the protagonist, Pepe Garcés, now thirty-five years of age, who has become a refugee. As he feels that his end is near, he clings to his memories, taking refuge in them in order to survive. The memories of his life as a student in Zaragoza constitute the narrative of this film.

The action occurs four years after the ending of the previous narrative. Classmates of fifteen-year-old Pepe (Miguel Molina), chant Valentina's name; this confirms that she is still Pepe's girlfriend, thus picking up the action from the earlier film. The friction between Pepe and his father continues, but now takes on political nuances, as the former accuses Pepe, who is holding a newspaper, of reading liberal publications. This political element continues in the following sequence, as Pepe stops by a newspaper stand as close-ups show the headlines of radical newspapers of the period—*El fusil* (*The Rifle*), *El motín* (*The Revolt*)—and Lucas (José Antonio Correa) informs the newspaper man Checa (Walter Vidarte) that a Catalan labor leader was assassinated. In the general strike sequence, Betancor gradually increases the level of authoritarian repression of workers: a long shot of the mounted Civil Guard, metonymic shots of their horses' hooves, a high-angle shot (from the perspective of Pepe's third-floor window) of people running in the street, the pursuit by mounted guards, and long shots of guards shooting into the air, all culminate in the shooting of a worker by the guards in front of Pepe's apartment. Pepe's reaction manifests his growing solidarity with the working class; although his father prohibits him from leaving the apartment, Pepe mocks his superficial Christianity and rushes—too late—to the worker's aid.

When Pepe goes to work in Zaragoza as an apprentice in a pharmacy his life revolves around his work and his revolutionary and erotic activities. The close-up profile shot of Garcés next to Isabel (Cristina Marsillach) at the movies parallels the close-up profile shot that they are watching on screen, as Svengali hypnotizes a woman to be under his spell. Pepe and Isabel likewise "hypnotize" each other; Pepe's advances during the next movie scene lead to a night of lovemaking during which they both admit to losing their virginity.

Although Pepe's co-workers in the pharmacy warn him that Isabel's cousin is a whore, Pepe continues the relationship. Isabel falls in love, saying, "Quisiera ser tu novia toda la vida" (I would like to be your girlfriend for my entire life), but Pepe counters with, "Mi amante" (My lover). For Pepe, his true love is still Valentina, to whom he writes letters (rendered in voice-over), and whom he visits in Bilbao. Circumstances have changed, however, and Valentina is now at the strict School of the Sacred Heart. When Pepe visits her, it is obvious that they are virtually speaking two languages when Pepe says, "No puedes imaginar, Valentina, lo que es el amor. Yo lo he descubierto ya del todo" (You can't imagine, Valentina, what love is. I have now discovered it in its entirety), and she responds, "Yo también. Debe ser por estar tanto tiempo separados" (I have, too. It must be from being separated for so long). Their separation in the hallway of the school, rendered by cross-cut close-ups as a nun leads Valentina away, parallels the farewell at the end of the previous film, but lacks the poignancy of that earlier scene. This farewell, however, is definitive, as the voice-over of Valentina's mother reading her letter to Pepe expresses her desire that he not see Valentina again. Although Isabel was extremely upset by Pepe's visit to Valentina, she returns to be his lover, claiming to be honorable because she is not hypocritical.

Pepe's ideological tendencies are clear from the early sequence in which a close-up of an envelope he is mailing shows that he has written "Viva la Revolución" (Long Live the Revolution) where he will place the stamp. His conversations with Checa and Lucas introduce him to theories of egalitarianism—"que cada uno vale tanto como el otro" (everybody is worth the same as everybody else)—and anarchism—"hay que destruir el estado" (the state has to be destroyed). Pepe is ingenuous, however, and although he manifests a desire to take revenge for the death of the worker, his supposed means for doing so—the dagger he shows Lucas—manifests his naivete. Lucas's prediction that "La cosa está al punto" (Things are ripe) soon becomes true, as the pharmacist confirms that the sounds of bombs and shots represent an uprising. As earlier, Pepe runs out to the street in solidarity. The shallow-focused long shot of him running toward the camera with mounted Civil Guards approaching in the background lends a threatening air, but Pepe is a mere spectator as before. The Civil Guards attack the rebels with cannons, and as in the earlier sequence, Pepe obeys the guard who tells him to leave. When the fighting ends, Pepe returns, only to see the Civil Guard march off with their prisoners—including the wounded Lucas—and carry off the dead: Checa, and the Civil Guard with whom Pepe had shared a table at a bar. The close-ups of Pepe crying, and of his cutting out Checa's photograph from the newspaper, underscore the importance to Garcés of the loss of his friend and ideological mentor. As Pepe sits with his head in his hands with the camera shot through the grating of his window—a symbol of his future incarceration—the narrator's voice-over comments: "Aquel día hubiese querido morirse, pero la providencia fue piadosa, o tal vez cruel, quién sabe. Aprender a vivir no era más fácil ni más difícil que aprender a morir" (That day I had wanted to die, but Providence was merciful, or perhaps cruel, who knows. Learning how to live was no easier nor more difficult than learning how to die). The blue-tinted scenes of a concentration camp complete the framing of the film and underscore the message of the final titles. These explain that Sender himself was a prisoner of war, thus manifesting the autobiographical element of the narrative, which is further confirmed by the fact that Sender's maternal surname, Garcés, coincides with Pepe's surname.

Réquiem por un campesino español (*Requiem for a Spanish Peasant*) is a film from 1985 directed by Francesc Betriu, and based on the novel of the same name by Ramón Sender, which first appeared in 1950 with the title *Mosén Millán*. The cinematographic story has the same structure as does the novel: the present time frame consists of the mass that Mosén Millán (Antonio Ferrandis), the village priest, says for the soul of Paco (Antonio Banderas); prior events are subordinated to this moment in flashbacks, with close-ups and often zoom-ins to the priest signalling a return to the past. The first flashback shows how artfully Betriu handles these temporal transitions. The camera slowly zooms-in to the priest, but continues past him to the windowpanes of the sacristy window and beyond, an image that will later relate to the iron grating on the window of Mosén Millán's bedroom. The soundtrack provides a bridge between the two temporal planes, because as the scene shifts from the interior of the sacristy to the exterior of the plaza, the ringing of the church bells for the requiem mass becomes the ringing of the bells for Paco's baptism.

This baptismal ceremony represents the earliest point of the plot, and manifests that the relationship between the peasant and the priest is inexorably linked from the beginning of the former's existence. Since he serves as an altar boy for the priest, this relationship grows during Paco's youth, a period that manifests the fundamental characteristics that will mark Paco's future. As an eight-year-old altar boy, he invokes the priest's ire when his wooden pistol falls from his pants to the floor during mass. The pistol itself serves as a symbol of the violent end that will meet Paco, and his defense of the incident before the priest, placing himself in the position of scapegoat, is actually a subconscious attempt to defer guilt: "Si lo tengo yo, no lo tienen otros chavales peores que yo" (If I have it, then other kids who are worse than I won't have it). The film adaptation underscores the symbolism of the pistol, since in the novel, the priest gives up trying to get the pistol from the boy (26), whereas in the movie, young Paco hands it over to him. The priest places it in his drawer in the sacristy, where it is still visible before the requiem mass—together with Paco's watch and handkerchief that the Fascists gave to the priest after Paco's execution. These objects metonymically represent the two main components of Paco's life—the toy of youth and the timepiece and handkerchief of adulthood. (Paco wore a handkerchief on his head while working in the fields and discussing social justice with his father.) Unlike the novel, the pistol in the film is merely a wooden toy, and Mosén Millán examines it in his drawer and pulls its rubber band without ammunition, an act that symbolizes his indirect role in Paco's death.

Later, during his confirmation ceremony, Paco tells the bishop that he wants to be a laborer like his father, and have three mules. The latter comment reflects his desire to improve his lot in life, a desire that will later inexorably cause him to clash with authorities. His visit to a cave when he accompanies Mosén Millán to give extreme unction to a parishioner is a seminal experience in Paco's life. (In the original narrative, later references to it (52-53; 69) show that it left an indelible imprint on Paco.) Close-up shots of Paco indicate his incredulity regarding the cave dweller's situation, and when he questions the priest about the man's poverty, Mosén Millán acknowledges the young boy's virtues, which will later form the basis of his social consciousness: "Tienes buen corazón. Tu compasión es virtuosa y caritativa" (You have a good heart. Your compassion is virtuous and charitable). The cave episode also manifests an important feature of Mosén Millán's character. His comment to Paco that "Cuando Dios permite la miseria y el dolor sus razones tendrá" (When God permits misery and pain, he must have his reason) shows an air of resignation that will be crucial to the outcome of Paco's fate.

Paco's transition to manhood occurs in a scene in which he goes swimming naked in a pond across from where a group of women who are washing clothes comment, amid much laughter, that he is now "todo un hombre" (really a man). As Paco begins to work in the fields, he comes to realize the extent to which the landowners exploit the peasants. An evening in the village square provides him with the opportunity to question his mentor about such abuses, but the priest brushes his complaints aside as "alegatos peregrinos" (strange allegations) and says that he should worry more about himself and the scandal that he caused by bathing naked in front of the washerwomen. This scene constitutes an indictment against the role of the church in prewar Spain. More concerned with sexuality than social injustice, Mosén Millán contributes to the social turmoil that follows.

Paco's wedding occurs just as social tensions in the town and in the country begin to mount, and the narrative of the film interweaves the two. The priest's blessing during the ceremony, "Este humilde ministro del Señor ha bendecido vuestro lecho natal, bendice en este momento vuestro lecho nupcial . . . y bendecirá vuestro lecho mortal, si Dios lo dispone así" (This humble minister of the Lord blessed the bed where you were born, now blesses your wedding bed . . . and will bless your deathbed, if God ordains it so, cf. 54), constitutes a foreshadowing of Paco's tragic end. The shoemaker—representative of the popular social conscience—warns, "el rey se tambalea y si cae muchas cosas se van a caer con él" (the king is shaky, and if he falls, a lot of things are going to fall with him).

The local and national political situations intersect when Paco becomes involved in the elections of April 1931, much to the chagrin of landowners. The laborer tells Mosén Millán that these are new times, and that the renters plan to stop rent payments to the landowners. After a long shot of the town, a shot of Paco on his white horse symbolically contrasts with the entrance into the town square of two automobiles from which a band of youths dressed in black military uniforms emerges. These outsiders are Fascists who terrorize the town with beatings and murders. In one of the most poignant scenes in the film, they gather the townsfolk into the square and force them at pistol point to sing the Fascist hymn, "Cara al sol" ("Facing the Sun"). Paco eludes the Fascist manhunt and comes to town at night—again on his white steed—to inquire of his mentor about his family. This will cause his downfall, however, since the priest collaborates with the Fascists and betrays Paco's whereabouts.

The close-up shots of Mosén Millán crying—both as the authorities interrogate him, and when Paco is about to be executed—show how actor Antonio Ferrandis attempted to imbue his role with an emotional depth worthy of the Sender character. The same moral justification for suffering that the priest showed in the early scene at the cave of the dying parishioner resurfaces when Paco asks him why he must die: Mosén Millán ignores both the injustice of the Fascist executions and his own complicity, only responding, "A veces Dios permite morir a un inocente" (Sometimes God permits an innocent man to die), a comment that imbues Paco with Christ symbolism. The priest not only ignores the righteousness of the laborers' protests, but overtly sides with the landowners from early on. Only the priest's guilty conscience causes him not to accept payment for the requiem by Paco's enemies, who are representatives of the Spanish oligarchy: the landlord's administrator, Don

Valeriano (Fernando Fernán Gómez), Don Cástulo (Simón Andreu) and Don Gumersindo (Eduardo Calvo). Betriu visually captures the collusion of the church and the oligarchy in the last scene of the film, when Mosén Millán enters the church to say the mass for Paco: although there are no townspeople, the landlord's administrator is conspicuously present. However, the intrusion moments before of Paco's white horse, poetic symbol of the peasant's goodness, freedom, and strength, into the church, shows that Paco's spiritual presence lives on in the town. The intrusion is seen as a sacrilege, just as Paco's struggle for justice was viewed as a violation of a God-given social order. The presence of the riderless horse in the church serves as a foreshadowing of the ending—the capture and assassination of Paco—as well as a haunting reminder to the priest of the tragic error that he has committed, since this scene immediately follows that in which the priest confesses Paco's hiding place to the Fascists. In addition, Betriu and photographer Raúl Artigot make excellent use of dark lighting throughout the film to presage the denouement.

Is Mosén Millán a base, repugnant figure who should be reviled for his lack of compassion over gross social inequities and his direct role in the death of Paco, or is he a victim in his own right, a man who is as trapped in his guilty conscience as the grasshopper in the opening page of the narration? Why do movie audiences invariably feel more compassion and empathy for the priest of the film than for Mosén Millán in the novel? The reason is that Betriu has made some subtle but important transformations in the priest's character and his circumstances. Certainly the film version places more emphasis on Mosén Millán's relationship with the oligarchy. During the dance scene, Mosén Millán is seated at a table in the background with Don Valeriano, Don Gumersindo, and a Civil Guard. In a scene not in the original narrative, Valeriano and Gumersindo visit Mosén Millán after the elections, and the duke's administrator warns against difficult times ahead, saying that they should "remain united." After Paco successfully gains access to the duke's land—a high-angle shot shows how the sheep enter between the stone pillars that mark the entrance to the land symbolizes the social victory for the lower class—Don

Valeriano decides to leave town. His angry statement to Mosén Millán before departing, "Dios que permite lo que está pasando no merece tantos miramientos" (A God who permits such things to happen does not deserve such consideration), is replete with irony. When the Fascist thugs come to town and assemble people in the plaza, a low-angle shot shows the Fascist captain (Emilio Gutiérrez Caba) on the balcony flanked by Cástulo and Gumersindo, and the reverse high angle shot shows Valeriano and Mosén Millán in the second row; the priest raises his arm in the Fascist salute when they sing the Fascist hymn, "Cara al sol." The cut to the shot of vultures near the cadavers of assassinated townsfolk is accompanied by an ironic rendition of this Fascist hymn in slow tempo on the mandolin. And yet, the film also portrays Mosén Millán as more of a victim. The Christ symbolism associated with Paco in the novel that begins with the use of the word *centurión* both in the ballad (12) and in references to the Fascist captain (86, 88, 90), shifts in the film to Mosén Millán. From the very beginning of the film, there are repeated shots of the priest that include images of Christ: the painting in the sacristy, and the crucifix seen above the priest in the low angle shot during his conversation with Paco about the toy pistol. Nevertheless, the film subtly underscores Paco's Christ symbolism on the soundtrack. The opening theme music associated with Paco (mandolin music played during the initial sequence of long shots of Paco's horse galloping through town) is repeated at the end of the film, but accompanied this time with the drumbeat associated with the Holy Week processions from the middle of the film.

Although the ballad does not have the same narrative importance in the film as in the novel—Betriu incorporates only the initial verses that the altar boy sings as he rings the bell for mass. Nevertheless, the director incorporates numerous images that underscore the mythic dimensions of the triadic narrative pattern found in folk narratives involving heroes. Besides the three enemies of Paco who offer to pay for his mass, they include the three guards of the duke's lands, and the three women with shaved heads in the plaza who are humiliated by the Fascists. In addition, the town festivities—a narrative sequence not in the original novel—serve to elevate Paco to the level of hero when he alone triumphs in the contest to obtain the roosters, and the explosions of the firecrackers during the festivities also provide a foreshadowing of the violence that will soon decimate the town.

In an important change from the original narrative, Mosén Millán learns of Paco's hiding place from Paco himself. In the novel, Mosén Millán discovers this information during a visit to Paco's family because of his egoism, giving the impression that he already knows where Paco is located (85). In the film adaptation, Paco sneaks into town at night to inquire about his family and pregnant wife. The image of Paco speaking through the iron grating of Mosén Millán's window is like that of a confessional. In the moment when Paco is about to reveal his hiding place, he pauses and looks down the street to see if anyone is listening, and the reverse angle shots show the priest shaking his head "no" with a terrified look on his face, not wanting to be entrusted with the information. The image of Mosén Millán behind the iron grating now connotes a prison, and relates to the earlier image of the window in the sacristy.

When interrogated by the Fascist captain, the three representatives of the oligarchy—Valeriano, Gumersindo, and Cástulo—are much more prominent than in the novel, and they help badger him into submission, with the latter reminding Mosén Millán that remaining silent is a sin of omission (cf. 89). As Dorward notes, the Fascist captain's interrogation is also much less subtle in the film (280). This certainly makes the priest more a victim of the others than of himself. In addition, the priest's protests concerning the Fascists' crimes are much stronger in the film—"Han (sic) muerto gente honrada. . . . Hay que acabar con esta locura" (Honorable people have died. . . . This madness must stop). The novel's ironic complaint is merely that the assassinations were carried out without giving the victims time to confess (81). The compelling confessional scene before Paco's assassination faithfully captures the tone of the original. Here, Mosén Millán is also a victim: "Me han engañado a mí también" (They deceived me, too). A slight change in the priest's words, from "Piensa, hijo, en tu alma, y olvida, si puedes, todo lo demás" (Think about your soul, my son, and forget everything else, if you can) to "Olvida, hijo, olvida. Piensa en tu alma y olvidas todo lo demás" (Forget, my son, forget. Think about your soul and forget everything else), more strongly underscores the words that Valeriano ascribes to Mosén Millán's latest sermon (47), and more importantly, what Robert Havard terms "the central issue of remembering" (90). It is ironic that Mosén Millán says to forget, but he himself cannot, which is the basis for the structure of the narrative: the flashbacks in Mosén Millán's memory (introduced in the novel with the verb "recordar") as he waits in the sacristy before mass. As Dorward points out, "the Judas element in Sender's Mosén Millán is finally dispensed with in the film's significant omission of three of Paco's key last words: 'El me denunció'" (281). Consequently, "the film seems to try to absolve Mosén Millán of much of the guilt that forms such a key part of the novel's psychological analysis" since "Betriu's priest is . . . more perceptive, more intelligent, more consciously aware, and more consistently pressurized into acting as he does" (Dorward 279, 281).

The film captures the frequent allusions to Paco's virility that are in the original: Jerónima's comment over the newborn, "Vaya zagal. Seguro que no te echarán del baile" (Some guy. They surely won't kick you out of the dance, cf. 16), or the comment among the women folk that Paco "los tenía bien puestos" (they are hanging well on him, cf. 77), can only be seen in contrast to the spineless priest who ironically speaks to Paco of his own martyrdom (77-78), and to the final adjectives that describe the priest as he performs the requiem mass: "aterrado y enternecido" (frightened and touched, 105). In a significant change from the novel, Mosén Millán confronts Paco as he labors in the fields after his confrontation with Valeriano. The priest tries to hold back Paco and his social changes, but when Paco hints at the possibility of a misfortune, the priest exclaims, "¿Desgracia? Que sea yo el primero en recibirla. Miedo no tengo, que Dios siempre me protegerá" (Misfortune? Let me be the first one to receive it. I'm not afraid, since God will always protect me). This change in character, together with the aforementioned social pressures not in the original narrative, make Mosén Millán somewhat more of a tragic figure in this excellent film adaptation of Sender's novel.

Ramón Solís

Angel del Pozo's *El alijo* (*The Smuggled Goods*, 1976) is based on the 1965 novel by Ramón Solís (b. 1923). Quesada (405) notes that this novel about contraband undergoes a fundamental transformation in its cinematographic adaptation: the change in the smuggled goods from tobacco to human contraband—Portuguese laborers trying to cross Spain in order to reach France—adds a note of social criticism to the narrative, and it also changes the geography of the narrative from Gibraltar and its environs to Extremadura, Castile, and finally, the mountainous Basque country near the French border.

The protagonists of the narrative are the two truck drivers, Curro (Juan Luis Galiardo) and Paco (Fernando Sancho), and their portrayal is fundamental to both novel and film. From the beginning, Paco (a middle-aged widower) is portrayed as a religious man: he lights a candle in church and thanks Saint Christopher for a good trip. After receiving the human contraband, he is compassionate toward them, often referring to the "pobre gente" (poor folks) that are packed into the truck, and trying to provide for their well-being with water, food, or blankets on different occasions. Curro, a young bachelor, is more concerned with earning money so he can marry his girlfriend, Araceli.

A second narrative thread of the film consists of the difficult situation for the human contraband inside the truck. The Portuguese are both religious (they pray to the Virgin of Fátima) and wary (one man apprehensively brandishes his knife). The discomfort that they put up with is in exchange for the hope of a better life, but this dream is smashed when an elderly man becomes ill and dies during the journey.

As might be expected in a film about contraband, the suspense comes from the recurring threat of discovery. The Civil Guard constitutes the main threat; for years, members of this Spanish rural police force commanded respect that bordered on fear.[1] While stopped on the highway because of overheating in the engine, a pair of guards appears, but Curro's ingenuity—shouting about the stupidity of not putting the radiator cap on correctly—distracts the guards. Later appearances by the police—in Avila, when the truck is illegally parked, or guards at a gas station who ask the truckers the favor of giving a man a ride—repeat this motif.

While Paco drinks in excess in order to forget the misery of his human contraband, Curro is on the prowl, but ends up being the victim of Mirna, the brains behind the contraband operation who has arrived to keep tabs on the "merchandise." She manifests a condescending attitude toward the young trucker, calling him a pig, and ordering him to take a shower before he comes to bed with her. The next morning, when Curro uses the informal "tú" form in his conversation with Mirna, she indignantly puts him in his place: "Se acabó el tuteo" (No more using the informal "tú").

The final segment of the trip, with long shots of the truck climbing the steep, curving roads of the Pyrenees, seems to drag. The ice and snow prove an insurmountable obstacle for the truck, and the illegal Portuguese have to walk final kilometers. The cross-cut close-ups of their feet and faces—especially that of the old woman whose husband has died during the trip—capture the despair of these unfortunate immigrants, which is underscored by the nostalgic soundtrack of Portuguese *fado* music. Poetic justice prevails at the end of the film, as a dispute between Mirna and her male assistant over the briefcase filled with the money for the contraband causes their car to veer off a cliff. The high-angle shot of the wrecked car in flames is a point of view shot for the truckers. They realize that their money is going up in flames, but not so their dreams. They philosophically plan to get on with their lives, including the wedding that Curro had planned.

---

[1]The Civil Guard often appears in poems by Federico García Lorca as a force of brutal repression. Michener (63-67) relates anecdotes that confirm this perception. Recent reforms in the Civil Guard—there are now women guards as well as men—have caused these perceptions to change.

The film is clearly a product of the waning years of the Franco regime (although it had its debut shortly after the death of the *caudillo*). Both the ethical and religious elements, as well as the implicit message regarding material well-being (human contraband from the neighboring country makes Spaniards look comparatively well-off) are reflections of Spanish society in the mid-1970s.

Pablo Sorozábal

Jaime Chávarri's film *Tierno verano de lujurias y azoteas* (*Tender Summer of Lust and Rooftops*, 1992) is based on *La última palabra* (*The Last Word*) written by Pablo Sorozábal. The film explores the sexual awakening of the young male protagonist, as well as different manifestations of love. Pablo (Gabino Diego) is obsessed with his cousin Olga (Marisa Paredes), in spite of the fact that she is much older than he. Indeed, in their first encounter, she is taken aback by his forwardness. When he throws his glass over his shoulder and declares, "Mi sed, sólo tu alma puede calmar mi sed" (My thirst, only your soul can quench my thirst) her reaction is subdued: "Creo que ha sido un error inivtarte" (I think that it was a mistake to invite you). But when he suddenly becomes more brazen, saying, "Quiero hacerte el amor. Quiero penetrarte" (I want to make love to you. I want to penetrate you), she responds, "Pero tú eres un imbécil" (But you are an imbecile). Indeed, Pablo's character never gels throughout the film as a plausible one; ironically, the filmmaker even underscores some of his shortcomings, such as his overly literary speech. Olga complains, "Mira que hablas raro, ¿eh?" (You speak strangely, you know?), and Pablo explains, "He aprendido a hablar en los libros donde reside la verdad del lenguaje" (I learned to speak from books, where language's truth resides). Her other reproach, "Hablas en clichés" (You speak in clichés) does not have a defensible response, however, and although this objection is voiced toward the protagonist, it is also a self-reflexive criticism of the work.

Pablo's background is not merely literary, however. He is an immigrant from Russia, where his father went during the Spanish civil war. The film "shows" stories that Pablo "tells" his cousin Olga regarding his past, and the common thread of these stories is Pablo's past loves and sexual experiences. "Te contaré la historia de la comarada oscura, mi primer amor" (I'll tell you the story of comrade Oscura, my first love) takes us in a flashback to Odessa, where Pablo was in love with the physical education trainer at a school. Although she seduces him during an evening campfire ("Vamos, tómame. No quiero

morir virgen" [Come on, take me. I don't want to die a virgin]),
the chiaroscuro lighting used in the sequence, especially in the
close-ups of Oscura (whose name in Spanish means "Dark")
reveals that there is another side to this character. Indeed,
Oscura deceived Pablo and used him to get the physical
education instructor, a denouement hinted at by the earlier cut
from the close-up of Oscura to that of the male instructor as
they sat around the campfire.

Pablo's second story occurs in Paris, amid jazz nightclubs,
where he meets Laura, who has the "lips of a perverse nun,"
and Aída, a black photographer. In their first encounter, Aída
spanks Laura's rear end as Pablo takes photographs. Pablo
laments that on that occasion, he found her body, but Aída
found her soul. After Olga complains about the story, Pablo
recounts their second encounter. The relationship takes on a
somewhat perverse nature, as Pablo and Laura act out roles as
both a baron and his butler together with the woman who must
accept her punishment. Pablo, who comes into the room as a
hunchback with a beret, gives orders to Laura using the archaic
linguistic forms, "Besadme. Seguidme" (Kisseth me. Followeth
me), puts a handkerchief gag in her mouth, and carries her off
naked through his "labyrinthian castle."

Olga has a story of her own, since she is an actress and is
working with Doria (Imanol Arias) on a representation of *A
Midsummer Night's Dream*, which constitutes an apt intertextual reference to the follies of love. The love triangle never
fully develops here, however. Although Pablo asks Olga if
Doria is good in bed, she evades the question, responding
simply that they lived together for a while. When Doria is
visiting Olga and Pablo rings the doorbell, Doria angrily says,
"Le voy a mandar a la mierda" (I'm going to send him to hell),
but Olga mollifies the situation, saying "No seas antipático con
él" (Don't be rude to him). Even after Pablo makes love to Olga
(preceded in the film by a delightful rooftop dinner), Doria's
aggression toward Pablo is limited to his quip, "Creía que
tenías más facilidad de palabra" (I thought that you had a
better way with words). The new sexual freedom depicted in
the film seems to be accompanied by a mitigation of jealousy.

With Gabino Diego as the leading actor and the film's exploration of early sexual and sentimental experiences, there are echoes of his earlier performance in *Las bicicletas son para el verano* (*Bicycles Are for Summer*), but *Tierno verano de lujurias y azoteas* is without the profound social dimension of the latter film. Voice-overs by Pablo dominate the film narrative from the very beginning and are an attempt to capture the first-person narrative of the novel. Pablo's comment, "La amé y quizá ella me amó. Fue un verano de lujura y azoteas" (I loved her, and perhaps she loved me. It was a summer of lust and rooftops), justifies the title change from novel to film, and synthesizes Pablo's memories of his relationship with his cousin Olga.

Gonzalo Suárez

Gonzalo Suárez (b. 1934) is a multifaceted individual who is a writer, actor (he appears as Lucas in Pedro Almodóvar's *¿Qué he hecho yo para merecer esto?* [*What Have I Done to Deserve This?*]), and director of critically acclaimed films such as *Remando al viento* (*Rowing With the Wind*) and *Don Juan en los infiernos* (*Don Juan in Hell*). Several of his novels and short stories have been adapted for the screen, either by other directors or by himself. Early adaptations of his works did not meet with much success. *De cuerpo presente* (*Public Viewing*, 1963) was filmed the following year by Antonio Eceiza, but did not have its debut until 1967. Vicente Aranda's version of Suárez's short story, "Fata Morgana," also had its debut in 1967. Cohn calls it a "labyrinthine film based on the most diabolical script that you could imagine" (Quesada 446) and the Spanish critic notes that director Aranda's considerable amplification of the original story was the object of arguments between author and filmmaker, and that Suárez decided that in the future he would film his own narratives (447). Nevertheless, Quesada (447-49) further notes that Aranda also filmed an adaptation of Suárez's short story, "Bailando para Parker" ("Dancing for Parker"), which was shown at the 1969 San Sebastián Film Festival with the title *El cadáver exquisito* (*The Exquisite Corpse*), and which did not have its commercial debut until two years later—perhaps because of the unfavorable reaction by critics at the festival—with a change in title: *Las crueles* (*The Cruel Women*).

After filming a short version of his own novel, *Rocabruno bate a Ditirambo* (*Rocabruno Batters Ditirambo*, 1966), Suárez made it into a feature length film in 1969 entitled simply *Ditirambo*. The layering of narratives that is fundamental to his later work, *Epílogo* (*Epilogue*), is incipient here. José Ditirambo (Gonzalo Suárez) is an out of work journalist who accepts a detective assignment from the widow of José Urdiales (Angela Yelena) to find Ana Carmona (Charo López), the woman with whom her late husband was in love, and destroy her life. The narrative thus takes on the trappings of detective fiction, as Ditirambo follows clues that will lead him to the end of his mission. Each step of the way also brings an element of mystery: the suitcase filled with money that the wealthy Eduardo gives Ditirambo for Ana; the boxer's warning that Jaime Normando is dangerous and controls everyone's life; Dalmás's dream that Ditirambo would kill him. When Ditirambo finally wins Ana away from Normando (José Prado)—here the narrative changes tone, with a ridiculous boxing match between the two—he is not sure that he can finish his mission, because he loves her. Normando's jealousy ironically fulfills the widow's desire for revenge when he kills Ana. The widow chose Ditirambo because he was an honorable man, and this quality leads him to follow the gangster Dalmás (Angel Carmona) in order to recover the money for Ana's daughter. Another plot twist ironically fulfills the gangster's dream when his own hit man decides to kill his boss instead of Ditirambo. Ditirambo, who is wounded, miraculously leaves with the suitcase full of money, and now the widow confesses her game. She collaborated with her writer husband in selecting characters from "authentic human specimens," and both Ana and Ditirambo were her choices. After her husband's death, she decided to write the story "en el tiempo y el espacio sin condenarla a las páginas muertas de un libro" (in time and space without condemning it to the dead pages of a book). Here the narrative seems to switch to the fairy tale, as Ditirambo gives the suitcase to a girl in the countryside who is standing beside a tree and a cow before he and the widow return home. As Suárez's first feature-length film, *Ditirambo* manifests many of the themes that are found in his later works.

Epílogo (1984) won the Prix Jeunesse for best foreign film at the 1984 Cannes Film Festival. The film seems to epitomize Barthes's rhetorical question, "Isn't every story basically the Oedipus story?" (75), especially as broadly interpreted by Porter that "all tales are tales of thwarted desire in which an obstacle comparable to the incest taboo obliges a character to take a circuitous path to fulfillment" (104-105). When two writers who collaborate separate, they find that they are unable to continue writing. The younger Ditirambo (José

Sacristán) seeks out the elder Rocabruno (Francisco Rabal) in order to get one last story, an epilogue to their earlier writing. The layering of narratives begins with the very first sequence in which the camera pans from a street scene to a storefront filled with television sets that show different programs (narratives), and the camera zooms into one of the scenes depicting a hallway of a hotel; it tracks in—entering this other narrative—toward a pair of women's shoes on the floor, a metonymical device that symbolizes the woman who is the object of both writers' desire. The metanarrative of *Epílogo* tells stories about telling stories, and in each of the embedded tales, the rivalry between the father figure and the son is clear: in the first, written by the younger Ditirambo, he complains that Rocabruno's dog has bitten his own dog, and a series of actions and statements by the former "prove" to the latter that they are father and son. Male rivalry often appears in the form of boxing—Rocabruno's first story is "Cómo ganar un combate inútil" (How to win a useless fight)—and his final narrative ends with the slow-motion boxing scenes between Pacheco and Baby Face that occur in the primal setting of shallow ocean waters. The long shot of the victorious Baby Face and his shadow in the water recalls the earlier shadow of the boxer cast on the wall in the first narrative.

The radio broadcast of *Hamlet* that Rocabruno turns off in order to begin his own story is really a master narrative that comes alive again in this modern variant that is replete with fictive layering: there are intercut shots of the typewriter at which Rocabruno is composing the tale; after the boy witnesses the primal scene of sex between his mother and his uncle, he and another child theatrically reenact his father's murder; this play cuts to Rocabruno, Ditirambo, and his wife (Charo López) in a restaurant where Rocabruno plays the uncle, Ditirambo the child, and Ditirambo's wife, the mother; and the maid in the embedded story is Ana, the maid that Ditirambo meets in his former companion's house.

Although Ditirambo sacrifices something dear in order to get Rocabruno's last story—he allows his wife to live with the older writer—in the end he learns that fulfillment must come from within. After the disappearance of the father figure

(Rocabruno commits suicide), Ana gives Ditirambo a packet that the latter supposes will be his magnificent final story. The blank sheets do not represent a frustration of Ditirambo's desire, but a rite of passage, as his wife explains, "ahora si quieres historias, tendrás que escribirlas tú" (now if you want any stories, you will have to write them).

Rocabruno's symbol to show that writing is dead—the author as a dinosaur biting his own tail—implies a circularity both of his own reasoning—what remains is that "el arte imitará el arte porque el arte será el arte de imitar" (art will imitate art because art will be the art of imitating)—and of the entire film narrative. The dialogue of the final boxing story repeats itself: first the creators "tell" the story around the kitchen table, then we are "shown" the story. The final sequence brings us back to the initial sequence in the hallway of the hotel, now showing us the student who interviews Ditirambo's wife for her thesis on Spanish literature, and Rocabruno's voice-over insists that "cada vez que la puerta se abra, la historia sucederá" (each time that the door opens, the story will happen). All stories are variants of the master narrative.

Daniel Sueiro

El puente (*The Long Weekend*, 1977) is a film by Juan Antonio Bardem that is based on the novel *Solo de moto* (*Alone on a Motorcycle*, 1967) and some short stories by Daniel Sueiro (b. 1931). This road film narrates a journey that occurs on two levels: the outer journey, the trip that Juan Gómez makes from Madrid to Torremolinos on a long weekend, and the inner journey, the transformation that occurs in Juan during his excursion.

Juan (Alfredo Landa) is a mechanic who leaves his garage to begin his long weekend with his girlfriend and his motorcycle—a "museum piece" that he affectionately calls "Poderosilla" (Powerful Little Machine). Juan's co-workers urge him to attend the next day's labor union meeting in order to achieve raises in salary, and their repetition of the word "todos" (everyone together) initiates the solidarity theme, but Juan's reaction is to give them the finger. The shot of Juan in front of the mirror, however, hints that perhaps a second or new Juan will develop. Juan's first setback occurs when his girlfriend breaks their date and goes off with other guys who, if not socially superior, at least have better hygiene than the mechanic, since his (ex-)girlfriend exclaims that they smell better and have cleaner hands. (Along with *Solo de moto*, a collection of short stories by Sueiro that influenced Bardem is *El cuidado de las manos* [*Hand Care*], and this motif recurs throughout the film). As Juan aimlessly rides around Madrid, a chance encounter with two English girls in a sports car who want directions to Torremolinos, the beach resort on the southern coast of Spain, inspires Juan to also head for fun in the sun. But the English girls zoom off, leaving Juan and his old motorcycle in the dust with a curt "So long, sucker," dealing Juan another blow to his self-esteem. The motorcycle metonymically represents its owner: the bravado of its nickname belies the empty reality behind the façade. As in a picaresque narrative, Juan continues to encounter a series of characters during his journey; almost all function in relation to Juan's inner journey, as the humiliations that he suffers in relation to some is offset by the lessons on new values that he receives from others.

After the initial humiliations, Juan suffers a bit more on the road. During a rest stop in a roadside bar, Juan encounters old friends who emigrated to Germany and prospered: Rafael (Germán Cobos) now drives a Mercedes and only returns to Spain for vacation, since Spain lacks both comforts and freedom. Juan's comparatively worse economic state humiliates him, and he lies about his current status, saying that he sells motorcycles.

The lessons on new values that Juan receives mainly have to do with solidarity, but new sensitivity training is also evident. When the Civil Guard asks Juan to do a favor for someone with mechanical troubles, Juan meets a family from Durango, in northern Spain, who have a relative in jail because of his participation in a metal workers strike. The woman's comment, "Está todo muy mal, hijo," (Everything is in bad shape, son), helps drive home the lesson that Spain has many socioeconomic difficulties. When they inquire if Juan was also involved, he lies to save face. Their final comment to Juan before he leaves echoes the solidarity theme enunciated by Juan's fellow garage workers: "A ver si le sacamos entre todos" (Let's see if we can get him out by working all together).

Three other instances manifest the economic hardship in Spain as well. When Juan stops for some melon, an Andalusian man complains about how the men that he knows are unemployed nine months out of the year. Their economic hardship does not preclude their generosity, however, as they do not charge Juan for the melon. A similar situation occurs near the end of the film when a man helps Juan with his flat tire, saying, "Hoy por ti mañana por ti" (Today it's your turn to be helped, tomorrow it's mine), but also laments the fact that the men in the plaza have not been able to find work since the end of the olive harvest.

The economic difficulties do not affect just Spaniards; when an Algerian asks for work at a bar and is refused, Juan's actions represents the beginning of a change in attitude: when he receives his change, he collects his coins one by one, leaving only a single peseta as a tip for the barman in retaliation for his rude treatment of the Algerian. This constitutes one of the early cases in Spanish cinema of the representation of racism and the immigrant situation, thus presaging this theme in later films, such as Montxo Armendariz's *Cartas de Alou* (*Letters from Alou*)and Imanol Uribe's *Bwana*.

Juan then receives a more profound lesson when he encounters a group of actors who surround him and announce, "Clase obrera, te abriremos los ojos" (Working class, we will open your eyes), as they equate Torremolinos with real estate speculation and corruption. Juan, however, dismisses them as a bunch of funny crazies. Their dramatic performance, which takes place in the famous seventeenth-century theater in the town of Almagro, is an allegory about Spanish democracy. Their parody of the peace and order provided by the Franco regime (with policemen beating citizens) is too much for the conservative audience of this town in La Mancha, and the ensuing turmoil results in the confirmation of the repression that is ridiculed in their play: the civil guards arrest the entire dramatic company. The actors' song of solidarity, "No nos moverán" ("We Shall Not Be Moved") elicits a negative reaction in the as yet unchanged auto mechanic: he complains that they are ruining his trip, and asks "¿Qué tengo que hacer con vosotros? (What do I have to do with you?) Their responses doubly underscore the solidarity theme, relating it thematically to the earlier vocabulary—"La represión es cosa de todos" (Repression is everybody's business)—as well as to their special dramatic context, saying that Juan's lack of involvement makes him merely a spectator in life.

Besides the solidarity theme, Juan also receives lessons in sensitivity. Juan often personifies the Spanish macho, a somewhat brutish type who considers himself a Don Juan. When he initially meets the English girls in Madrid, he proclaims to them, "Estáis ligadas" (You've got your date), but they leave him in the dust. As he is initially about to take leave of the actors, he says, "Me esperan mis suecas, machos" (My Swedish gals are waiting for me, dudes), alluding to the myth of sexually liberated northern Europeans who began to flock to Spanish beach resorts in the 1960s. His sexual bravado is again deflated when a van of marijuana smoking hippies picks up the hitchhiking mechanic; his overaggressiveness with Sally causes a tear in her clothing, and she complains, "Look what you've done to my dress. Why?" She also admonishes him to keep his hands clean, following the earlier motif.

Juan finally reaches his destination, and sits on the beach at Torremolinos, smoking and watching the waves; this provides a more satisfying completion of his difficult journey than in the novel, where he turns back as soon as he can see the Mediterranean, eight kilometers from the coast. With the weekend more than half over, however, there is still irony in the fact that he must return home immediately. Bardem synthesizes the return trip with a montage sequence of flashbacks to the first half of the journey. At work, Juan now joins his fellow workers in their union discussions. Their gesture of offering him a light incorporates him into their group. Bardem repeats the mirror motif from the initial sequence to underscore Juan's inner transformation: the zoom-in to Juan in shallow focus standing in front of the mirror immediately before he joins his fellow workers signals the new Juan. (Bardem uses the mirror motif in the middle of the film as well. Just before Juan encounters his friends from Germany in the roadside restaurant, he washes his hands, and the camera pans up to the mirror image, where Juan speaks to himself: "Y tú eres un macho, una figura" [You are a macho man, a real character], an opinion that is totally deflated in the rest of the sequence.)

Bardem faithfully captures the idiomatic language of the original narrative in the many voice-overs that constitute Juan's thoughts as he travels the hundreds of kilometers on his motorcycle. He maintains the didactic elements from *Solo de moto* in the single reference in the filmic text to the dangers of the highway—the scene of crashed automobiles and a highway littered with their contents. This captures the message from the original without falling into the excessive preachiness of the novel. The film version magnifies some of the humor of the original: in the novel, Juan receives a traffic fine in a small town for riding in his bathing suit; in the movie, Juan is in his underwear, and has to stop in a long line of traffic for a funeral procession that crosses the highway.

Navales (181) notes that Sueiro's novel explores a fundamental human problem: the frustration that results from the disproportion between a desire and the means to carry it out. Constant references to time—or lack thereof—exist in both narratives, and certainly the lack of power in Juan's ironically named motorcycle, and the many obstacles that he encounters on his journey lead to Juan's failure to spend the weekend at the beach resort. But there is only a "failure" in the superficial sense, because in Juan's inner journey there is great success. Bardem's adaptation of Sueiro's novel foregrounds the solidarity theme, and eschews the tone of pessimism that is present at the end of the original in the negative metaphors (a miserable insect, a raging panther) that Sueiro uses to describe Juan on his return trip (125-26). This conforms to Bardem's own political ideology, and perhaps helped to win first prize for the film at the 1977 Moscow International Film Festival.

Quesada (436) notes that *El puente* represents a resurgence in director Bardem's career after a long period of mediocrity. The film also represents a dramatic change in the career of actor Alfredo Landa. Up until this point, Landa had made a career of sex farces, to the extent that the term "landismo" was coined. The change in direction following this film saw Landa go on to such marvelous roles as Paco in *Los santos inocentes* (*The Holy Innocents*) and Fendetestas in *El bosque animado* (*The Animated Forest*).

José Luis de Tomás

Javier Elorrieta's *Cautivos de la sombra* (*Captives of the Shadow*, 1993) is based on the novel *La otra orilla de la droga* (*The Other Side of Drugs*), by José Luis de Tomás. The film manifests the dark underworld of petty criminals, drug addicts, and prostitutes, a world which also appears in Uribe's *Días contados* (*Running Out of Time*). Elorrieta's movie, however, is not of the same quality as Uribe's Goya-winning film.

The protagonists, Toni (Manuel Bandera) and his girlfriend Maica (Beatriz Santana), appear trapped in a world in which their past pulls them down and does not let them begin new lives. Toni reveals that his father committed suicide when he was seven because of his mother's infidelity. Although this superficially appears to have marked Toni, it is never fully developed in the film narrative. A more important component of his past, however, is the flashback/dream sequence of his stint in prison, where he slashes the face of el Uruguayo, the prison bully who rapes other prisoners. This naturally leads to the vengeance theme, with threatening phone calls leading up to the kidnapping and gang rape of Toni's girlfriend, a sequence that is exacerbated with its fade-outs and slow motion. Maica's victimization is meant to be compelling because it follows changes in her life that seem to indicate a revindication. Now pregnant by Toni, she meets with her parents who tell her that the future has many doors and that she should open one; she decides to do so, and shows her commitment to give up prostitution and drugs in order to become an actress. Her brutal violation, however, negates this seeming escape from her entrapment of the past, and it confirms Toni's earlier pronouncements that she is in the sewer with him and that it is hard to leave hell.

The attack on Maica in turn necessitates vengeance on Toni's part, but the confrontation of the two criminals unfortunately reaches the limits of the ludicrous. After shooting el Uruguayo in the leg, he is able to limp off and then ambush Toni with his knife. Even after shooting him again—this time in the chest/heart, this seemingly invincible bad guy is able to get up and run away for a final rooftop encounter. El Uruguayo maintains his bravado until the very end, challenging Toni, "Dispara, cobarde" (Shoot, coward) as he grabs his crotch in a freeze frame. Shoot he does, with two bullets to the crotch constituting the just deserts for the rape of Toni's girlfriend that el Uruguayo had boasted of in a vengeful telephone call.

The other criminal elements also meet their just deserts. The egotistical drug addict Nano (Juan Rubio), who cuts out newspaper clippings of his crimes, is wounded in a shoot-out with police during a chase sequence following Nano's robbery of a pharmacy. Even Toni ends up in jail, where a final voice-over, "Hoy se cumplen mis primeros dos años de infierno" (Today marks my first two years of hell), indicates little hope for the future.

Both the dialogue and the overall plot indicate a clear didactic element in the narrative. The author of the novel is a former policeman who surely saw enough wasted young lives to prompt his writing of this moral tale. However, the crude violence of the film version, especially in the rape sc enes—both in prison and in the violation of Maica—is simply too much. The film version seems simplistic and tries too hard to be didactic.

Gonzalo Torrente Ballester

El rey pasmado (*The Dumbfounded King*) is Imanol Uribe's 1991 award-winning film adaptation of Gonzalo Torrente Ballester's recent novel, *Crónica del rey pasmado* (*Chronicle of the Dumbfounded King*, 1989). Although Torrente Ballester has an illustrious literary career that spans decades, and his trilogy *Los gozos y las sombras* was made into a very successful television series, this is his first novel that has been adapted as a feature-length film. *El rey pasmado* captured seven Goyas from the Spanish Film Academy in 1992: best supporting actor (Juan Diego), best original music (José Nieto), best artistic direction (Félix Murcia), best costume design (Javier Artiñano), best sound (Gilles Ortion, Ricard Casals), best make-up (R. González and J. Morales), and best production director (Andrés Santana). The iconography of the poster that advertised the movie manifests key elements of the film: Velázquez's *Venus with the Mirror* with the image of King Philip IV replacing that of the goddess of love in the mirror indicates not only the temporal framework of the narrative, but also the importance of the male gaze in an erotic setting. The desire by the king to see his wife in the nude imbues the narrative with a voyeuristic quality that is heightened because of the conflict between natural human sexuality and oppressive religion. The mise-en-scène of the film visually exploits the libidinous gaze as a fundamental thematic component of the narrative while it distinguishes between the gaze of the male character and that of the (male) spectator.

The male gaze is manifest in the early sequence when the king (Gabino Diego), visits Marfisa (Laura del Sol), the most expensive prostitute of the realm. The king's gaze is libidinous, as he contemplates the nude Marfisa, whose posture on the bed with her nude back and buttocks imitates that of the *Venus with the Mirror*, with the modification of her wearing red stockings. That Uribe used a mirror to shoot this shot also recalls Velazquez's masterpiece, *Las Meninas*. The king's comment, "Qué belleza. Es la primera vez que veo a una mujer desnuda" (What beauty. It's the first time that I've seen a nude woman), underscores both the importance of the male gaze as an erotic construct, as well as the monarch's lack of power in the face of protocol, since it implies that he has never even been able to see his own wife's body. The conflict between free will and obeying of courtly ceremony is reinforced when the ingenuous young monarch tries to give the lady one half ducat in recompense for her services, the amount that protocol indicates for the circumstances. When the count points out that a woman of Marfisa's category deserves a full ten ducats, the king's response, "Pero si yo nunca he tenido en mano tanto dinero" (But I've never held so much money before), manifests the king's lack of power, a theme that will recur throughout the film. The image of the nude Marfisa causes astonishment in the young king, and when the Count of Peña Andrada (Eusebio Poncela) asks the enthralled monarch what he is looking at during their coach ride to the palace, he replies that he only "sees" Marfisa's body.

This stupefaction not only explains the title, but introduces the fundamental narrative strategy of displacement, which in this case is visual. (Displacement in the film version generally entails a substitution of one person for another [Venus/queen, Valido/king, prostitute/queen, etc.] so as to underscore the thematic component of the libidinous gaze or to treat the queen with a modicum of decorum. The visual displacement here is a direct result of the king's mental state of astonishment. It is elliptical in that Uribe does not cut to a shot of Marfisa's body, yet it emphasizes the libidinous gaze, since the visualization on the part of the king prompts the [male] spectator to do the same.) His first act when he arrives at the palace is to ask for the keys to the "cuarto prohibido" (off-limits room) whose very name connotes a limitation on royal power. The king opens the curtain to allow light to flood into the room, a gesture of both literal and metaphorical significance, and he then draws back the curtain that covers the gigantic nudes of Titian: *Venus with the Organist*, and the *Danäe*. The novel refers to the paintings as "las mitologías que su abuelo había coleccionado" (the mythological [paintings] that my grandfather had collected, 26), and the choice of precisely these two works underscores the importance of the male gaze in the film narrative. The close-up of the open-mouthed king again visually captures the monarch's emotional state as manifested in the

The desire to gaze: Gabino Diego in Imanol Uribe's *El rey pasmado*.
Courtesy Aiete Films.

narrative's title, and Uribe further emphasizes this element in
the following sequence when Padre Villaescusa (Juan Diego),
the fanatic Capuchin monk and antagonist in both film and
novel, notes that "el Rey anda como pasmado" (the king is

going around sort of dumbfounded), and also when the narrative then returns to the off-limits room, where a servant has to call the king three times to get his attention. The subjective or point of view close-up shot that pans the nude body of Venus and lingers on her sexual organs again underscores the libidinous gaze, here displaced onto the painting.

The intertextual reference to this particular painting by Titian contains another type of displacement as well. The camera pans from right to left but stops at the middle of the painting (above Venus's groin); thus the king's gaze displaces the libidinous gaze of the musician, clad with his phallic sword, and straining his neck away from the organ to view the nude goddess. The *Danäe*, which portrays a scene of "active eroticism" (Williams 145) reinforces the theme of the libidinous gaze, except that in this case, it is feminine. But it is not just the libidinous gaze of the monarch that is in question here, since, as Laura Mulvey points out, the erotization of women on screen is constituted by three different types of male gaze: the look of the camera (which is male insomuch as a man usually does the directing and actual filming); the look of men on screen, within the film narrative, that is directed toward women on screen; and the look of the male spectator that copies the first two looks (6-18).

After the sequence in the off-limits room, the monarch attends morning mass, in which Padre Villaescusa gives a sermon against fornication. The male gaze again acquires importance, as the king now stares at the queen (played by Anne Roussel; although never named, the historical framework of the narrative and the fact that she speaks with a heavy French accent identify her as Isabelle de Bourbon, Felipe IV's first wife). The beautiful costuming of the members of the court provides a visual richness to the movie, and the dwarfs in this scene, who gossip about the king's whoring, constitute another intertextual reference to the paintings by Velazquez of court jesters such as Sebastián de Morra or Diego de Acedo, and further establish the historical authenticity of the film, since, as Hume notes, King Felipe's early introduction into profligacy was the cause of gossip mongering and scandal (54-55). The tight protocol and sense of etiquette in the Hapsburg court, and

The object of desire: Anne Roussel in Imanol Uribe's *El rey pasmado*. *Courtesy Aiete Films*.

especially the close scrutiny under which the young Felipe IV lived, may have ironically contributed to his profligacy. Hume notes that this profligacy was "the curse of his life, and the endless subject of his remorse in later years" (55); and that of his more than thirty illegitimate children, he officially recognized eight (207). The king's announcement that he wants to see the queen nude not only provokes murmurs in court and in the streets of the capital, but manifests the main theme of the narrative: the repression of human nature, and most especially, natural human sexuality. The conflict in both novel and film, then, is between this sexuality and a religion that represses or demands that one conceal it. Concretely, the narrative tension arises from the conflict stemming from the attempt by the king and those who help him to carry out his desire (the count, Marfisa, and Padre Almeida) against those who would not allow him to do so, led by Padre Villaescusa.

A fundamental aspect of the novel's tone is the humor and irony that pervade the narrative, an aspect that is apparent from the subtitle of the novel, "Scherzo en Re(y) mayor. Alegre, mas no demasiado" (Scherzo in Re(x) major. Allegro, ma non troppo). (Torrente's humor in the subtitle revolves around the play on words with Re, the second note of the musical scale, and Rey, which means king.) Although Quim Casas (79) observes that the division of characters in the film is one of "buenos" and "malos" (good guys and bad guys), the humorous tone of the narrative helps to overcome the limitations of this simplistic dichotomy. Much of the humor in the narrative is based on a satire of the zealot clergyman Villaescusa. The latter calls for a theological discussion of the king's sins, and the debate regarding the moral transgression is replete with satire. The sequence begins with what is perhaps the most visually striking image of the entire film: an overhead shot taken from the cupola over the assemblage shows the beautiful black-and-white design on the marble floor of the great hall, a design which symbolizes the dialectic nature of the proceedings. The antagonists are Padre Villaescusa, who accuses the king of mortal sins that profane the holy sacrament of marriage, and Padre Almeida, who doubts that adultery was committed, since he contends that the king and queen were not freely married, but rather, simply adolescents joined together out of sociopolitical obligations.[1] Indeed, the sociopolitical element of the

---

1The concept of free will (libre albedrío) was an important theme in the Spanish baroque period, and it should be noted that no one seems to be able to exercise it in either version of the narrative. This is directly related to the etiquette and social conventions of the court that stifled free will. Counsellor Bertaut observed of Felipe IV, "There is no prince who lives like the king of Spain. His actions and preoccupations never

debate transcends its original focus. Padre Villaescusa tries to give the king's private sins sociopolitical transcendence with his argument, "¿No es lógico y natural que Dios, indignado por los pecados de nuestro Rey, nos castigue haciéndonos perder la batalla y dejando que nuestra flota sea asaltada por los corsarios ingleses?" (Isn't it logical and natural that God, indignant about our king's sins, should punish us by making us lose the battle and letting our fleet be assaulted by the English pirates? [cf. 79]). However, Peña Andrada retorts, "No veo la lógica por ninguna parte. . . . Más bien creo que Dios los castiga [a los pueblos] por su estupidez y la de sus gobernantes" (I don't see the logic at all. . . . Rather, I believe that God punishes people for their stupidity and that of their rulers, cf. 79). Padre Almeida lends another dimension to the sociopolitical aspect of the debate when he states that misgovernment consists of "Quemar judíos, brujas y herejes; quemar moriscos; atentar contra la libertad de los pueblos; hacer esclavos a los hombres; explotarles con impuestos excesivos; pensar que no todos somos iguales . . ." (Burning Jews, witches, and heretics; committing outrages against people's freedom; making men slaves; exploiting them with excessive taxes, thinking that we are not all equal . . . , cf. 85)—which causes a swelling of murmurs from the assembled priests (the novel describes them as "estupefactos" [thunderstruck, 85]). The *Gran Inquisidor* (Fernando Fernán Gómez) who oversees the tribunal is located at the top of a pyramid of other inquisitors; this physical location conveys power both to his person and to his gaze, which is free to roam the proceedings.

The male gaze again gains importance as he brings the debate around to its raison d'être: whether the king's viewing of the nude queen is a right, or a sin. Padre Almeida contends that it is not only a right, but leads to the conferring of divine grace. Padre Villaescusa's retort combines the sexual frustration inherent in the only character who seems to take his vow of chastity seriously, together with a dosage of misogyny:

---

vary. They march forward with such a sure step, day by day, that he knows exactly where he is going every day of his life" (Defourneaux, 48-49). The concept of free will in Torrente's novel may also come by way of Cervantes's *Don Quixote*, which has deeply influenced his writing.

"¿Encuentra que la gracia del Señor se manifiesta en el coito? ¿O en la contemplación de ésos horrible colgajos de las hembras que se llaman mamas, o en la visión *contra natura* por la espalda de sus . . . de sus nalgas"? (Do you find the Lord's grace manifested in coitus? Or in the contemplation of those horrible female tatters called breasts, or in the sight from her back, *contra natura,* of her . . . her buttocks?) The final humorous deflation of Padre Villaescusa occurs when the count mentions that over half of the women on earth go around naked, and Padre Almeida notes that the women of the tribes that he christianized were, and still are, naked. This implies that nakedness is not unnatural, and that over half of the men on earth view naked women without astonishment. The image with which the sequence began—the overhead shot of the black-and-white marble floor—set the conceptual framework for the entire sequence: the "good" guy with logic and humor completely deflates the "bad" guy. Although Almeida wins the debate, he does not convince the Capuchin, who continues to view sex as something dark and evil; the black and white dichotomy between the two remains.

Both the film's montage as well as its mise-en-scène beautifully capture the power theme that is intertwined with the conflict of sexuality versus oppressive religion. The cut from the king's erotic gaze of the painting of *Venus with the Organist* to a close-up of Padre Villaescusa establishes the conflict of sexual passion (as manifested in the erotic gaze) and oppressive religion; the soundtrack further underscores the dichotomy with a switch from the musical motif associated with the erotic gaze to ecclesiastical organ music. When Padre Villaescusa is informed of the king's desires, he runs through the palace halls with a crucifix raised high, and when the king attempts to enter the queen's chamber, the crucifix blocks his way both literally and symbolically. After the king arranges a nocturnal meeting with the queen, he is frustrated by a series of locked doors. When he is finally able to open one, it leads to the wake for his deceased confessor. After saying prayers, the king attempts to leave through another door, but the circle of praying monks does not give way. The scene of the king vainly attempting to impose his will—"Déjame pasar, soy

Oppressive religion: Juan Diego and Fernando Fernán Gómez in Imanol Uribe's *El rey pasmado. Courtesy Aiete Films.*

el Rey" (Let me through, I am the king)—was shot with a high-angle long shot, and the cut to the low-angle shot of Padre Villaescusa visually diminishes the sense of power of the former, and adds to that of the latter, who seems to have not only observed the king's lack of authority, but indeed orchestrated it. The king is reduced to a solitary, crying youth in the empty halls of the palace.

This conflict between sexuality and repressive religion materializes on a secondary level as well, as the *Valido* (an admirably costumed Javier Gurruchaga who plays the role of the Count-Duke of Olivares) complains to Padre Villaescusa that he needs an heir, and that the Lord does not seem to listen to his prayers. Padre Villaescusa offers to help on the condition that the *Valido* and his wife, Doña Bárbara, renounce pleasure while they have sex. The film text adds a scene in order to underscore this second level of the conflict: at the hour of the *siesta*, Doña Bárbara stands in the doorway with her hands enticingly placed on her dress and asks her husband, "¿No te gustaría verme desnuda, completamente desnuda?" (Wouldn't you like to see me nude, completely nude?) Under the influence of Padre Villaescusa, the *Valido* believes that God has punished his lust with a fruitless relationship, and that he must follow Padre Villaescusa's plan, but the mise-en-scène visually manifests the eros/religion conflict and humorously undermines the religious argument as the *Valido* says that he must remain chaste, while at the same time he places his hand on Doña Bárbara's breast and leans over to overtly gaze at her cleavage. The exact nature of Padre Villaescusa's plan to force Providence is suppressed in the text so as to create curiosity or suspense: the priest tells the *Valido*, "Mañana se lo diré" (I'll tell you tomorrow). After devising his plan and discussing it with the abbess, who declares it to be blasphemy, Padre Villaescusa counters that it was "un medio indicado direc-tamente por el Altísimo" (a means indicated directly by the Almighty). Doña Bárbara's enigmatic question—"¿Seremos capaces?" (Will we be capable?)—as she and the Valido enter church the next morning, is the final element of mystery before the realization of Padre Villaescusa's plan. This underscores the fact that concealment is a fundamental narrative device in the film. After hearing their confession, the priest warns the couple that "el Señor les estará mirando" (the Lord will be watching you). The filmic rendition of the "ceremony" increases the irony contained in the novelistic narrative. In the latter, the sexual act is performed to the accompaniment of the Benedictus, but in an "ámbito secreto" (secret confines, 209); in the film, Doña Bárbara lies on the floor and the singing nuns form a circle around the couple with their backs toward them. The high-angled long shot of this ceremony provides an even greater Freudian symbolism to the act, and the montage of intercut high and low-angle medium and close-up shots that manifest the pleasure of the couple as they copulate, contrasted with the long shot of Padre Villaescusa on the altar as he says mass, creates a greater sense of irony (and perversion) in the film version. In addition, it is not only Doña Bárbara who gives "un suspiro prolongado y feliz" (a prolonged and happy sigh) as in the novel (209), but the *Valido*'s cry of ecstasy off screen as we see Padre Villaescusa on the altar leads the priest to exclaim, "No hay manera" (It's no use), thus humorously undercutting the absurdity of his plan.

The queen's nude body is the obscure object of desire for both the king and the (male) spectator; the voyeuristic nature of the novel is magnified in the screen adaptation, since film is inherently a voyeuristic medium, as spectators in a darkened room view the activities of characters on screen. The tension inherent in desire is heightened in the film version of the narrative because, like in the myth of Tantalus, the object of desire is always just out of reach for the spectator: the fulfillment of the king's desire occurs through ellipsis, again underscoring the narrative's fundamental technique of concealment. (And concealment enhances our desire to gaze, as Velázquez shows us with his *Venus with the Mirror*. Brown notes that "Velázquez heightens the charged eroticism of the painting" when he "shows the back of the figure in its entirety, but reveals the front only partially in the mirror" [182]). There is, then, a divergence between the look of the male narrative character and the look of the (male) spectator, since the erotic component of the amorous rendezvous occurs for the king off screen, and is displaced through the simultaneity of the consummation of the relationship between the *Valido* and Doña Bárbara. This is achieved through the film narrative's structure of rhythmic montage, and heightened through the spatial concurrence of the two events, as the church belongs to the same convent where the king and queen carry out their amorous encounter. The clock (Torrente 182) that Marfisa tells the abbess that she will request of the king in compensation for allowing the amorous rendezvous to occur in the convent has its historical foundation; Hume notes that the clock of the convent of San Plácido was said to have been a gift as "one of the king's peace offerings" (351) for the scandal that he caused there in 1632.

The appearance of the king and queen following their amorous rendezvous confirms the achievement of the object of desire, and faithfully captures the description in the novel: they appear "muy cogidos del brazo y con rostro sonriente. Todo el mundo comprendió lo que había pasado" (walking very closely arm in arm and with a happy face. Everyone understood what had happened, 212). The concealment of the object of desire functions even better in the film than in the novel, since the screen version of the narrative eliminates the scene in which the naked queen steps into her bathtub; the reader thus achieves the goal before the king, and the level of voyeuristic desire is deflated. (The bath scene with Marfisa represents a displacement of this motif.) Another possible factor in the elimination of the bath scene might be a sense of respect toward the queen that the film conveys. In the novel, when the king stares at the queen's cleavage, the dwarfs' joke regarding the king's wishes—"'Quiere saber si la Reina tiene tetas'—exclamó un bufón malicioso" ('He wants to know if the queen has tits,' a mischievous jester exclaimed, 42); the film version, however, displaces the lascivious stare to the *Valido* and his wife, and the buffoon's coarse humor is eliminated in favor of a simple comment that the king had gone to a whore.

The good news that the Spanish troops have been victorious and the fleet has arrived from the Indies further deflates Padre Villaescusa's ridiculous logic and leads to a happy ending. The arrival of silver and gold into the royal coffers will allow the king to buy the queen a new dress. This idea also allowed the scriptwriters to include a final scene that further provides thematic and structural coherence to the film. In this added final scene, the king enters the queen's bedroom, and they both look at a mirror, which, as the queen notes, was installed that day at the express order of His Majesty. The king offers a present of red stockings to the queen, and she puts them on and reclines on her bed with her back to the king, who observes her in the mirror. This, of course, repeats the Velázquez-like imagery of Marfisa at the beginning of the film. Again, there is greater discretion shown toward the monarchs, as we do not see the bared buttocks that we saw with the prostitute.   The red stockings are a fetish, and their erotic connotations acquire their full meaning through the syntagmatic relationship with their other occurrences in the narrative in which they are worn by the most expensive prostitute of the realm. Marfisa wears them in the initial sequence, and also later, when, disguised as a nun, she helps

Accomplices to desire: Laura del Sol and Joaquim Almeida in Imanol Uribe's *El rey pasmado. Courtesy Aiete Films.*

arrange the amorous rendezvous between the king and the queen in the convent. Uribe's use of a slow-motion shot of the red stockings that appear under Marfisa's habit as she runs through the cloister underscores their erotic nature somewhat more than the description in the novel: "El Rey la vio marchar, y juraría haber descubierto, entre el vuelo de la falda, unos zapatos de hebilla y unas medias granate" (The king saw her leave, and he would swear that he had seen, as her skirt flew about, buckle shoes and garnet stockings, 198). The slow-motion shot serves to prolong and intensify the libidinous stare of both the king and the (male) spectator.

The shot of the queen in the mirror transcends its intertextual reference to Velázquez, however, and performs an aesthetic function analogous to that of Renaissance paintings with the same motif. Art historian John Berger notes that in the Renaissance painting of nudes with mirrors, "the real function of the mirror was . . . to make the woman connive in treating herself as, first and foremost, a sight" (51) and she becomes objectified, is transformed from being simply naked to being nude, since "to be naked is to be oneself. To be nude is to be seen naked by others and yet not recognized for oneself. A naked body has to be seen as an object in order to become nude. (The sight of it as an object stimulates the use of it as an object.) Nakedness reveals itself. Nudity is placed on display" (54). This final male gaze doubly reifies or objectifies the queen, since wearing the red stockings equates her with the eroticism of the best prostitute of the realm. The gaze inherently objectifies the other, but, as E. Ann Kaplin notes, objectification "may be an inherent component of both male and female eroticism as constructed in western culture" (31). Human nature and common sense (with some help from the underworld) have triumphed; the zealot Capuchin was foiled, and the boyish king has achieved his goal.

Now that the "gaze" has been accomplished by the king in the amorous encounter in the convent, he has acquired a position of power, and the queen acquiesces to his desire. Nevertheless, the queen does not represent passive erotic reification in the narrative, since she takes an active role in the consummation of desire, first inviting His Majesty to come to her room at 11:00 p.m. and then deciding with Colette on which negligee would be the most appropriate for the occasion. (Foreign visitors to the court of Felipe IV were often amazed at the relative freedom exercised by the queen and the ladies of court with regard to their social interaction with males.) The final iris to the darkened screen with the image of the smiling king in the upper left hand corner as the credits begin no longer shows astonishment, but joy; the eroticism is controlled within the confines of the socially approved paradigm of marriage, and thus allows the film narrative to have a "happy ending." (The ending may be somewhat "bittersweet," since the Spanish spectator is well aware that Felipe would have another wife, Mariana de Austria, and numerous lovers.)

The supernatural assistance in achieving the king's goal comes from the Count of Peña Andrada, and the film version does a marvelous rendition of the count's supernatural qualities, beginning with the symbolic color of his red attire. Padre Villaescusa's comment that 90 percent of all Galicians go to hell is ironic in the extratextual context that Torrente himself is from Galicia, but also refers to the count, since the *Valido* has already ascertained that the Count of Peña Andrada is from Galicia, "tierra de brujas" (land of witches). (Of course, Galicians refer to their homeland in that way—"terra meiga" —which could also be translated as "bewitched land".) Both of these comments characterize the count early in the narrative as a somewhat suspicious and perhaps supernatural character, and therefore capture the novel's early characterization of the count's supernatural element that appears in the description, "La carroza corría por la calle, llena de baches, como por la superficie de un espejo" (The carriage flew through the pot-holed street as if over the surface of a mirror, 15), as well as the comment, "Todo es muy raro" (Everything is strange, 17). Lucrecia's observation that the count's eyes "alumbraban toda la habitación" (lighted up the entire room, 23), can be taken as a supernatural element, but it is also certainly another example of the male libidinous gaze. With the camera at ground level, a tracking shot of chickens introduces the sequence in which the devil appears to Padre Rivadesella. As the count as devil /rooster chases the chickens, he is gazing at their rears, much like the king with his women. The voice off screen that begins "Siento haberte hecho esperar" (Sorry I made you wait) is clearly that of the count, and the shot of a rooster in the window of the monastery cuts to that of the devil in human form. This rings true to the novel; when Padre Rivadesella first observes the count, "Buscó una referencia en su memoria, y lo único que se le recordó fue un gallo . . . con algo raro, quizá en la cresta" (He searched his memory for a reference, and the only thing that he remembered was a rooster . . . with something strange, perhaps on his crest, 87). When the devil takes his leave, "Al Padre Rivadesella le recordó algo, pero, al igual que aquella tarde en la sala de los consejos del Santo Tribunal, lo único que se le representó en la mente fue la figura de un gallo" (It reminded Father Rivadesella of something, but, just as on that afternoon in the council room of the Holy Tribunal, the only thing that came to mind was the figure of a rooster, 135). Shot through a blue filter, the count/devil's face is always in the shadows, and when the conversation with the friar ends, he slowly vanishes.

The mise-en-scène allows this devil/count to suddenly appear with equal facility. After the king's attempt to visit the queen's chamber was thwarted, a tracking shot follows him down the hallway, and when another locked door frustrates him, the camera pans from left to right as he crosses the empty hallway to sit and cry; when the camera pulls back and pans left, the count is unexpectedly there, as if by magic, thus further imbuing him with supernatural qualities. When the count appears in the ballroom, he throws his hat up into the air, and it magically flies in a circle and returns to him. After dancing with the Portuguese lady, Francisca Tavora, they plan a midnight rendezvous, but their lovemaking is interrupted by Padre Villaescusa and soldiers who have come to arrest the count and thwart the king's plans. The count hides behind the door, and when Padre Villaescusa leaves after not finding his victim, Francisca shuts the door but finds no one there. The novel's description is unequivocal: "Le pareció [a Francisca Tavora] ver en la pared la silueta de un hombre alto, con espada y sombrero de larga pluma, como el conde: la silueta que hubiera dejado alguien al filtrarse por la pared, no muy clara, por supuesto . . . el conde parecía sonreírle desde el fondo de los tiempos" ([Francisca Tavora] seemed to see on the wall the silhouette of a tall man with a sword and a hat with a long feather, like the count: the silhouette that someone who had filtered through the wall would leave, not very clear, of course . . . the count seemed to smile at her from the depth of time), and Tavora shouts "¡Me acosté con el diablo!" (I went to bed with the devil, 168). In the film version, Tavora merely looks around the room calling "¿Conde?, ¿Conde?" (Count? Count?) In this scene, then, the screen adaptation is less explicit than the novel, allowing the viewer to take a more active role in the creation of the film text's meaning. It is not without irony that Padre Villaescusa has a slip of the tongue when he declares before the assembled theologians that "Esta reunión el diablo la convocó, perdón, señoría, quiero decir, la provocó" (The devil called, excuse me, your lordship, I mean provoked, this meeting), since he himself called for the debate. To further connote the diabolical aspect of the count in the film version, Padre Villaescusa says, "Ese infernal Peña Andrada le ha prometido arreglarle una cita con la Reina . . . es, sin duda, un instrumento del diablo" (That infernal Peña Andrada has promised to arrange a date with the queen for him . . . he is, without doubt, an instrument of the devil). At the end of the film, after Marfisa and Lucrecia escape with Padre Almeida and Peña Andrada in a carriage, a shot of the carriage stopped on a foggy road cuts to the interior where the maid asks Marfisa where the priest and Peña Andrada have gone, and she replies, "Al infierno, seguramente" (To hell, surely).

The release of *El rey pasmado* in late 1991 is not without certain irony. As the country prepared to host the Olympics, the Expo-92, and a host of cultural events in commemoration of the "discovery" of America, this portrait of a powerless king and religious fanatics constitutes a deflation or demythification of Spain's hegemony and cultural unity based on empty dogmatism. The ridicule of Padre Villaescusa, and—in the words of the Duchess of the Maestrazgo—all the "imbeciles" who believe in the nonsense espoused by the likes of the Capuchin priest could not have been more timely.

Torrente Ballester's *Crónica del rey pasmado* has a structure that is extremely cinematographic, following a pattern of rhythmic montage. Together with the fact that it is very much a "novela dialogada," it must have been easy for scriptwriters Juan Potau and Gonzalo Torrente Malvido and director Uribe to maintain the tone and spirit of the original in the film adaptation. At the same time, Uribe exploits the voyeuristic aspects of the original narrative, especially with intertextual references to painting, and thus uses what Bazin refers to as the creativity necessary for a successful transition from page to screen in his interpretation of the novel (55). Joy Gould Boyum's theory that a screen adaptation "is always, whatever else it may be, an interpretation" (61-62) applies well in this case. Uribe's film version of Torrente Ballester's *Crónica del rey pasmado* is a superb reading of the original text, and represents one of the best examples in recent Spanish cinema of the adaptation from page to screen.

José María Vaz de Soto

José M. Gutiérrez Santos's 1978 film, *Arriba Hazaña* (*Up with Hazaña*), is based on the 1969 novel *El infierno y la brisa* (*Hell and the Wind*) by José María Vaz de Soto (b. 1938). The title of the film is a play on words; "Hazaña" means "feat" or "deed," but it is also a homonym for (Manuel) Azaña, who served as president of Spain during the Republic, and under whose leadership the Catholic church lost a great deal of power in Spain. The film portrays the religious education system during the Franco regime, and in a broader sense, political repression and the transition to democracy.

The priests who represent the oppressors at the school are Brother Ramiro (Fernando Fernán Gómez) and Brother Eluterio (Héctor Alterio). The former represents the hard-line approach and often metes out physical punishment to the students; his bywords are "disciplina y autoridad" (discipline and authority). The latter represents a more subtle, psychological type of repression. Indeed, Méndez Leite notes that in the film there is a "suggestive duel between two forms of oppression" represented by these two characters (23).

The male teenage students become more and more rebellious as the film progresses. Some of their rebellious acts have a specific motivation against the system; in this case the system is, superficially at least, religion, and the pranks border on blasphemy (putting a dead bird on a crucifix, placing hosts and a chalice with Coca-Cola in someone's bed, letting a d ove—symbol of the Holy Spirit—loose during chapel and then shooting it). Others are typical teenage pranks—smoke bombs and writing slogans on the blackboards—but barricading themselves into the dormitory quarters takes on specific political connotations as the act is carried out with the anarchist tune "A las barricadas" ("To the Barricades") repeating itself on the soundtrack, and as the students use terms like "la primera jornada revolucionaria" (the first day of the revolution) and "camarada" (comrade). The resolution of the conflict—expulsion of the ringleaders, and a new director who implements some superficial reforms such as student referenda—points allegorically to the transition to democracy in

Spain after the death of Franco. The final shot of the students singing the same song with which the film began hints that nothing has really changed.

The character of Brother Ramiro manifests the effects of the civil war on this segment of Spanish society. During an early crisis in which a student who has been locked in a closet starts a fire and almost dies of smoke inhalation, Ramiro quips "bastante sufrí en la guerra" (I suffered enough in the war). When he enters a classroom to punish the students, Brother Ramiro clearly carries a book with him entitled *La legión* (*The Legion*), which refers to soldiers of Franco's Nationalist army. The director tries to assuage Brother Ramiro at one point, saying, "Yo sé que usted ha sufrido mucho en la guerra, pero los tiempos han cambiado" (I know that you suffered a lot in the war, but times have changed)—a point that Ramiro and many like him during the regime found difficult to acknowledge. Indeed, even the terminology used by the priests reflects a wartime mentality: when the students carry out another prank and have someone call the priests' residence inquiring about a massage parlor, a priest reacts, "atacan por todos los frentes" (they are attacking on every front). During a search of students' quarters, two brothers lament that perhaps the overexertion of authority is the cause of the rebellion among the students: "La culpa la tiene el Hermano Ramiro que cree que todavía es sargento de la Legión" (Brother Ramiro, who thinks he's still a sergeant in the Legion, is to blame). Thus, the civil war imposes itself on the psyche of its participants and shapes their interaction with others for years to come.

Angel Vázquez

Javier Aguirre's cinematographic adaptation of Angel Vázquez's *La vida perra de Juanita Narboni* (*The Dog's Life of Juanita Narboni*, 1976) was entitled *Vida/perra* (*Life/Bitch*, 1981). It is an audacious filmic experiment, because the entire movie consists of a monologue by Esperanza Roy, who portrays Juanita. Although there are several examples of dramatic monologues that have been great successes in contemporary Spanish theater (*Cinco horas con Mario* [*Five Hours with Mario*] and *La guerra de nuestros antepasados* [*Wars of Our Ancestors*]—both dramatic adaptations of novels by Miguel Delibes), it is rare indeed to encounter this narrative vehicle in film, and it inevitably leads to a division in opinion: those who deem it a daring and brilliant artistic rendition, and those who believe this form to be untenable and doomed to failure. Although critics of the latter opinion are certainly right in that such a film would be unlikely to gain much commercial success, Esperanza Roy's gripping performance must be recognized as one that brilliantly delves into the soul of the character that she portrays.

The voice-over with which the film begins, "En la soledad están los otros más presentes que nunca" (In solitude, the others are more present than ever), announces the main themes of the narrative: solitude, memories, and the attempt to come to terms with people who are no longer with us. The initial visual image of the film is an extreme close-up of a woman's eyes in an old photograph; the camera pulls back to show a woman from the 1940s. The cut to the long shot of a middle-aged Juanita alone on a beach underscores that the relationship between the two women, a daughter and her deceased mother, will be fundamental to the film. Juanita addresses her mother and others in impassioned second-person discourse, but her mother is always the person to whom she returns.

Little by little, we glimpse into the past and view the characters who shape Juanita's life: an egotistical father who drank, never made her mother happy, and finally abandoned the family; a sister who was at once despised and envied; a boyfriend who abandons her; and above all, her domineering mother. Her hatred of her father is extrapolated to that of all men—"Papá es un egoísta como todos los hombres" (Dad is an egotist like all men)—and she later accuses the boyfriend who abandoned her of being a queer.

All of the filmic spaces echo her solitude: the beach, her bed, the living room, an empty staircase, her bathroom, a church, Roman ruins, a cemetery. Each of the locales has a special significance. The latter two in particular connote loss, and underscore her solitude, as her black garb connotes a deep mourning for her lost loved ones. Lamenting that they are all gone, she anguishes, "Lo importante es morir a tiempo" (The important thing is to die on time). The living room, with the couch on which Juanita sits, seems to become a psychiatrist's office in which her intimate confessions are revealed. Her comment while facing her bathroom mirror, "parezco una máscara" (I seem like a mask), reveals the dichotomy between the inner and outer self of this character—and of us all.

Sibling rivalry surfaces throughout these confessions. Juanita expresses her hatred of her sister, claiming that she (Juanita) was their parents' only real child, her sister being merely "un error de la naturaleza" (a mistake of nature). She accuses her sister of being obsessed with sex, and repeatedly calls her a whore. Nevertheless, she confesses, "A mí me gustaría ser como tú" (I would like to be like you). Her frustrated sexuality leads her to admit, "Un hombre es lo que me hace falta" (What I need is a man), and the double bed on which she sleeps alone connotes solitude through the absence of the other. This same frustration causes her to imagine a mouse running up her legs, which paralyzes her, but also causes her to fantasize, "Acabará metiéndose en el chisme" (It will end up sticking itself into the thing). The discovery that it is merely an ant results in an emotional outburst, as she cries in a combination of anger and frustration, "Te arranco la cabeza, te pisoteo, te pisoteo" (I'll rip your head off, I'll step on you, I'll step on you). Her bed also symbolizes the dichotomy between passivity (sleeping) and activity (waking); her life is so miserable that at times she does not dare get up, and she prays God for sleep, hoping that when she awakes, everything would be different. Indeed, Juanita often complains of being tired, and her existential ennui culminates in her confession during the final beach scene, "Cada día me cuesta más ponerme las medias" (Each day it is harder for me to put my stockings on). The dissolve to the initial photograph of her mother brings the narrative full circle, although the black shading is now greater as if to emphasize the dark relationship between mother and daughter. The final zoom-in to the extreme close-up of her mother's eyes underscores both the mother's dominance and the visual aspect of Juanita's—and our—memories. Indeed, the past holds her hostage; although she rips up old papers, it is a vain attempt to break with the past, and she admits that losing the photograph of her mother would have horrible consequences, since the absence of her image would break the tenuous link to the past and leave her completely, eternally alone. She can only lament, "Cuánto daño me has hecho, Mamá" (You caused me so much harm, Mama).

Esperanza Roy expresses a magnificent range of frustrated emotions, as she cries from despair, whispers from loneliness, and curses from anger. The changes in locale and the varied camera angles and shots relieve what otherwise might have resulted in monotony in this audacious film adaptation.

Manuel Vázquez Montalbán

Manuel Vázquez Montalbán (b. 1939) is a novelist whose fame for the general public rests on the creation of Pepe Carvalho, a private detective, gourmet, and ex-CIA agent based in Barcelona who is the star of both a Spanish television series as well as feature-length films—*Tatuaje, Asesinato en el comité central, El laberinto griego,* and *Los mares del sur*.[1]

Tatuaje (*Tattoo*, 1977) was brought to the screen by Juan José Bigas Luna three years after the appearance of the novel. The appearance of a cadaver washed up on a beach in the initial sequence provides a note of mystery, as well as the name of the narrative: the tattoo, "I was born to revolutionize hell" appears on the dead man's shoulder. Detective Pepe Carvalho (Carlos Ballesteros) is hired by Ramón (Carlos Lucena), the owner of a beauty salon, in order to find out the dead man's identity. Pepe's lifestyle—he is the lover of Charo (Pilar Velázquez), a prostitute who works in Barcelona's red-light district—allows him to move about the sordid world of lowlifes and criminals with ease, and also provides him with important tips: the police begin to round up prostitutes in order to get information about the dead man, who appears to have been involved in drug trafficking. His involvement with Charo also manifests his tough character—when he discovers the "boyfriend" of another prostitute in Charo's house, he punches and throws him down the stairway. Pepe represents the macho, hard-boiled detective who handles things with his fists instead of resorting to the easy violence of guns.

Pepe's visit to a tattoo artist in Barcelona provides him with a lead, which takes him to Holland. The shots of the boats and canals of Amsterdam, together with striking long shots of Barcelona, constitute the urban landscapes that provide visual appeal for the film. The canals of Amsterdam are also the locale for action and suspense in the film: Pepe learns more about the identity of the dead man from Spaniards who work at a Phillips factory: his name is Julio Chesma.

---

[1] I have been unable to view the latter two films.

Someone thinks that the detective is getting too close to the truth, however, and decides to scare him off by attacking him and throwing him in the canal. The multiple channels of information in cinema that Metz postulates are manifest here: the film version of the narrative can capture the atmosphere of the Dutch capital in a way that the novel could not, since the thugs speak to each other in Dutch, with translations provided by subtitles. The laughter of the female thug, and the fact that she grabs Pepe's ass before the others slash his face represents a demythification of the macho detective.

In spite of this "warning," Pepe stays on the trail, and information from Julio's lover takes him back to Barcelona to another sometimes lover, sometimes friend, Teresa (Mónica Randall), who let Julio use her parents' house in Caldetas, outside Barcelona. Pepe's tough guy character again comes through, as he manhandles Teresa in order to get information from her. The close-up of her face signals the flashback to the house in Caldetas, where Teresa found bloodstains, but no victim. A second flashback provides another key bit of information: she once found Julio in Caldetas in bed with a red-head. Pepe can now put another piece of the puzzle together: Julio's lover was Queta, Ramón's wife. Pepe goes to Ramón for his payment, and the final flashback represents what the beauty salon owner tells the detective: when he found Queta and Julio in bed, his thugs beat up the lover, and he then obliged his wife to provide the deathblows with a small bronze statue. The film expands somewhat on the ending of the novel using the typical transition from telling to showing. In the original narrative, Pepe reads in the paper that Ramón was found dead with scissors through his neck, and that Queta had disappeared; the film shows Ramón attempting to strangle his unfaithful wife—"Basura, eres una auténtica basura" (Garbage, you are real garbage)—and she stabs him.

Pepe's comment regarding circularity when he leaves Holland for his starting point—Barcelona— should be taken on two levels. There is certainly the obvious level of physical, geographical return, but there is also an ironic circularity in the narrative in that Ramón is at once the client who pays for the discovery of the victim's identity, the "author" of his murder, as well as a victim himself.

Although Pepe claims that he discovered that Queta was the lover of the blond man with the tattoo because of the song of that name, Piquer's rendition of "Tatuaje" is heard only sparingly on the soundtrack. In the novel, Pepe's memory of the lyrics, as well as the epigraph containing lyrics from the song, make a clearer connection.

Tatuaje is Bigas Luna's first feature-length film and marks the beginning of an important cinematic career.

Vicente Aranda adapted *Asesinato en el comité central* (*Assassination in the Central Committee*, 1982) for the screen the year after its publication. Here, the detective travels from Barcelona to Madrid to discover the identity of the assassin of the leader of the Spanish Communist party who is stabbed during a blackout while presiding over a meeting of the party's central committee. The change in locale is significant and underscores the importance of the political theme in the film.

Carvalho's investigation is set against the background of Spain's transition from dictatorship to democracy. Indeed, Alvares and Frías note that Aranda was more interested in the representation of this period of Spanish history than in the detective himself (131), whom he considers very unpleasant: "I detest Carvalho's morals, his cynicism, the use he makes of women . . ." (Vera 133). Carvalho, then, is merely an instrument for Aranda to tell this chronicle. The director states, "He only interests me from the point of view that he drives the narration. Practically nothing happens to him throughout the film; he is watching what happens to others" (Alvares and Frías 136).

One technique that Aranda uses to lend credence to this historical chronicle is constant references to the media: close-ups of headlines in well-known Spanish newspapers, photographs of famous politicians such as Communist party leader Santiago Carrillo, and above all, television images, all underscore the period of transition to democracy. The events surrounding the death of Franco (with televisions everywhere transmitting images of that historical moment) inspired

Aranda to use the television images to obtain what he calls a "multivision" in which the spectator "could be in that way in two places at the same time, in the real and in the retransmitted" (Vera 136). But even this element of the historical chronicle does not escape the satirical gaze of the director, since the television images of the funeral of the assassinated Communist leader were in reality those of Franco's funeral.

Aranda satirizes both ends of the political spectrum in the film. When Carvalho meets Fonseca, the Fascist policeman in charge of the investigation, a close-up of the detective's hand as he wipes it off shows a gesture of sheer disdain. Fonseca ironically considers himself a professional, but his statement, "Ayer perseguí a rojos, hoy a amarillos y quizá mañana a violetas" (Yesterday I persecuted reds; today, yellows; and tomorrow, maybe violets), constitutes a ludicrous deflation of this character. The wheelchaired ex-CIA chief and his female companion, Marilyn—characters that are not in the novel and which Aranda admits as being "all my invention" (Vera 134) also constitute a satirical element. The ex-CIA chief refuses to help Carvalho by confirming the identity of the assassin until the detective decides to play hardball, filling the handicapped man's mouth with bullets and pushing his wheelchair out into the street among traffic. He whispers the name to Carvalho, after having swallowed the bullets out of fear! The main demythification of the Left arises from the question that the detective asks all of the Communist party members whom he investigates: why are you in the party? Their evasive answers manifest a lack of real conviction. So too do comments such as that by Juan Sepúlveda (Héctor Alterio): in order to take political meetings, "hay que tener el culo de hierro" (you have to have an ass of steel), or the common leftist joke during the early years of democracy, "contra Franco andábamos mejor" (we were better off against Franco). The soundtrack adds to the comic, satirical tone of the film, since the music consists of variations on the "Internationale"—played on everything from flute to organ to bagpipes. Aranda intentionally filmed the movie with a comic strip tone, but Alvares and Frías believe that the comic strip tone that Aranda imbued in the film detracts from the chronicle that he intended to carry out (132).

Alvares and Frías (132) note that the script eliminates the sequences of the novel that occur in Barcelona, so as to concentrate on Madrid. The final sequence also differs from the novel, where Carvalho meets with Gladis in the airport and has a sexual encounter with her—a sequence that was in the original script, but which Aranda substituted with the freeze frame of Carmela that merely hints at a future sexual encounter with the detective. Aranda also decided to change actors to represent the protagonist Carvalho. Carlos Ballesteros played Carvalho in Bigas Luna's first Carvalho film, *Tatuaje*, in 1977, and in the series on Spanish television, actor Eusebio Poncela played the detective. In Aranda's case, the decision was based on economic reasons as much as anything else: both Patxi Andión and Victoria Abril were under contract by Aranda's producer for another project that fell through, and they consequently were incorporated into *Asesinato en el comité central*. Although the incorporation of Abril into the cast may have been positive—Alvares and Frías (136) believe that the change in the character of Carmela and in Carvalho's relationship with her is the best part of the film—Andión's portrayal of the detective is not Oscar (or even Goya) material. Perhaps it is difficult to value the performance of an actor who is almost always speaking through the cigarette holder in his mouth.

Fernando Vizcaíno Casas

Fernando Vizcaíno Casas (b. 1926) is the author of several best-selling works that satirize the contemporary social and political situation in Spain from the point of view of someone who was closely allied with the Franco regime. Consequently, changes under the democratic governments of the transition and the Socialist era are the targets of the author's ridicule. Lawyer, newspaper columnist, novelist, and film critic (he is the author of the *Diccionario del cine español*), Vizcaíno Casas's works hit a chord among Spaniards who are nostalgic for the seemingly less complicated days under Franco; both his novels and their screen adaptations have had massive commercial success, although they have not received favorable reviews by Spanish film critics.

Niñas . . . al salón (Girls . . . to the Living Room, 1976) appeared on screen only a year after it appeared in print. Director Vicente Escrivá undoubtedly wanted to take advantage of the immense popularity of the book, as well as the changes in censorship laws that allow nudity on screen and make this film a good example of the *destape* phenomenon. The living room of the title is actually in a brothel, which is the focal point through which a variety of characters pass, providing a commentary on post–civil war Spain. The brothel is permitted to function due to the fact that the madam had given refuge to a man during the fratricidal conflict who ironically turned out to be none other than a bishop. The wide variety of clients includes a Galician (Francisco Algora) who is looking for a wife. Since he comes from the countryside, he is able to provide fresh food, a motif that underscores the difficult time that residents in Madrid had during these "years of hunger." There is criticism in the film toward the hypocrisy in post–civil war Spanish society, as a bourgeois husband with a fetish for young girls dies while having sex, and his wife refuses to accept the news, insisting that he is in Toledo. The best criticism in the film comes in the character of Don Acadio (José Luis López Vázquez), a government censor, who declares that his job is to defend Spaniards' morals. Although he censors elements of a cabaret routine, he himself is an assiduous client of the brothel.

The strongest irony in the film comes when Acadio reviews a Western filmed by Félix (José Sacristán). The passionate dialogue of the couple on screen in the original version is completely changed in the fixed version; instead of erotic desire, they talk of purchasing a horse and cattle. The kisses remain, however, and when another censor complains that the fixed version is now worse because they are made out to be brother and sister, Acadio retorts that's just what you can expect from Americans, who are a bunch of degenerates. This humorous scene alludes to the actual case of censorship regarding John Ford's *Mogambo*, where Franco regime censors attempted to avoid an insinuation of adultery with the result that they insinuated incest instead!

Aside from the visits by myriad clients, the film includes two melodramatic subplots regarding the madam, Laura (María Vico). The first involves her lover Antonio (Simón Andreu), an ex-Republican doctor who must leave Madrid and begin to practice medicine in Barcelona. Antonio is seduced by the young daughter of the director of the hospital where he works, and he hypocritically chooses the young nurse—and professional advancement—over the woman he loved. The other melodramatic subplot interweaves the hypocrisy theme, and concerns Laura's son, Luis. The teenager has been in a Jesuit school in San Sebastián in northern Spain during the war, and two montage sequences underscore the hypocrisy of those years. After a priest confirms that his schooling has solidified his religious and moral base, Escrivá cuts to a scene of the boys huddling around a pornographic novel. The subsequent scene of his host family declaring that Luis and their son Nacho represent "the yeast of the new Spain" ironically cuts to the brothel where the girls are called "down to the living room" to show their stuff. The discovery by Nacho's parents that Laura is a madam ruins both Luis's friendship with his schoolmate, as well as his relationship with his girlfriend, and this leads to a lachrymose confrontation between mother and son. Although Laura maintains that running the brothel was for her son's sake, the disgraced Luis refuses to pardon her. Nevertheless, the comedy could not end on that note, and following the conciliatory and moralizing "Aprenderemos a vivir juntos"

(We'll learn to live together), there is a cut to the final scene in which two clients, father and son, argue over the girls.

Unlike his other works, Vizcaíno Casas did not write *La boda del señor cura* (*The Priest's Wedding*, 1977) in a comic vein. Like his *De camisa vieja a chaqueta nueva* (*Turncoat*), however, the work deals with the transformation of an individual Spaniard as Spanish society as a whole undergoes the major transition from dictatorship to democracy. As the title hints, the social transformation is exemplified by a priest who decides to leave the priesthood and marry. The film version of the novel, directed by Rafael Gil in 1979, follows a twenty-five-year trajectory in the life of Juan Caní (José Sancho). The narrative begins in a Catholic boys school in which the Fascist ideology of the Franco regime dominates the pedagogy: the priest invokes the notion of "interior discipline" as espoused in the *Formación de selectos* (*Formation of the Select*) and the students sing Fascist hymns with arms raised in fascist salutes.

Once Caní becomes a Jesuit, his troubles begin, as he rebels against the orders of the tyrannical rector of the school where he is assigned. This rebellion against conservative society grows with each new assignment for the Jesuit: as parish priest in a small town, he confronts the mayor who wants to run things as if he were a *cacique* (political boss); in a mining town, he joins the workers in a strike and ends up in prison; he then works in a factory where he becomes part of the "central committee" of the Communist party, which orders him to subvert the Church from the inside by giving Marxist sermons. His rebellion culminates in his announcement from the altar that he is rejecting his priesthood in order to marry his lover. His claim of being a victim of a hypocritical society ironically proves true when his lover rejects him due to family pressures in order to marry a wealthy seventy-year-old man. However, he finally does marry a flamenco artist who became a stripper on his recommendation—one of the many grotesque and absurd details of this narrative. Indeed, the grotesque and the absurd predominate in the film. There are just too many incredible and disconnected elements to make the narrative believable.

As in other films based on works by Vizcaíno Casas that were done early on in the transition, the sexual theme is of primary importance, appearing throughout: the sexual encounter between the "señorito" and a maid, the visit to the brothel, the details that the priest extracts from one of the students regarding his sins of impure thoughts and masturbation, the zoom-in to the penis of Popi, the monkey in the Madrid zoo that the school boys visit in order to scandalize girls, and the affair between the priest and his fellow factory worker. This culminates in the *destape* of the two striptease acts. The first occurs when old classmates of the Catholic school plan their twenty-fifth reunion, and it serves to reunite the former students with their erstwhile spiritual mentor; the second occurs when wedding guests encourage the bride to perform a "number," which she does with Caní's permission. The final montage sequence has the clear purpose of implying a moral superiority of the past: the film cuts back and forth between the bride's striptease, and the two men (former students) who observe it in disdain, together with black-and-white "flashbacks" to their memories of themselves as young students singing hymns and to the ceremony of Caní becoming a priest. But the past was morally bankrupt: students passed their examinations by cheating or because of family influence, and a hypocritical bourgeois maintained its material well-being through its own prostitution (Mrs. Cuéllar). Their present day lives are also morally bankrupt: they enthusiastically attend the stripper's performance, and they are eager to attempt a pickup, yet they look with disgust at the uninhibited entertainment of the wedding party. Although morally bankrupt, they are not materially bankrupt; the classmates' homes are reflections of the affluent society to which they belong, and it is significant that a photograph of Fascist leader José Antonio is prominently displayed on a table in the house of José Lloret (Juan Luis Galiardo).

Rafael Gil also directed *De camisa vieja a chaqueta nueva* (*Turncoat*, 1982), a satire of politicians who, lacking real convictions, enter into the transition to democracy for their own personal gain. Manolo (José Luis López Vázquez) begins as a devoted Fascist: the close-up of this mustachioed character offering a toast to Hitler in front of a huge photograph of the

Führer offers a parallelism of images to show an affinity of ideology. However, Manolo ends up a bearded democratic activist and protester.

The film makes extensive use of news footage from the official NO-DO archives of the Franco regime. The images chosen reflect some of the most important moments in contemporary Spanish history, and trace the changes in the regime, which are analogous to the transformations in the protagonist. Paralleling the image of Franco meeting with Hitler, Manolo's Fascist ideology is impeccable, as he works at the headquarters of the Falange as a censor responsible for the "moral formation of the country." Although he is expert at deleting words such as "panties, garter, homosexual," or changing photographs, such as adding tee shirts to the bare torsos of boxers (as was actually done), he hypocritically has an affair with a married woman, Antonia Brillas (Charo López), thus reiterating the motif of the hypocritical censor that also appeared in *Niñas . . . al salón*.

Footage of Spanish troops of the Blue Division—who fought on the side of the Nazis on the Russian front—as they board trains follows a conversation between Manolo and his boss regarding why they themselves were unable to enlist. Again, hypocrisy is the principal motif, as their excuses ring hollow. Images of the allied invasion begin with the firing of the giant guns on a battleship.

This image follows a shot of Manolo and Antonia falling on a bed together, and in case the Freudian symbolism escapes a particularly dense spectator, the film hits the viewer over the head with the narrator proclaiming in a voice off screen that they are having their "own little erotic battle" while the allies invade. Of course, this also changes Manolo's sociopolitical direction, as he now plans to take English classes. Footage of the atom bomb and the famous meeting at Malta mark the allied victory, and Manolo now dictates press articles that adapt to the times: Hitler's "heretical pantheism" was what led to his defeat. Newsreel of Eisenhower visiting Franco means international recognition of the regime, and an opening up of the economy. Manolo, now a bank board member, attends social gatherings with Americans. When the NO-DO shows

Prince Juan Carlos swearing loyalty to the National Movement, we know that he will soon become king, so Manolo asks for a book on King Alfonso XIII in order to give the impression of always having been a monarchist—again, the façade underscores the hypocrisy theme. The most important event near the end of the Franco regime is the assassination of Franco's successor, Admiral Carrero Blanco. Although he fears political and economic instability, Manolo's financial advisor, Daniel (Agustín González) tells him not to worry, since he already has a large amount of money in Switzerland. The final NO-DO announces the death of Franco and shows his burial. Manolo must now "bury" the past, and he places the photograph of himself with the Caudillo (shown in close-up) in a drawer. His business partner, Alfonso, with whom he has grown rich through decades of shady deals representing conflicts of interest, decides to retire to Galicia (also home of Franco) where priests still wear cassocks—a sign of conservatism that contrasts with the character of Father Llaneza, who appears with a beard and sport coat as a representative of the Communist union. Of course, the change in attire alluded to in the title is metaphorical, but director Gil unnecessarily makes it literal as well, both in Carmiña's exhortation to Manolo, "Cámbiate de chaqueta" (Change your jacket) as he prepares to attend a protest rally, as well as in the superfluous and inane montage sequence with which the film ends: Manolo, beginning in longjohns, is dressed in a series of other types of attire that unnecessarily underscore his ideological progression, all linked through visual flips. Certainly the opening sequence with Vizcaíno Casas's cameo appearance—Manolo pees into the hat of a mayor just before he puts it on—sets the general tone for the rest of the film.

Director Gil also adapted Vizcaíno Casas's *Las autonosuyas* (*The Autonotheirs*, 1983). The title is a play on words with "Autonomies," and the film satirizes the transition from the centrist, monolithic state maintained by the Franco regime to the pluralistic democratic government whose representation was based on autonomous regions that represent the linguistic and cultural differences within Spain. Although the initial disclaimer in the film states that it does not propose any irony toward any regions that are "historically endorsed," the film did indeed cause some rancor in Catalonia and the Basque country. The Basque terrorist organization ETA threatened movie theaters in San Sebastián, so the film was withdrawn and later prohibited. The film's debut in Barcelona was delayed several months. Following the disclaimer, there is a close-up of a newspaper article quoting then Socialist Vice President Alfonso Guerra as saying that "the autonomies are a joke." Although this quote is surely a shield for criticism from the Left, it was not altogether successful, as Diego Galán criticized what he called "Fascist applause" during the showings of the film when allusions were made to the unity of Spain.

Following his cameo appearance in *De camisa vieja a chaqueta nueva*, author Vizcaíno Casas again appears in the opening of this film: he serves as the narrator who introduces the characters, appearing as a television reporter who faces the camera and announces that he will disappear so that the film can tell itself.

The action takes place in Rebollar de la Mata, a town in the mountains of central Spain, where the mayor (Alfredo Landa) decides that forming an autonomous region of his own will provide enormous benefits. The film comically undermines many of the cultural components that constituted the justification for autonomies. The most important of these is the linguistic situation in Spain: the Basque country (Euskadi), Galicia, and Catalonia have their own languages, and so as not to be left behind, this "autonomous mountain entity" adapts "Farfullo" as their official language. This is a running gag throughout the film, since it is based on a speech defect that the mayor has whereby he cannot pronounce the letter "p," making an "f" sound in its place. Following what happened in other regions, all signs are changed to the autonomous language, and this results in sight gags such as when the Calle del Palo (Stick Street) becomes the Calle del Falo (Phallus Street). The mayor's declaration that "autonomy" comes from "auto(mobile)," and the desire to have "autochthonous pigs" are other examples of the satirical humor in the film.

The best satire comes from the Franquista colonel, who is a takeoff on Colonel Tejero, the leader of the foiled coup d'état in 1983. His home is a satirical symbol of the intransigent ultraright, complete with a machine gun among sandbags, Fascist flags, and a painting of Franco. Opposed to the transformations occurring under democracy, he declares the autonomy idea to be "demonic inventions." When the colonel breaks into the Mountain Beauty contest, it parodies Tejero's breaking into Spanish parliament. The rebel colonel's order to lawmakers was "Al suelo" (Hit the floor), parodied here when the colonel gives the same command to a dog, and all present dive to the floor.

The inauguration of a new building is scheduled for the symbolic date of July 18th (date of the "glorious invasion" by Franco), but its sudden collapse is seen as a divine punishment. The only piece of the building that remains intact is its eagle coat of arms, which was the symbol of the Franco regime. The film ends with a close-up of the coat of arms symbolizing the enduring attachment to the Franco regime among certain segments of Spanish society. Although the film was panned by Spanish critics, caused a negative reaction among members of the intellectual Left in Spain, and raised ire in the legitimate autonomous regions, it was a phenomenal box office success.

Y al tercer año resucitó (*And in the Third Year, He Has Been Resurrected*, 1978) was adapted for the screen by Rafael Gil in 1980. Unlike the book, in which a drunken sexton at Franco's tomb starts the rumor that the Caudillo has been resurrected, the film version bases this rumor on the play on words between the dictator's surname and the Spanish word for the French monetary unit. A government worker who is going to transcribe a tape recording about economic news is interrupted and misses the definite article, "*el* franco" (*the* franc); instead of understanding that the French currency has "resuscitated" and regained value, he believes that a miracle has occurred and that Franco is back from the dead.

The film satirizes the process of the transition to democracy and the key figures of that process: Communist leader Santiago Carrillo runs away with his wig on (a disguise that

he used to enter Spain during the Franco regime); Socialist
Felipe González and President Suárez are depicted as targets at
a carnival; Isidoro (the code name for González) plucks the
petals of a rose (symbol of the Socialist party in Spain). As in
the previous movie, this film also tries to satirize both the
process of moving from a centralized government to one of
autonomies and the liberalization in the film industry.
However, the debate and voting in the "Organization of
Iberian States" is ridiculous, and the sequence on the filming of
a porno movie is weak. The clergy is not above being a target of
satire as well. A liberal priest refuses to baptize a baby with
the name José Antonio (which is associated with the founder of
the Falange, or Spanish Fascist party), but when he learns of
the resurrection, he puts on his cassock and gets out the canopy
for a religious procession. The author makes his usual appearance in the film, showing a postcard of the presidential
residence (La Moncloa Palace), since filmmakers were denied
permission to shoot on location.

While the movie ridicules democratic figures, it makes
people associated with the regime appear in a positive light.
One character has the audacity to say, "Franco siempre fue
democrático—a su manera" (Franco was always democratic—in
his own way), and another confirms, "Franco lo hizo bien, o
quizá estos de ahora lo están haciendo mal" (Franco did a good
job, or perhaps these guys today are doing a bad one). After the
initial misunderstanding is rectified, the grandfatherly figure
resembling Franco who opened the film finally returns amidst
the snow to the basilica where the *Caudillo* is buried—an
ambiguous ending that surely left some spectators hoping for
such a miracle. Quesada notes that in spite of its commercial
success, the book was a poorly organized series of vignettes that
had little basis for a film adaptation, so director Gil had to
improvise a plot, and the resulting movie is an example of
"political and commercial opportunism" (422).

None of the movies based on works by Vizcaíno Casas
received critical acclaim. Although they contain some
genuinely comic moments that link into a deep tradition of
Spanish humor, they generally look for an easy laugh from an
audience that may be nostalgic about the Franco regime. In

spite of lacking aesthetic importance, their massive success makes them an important social phenomenon.

Juan Antonio Zunzúnegui

Rafael Gil's *Dos hombres . . . y en medio dos mujeres* (*Two men . . . and Two Women in the Middle*, 1972) is a film based on the short story by Juan Antonio Zunzúnegui (b. 1944). From its title, we know that the narrative is about crossed relationships. The traditional lover's triangle is amplified here, however, to include a somewhat bizarre fourth member; in addition to the conventional married man, Martín (Alberto Closas), his wife Carmen (Gemma Cuervo), and his lover Mary (Nadiuska), the triangle is enlarged to include Martín and Carmen's son Ramón (Alfredo Alba). Martín is the president of a shipping company, and he pays an indemnity to Mary, whose husband, a ship captain, has recently died. The young widow is the daughter of an Englishman and a Spanish woman, and this somewhat foreign identity can be seen as the justification for her immoral behavior, which is the opposite of that of the archetypical loving Spanish wife. (In the original narrative, Zunzúnegui insists on referring to her as an "española-inglesa" or Spanish-English woman, 59.)

Martín's conventional domestic life—exemplified by the image of him sitting with pipe in mouth, surrounded by his loving children—is precisely too conventional, yet the film does not manifest the domestic difficulties and inner conflict in Martín before the young widow is even introduced into the original narrative (58-59), perhaps because there is no profound psychological development in the short story. His successive meetings with the widow increase the sexual tension between the two, and director Gil's adaptation of Zunzúnegui's text manifests the greater sexual freedom stemming from the fact that twenty-eight years elapsed between short story and film adaptation, which was made in the waning years of the Franco regime. Whereas in the original narrative, Mary, dressed in a short robe, takes his hand and the narrator intervenes to elliptically comment that "one knows what happens" under such circumstances, the film version is much more explicit: after she steps out of the shower and he brings her a towel, she opens her robe, exemplifying the early seventies phenomenon of *destape*. At that time, bare breasts were the limit however, their kiss leads to a cut to the contrasting domestic scene in which Carmen complains that he should leave his worries at the office. To add to the erotic tone of the narrative, Gil adds a lovers' tryst to Hamburg, where Martín and Mary stroll along the streets of the St. Pauli district, filled with sex shops, posters of bare-breasted women, and prostitutes. Martín's hypocrisy culminates in a phone call to his wife from his hotel room during which he kisses his lover and tickles her with the fur stole that he has purchased her.

Carmen, convinced that her husband has a lover, is unable to find solace nor assistance from the Church or her friends, and this lack of support leads to the change in the traditional narrative structure: Carmen turns to her son Ramón for assistance. Carmen's initial plan—to have Ramón speak to Mary, or even to offer her money to end the relationship with Martín—backfires when her son also falls into the widow's web. The father's generosity (he buys Ramón a Jaguar) likewise turns ironically against him, as Ramón and Mary use it to run off to the beach resort of San Sebastián together, seeking at least an illusion of happiness. The high-angle long shot of the Jaguar on the deserted beach underscores the sentiment that "No hay nadie más que tú y yo en el mundo" (There is no one but you and I in the world), but of course this is false, since the continued presence in the background of Ramón's father and mother maintains the triangle/quadrilateral of these tangled relations.   Ramón is jealous of his own father, and the generational conflict expressed in the original ("I am the truth and He is falsity . . . I am love and He is monotony," 93) plays out on the screen. Ramón wants Mary to choose between them—and his jealousy culminates when Mary divulges that she is pregnant. She insists that the father must be the older Martín, since she asks Ramón, "¿Tú, qué puedes ofrecerme?" (You, what can you offer me?) Just as in the case of the earlier *destape*, Gil has chosen to be less elliptical than the original text, where the response is merely, "An ashen, devilish look froze her smile" (104). Ramón's rage about Mary's choice of Martín's money over his own love leads him to strangle Mary to death. The final telephone call to his mother while in police custody muddies the waters, however, as Carmen says, "Por mí, lo has hecho por mí, hijo" (For me, you did it for me, son), and Ramón responds, "Por ti, por que si no, ¿por quién podría hacerlo?" (For you, because if not, for whom could I do it?) The slight change from the original narrative, in which Ramón flees the scene of the crime and returns home to embrace his mother before the final conversation and the doorbell announcing the arrival of the police, seems to work better in the film adaptation. However, the tragic ending of the film does not jibe with the opening tone, which corresponds to that of a *destape* comedy (Quesada 321).

Twice-Told Tales

Great books do not always make great films, and some second-rate novels become magnificent movies. As to be expected, screen adaptations of contemporary Spanish narratives run the gamut. It is important to recognize that many of Spain's twentieth-century "classics" have film adaptations: Cela's *La familia de Pascual Duarte* (*The Family of Pascual Duarte*)and *La colmena* (*The Hive*); Martín Santos's *Tiempo de silencio* (*Time of Silence*); Delibes's *Los santos inocentes* (*The Holy Innocents*); Marsé's *Si te dicen que caí* (*If They Tell You I Have Fallen*); Mendoza's *La verdad sobre el caso Savolta* (*The Truth About the Savolta Case*). Some of these films received considerable subsidies from the Spanish government. We have noted that adaptations such as those of Sender's *Crónica del alba* (*Chronicle of Dawn*) into *Valentina* and *1919 Crónica del alba* (*1919 Chronicle of Dawn*) were part of an initiative taken by the Spanish Ministry of Culture to bring important works of Spanish literature to the silver screen. Literary adaptations, and particularly screen versions of modern classics, would seem to confirm within a Spanish context the comment by Elsaesser regarding screen adaptations in Germany: "filmed literature sells German culture twice over, as film and as literature, while also going down well on television and even abroad in literature classes of modern language departments" (107).

Although adaptations of Spanish novels often do receive subsidies, there is no pattern that would show a favoring of this particular type of film over original scripts. For example, Payan (30) lists thirty-four films that received subsidies during 1986, and only eight of them are screen adaptations of literary works. Nevertheless, subsidizing film adaptations of Spanish novels is a way in which the Spanish state underscores its manifestation of the national as an ideological construct. The twice-told tale (whether subsidized or not) becomes a double affirmation of Spanish cultural production. What kind of Spain do screen adaptations of contemporary narratives portray?

Film adaptations of contemporary Spanish novels often

have a historical context that is fundamental to the narrative. Rarely, however, do these narratives deal with a historical framework prior to the twentieth century. Spain's Golden Age—the sixteenth and seventeenth centuries—provides the historical background for only two films—*Extramuros* (1985) and *El rey pasmado* (*The Dumbfounded King*, 1991). Both of these tales pit the mores of a repressive and structured society against the freedom of the individual. The construction of desire in the homosexual context has a different result from that of the heterosexual context —the tragic repression in *Extramuros* contrasts with the happy ending of *El rey pasmado*. And yet *Extramuros*, which was released in 1985, treats homosexuality in a way that few American films of the time would do; the dramatic changes in Spanish society following Franco's death make it much more open than American society in many ways. Almodóvar, whose first feature-length film was in 1980, is both a reflection of and a contributor to this transformation in which marginality shifts to the center.

The other two films that have an early historical context are set in the nineteenth century and are both by director Pedro Olea. *El bosque del lobo* (*Wolf Forest*, 1971) is based on a historical occurrence and exemplifies what Soldevilla Durante (122) calls the *tremendismo* or extremism in Spanish literature in the 1940s. The portrayal of regional culture of Galicia in this film is a forerunner of the microregionalism that emerges in Spanish cinema in the 1980s and 1990s. *El maestro de esgrima* (*The Fencing Master*, 1992) is set in a period of scandal and social change that parallels contemporary Spanish society, but Olea concentrates on the narrative threads of impossible love and intrigue in what is essentially a detective tale.

The early twentieth century (1900-1939) is a period often depicted on screen and almost all of these narratives deal with the pivotal experience of the Spanish civil war or the events that led up to that fratricidal conflict. An exception is Rosa Chacel's novel from 1946, *Las memorias de Leticia Valle* (*The Memoirs of Leticia Valle*, adapted for the screen in 1979 by Miguel Angel Rivas), an autobiographical narrative that portrays the coming of age of a young Spanish girl and captures Spanish provincial life at the beginning of the century. The filmic readings of both *La verdad sobre el caso Savolta* (1975) and *Pascual Duarte* (1977) foreground the sociopolitical conflicts of the early decades of this century in Spain that led to the Spanish civil war. Adaptations of Sender's *Valentina* (1982) and *1919 Crónica del alba* (1983) also manifest these tensions and relate them to the civil war; the repression of workers and the protagonist's revolutionary tendencies in the latter, and the framing devices in both films underscore Pepe's tragic end in a concentration camp. After the success of other adaptations of novels by Delibes, it was perhaps inevitable that his first novel, *La sombra del ciprés es alargada* (*The Cypress's Shadow Is Elongated*), would finally be brought to the screen in 1989. The inclusion of a sequence regarding the Spanish civil war is a transformation of the original text that manifests an important tendency in contemporary Spanish cinema: the *cainismo* or fratricidal conflict as a fundamental thematic component. The civil war itself is the historical context for several film adaptations: *El otro arbol de Guernica* (*Guernica's Other Tree*, 1969), *La casa de las chivas* (*The Bitches' House*, 1971), *La montaña rebelde* (*Rebel Mountain*, 1972), *Retrato de familia* (*Family Portrait*, 1976), *Soldados* (*Soldiers*, 1978), *Réquiem por un campesino español* (*Requiem for a Spanish Peasant*, 1985), and *El hermano bastardo de Dios* (*God's Bastard Brother*, 1986). The changes of titles in the adaptations of Max Aub's novel, from *Las buenas intenciones* (*Good Intentions*) to *Soldados* (*Soldiers*), and of Delibes's novel, from *Mi idolatrado hijo Sisí* (*My Adored Son Sisí*))to *Retrato de familia* (*Family Portrait*),indicate substantial transformations, and these filmic readings both foreground the civil war by dramatically altering the temporality of the original narratives. The death of Franco allowed a striking change in the perspective on the war, as Spanish filmmakers attempted to deconstruct the official version of the conflict that the Franco regime had maintained.

The period of the Franco regime, which lasted until the *Caudillo*'s death in 1975, constitutes the historical context for the largest group of contemporary film adaptations. The postwar period in particular, with its economic hardships (the "years of hunger"), corruption (the black market was rampant), and repression is important in *Arriba Hazaña* (*Up with Hazaña*, 1971), *La guerra de papá* (*Daddy's War*, 1977), *La muchacha de las bragas de oro* (*The Girl with the Golden Panties*, 1979), *La colmena* (*The Hive*, 1982), *El sur* (1983), *Luna de lobos* (1987), and *Si te dicen que caí* (1989). The changes in title for the first two of these movies—from *El infierno y la brisa* (*Hell and the Wind*) and *El príncipe destronado* (*The Dethroned Prince*), respectively—indicate a filmic reading that emphasizes the sociopolitical element. This also occurs in *El sur*, where a scant mention of the civil war in the novel becomes an important thematic element of the film. An analysis of the historical inscription or the act of remembering the postwar period is crucial in *La muchacha de las bragas de oro* and *El viaje a ninguna parte* (*The Trip to Nowhere*, 1989). These filmic narratives realize this through a bipartite temporal structure that contrasts the present with the past. This feature also appears in *Beltenebros* (1990). Marginalized, underclass characters are predominant in many narratives that illustrate this historical period: we see itinerant actors in *El viaje a ninguna parte* (1986), gypsies in *Con el viento solano* (*With the Easterly Wind*, 1966), human contraband in *El alijo* (*The Smuggled Goods*, 1976), fishermen in *Gran sol* (*Great Sole*, 1988), and *gancheros* in *El río que nos lleva* (*The River that Carries Us*, 1989). Quite often the narratives contrast these marginalized characters with the upper class in both a rural context—*Los santos inocentes* (1984)—or an urban one—*La oscura historia de la prima Montse* (*The Dark Story of Cousin Montse*, 1977), *Ultimas tardes con Teresa* (*The Last Afternoons with Teresa*, 1984), or *Tiempo de silencio* (1986). The sociopolitical problems that result from oppression at the end of the Franco regime appear in *La noche más larga* (*The Longest Night*, 1991). Just as Spanish intellectuals of the Generation of '98 critically reevaluated the country's past following the important historical events of Spain's defeat in the Spanish-American War, contemporary Spaniards reevaluated the years of the Franco regime after the *caudillo*'s death. This is one of the main elements in contemporary Spanish cinema as a whole, so it is not surprising that the largest group of film adaptations also deals with that thematic component. This reexamination continues with films set in the post-Franco regime.

Modern Spain of the Democratic period is the historical context for another large group of films. Some of these films deal with the difficulties of the transition from dictatorship to democracy. Bardem transforms Sueiro's *Solo de moto* (*Alone on a Motorcycle*) to *El puente* (*The Long Weekend*, 1977) in order to show the growth of political consciousness in the motorcycle mechanic protagonist, and *Emilia, parada y fonda* (*Emilia, a Stop and an Inn*, 1976) manifests the desires for new freedom, especially for women. *La rusa* (*The Russian Woman*, 1987), however, shows the hidden forces that make the transition to democracy difficult. *El disputado voto del señor Cayo* (*The Disputed Vote of Mr. Cayo*, 1986) contrasts "progressive" urban life with traditional country life, while capturing the transformation of the enthusiastic young democratic politicians once in power. *El mar y el tiempo* (*The Sea and Time*, 1989) captures the problems of Spaniards who had to escape the dictatorship and who find that returning to a country that is now a democracy has unimagined psychological pitfalls. And many of the films based on works by Vizcaíno Casas—*Las autonosuyas* (*The Autonotheirs*), *Y al tercer año resucitó* (*And in the Third Year, He Has Been Resurrected*)—satirize the transition to democracy. Some of the more recent films no longer deal with problems that stem from the civil war and the Franco regime: those based on the works of Carmen Rico Godoy try to capture the vissicitudes of women in modern Spain, and films such as *Bueno y tierno como un ángel* (*Good and Tender Like an Angel*, 1988) or *El tesoro* (*The Treasure*, 1990) have nothing to do with the dictatorship. And yet, the consequences of forty years of the regime are hard to completely overcome: the transformation from novel to screen of the protagonist of *Dias contados* (*Running Out of Time*, 1995)—from a photographer to a Basque terrorist—shows that the social scars left by the dictatorship run deep.

The erotic theme comes to the forefront in films such as *Sinatra* (1988), *El pecador impecable* (*The Sinless Sinner*, 1987), *Las edades de Lulú* (*Lulu's Ages*, 1990), *Tierno verano de lujurias y azoteas* (*Tender Summer of Lust and Rooftops*, 1992), and *La pasión turca* (*The Turkish Passion*, 1994). Although earlier movies—*La mujer de otro* (*Another Man's Wife*, 1967), as well as *No encontré rosas para mi madre* (*I Didn't Find Roses for My Mother*), *Dos hombres . . . y en medio dos mujeres* (*Two Men . . . and Two Women in the Middle*), both from 1972—also deal with themes of passion and impossible love, the more recent films tend to be much more graphically open in the portrayal of sex on screen because of the changes in censorship laws and social outlook that resulted in the *destape* phenomenon of the late 1970s and which continue to manifest themselves in a much more tolerant attitude toward nudity and sex on the Spanish screen. Sometimes, however, directors are quite discreet. Pedro Olea's tales of impossible love in *El maestro de esgrima* (1992) and *Morirás en Chafarinas* (*You Will Die in Chafarinas*, 1995) are marked by their restraint; Víctor Erice's adaptation of *El sur* (1983) magnificently captures the suffering caused by a lost love without any sexual scenes whatsoever.

The drug scene constitutes a thematic component of several recent film adaptations. *La muchacha de las bragas de oro* (1978) and *Los invitados* (*The Guests*, 1987) deal with marijuana as a sign of the new freedom that Spaniards have under democracy, or as a manifestation of the power and ruthlessness of organized crime. Films from the 1990s, however, show the world of hard drugs. *Cautivos de la sombra* (*Captives of the Shadow*, 1993), *Días contados* (1995), *Historias del Kronan* (*Stories from the Kronan Bar*, 1994), and *Morirás en Chafarinas* (1995) are populated by characters with wasted lives who meet untimely deaths because of their addictions. The term "yonki" (junkie) has reached the Spanish screen.

Often related to this world of crime is the detective story, and the popularity of this genre on screen is directly related to its popularity in print. Vázquez Montalbán's sleuth, Pepe Carvalho, heads the list, beginning in*Tatuaje* (*Tattoo*, 1974) and continuing with *Los mares del sur* (*South Seas*, 1991) and *Asesinato en el comité central* (*Assassination in the Central Committee*, 1982). Many of the novelistic/film narratives, however, manifest an important postmodern characteristic of the genre: the detective is not a traditional sleuth. In *La cripta* (*The Crypt*, 1979), he is an insane asylum patient; in *La verdad* *sobre el caso Savolta* (1980) he is an anarchist newspaper writer; the fencing master solves the mystery in *El maestro de esgrima* (1992); and soldiers are sleuths in *El aire de un crimen* (*The Air of a Crime*, 1988) and *Morirás en Chafarinas* (1995). Crime fiction also appears on screen in *Fanny Pelopaja* (*Fanny with the Straw-colored Hair*, 1984), *Nada que hacer* (*Nothing to Do*, 1988), and *Cautivos de la sombra* (1993). Since solving a mystery or a crime is the central narrative thrust of this genre, perhaps the "second telling" of the tale on screen inevitably invites greater disappointment, unless you are one of Boyum's "ideal" spectators who has not yet read the original novel.

The two Spanish novelists whose works have most been adapted to the screen are Miguel Delibes and Juan Marsé. Director Ana Mariscal (72) notes that Delibes's pen often seems like a camera, and some of his novels, notably *El camino* (*The Road*) and *Los santos inocentes*, have become superb screen adaptations. Marsé's novels have met with less success, although Aranda's rendition of *Si te dicen que caí* is an audacious attempt to film an extremely difficult text, and his *El amante bilingüe* (*The Bilingual Lover*) is a very successful film. Orr (3) believes that "the novella and the short story are more often the right length for a two-hour feature film," and some of the best screen adaptations in contemporary Spanish cinema are indeed based on shorter works: *El sur*, *Los santos inocentes*, *El amante bilingüe*.

One noticeable aspect of contemporary screen adaptation is the relative paucity of works by Spanish women authors. In spite of the critical and commercial success by authors such as Soledad Puértolas, Rosa Montero, and Paloma Díaz Mas, none of their works have had film adaptations. Of the fifty-seven authors that have film adaptations of their works between 1965 and 1995, only six are women: Carmen Martín Gaite ("Un alto en el camino," made into *Emilia, parada y fonda*); Rosa Chacel (*Memorias de Leticia Valle*); Ana María Matute (*El polizón del Ulises*) [*Ulysses's Cabin Boy*]; Rico Godoy's three works—*Cómo ser mujer y no morir en el intento* (*How to Be a Woman and Not Die Trying*), *Cómo ser infeliz y disfrutarlo* (*How to Be Unhappy and Enjoy It*), and *Cuernos de mujer* (*Cuckold Woman*); Almudena Grandes, (*Las edades de Lulú*);

and Adelaida García Morales (*El sur*). The mediocre film adaptations of works by Rico Godoy and Grandes produced by Andrés Vicente Gómez seem geared toward making a fast peseta. On the other hand, the Fons adaptation of Martín Gaite contains an interesting cultural commentary on the Spain of that period, and Erice's version of García Morales's work is magnificent. When will Spanish producers and directors begin to take a serious interest in narratives by Spanish women authors?

Since one of the important aesthetic tendencies in the contemporary Spanish novel is the tension between realism and formalism, how does this tension translate to the cinematographic adaptation of contemporary novels? In novels themselves, the realist mode clearly dominates, and the realist aesthetic dominates screen narratives as well. Although some films (*El sur, Los santos inocentes*) have strong poetic qualities, few adaptations match the formal qualities of texts such as Martín Santos's *Tiempo de silencio*, Mendoza's *La verdad del caso Savolta*, or Marsé's *Si te dicen que caí*. It is to his credit that director Vicente Aranda even attempted to adapt two of these titles. Flawed as they may be, Aranda shows that he is one of the most daring filmmakers in Spain today.

Some directors, notably Aranda (seven adaptations) and Camus (five adaptations), developed major phases of their careers around bringing literary works to the screen, and their works constitute some of the best examples of this enterprise. Rafael Gil also had six adaptations of contemporary novels, including a 1970 remake of his own earlier *El hombre que se quiso matar* (*The Man Who Wanted to Kill Himself*) and ending with three adaptations of novels by Vizcaíno Casas. In addition, Gil's adaptation of Galdos's *El abuelo* (*The Grandfather*), called *La duda* (*Doubt*), was one of several adaptations of nineteenth-century texts that followed Buñuel's adaptation of *Tristana*. However, literary adaptations represent a small portion of Gil's total output, which numbered some seventy films. Pedro Olea has made three adaptations, and several other directors—Betancor, Betriu, Cuerda, Fernán Gómez, Herralde, Nieves Conde, Uribe, and Uribizu—have made two. And of course, some of the best adaptations have been made by directors who have brought only one text to the screen, such as Víctor Erice's *El sur*. The motivations for adapting novels range from a passion to bring excellent literary works to the screen to merely paid assignments.

Aranda's attitude toward adaptations is similar to that of many filmmakers, both in Spain and worldwide. He states, "I don't aspire to have the writers that I adapt feel enthusiastic; I think that it is logical that someone who writes a novel not be in total agreement with the cinematographic adaptation, which, after all, is another interpretation of the novel (Alvares and Frías 121). Aranda admits that his frequent adaptation of literary works is due to the fact that it is easier to use a preexisting narrative, but he adds that he uses the original literary work "as material; I do not consider it as a novel. For me, it is a question of raw material with which I can make a movie" (Vera 29). Aranda believes that the ease of adaptation does not always depend on the original. *Asesinato en el comité central*, a novel with easy scenes and abundant dialogue, was more difficult to film than *La muchacha de las bragas de oro*, a novel with less dialogue and a difficult structure (Vera 30). Aranda also stresses the importance of his own reading of the original tale: "I don't have any need to be faithful or unfaithful to the novel, but I should be faithful, as best I can, to the interpretation that I have made of that novel" (Vera 31). These comments compare to a more universal context as described by Bluestone (62): "What happens, therefore, when the filmist undertakes the adaptation of a novel, given the inevitable mutation, is that he does not convert the novel at all. What he adapts is a kind of paraphrase of the novel—the novel viewed as raw material. He looks not to the organic novel, whose language is inseparable from its theme, but to characters and incidents which have somehow detached themselves from language and, like the heroes of folk legends, have achieved a mythic life of their own." Colmena remarks that in Vicente Aranda's numerous screen adaptations of novels, all the literary material loses its original meaning and is transformed into a series of thematic and aesthetic elements that pertain to the director (74).

There is an increasing tendency over the past three decades to film recent narratives, especially best-sellers. If we use a twenty-year benchmark as one criterion for considering a work a "classic," then statistics show an inverse tendency: a decreasing number of classics and an increasing number of recent works. From 1965-1975, there are four classic adaptations: Fernández Flórez's *El hombre que se quiso matar*, Zunzúnegui's *Dos hombres . . . y en medio dos mujeres*, Martínez Barbeito's *El bosque de Ancines* (*Ancines Forest*), and Cela's *La familia de Pascual Duarte*. Two of these are by the same director—Rafael Gil—and the first is a remake of his earlier film version of the narrative. This represents 25 percent of the film adaptations from this period. During the next decade (1976-85), there are six classics filmed: Aldecoa's *Los pájaros de Baden-Baden* (*The Birds of Baden-Baden*), Delibes's *Mi idolatrado hijo Sisí*, Aub's *Las buenas intenciones*, Chacel's *Memorias de Leticia Valle*, Cela's *La colmena*, and Sender's *Requiem por un campesino español*. The percentage decreases to 18 percent of the film adaptations of that period. Although there were also six during the next decade (1986-1995)—Matute's *El polizón del Ulises*, Martín Santos's *Tiempo de silencio*, Fernández Flórez's *El bosque animado*, Aldecoa's *Gran sol*, Sampedro's *El río que nos lleva*, and Delibes's *La sombra del ciprés es alargada*—they only represent 11 percent of the film adaptations from that decade. On the other hand, the average length of time between publication of the novel and debut of the film is eleven years, twelve years, and five years for the three respective periods. The trend continues as numerous best-sellers from the 1990s are current projects.

During the 1980s, Spanish films progressively lost their domestic market share. In 1982, Spanish films captured 30 percent of the market with 39 million spectators; by 1989, that figure had dropped to 8 percent and only six million spectators (Alberich 210-211). In 1995, Spanish films had four million spectators more than the previous year, with over ten million tickets sold. Although this still accounts for only about 12 percent of the market in Spain, with American cinema dominating the market share ("El cine en España" 78), it appears that Spanish cinema is entering a period of relative good health, and screen adaptations both contribute to and take advantage of this situation.

Nevertheless, in the opening line of Cela's *La colmena*, Doña Rosa exhorts the other characters—and us—not to lose our perspective on things. We should not forget that all of these films adaptations, both good and bad, represent only a fraction of Spanish cinema. During the period of 1965-1975, screen adaptations of contemporary Spanish narratives constitute only 2 percent of all Spanish film production.[1] From 1976-1985, this figure is 4 percent, and from 1986-1995, it is almost 8 percent. Consequently, each decade doubled the percentage of screen adaptations of post–civil war Spanish narratives. The cinematographic adaptation of Spanish narratives continues beyond the span of the three decades of our study. Recently, several other adaptations had their debut or were announced as projects. These works continue the trend of adapting the most contemporary fiction, since the majority are based on recent best-sellers. Titles include Juan Marsé's *El embrujo de Shangai* (*The Bewitchment of Shanghai*, to be directed by Víctor Erice), Julio Llamazares's *Escenas del cine mudo* (*Scenes from the Silent Movies*), Antonio Gala's *Más allá del jardín* (*Beyond the Garden*), Fernando Delgado's *La mirada del otro* (*The Other's Look*), Arturo Perez-Reverte's *La piel del tambor* (*The Skin of the Drum*), and *Territorio Comanche* (*Comanche Territory*), Antonio Muñoz Molina's *Ardor guerrero* (*Fighting Fever*), Miguel Delibes's *Diario de un jubilado* (*Diary of a Retiree*), Manuel Vázquez Montalbán's *Galíndez*, Almudena Grandes's

---

[1]Spanish cinema certainly does film adaptations of literary works other than contemporary Spanish narratives. In that regard, 1989 was a banner year, with four adaptations of contemporary Spanish works, and five adaptations of other types. These included an American novel (Christopher Frank's *The Mad Monkey*), a French novel (*The Return of the Musketeers*, based on Dumas), a Catalan novel (Manuel de Pedrolo's *Procès de contradicció suficient*, made into *Garum*), a Spanish play (Buero Vallejo's *Esquilache*), and an earlier Spanish novel (Javier Elorrieta's version of Blasco Ibañez's *Sangre y arena*, starring Christopher Rydell and Sharon Stone). There was also a Spanish-American coproduction of Alberto Vázquez Figueroa's novel *La iguana*, which was directed by Monty Hellman.

Malena es nombre de tango (*Malena is the Name of a Tango*), Ferrán Torrent's *Gracias por la propina* (*Thanks for the Tip*), and Ignacio Martínez de Pisón's *Carreteras secundarias* (*Secondary Roads*). There is also the occasional classic title, such as Miguel Delibes's *Las ratas* (*The Rats*). It appears that in Spain telling tales twice has a vibrant future.

Appendix A
Spanish Post-Civil War Narratives to Films
(1965-1995)

Chronological list of years in which films appeared
by author of narrative, date of publication, and film
director

1965

Delibes, M. *El camino*, 1950. Mariscal, Ana.

1966

Fernández Flórez, Dario. *Lola espejo obscuro*, 1950. Merino, Fernando.

1967

Aldecoa, Ignacio. *Con el viento solano*, 1962. Camus, Mario.
García Serrano, Rafael. *Los ojos perdidos*, 1958. García Serrano, Rafael.
Lúca de Tena, Torcuato. *La mujer de otro*, 1961. Gil, Rafael.
Suárez, Gonzalo. *Fata morgana*, 1964. Aranda, Vicente.

1968

Suárez, Gonzalo. *Rocabruno bate a Ditirambo*, 1966. Suárez, Gonzalo. *Ditirambo*.

1969

Castresana, Luis de. *El otro árbol de Guernica*, 1968. Lazaga, Pedro.

1970

Fernández Florez, Wenceslao. *El hombre que se quiso matar.* Gil, Rafael.

1971

Martínez Barbeito, Carlos. *El bosque de Ancines*, 1947. Olea, Pedro. *El bosque del lobo.*
Súarez, Gonzalo. "Bailando para Parker," 1964. Aranda, Vicente. *Las crueles.*

1972

Cabezas, Juan Antonio. *La montaña rebelde*, 1960. Torrado, Ramón.
García Blázquez, José Antonio. *No encontré rosas para mi madre*, 1968. Rovira Beleta, Francisco.
Zunzúnegui, Juan Antonio. *Dos hombres . . . y dos mujeres en medio*, 1944. Gil, Rafael.

1973

None

1974

None

1975

Cela, Camilo José. *La familia de Pascual Duarte*, 1942. Franco, Ricardo. *Pascual Duarte.*

1976

Aldecoa, Ignacio. "Los pájaros de Baden-Baden," 1955. Camus, Mario.
Barrios, Manuel. *La espuela*, 1965. Fandiño, Roberto.

Delibes, Miguel. *Mi idolatrado hijo Sisí*, 1953. Giménez Rico, Antonio. *Retrato de familia*.

Martín Gaite, Carmen. "Un alto en el camino," 1960. Fons, Angelino. *Emilia, parada y fonda*.

Palomino, Angel. *Madrid, Costa Fleming*, 1973. Forqué, José María.

Solís, Ramón. *El alijo*, 1965. Del Pozo, Angel.

1977

Delibes, Miguel. "El príncipe destronado," 1973. Mercero, Antonio. *La guerra de papá*.

Marsé , Juan. *La oscura historia de la prima Montse*, 1970. Cadena, Jordi.

Sueiro, Daniel. *Solo de moto*, 1967. Bardem, Antonio. *El puente*.

Vázquez Montalbán, Manuel. *Tatuaje*, 1974. Bigas Luna, Juan José.

Vizcaino Casas, Fernando. *Niñas, al salón*, 1976. Escrivá, Vicente.

1978

Aub, Max. *Las buenas intenciones*, 1954. Ungría, Alfonso. *Soldados*.

Vaz de Soto, José María. *El infierno y la brisa*, 1969. Gutiérrez Santos, J. M. *Arriba Hazaña*.

1979

Chacel, Rosa. *Memorias de Leticia Valle*, 1946. Rivas, Miguel Angel.

Laiglesia, Alvaro de. *Yo soy fulana de tal*, 1963. Lazaga, Pedro.

Vizcaino Casas, Fernando. *La boda del señor cura*, 1977. Gil, Rafael.

1980

Marsé, Juan. *La muchacha de las bragas de oro*, 1978. Aranda, Vicente.
Mendoza, Eduardo. *La verdad sobre el caso Savolta*, 1975. Drove, Antonio.
Romero, Emilio. *Casa manchada*, 1969. Nieves Conde, Jose Antonio.
Vizcaino Casas, Fernando. *Y al tercer año resucitó*, 1978. Gil, Rafael.

1981

Delibes, Miguel. *Cinco horas con Mario*, 1968. Molina, Josefina. *Función de noche*.
Mendoza, Eduardo. *El misterio de al cripta embrujada*, 1979. Del Real, Cayetano. *La cripta*.
Vázquez, Angel. *La vida perra de Juanita Narboni*, 1976. Aguirre, Javier. *Vida/perra*.

1982

Cela, Camilo José. *La colmena*, 1951. Camus, Mario.
Sender, Ramón. *Crónica del alba*. 1963. Betancor, Antonio. *Valentina*.
Vázquez Montalbán, Manuel. *Asesinato en el comité central*, 1981. Aranda, Vicente.
Vizcaíno Casas, Fernando. *De camisa vieja a chaqueta nueva*, 1979. Gil, Rafael.

1983

García Morales, Adelaida. *El sur*, 1985. Erice, Víctor.
Sender, Ramon. *1919 Crónica del alba*, 1963. Betancor, Antonio.
Vizcaino Casas, Fernando. *Las autonosuyas*, 1981. Gil, Rafael.

1984

Delibes, Miguel. *Los santos inocentes*, 1981. Camus, Mario.

Marsé, Juan. *Ultimas tardes con Teresa*, 1966. Herralde, Gonzalo.

Martín, Andreu. *Protesis*, 1980. Aranda, Vicente. *Fanny Pelopaja*.

1985

Fernández Santos, Jesús. *Extramuros*, 1978. Picazo, Miguel.

Sender, Ramón. *Requiem por un campesino español*, 1950. Betriu, Francesc.

1986

Coll, José Luis. *El hermano bastardo de Dios*, 1984. Rabal, Benito.

Delibes, Miguel. *El disputado voto del señor Cayo*, 1978. Giménez Rico, Antonio.

Fernán Gómez, Fernando. *El viaje a ninguna parte*, 1985. Fernán Gómez, Fernando.

Martín Santos, Luis. *Tiempo de silencio*, 1962. Aranda, Vicente.

1987

Cebrián, Juan Luis. *La rusa*, 1986. Camus, Mario.

Fernández Florez, Wenceslao. *El bosque animado*, 1943, Cuerda, José Luis.

Grosso, Alfonso. *Los invitados*, 1978. Barrera, Víctor.

Hidalgo, Manuel. *El pecador impecable*, 1986. Torres, Augusto M.

Llamazares, Julio. *Luna de lobos*, 1985. Sánchez Valdés, Julio.

Matute, Ana María. *El polizón del Ulises*, 1965. Aguirre, Javier.

1988

Benet, Juan. *El aire de un crimen*, 1980. Isasi, Antonio.

Madrid, Juan. *Nada que hacer*, 1984. Herrero, Gerardo. *Al acecho*.

Núñez, Raúl. *Sinatra*, 1984. Betriu, Francesc.
Pérez Merinero, Carlos. *El angel triste*, 1983. Blanco, José
María. *Bueno y tierno como un angel*.

1989

Aldecoa, Ignacio. *Gran sol*, 1957. Llagoster, Ferrán.
Fernán Gómez, Fernando. *El mar y el tiempo*, 1988.
Marsé, Juan. *Si te dicen que caí* (Mexico, 1973; Spain, 1976).
Aranda, Vicente.
Sampedro, José Luis. *El río que nos lleva*, 1961. Del Real,
Antonio.

1990

Delibes, Miguel. *La sombra del ciprés es alargada*, 1948.
Alcoriza, Luis.
Delibes, Miguel. *El tesoro*, 1985. Mercero, Antonio.
Grandes, Almudena. *Las edades de Lulú*, 1989. Bigas Luna, J. J.
Muñoz Molina, Antonio. *Invierno en Lisboa*, 1987. Zorrilla,
Antonio.

1991

García Montalvo, Pedro. *Una historia madrileña*, 1988.
Cuerda, José Luis. *La viuda del Capitán Estrada*.
Muñoz Molina, Antonio. *Beltenebros*, 1990. Miró, Pilar.
Pombo, Alvaro. *El hijo adoptivo*, 1984. Pinzas, Juan. *El juego de
los mensajes invisibles*.
Ramírez, Pedro J. *El año en que murió Franco*, 1985. García
Sánchez, José Luis. *La noche más larga*.
Rico Godoy, Carmen. *Cómo ser mujer y no morir en el intento*,
1990. Belén, Ana.
Torrente Ballester, Gonzalo. *La crónica del rey pasmado*, 1989.
Uribe, Imanol. *El rey pasmado*.

1992

Pérez Reverte, Arturo. *El maestro de esgrima*, 1988. Olea, Pedro.
Vázquez Montalbán, Manuel. *El laberinto griego*, 1991. Alcázar, Rafael.
Vázquez Montalbán, Manuel. *Los mares del sur*, 1979. Marquilles, Manuel Esteban.

1993

Marsé, Juan. *El amante bilingüe*, 1991. Aranda, Vicente.
Sorozábel, Pablo. *La última palabra*, 1987. Chávarri, Jaime. *Tierno verano de lujurias y azoteas*.
Tomás, José Luis de. *La otra orilla de la droga*, 1985. Elorrieta, Javier. *Cautivos de la sombra*.

1994

Gala, Antonio. *La pasión turca*, 1993. Aranda, Vicente.
Madrid, Juan. *Los días contados*, 1993. Uribe, Imanol.
Rico Godoy, Carmen. *Cómo ser infeliz y disfrutarlo*, 1992. Urbizu, Eduardo.
Rico Godoy, Carmen. *Cuernos de mujer*, 1992. Urbizu, Eduardo.

1995

Lalana, Fernando. *Historias del Kronan*, 1994. Armendáriz, Montxo.
Mañas, José Angel. *Morirás en Chafarinas*, 1989. Olea, Pedro.
Mendicutti, Eduardo. *El palomo cojo*, 1991. Armiñán, Jaime de.

Appendix B: Percentage of Film Adaptations

The following table shows the number of Spanish films made from contemporary narratives (post–civil war novels and short stories) from 1965-1995. The source for the years 1965-1977 is the annual *Cine español* published by Uniespaña; for 1982-1995, it is the annual *Cine español* published by the Ministerio de Cultura. (Pornographic films rated "S" in the early 1980s are not counted in the total number of films for each year; adaptations of literary works other than contemporary narratives do not enter into the number of film adaptations.)

Year	Total films	Adaptations	Percentage
1965	36	1	3%
1966	131	2	2%
1967	155	3	2%
1968	134	1	1%
1969	115	1	1%
1970	123	1	1%
1971	105	2	2%
1972	95	3	3%
1973	87	0	0%
1974	44	0	0%
1975	45	1	3%
1976	89	6	7%

Year	Total films	Adaptations	Percentage
1977	63	5	8%
1978	102	2	2%
1979	102	3	3%
1980	87	4	5%
1981	88	3	3%
1982	92	4	4%
1983	90	3	3%
1984	75	3	4%
1985	65	2	3%
1986	56	4	7%
1987	66	3	9%
1988	63	2	6%
1989	47	3	9%
1990	42	4	10%
1991	64	3	9%
1992	53	4	6%
1993	56	3	5%
1994	44	4	9%
1995	49	3	5%

Bibliography of Spanish Post–Civil War Narratives Made into Films

Alphabetical list by author of novel, publisher, date of publication, followed by film director, date of debut of the film adaptation, and name of film (if different from the original narrative). Years within brackets indicate original publication dates.

Aldecoa, Ignacio. *Con el viento solano*. Barcelona: Planeta, 1956. Camus, Mario. 1966.

———. *Gran sol*. Barcelona: Noguer, 1963. Llagoster, Ferrán. 1988.

———. *Los pájaros de Baden-Baden*. Madrid: Ediciones Cid, 1965 [1955] . Camus, Mario. 1975.

Aub, Max. *Las buenas intenciones*. Madrid: Alianza, 1986 [1954]. Ungría, Alfonso. *Soldados*, 1978.

Barrios, Manuel. *La espuela*. Barcelona: Argos, 1965. Fandiño, Roberto. 1976.

Benet, Juan. *El aire de un crimen*. Barcelona: Planeta, 1980. Isasi, Antonio. 1989.

Cabezas, Juan Antonio. *La montaña rebelde*. Madrid: Espasa-Calpe, 1960. Torrado, Ramón. 1972.

Castresana, Luis de. *El otro árbol de Guernica*. 6th ed. Madrid: Prensa Española, 1968. Lazaga, Pedro. 1969.

Cebrián, Juan Luis. *La rusa*. Madrid: Alfaguara, 1986. Camus, Mario. 1987.

Cela, Camilo José. *La colmena*. Ed. Darío Villanueva. 43rd ed. Barcelona: Noguer, 1986 [1951]. Camus, Mario. 1982.

———. *La familia de Pascual Duarte*. 18th ed. Barcelona: Noguer, 1988 [1942] . Franco, Ricardo. *Pascual Duarte*, 1975.

Chacel, Rosa. *Memorias de Leticia Valle*. Madrid: Lumen, 1946. Rivas, Miguel Angel. 1979.

Coll, José Luis. *El hermano bastardo de Dios*. Barcelona: Planeta, 1984. Rabal, Benito. 1986.

Delibes, Miguel. *El camino*. 8th ed. Barcelona: Destino, 1968 [1950]. Mariscal, Ana. 1965.

———. *Cinco horas con Mario*. Barcelona: Destino, 1968. Molina, Josefina. *Función de noche*, 1981.

———. *El disputado voto del señor Cayo*. 10th ed. Barcelona: Destino, 1980 [1978]. Giménez Rico, Antonio. 1986.

———. *Mi idolatrado hijo Sisí. La obra completa de Miguel Delibes*.

Barcelona: Destino, 1964-1968 [1953]. Giménez Rico, Antonio. *Retrato de familia*, 1976.

———. *El príncipe destronado*. Barcelona: Destino, 1973. Mercero, Antonio. *La guerra de papá*, 1977.

———. *Los santos inocentes*. 17th ed. Barcelona: Destino, 1988 [1981]. Camus, Mario. 1984.

———. *La sombra del ciprés es alargada. La obra completa de Miguel Delibes*. Barcelona: Destino, 1964-1968 [1948]. Alcoriza, Luis. 1990.

———. *El tesoro*. Barcelona: Planeta, 1985. Mercero, Antonio. 1990.

Fernán Gómez, Fernando. *El mar y el tiempo*. Barcelona: Planeta, 1988. Fernán Gómez, Fernando. 1989.

———. *El viaje a ninguna parte*. Madrid: Debate, 1985. Fernán Gómez, Fernando. 1986.

Fernández Flórez, Wenceslao. *El bosque animado*. Madrid: Espasa-Calpe, 1965 [1943]. Cuerda, José Luis. 1987.

———. *El hombre que se quiso matar*. In *Obras completas IV*. Madrid: Aguilar, 1964. Gil, Rafael, 1970.

Fernández Santos, Jesús. *Extramuros*. Barcelona: Seix Barral, 1989 [1978]. Picazo, Miguel. 1985.

Gala, Antonio. *La pasión turca*. 13th ed. Barcelona: Planeta, 1994 [1993] . Aranda, Vicente. 1994.

García Blázquez, José Antonio. *No encontré rosas para mi madre*. Madrid: Alfaguara, 1968. Rovira Beleta, Francisco. 1972.

García Montalvo, Pedro. *Una historia madrileña*. Barcelona: Seix Barral, 1988. Cuerda, José Luis. *La viuda del capitán Estrada*, 1991.

García Morales. *El sur*. 6th ed. Barcelona: Anagrama, 1985. Erice, Víctor. 1983.

García Serrano, Rafael. *Los ojos perdidos*. Barcelona: Planeta, 1967 [1958]. García Serrano, Rafael. 1967.

Grandes, Almudena. *Las edades de Lulú*. Barcelona: Tusquets, 1989. Bigas Luna, J. J. 1990.

Grosso, Alfonso. *Los invitados*. Barcelona: Planeta, 1978. Barrera, Víctor. 1987.

Guzmán, Eduardo de. *Aurora de sangre (Vida y muerte de Hildegart)*. Madrid: G. del Toro, 1972. Fernán Gómez, Fernando. *Mi hija Hildegart*, 1977.

Hidalgo, Manuel. *El pecador impecable*. Barcelona: Tusquets, 1986. Torres, Augusto M. 1987.

Laiglesia, Alvaro de. *Yo soy fulana de tal*. Barcelona: Planeta, 1964. Lazaga, Pedro. 1979.

Lalana, Fernando. *Morirás en Chafarinas*. Madrid: SM, 1989. Olea, Pedro. 1995.

Llamazares, Julio. *Luna de lobos*. Barcelona: Seix Barral, 1985. Sánchez Valdés, Julio. 1987.

Luca de Tena, T. *La mujer de otro*. Barcelona: Planeta, 1961. Gil, Rafael. 1967.

Madrid, Juan. *Días contados*. 5th ed. Madrid: Alfaguara Hispánica, 1994 [1993] . Uribe, Imanol. 1995.

———.*Nada que hacer*. Barcelona: Seix Barral, 1984. Herrero, Gerardo. *Al acecho*, 1988.

Mañas, José Angel. *Historias del Kronan*. 4th ed. Barcelona: Destino, 1994. Armendáriz, Montxo. 1995.

Marsé, Juan. *El amante bilingüe*. Barcelona: Planeta, 1991. Aranda, Vicente. 1993.

———. *La muchacha de las bragas de oro*. Barcelona: Planeta, 1978. Aranda, Vicente. 1980.

———. *La oscura historia de la prima Montse*. Barcelona: Seix Barral, 1970. Cadena, Jordi. 1977.

———. *Si te dicen que caí*. Ed. William Scherzer. Madrid: Cátedra, 1985 [Mexico, 1973]. Aranda, Vicente. 1989.

———. *Ultimas tardes con Teresa*. 21st ed. Barcelona: Seix Barral, 1990 [1966]. Herralde, Gonzalo. 1984.

Martín, Andreu. *Protesis*. Madrid: Sedmay, 1980. Aranda, Vicente. *Fanny Pelopaja*, 1984.

Martín Gaite, Carmen. "Un alto en el camino." In *Ataduras*. Barcelona: Destino, 1960. Fons, Angelino. *Emilia, parada y fonda*, 1976.

Martín Santos, Luis. *Tiempo de silencio*. 11th ed. Barcelona: Seix Barral, 1976 [1961] . Aranda, Vicente. 1986.

Martínez Barbeito, Carlos. *El bosque de Ancines*. 2nd ed. Barcelona: Destino, 1966 [1947]. Olea, Pedro. *El bosque del lobo*, 1971.

Mendicutti, Eduardo. *El palomo cojo*. Barcelona: Tusquets, 1991. Armiñán, Jaime de.

Mendoza, Eduardo. *El misterio de al cripta embrujada* . 18th ed. Barcelona: Seix Barral, 1989 [1979]. Del Real, Cayetano. *La cripta*, 1981.

———. *La verdad sobre el caso Savolta*. Barcelona: Seix Barral, 1975. Drove, Antonio, 1980.

Muñoz Molina, Antonio. *Invierno en Lisboa*. Barcelona: Seix Barral, 1987. Zorrilla, Antonio. 1990.

———. *Beltenebros*. Barcelona: Seix Barral, 1990. Miró, Pilar. 1991.

Núñez, Raúl. *Sinatra*. Barcelona: Anagrama, 1984. Betriu, Francesc. 1988.

Palomino, Angel. *Madrid, Costa Fleming*. Barcelona: Planeta, 1973. Forqué, José María. 1976.

Pérez Merinero, Carlos. *El angel triste*. Barcelona: Bruguera, 1983. Blanco, José María. *Bueno y tierno como un angel*, 1988.

Pérez Reverte, Arturo. *El maestro de esgrima*. Barcelona: Alfaguara, 1988. Olea, Pedro. 1992.

Ramírez, Pedro J. *El año en que murió Franco*. Esplugues de Llobregat (Barcelona): Plaza & Janes: 1985. García Sánchez, José Luis. *La noche más larga*, 1991.

Rico Godoy, Carmen. *Cómo ser mujer y no morir en el intento*. Madrid: Temas de Hoy, 1990. Belén, Ana. 1991.

———. *Cómo ser infeliz y disfrutarlo*. Madrid: Temas de Hoy, 1992. Urbizu, Eduardo. 1993.

———. *Cuernos de mujer*. Madrid: Temas de Hoy, 1992. Urbizu, Eduardo. 1994.

Romero, Emilio. *Todos morirán en casa manchada*. Barcelona: Planeta, 1969. Nieves Conde, Jose Antonio. *Casa manchada*, 1980.

Sampedro, José Luis. *El río que nos lleva*. Madrid: Aguilar, 1961. Del Real, Antonio. 1989.

Sender, Ramón. *Requiem por un campesino español*. 13th ed. Barcelona: Destino, 1986 [1950]. Betriu, Francesc. 1985.

———. *Crónica del alba*. Barcelona: Destino, 1973 [1963]. Betancor, Antonio. *Valentina/1919 Crónica del alba*, 1983.

Solís, Ramón. *El alijo y otros relatos*. Barcelona: Planeta, 1965. Del Pozo, Angel. 1976.

Sorozábal, Pablo. *La última palabra*. Barcelona: Anthropos, 1987. Chávarri, Jaime. *Tierno verano de lujurias y azoteas*, 1992.

Suárez, Gonzalo. *De cuerpo presente*. Barcelona: L. de Caralt, 1963. Suárez, Gonzalo, 1964.

———. "Fata Morgana." Aranda, Vicente. 1967.

———. *Rocabruno bate a Ditirambo*. Barcelona: Ferró, 1966. Suárez, Gonzalo. *Ditirambo*, 1968.

———. "Bailando para Parker" de *Trece veces trece*. La Bonanova (Palma de Mallorca): Papeles de Sons Armadans, 1972 [1964]. Aranda, Vicente. *Las crueles*, 1971.

Sueiro, Daniel. *Solo de moto*. Madrid: Alfaguara, 1967. Bardem, Antonio. *El puente*, 1977.

Tomás, Juan Luis de. *Cautivos de la sombra*. Barcelona: Destino, 1985. Elorrieta, Javier. 1993.

Torrente Ballester, Gonzalo. *Crónica del rey pasmado*, 1989. Uribe, Imanol. *El rey pasmado*, 1991.

Vaz de Soto, José María. *El infierno y la brisa*. Barcelona: Argos Vargara, 1982 [1969]. Gutiérrez Santos, J. M. *Arriba Hazaña*, 1978.

Vázquez, Angel. *La vida perra de Juanita Narboni*. Barcelona: Planeta, 1976. Aguirre, Juan. *Vida/perra*, 1981.

Vázquez Montalbán, Manuel. *Asesinato en el comité central*. Barcelona: Planeta, 1981. Aranda, Vicente. 1982.

———. *El laberinto griego*. Barcelona: Planeta, 1991. Alcázar, Rafael. 1992.

———. *Los mares del sur*. Barcelona: Planeta, 1979. Marquilles, Manuel Esteban. 1992.

———. *Tatuaje. Primera aventura de Pepe Carvalho*. Barcelona: J. Batlló, 1979 [1974]. Bigas Luna, Juan José. 1977.

Vizcaino Casas, Fernando. *Las autonomosuyas*. Barcelona: Planeta, 1981. Gil, Rafael. 1983.

———. *La boda del señor cura*. Bilbao: Albia, 1977. Gil, Rafael. 1979.

———. *De camisa vieja a chaqueta nueva*. Barcelona: Planeta, 1979. Gil, Rafael. 1982.

———. *Niñas, al salón*. Barcelona: Planeta, 1976. Escrivá, Vicente. 1977.

———. *Y al tercer año resucitó*. Barcelona: Planeta, 1978. Gil, Rafael. 1980.

Zunzúnegui, Juan Antonio. *Dos hombres . . . y dos mujeres en medio*. Madrid: Summa, 1944. Gil, Rafael. 1972.

Filmography

Aguirre, Javier. *Vida/perra*. Bermúdez de Castro, P.C., 1981. Script: Javier Aguirre, based on *La vida perra de Juanita Narboni*, by Angel Vázquez. Photography: Manuel Rojas. Music: Jésus Villa Rojo. Starring: Esperanza Roy.

Alcoriza, Luis. *La sombra del ciprés es alargada*. Rosa García, P.C., 1990. Script: Luis Alcoriza, based on the novel by Miguel Delibes. Photography: Hans Burmann. Music: Gregorio García Segura. Starring: Emilio Gutiérrez Caba, Fiorella Faltoyano, Juano Guerenabarrena, Dany Prius, María Roso, Claudia Gravy, Julián Pastor, M. Jesús Hoyos, Gustavo Ganema, M. Luisa San José.

Aranda, Vicente. *Si te dicen que caí*. I.P.C. Ideas y Producciones Cinematográficas, S.A., 1989. Script: Vicente Aranda, based on the novel by Juan Marsé. Photography: Juan Amorós. Music: José Nieto. Starring: Victoria Abril, Jorge Sanz, Antonio Banderas, Javier Gurruchaga, Guillermo Montesinos, Ferrán Rañe, Lluis Homar, María Bottó, Juan Diego Bottó, Luis Giralte, and Marc Barahona.

———. *Fanny pelopaja*. Lola Films S.A., Morgana Films S.A., Lima P.C., Carlton Films Export, 1984. Script: Vicente Aranda, based on the novel by Andreu Martín. Photography: Juan Amorós. Music: Manuel Camp. Starring: Fanny Cottençon, Bruno Cremer, Francisco Algora, Berta Cabré, Ian Sera, Paca Gabaldón, Eduardo MacGregor, Joaquín Cardona, Roberto Asla, Jordi Serrat, Marta Padovan, Carles Sales.

———. *El amante bilingüe*. Lola Films, Atrium Productions, 1993. Script: Vicente Aranda, based on the novel by Juan Marsé. Photography: Juan Amorós. Music: José Nieto. Starring: Imanol Arias, Ornella Muti, Loles León, Javier Bardem, Joan Lluis Bozzo, Pep Cruz.

———. *Asesinato en el comité central*. Morgana Films, Lola Films, Acuarius, S. A., 1982. Script: Vicente Aranda, based on the novel by Vázquez Montalbán. Photography: José Luis Alcaine. Music: Variations of the "Internationale." Starring: Patxi Andión, Victoria Abril, Héctor Alterio, Conrado San Martín, Rosa María Mateo, José Vivó, Carlos Plaza, Miguel Rellán, Francisco Vidal, Juan Jesús Valverde, José Cerro, Ramón Durán, Juan José Otegui, Palmiro Aranda, Aura María Rojas.

———. *La pasión turca*. Lolafilms, S.A., 1994. Script: Vicente Aranda, based on the novel by Antonio Gala. Photography: José Luis Alcaine. Music: José Nieto. Starring: Ana Belén, Georges Corraface, Silvia Munt, Francis Lorenzo, Ramón Madaula, Loles León.

———. *Tiempo de silencio*. Lola Films-Morgana Films, 1986. Script: Vicente Aranda and Antonio Rabinat, based on the novel by Luis Martín Santos. Photography: Juan Amorós. Starring: Imanol Arias, Paco Rabal, Victoria Abril, Paco Algora, Joaquín Hinojosa, Juan Echanove, Charo López.

———. *La muchacha de las bragas de oro*. Morgana, S. A., Prozesa, Proa Cinematográfica C.A., 1979. Script: Vicente Aranda, based on the novel by Juan Marsé. Photography: José Luis Alcaine. Music: Manuel Camps. Starring: Victoria Abril, Lautaro Murúa, Perla Vonacek, Pep Munné, Consuelo de Nieva.

Armendáriz, Montxo. *Historias del Kronan*. Elías Querejeta, P.C., S.L.; Claudie Ossard Producciones; Alert Film, 1995. Script: Montxo Armendáriz, José Angel Mañas, based on the novel by José Angel Mañas. Photography: Alfredo Mayo. Starring: Juan Diego Botto, Jordi Molla, Nuria Prims, Aitor Merino, Armando del Río, Diana Gálvez, Iñaki Méndez.

Armiñán, Jaime de. *El palomo cojo*. Lotus Films International, S.A., 1995. Script: Jaime de   Armiñán, based on the novel by Eduardo Mendicutti. Photography: Fernando Arribas. Starring: María Barranco, Carmen Maura, Francisco Rabal, Ana Torrent, Miguel Angel Muñoz, Joaquín Kremel, Valeriano Andrés, Amparo Baró, María Massip, Tomás Zori, María Galiana, Asunción Balaguer.

Barrera, Victor. *Los invitados*. PC/Impala, S.A., 1987. Script: Victor Barrera, based on the novel by Alfonso Grosso. Photography: José G. Galisteo. Music: Raúl Alcover. Starring: Amparo Muñoz, Pablo Carbonell, Raúl Fraire, Lola Flores, Pedro Reyes.

Belén, Ana. *Cómo ser mujer y no morir en el intento*. Iberoamericana Films, Atrium, S.A., 1991. Script: Carmen Rico Godoy, based on her novel, and adapted by Rafael Azcona and Emilio Martínez-Lázaro. Photography: Juan Amorós. Music: A. Garcia de Diego, P. Varona, and M. Díaz. Starring: Carmen Maura, Antonio Resines, Tina Sainz, Juan Diego Botto, Carmen Conesa, Juanjo Puigcorbé, Miguel Rellán, Enriqueta Carballeira, Victor García, Asunción Balaguer, José Carlos Plaza.

Betancor, Antonio José. *1919 Crónica del alba*. Ofelia Films, S.A., TVE, S.A., 1983. Script: Lautaro Murúa, Antonio José Betancor, Carlos

Escobedo, Javier Moro, based on the novel by Ramón Sender. Photography: Juan Antonio Ruiz Anchía. Starring: Miguel Molina, Cristina Marsillach, Walter Vidarte, José Antonio Correa, Emma Suárez, Saturno Ferra, Conchita Leza, Alfredo Lucchetti, Fernando Sancho.

——. *Valentina*. Ofelia Films-Kaktus P.C.-TVE, 1982. Script: Antonio Betancor, based on the novel *Crónica del alba* by Ramón Sender. Script: Lautaro Murúa, Antonio J. Betancor, Carlos Escobedo and Javier Moro. Photography: Juan Antonio Ruiz Anchía. Music: Riz Ortolani. Starring: Jorge Sanz, Paloma Gómez, Anthony Quinn, Saturno Ferra, Conchita Leza.

Betriu, Francesc. *Sinatra*. I.P.C. Ideas y Producciones Cinematográficas, S.A., 1988. Script: Raúl Ernesto and Francesc Betriu, based on the novel by Raúl Ernesto. Photography: Carlos Suárez. Music: Joaquín Sabina. Starring: Alfredo Landa, Ana Obregón, Maribel Verdú, Queta Claver, Mercedes Sampietro, Julita Martínez, Luis Ciges, Manuel Alexandre, Carlos Lucena.

——. *Requiem por un campesino español*. Nemo Films/Venus Producción S. A., 1985. Script: Raúl Artigot, Francisco Betriu and Gustav Hernández, based on the novel by Ramón Sender. Photography: Raúl Artigot. Music: Antón García Abril. Starring: Antonio Ferrandis, Antonio Banderas, Fernando Fernán Gómez, Simón Andréu, Amilio Gutiérrez Caba, María Luisa San José, Terere Pávez, Antonio Iranzo.

Bigas Luna, J. J. *Las edades de Lulú*. Iberoamericana Films, Apricot Films, 1990. Script: J. J. Bigas Luna and Almudena Grandes, based on the novel by Almudena Grandes. Photography: Fernando Arribas. Starring: Francesca Neri, Oscar Ladoire, María Barranco, Fernando Guíllen Cuervo, Pilar Bardem.

——. *Tatuaje*. Luna Films, 1976. Script: Manuel Vázquez Montalbán, Juan José Bigas Luna, and José Ulloa, based on the novel by Manuel Vázquez Montalbán. Photography: Tomás Pladevall. Music: Toni Miró and J. A. Amargos. Starring: Carlos Ballesteros, Pilar Velázquez, Mónica Randall, Carlos Lucena, Carmen Liaño, Luis Induni, Consol Turo, and Terele Pávez.

Blanco, José María. *Bueno y tierno como un ángel*. José María Blanco Film & Video, 1983. Script: José María Blanco, based on Carlos Pérez Merinero's *El ángel triste*. Photography: Francisco Peso and J. M. Blanco. Music: Manuel Palencia Lefler. Starring: José María Blanco, Montse Bayó, José María Cañete, Pilar Bardém, Amparo Moreno.

Cadena, Jordi. *La oscura historia de la prima Montse.* Opalo Films, 1977. Script: Ramón Font, Jordi Cadena, based on the novel by Juan Marsé. Music: Carles Santos. Starring: Ana Belén, Ovidi Montllor, Christa Lem, Xavier Elgorriaga, Gabriel Renom, Concha Bardem, Manuel Gas, Alfredo Luchetti.

Camus, Mario. *Los santos inocentes.* Ganesh S.A., 1984. Script: Antonio Larreta, Manuel Matji, Mario Camus, based on the novel by Miguel Delibes. Photography: Hans Burmann. Music: Antón García Abril. Starring: Alfredo Landa, Francisco Rabal, Terere Pávez, Juan Diego, Maribel Martín, Agustín González, Agata Lys, Mary Carrillo, Belén Ballesteros, Juan Sánchez, Susana Sánchez.

———. *Los pájaros de Baden-Baden.* Impala y Arvi, 1975. Script: M. Camus and Manuel Merinero, based on the narrative by Ignacio Aldecoa. Photography: Hans Burman. Starring: Catherine Spaak, Frederic de Pasquale, José Luis Alonso, Carlos Larrañaga, Andrés Mejuto, Cándida Losada, Antonio Iranzo, and Alejandro Enciso.

———. *La rusa.* Pedro Masó, 1987. Script: Mario Camus, and Juan Luis Cebrián, based on the novel by Cebrián. Photography: Hans Burmann. Music: Antón García Abril. Starring: Anjeli Van Os, Didier Flamand, Muntsa Alcañiz, Eusebio Lázaro, Fernando Guillén.

———. *Con el viento solano.* Pro Artis, Ibérica, 1966. Script: Mario Camus, based on the novel by Ignacio Aldecoa. Photography: J. J. Baena. Starring: Antonio Gades, María José Alfonso, María Luisa Ponte, Antonio Ferrandis, Fernando Sánchez Polak, Imperio Argentina.

———. *La colmena.* Agata Films, S.A., 1982. Script: José Luis Dibildos, based on the novel by Camilo José Cela. Photography: Hans Burman. Music: Antón García Abril. Starring: José Sacristán, Francisco Rabal, Francisco Algora, Agustín González, Imanol Arias, Victoria Abril, Concha Velasco, Ana Belén, Rafael Alonso, José Bódalo, Mary Carrillo, Queta Claver, Luis Escobar, Fiorella Faltoyano, Emilio Gutiérrez Caba, Charo López, José Luis López Vázquez, Mario Pardo, Encarna Pasó, María Luisa Ponte, Elvira Quintilla, Anatonio Resines, José Sazatornil, Elena María Tejeiro.

Chávarri, Jaime. *Tierno verano de lujurias y azoteas.* Jet Films, Sogetel, 1993. Script: Lola Salvador and Jaime Chávarri, based on the novel *La última palabra*, by Pablo Solozábel. Photography: José Luis López Linares. Music: Alejandro Massó. Starring: Marisa

Paredes, Gabino Diego, Imaonol Arias, Ana Alvarez, Laura Bayonas, Clara Sanchís, Sara Sanders, Gabriel Garbisu, Isabel Ruiz de la Prada.

Cuerda, José Luis. *La viuda del Capitán Estrada*. Classic Films, 1991. Script: José Luis Cuerda, and Eduardo Ducay, based on the novel *Una historia madrileña* by Pedro García Montalvo. Photography: Magí Torruella. Music: Salvador Bacarisse and Federico Morreno Torroba. Starring: Sergi Mateu, Anna Galiena, Nacho Martínez, Chema Mazo, José M. Escuer, Gabino Diego, Manuel de Blas.

———. *El bosque animado*. Classic Films Producción, S.A., 1987. Script: Rafael Azcona, based on the novel by Wenceslao Fernández Flórez. Photography: Xavier Aguirresarobe. Music: José Nieto. Starring: Alfredo Landa, Encarna Paso, Fernando Valverde, Alejandra Grepi, Miguel Rellán, Alicia Hermida, Amparo Baró, María Isbert, Luma Gómez, Laura Cisneros, José Esteban Jr., Fernando Rey.

Del Pozo, Angel. *El alijo*. Coral Films, 1976. Script: Angel del Pozo, based on the novel by Ramón Solís. Starring: Juan Luis Galiardo, Fernando Sancho, Helga Liné, Manuel Zarzo, Venancio Muro.

Del Real, Antonio. *El río que nos lleva*. Lauren Films, S.A., 1989. Based on the novel by José Luis Sampedro. Script: Antonio Larreta, José Luis Sampedro, and Antonio del Real. Photography: Federico Ribes. Music: Lluis Llach. Starring: Alfredo Landa, Tony Peck, Eulalia Ramón, Fernando Fernán Gómez, Santiago Ramos, Juanjo Artero, Mario Pardo, Antonio Gamero, Ovidi Montllor, Mikel Insúa.

Del Real, Cayetano. *La cripta*. Figaro Films, Kaktus, P. C. S. A., 1981. Script: Cayetano del Real, Francisco Siurana, and Eduardo Mendoza, based on the novel *El misterio de la cripta embrujada* by Eduardo Mendoza. Photography: Jaume Peracaula. Starring: José Sacristán, Rafaela Aparicio, Blanca Guerra, Carlos Lucena, Marta Molins.

Drove, Antonio. *La verdad sobre el caso Savolta*. P.C. Domingo Pedret, S.A., Filmalpha, NEF Diffusion, S.A., 1980. Script: Antonio Drove and Antonio Larreta, based on the novel by Eduardo Mendoza. Photography: Gilberto Azevedo. Music: Egisto Macchi. Starring: José Luis López Vázquez, Omero Antonutti, Charles Denner, Stefania Sandrelli, Ovidi Montllor, Ettore Manni, Alfredo Pea, Virginnie Billedoux.

Elorrieta, Javier. *Cautivos de la sombra*. Lotus Film International, S.L., Anem Films, S.A., 1993. Script: Santiago Moncada, based on the novel *La otra orilla de la droga*, by José Luis de Tomás. Photography: Eduardo Suárez. Music: A.D.V., S.A. Starring: Manuel Bandera, Beatriz Santana, Juan Ribó, Antonio Flores, Neus Asensi, Elena Nieto, Tony Isbert, Manuel Zarzo.

Erice, Víctor. *El sur*. Elías Querejeta, P. C., 1983. Script: Víctor Erice, based on the novel by Adelaida García Morales. Photography: José Luis Alcaine. Music: Ravel, Schubert, Granados. Starring: Omero Antonutti, Sonsoles Aranguren, Icíar Bollain, Lola Cardona, Rafaela Aparicio.

Escrivá, Vicente. *Niñas . . . al salón*. Aspa, P.C., Impala S.A., 1976. Script: Vicente Escrivá and Antonio Fos, based on the novel by Fernando Vizcaíno Casas. Music: Anton García Abril. Starring: Dagmar Lassender, Josele Román, Antonio Casas, María Vico, Luis Barbero, Emilio Fornet, Pilar Cansino, Rafael Hernández, María Alvarez, Ricardo Merino, Luis Lorenzo.

Esteban, Manuel. *Los mares del sur*. Pere Fages, CYRK Productions, 1990. Script: Manuel Esteban and Gustavo Hernández, based on the novel by Manuel Vázquez Montalbán. Photography: Carlos Suárez. Starring: Juan Luis Galiardo, Alejandra Grepi, Silvia Tortosa, Eulalia Ramón, Jean-Pierre Aumont, Carlos Lucena, Anne Alvaro, Albert Vidal, Muntsa Alcañiz, Mónica Duart.

Fandiño, Roberto. *La espuela*. Galgo Films, 1977. Script: Pancho Bautista, based on the novel by Manuel Barrios. Photography: Raúl Artigot. Starring: Javier Escrivá, Claudia Gravi, Simón Andreu, Mary Francis, Mario Pardo, Máximo Valverde.

Fernán Gómez, Fernando. *El mar y el tiempo*. Ion, 1989. Script: Fernando Fernán Gómez, based on his own novel. Photography: José Luis Alcaine. Starring: Fernando Fernán Gómez, José Soriano, Rafaela Aparicio, Aitana Sánchez Gijón, Cristina Marsillach, Inaki Miramón, Ramón Madaula, Eulalia Ramón, Gabino Diego, Fernando Guillén Cuervo, María Asquerino, Emma Cohen, Manuel Alexandre.

———. *Mi hija Hildegart*. Cámara P.C.-Jet Films, 1977. Script: Fernando Fernán Gómez and Rafael Azcona based on the novel *Aurora de sangre* by Eduardo de Guzmán. Photography: Cecilio Paniagua. Music: Luis Eduardo Aute. Starring: Amparo Soler Leal, Carmen Roldán, Pedro Díez del Corral, Manuel Galiana, José María Mompin, Guerllermo Marín.

S.A., 1983. Script: Lautaro Murúa, Antonio José Betancor, Carlos

——. *El viaje a ninguna parte*. Ganesh Producciones, 1986. Script: Fernando Fernán Gómez, based on his own novel. Photography: José Luis Alcaine. Music: Pedro Iturralde. Starring: Fernando Fernán Gómez, José Sacristán, Gabino Diego, Laura del Sol, Juan Diego, María Luisa Poncew, Nuria Gallardo.

Fons, Angelino. *Emilia, parada y fonda*. Cámara P.C., S. A.; 1966. Script: Juan Tebar and Carmen Martín Gaite, based on the short story, "Un alto en el camino" by Carmen Martín Gaite. Photography: Luis Cuadrado. Music: Luis Eduardo Aute. Starring: Ana Belén, Francisco Rabal, Juan Diego, Pilar Muñoz, Lina Canaleja, Georges Mansont.

Franco, Ricardo. *Pascual Duarte*. Elías Querejeta, P.C., 1975. Script: Ricardo Franco, Elías Querejeta, and Emilio Martínez Lázaro, based on the novel *La familia de Pascual Duarte* by Camilo José Cela. Photography: Luis Cuadrado. Music: Luis de Pablo. Starring: José Luis Gómez, Paca Ojea, Héctor Alterio, Diana Pérez de Guzmán, Eduardo Calvo, José Hinojosa, Maribel Ferrero, Eduardo Bea Boluda, Francisco Casares, Eugenio Navarro.

García, José Luis Sánchez. *La noche más larga*. Iberoamericana Films International, 1991. Script: José Luis García Sánchez, Manuel Gutiérrez Aragón, and Carmen Rico Godoy, based on the novel by Pedro J. Ramírez. Photography: Fernando Arribas. Music: Alejandro Massó. Starring: Juan Echanove, Carmen Conesa, Juan Diego, Gabino Diego, Fernando Guillén Cuervo, Alberto Alonso, Juan José Otegui, Paco Casares, Enrique Escudero, José Carlos Goméz, Concha Leza.

Gil, Rafael. *El hombre que se quiso matar*. Coral Films, 1970. Script: Rafael J. Salvia, based on the novel by Wenceslao Fernández Flórez. Photography: José F. Aguayo. Starring: Tony Leblanc, Antonio Garisa, Elisa Ramírez, Emma Cohen, Aurora Redondo, Julia Caba Alba, and José Sacristán.

——. *Las autonomosuyas*. Filmayar, S.A., Coral P.C., 1983. Script: Rafael Gil, based on the novel by Fernando Vizcaíno Casas. Photography: José F. Aguayo. Music: Gregorio Seguro. Starring: Alfredo Landa, María Casanova, Manolo Codesa, Antonio Garisa, Fernando Sancho, Ismael Merlo, José Bódalo, Tomás Blanco.

——. *Dos hombres . . . y en medio dos mujeres*. Coral P.C., 1972. Script: José López Rubio, based on the novel by Juan Antonio Zunzúnegui (1944). Starring: Alberto Closas, Nadiuska, Gemma Cuervo, Alfredo Alba.

———. *Y al tercer año resucitó*. 5 Films, 1978. Script: Rafael Gil, based on the novel by Fernando Vizcaíno Casas. Photography: José F. Aguayo. Music: Gregorio García Segura. Starring: José Bódalo, Mary Begoña, Francisco Cecilio, Florinda Chico, Juan L. Galiardo, Antonio Gansa, Isabel Luque, José Nieto, Adrián Ortega, Alfonso del Real, José Sancho, Fernando Sancho, Tip y Coll, Juan Santamaría, Pedro Valentín.

———. *La boda del señor cura*. Futuro Visión, S.A., 1979. Script: Rafael Gil and Fernando Vizcaíno Casas, based on the novel by Fernando Vizcaíno Casas. Photography: José F. Aguayo. Music: Antón García Abril. Starring: José Sancho, Juan Luis Galiardo, Manuel Tejada, José Bódalo, Blanca Estrada, Manuel Codeso, Gemma Cuervo, Fernando Sancho, Isabel Luque, Ricardo Merino, Carmen Platero, Juan Santamaría, Rafael Hernánez, Alfonso del Real.

———. *La mujer de otro*. Coral, P.C., 1967. Script: José López Rubio and Torcuato Luca de Tena, based on the novel by Torcuato Luca de Tena. Starring: Marta Hyer, John Rohane, Analía Gadé, Angel del Pozo, Fosco Giachetti.

Giménez Rico, Antonio. *Retrato de familia*. Sabre Films, S. A., 1976. Script: José Samano and Antonio Giménez Rico, based on *Mi idolatrado hijo Sisí*, by Miguel Delibes. Photography: José Luis Alcaine. Music: Carmelo Bernaola. Starring: Antonio Ferrandis, Amparo Soler Leal, Mónica Randall, Miguel Bosé, Gabriel Llopart, Encarna Pasó, Alberto Fernández, Mirta Miller, Carmen Lozano, Josefina Díaz.

———. *El disputado voto del señor Cayo*. Penélope, S.A., 1986. Script: Manuel Matji and Antonio Giménez Rico, based on the novel by Miguel Delibes. Photography: Alejandro Ulloa. Starring: Francisco Rabal, Juan Luis Galiardo, Iñaki Maramón, Lydia Bosch, Eusebio Lázaro, Mari Paz Molinero, Abel Vitón, Gabriel Renom, Paco Casares, Juan Jesús Valverde.

Gutiérrez Santos, José María. *Arriba hazaña*. CB Films, 1978. Script: José María Gutiérrez Santos and José Samano, based on the novel *El infierno y la brisa* by José María Vaz de Soto. Photography: Magi Torruela. Music: Luis Eduardo Aute. Starring: Fernando Fernán Gómez, Héctor Alterio, José Sacristán, Gabriel Llorpart, Luis Ciges, José Cerro.

Herralde, Gonzalo. *Ultimas tardes con Teresa*. Samba, P.C., 1983. Script: Gonzalo Herralde, based on the novel by Juan Marsé. Photography: Fernando Arribas. Music: José María Bardagi.

Starring: Maribel Martín, Angel Alcázar, Patricia Adriani, Cristina Marsillach, Juano Puigcorbe.

———. *Al acecho*. Malta Films, S.A., 1987. Script: Gerardo Herrero, based on the novel *Nada que hacer* by Juan Madrid. Photography: José L. López Linares. Music: Bernardo Bonezzi. Starring: Giulano Gemma, Amparo Muñoz, Mario Gas, Cristina Marcos, Cristina Gavi, Joaquín Hinojosa, Eduardo Calvo, Paco Catalá, Conrado Sanmartín, Joaquín Cayuela, Francisco Casares, Nuria Hosta, Hugo Blanco.

Isasi-Isasmendi, Antonio. *El aire de un crimen*. A. Isasi, 1988. Script: Gabriel Castro and Antonio Isasi based on the novel by Juan Benet. Photography: Juan Gelpin. Music: Pedro Agaurod. Starring: Paco Rabal, Chema Mazo, Fernando Rey, Maribel Verdú, Germán Cobos, Miguel Rellan, Agustín González, Rafaela Aparicio, María José Moreno, Ovidi Montllor, Alfred Luchetti, Terele Pávez.

Klimovsky, León. *La casa de las chivas*. Galaxia Films, 1971. Script: Manuel Villegas López, José Luis Garci, Carlos Pumares. Photography: Francisco Fraile. Music: Carlos Laporta. Starring: Charo Soriano, Simón Andréu, María Kosti, Ricardo Merino, Pedro María Sánchez, Rafael Hernández, Antonio Casas, José Canalejas, Simón Arriaga.

Lazaga, Pedro. *El otro árbol de Guernica*. CB Films, 1969. Script: Pedro Masó and Florentino Soria, based on the novel by Luis de Castresana. Music: Antón García Abril. Photography: Juan Marine. Starring: Juan Manuel Barrio, María Fernanda d'Ocon, Inma de Santi, Luis Miguel Toledano, Ramón Corroto, Marcelo Arroita-Jaúregui, José Montejano, Alicia Altabella.

Llagostera, Ferrán. *Gran sol*. Lauren Films, Mare Nostrum Films, Irati filmak, S.A., 1988. Script: F. Llagostera, based on the novel by Ignacio Aldecoa. Photography: Xavier Cami. Music: Luis Iriondo. Starring: Carlos Lucena, Agustín González, Luis Iriondo, Patxi Bisquert, Ovidi Montllor, Paco Casares, Paco Sagarzazu, Lola Gaos.

Mariscal, Ana. *El camino*. Bosco Films, 1965. Script: José Zamit and Ana Mariscal, based on the novel by Miguel Delibes. Photography: Valentín Javier. Music: Gerardo Gombau. Starring: José Antonio Mejías, Maribel Martín, Angel Díaz, Jesús Crespo, Julia Caba Alba, Mary Delgado, Mari Paz Pondal, Maruchi Fresno, Rafael Luis Calvo, Joaquín Roa, Antonio Casas, Adriano Domínguez, José Orjas, María Isbert, María Asunción Balaguer, Xan de Bolas, José Sepúlveda, Juan Luis Galiardo.

Martinez Torres, Augusto. *El pecador impecable*. Amparo Suárez Bárcena and Andrés Vicente Gómez, 1987. Script: Rafael Azcona and Augusto Martínez Torres, based on the novel by Manuel Hidalgo. Photography: Juan Amorós. Music: Alejandro Massó. Starring: Alfredo Landa, Chus Lampreave, Rafaela Aparicio, Julieta Serrano, Queta Claver, Alicia Sánchez, José Sazatornil, Rafael Alonso, Diana Peñalver, Tomás Zori, María Isbert, Manuel Zarzo.

Mercero, Antonio. *La guerra de papá*. J F Films, 1977. Script: Antonio Mercero and Horacio Valcárcel, based on *El príncipe destronado* by Miguel Delibes. Photography: Manuel Rojas. Starring: Lolo García, Teresa Gimpera, Héctor Alterio, Verónica Forqué, Queta Claver, Rosario García Ortega, Vicente Parra.

Miró, Pilar. *Beltenebros*. Iberoamericana Films, 1990. Script: Mario Camus, Juan Antonio Porto and Pilar Miró, based on the novel by Antonio Muñoz Molina. Photography: Javier Aguirresarobe. Starring: Terence Stamp, Patsy Kensit, José Luis Gómez, Geraldine James, John McEnery, Alexander Bardini, Jorge de Juan, Simón Andreu, Pedro Diez del Corral, Carlos Hipólito, Paco Casares, William Job, Queta Claver, Antonio Orengo, Magda Wojcik.

Molina, Josefina. *Función de noche*. Sabre Films, 1981. With fragments of *Cinco horas con Mario* by Miguel Delibes. Photography: Teo Escamilla. Musical Direction: Alejandro Massó. Starring: Lola Herrera, Daniel Dicente, Natalia Dicente Herrera, and Daniel Dicente Herrera.

Nieves-Conde, José Antonio. *Casa manchada*. Hidalgo, 1980. Script: Andrés Velasco Pedro Gil Paradela and J. A. Nieves-Conde, based on the novel *Todos morían en casa manchada*, by Emilio Romero. Starring: Stephen Boyd, Sara Lezana, Paola Senatore, Carmen de la Maza, Ricardo Merino.

———. *Más allá del deseo*. Azor Films, 1976. Photography: Francisco Sampere. Music: Antón García Abril. Starring: María Luisa San José, Ramiro Oliveros, Mónica Randall, Ricardo Merino, Patricia Granada, Isabel Mestres, Manuel Torremocha, Ricardo Palacios, Francisco Merino, Ricardo Sacristán, Ingrid Rabel, Enrique Karrión, Francisco Valledares.

Olea, Pedro. *Morirás en Chafarinas*. Altubak Filmeak, S.A., 1995. Script: Pedro Olea and Fernando Lalana based on the novel by Fernando Lalana. Photography: Paco Femenia. Music: Bernardo Bonezzi. Starring: Jorge Sanz, Oscar Ladoire, María Barranco, Toni Zenet, Esperanza Campuzano.

——. *El maestro de esgrima*. Origen P.C., Altube, S.L.,1992. Script: Arturo Pérez Reverte, Pedro Olea, Antonio Larreta and Francisco Prada, based on the novel by Arturo Pérez Reverte. Photography: Alfredo Mayo. Music: José Nieto. Starring: Omero Antonutti, Assumpta Serna, Joaquim de Almeida, Jose Luis López Vázquez, Alberto Closas, Miguel Rellán, Elisa Matilla, Ramón Goyanes, Marcos Tizón, Miguel Angel Salomón.

——. *El bosque del lobo*. Amboto, P.C. 1970. Script: Pedro Olea and Juan Antonio Porto, based on the novel *El bosque de Ancines*, by Carlos Martínez-Barbeito. Photography: Aurelio G. Larraya. Music: Antonio Pérez Olea. Starring: José Luis López Vázquez, Amparo Soler Leal, Antonio Casas, John Steiner, Nuria Torray, María Fernanda Ladrón de Guevara, Alfredo Mayo, Víctor Israel, María Vico, Fernando Sánchez Polak, Pedro Luis León.

Picazo, Miguel. *Extramuros*. Blau Films, S.A., 1985. Script: Miguel Picazo, based on the novel by Jesús Fernández Santos. Photography: Teo Escamilla. Music: José Nieto. Starring: Carmen Maura, Mercedes Sampietro, Aurora Bautista, Assumpta Serna, Antonio Ferrandis, Manuel Alexandre, Conrado San Martín, Marta Ferández Muro, Valentín Paredes, Beatriz Elorrieta, Cándida Losada.

Pinzás, Juan. *El juego de los mensajes invisibles*. Atlántico Films, 1991. Script: Juan Pinzás and Alvaro Pombo, based on the novel *El hijo adoptivo* by Alvaro Pombo. Photography: Carlos Suárez. Music: Juan Manuel Sueiro. Starring: Antonio Ferrandis, María Barranco, Eusebio Poncela, José Luis López Vázquez, Mayrata O'Wisiedo, Raúl Fraire, Pablo Corbacho, Luma Gómez.

Rabal, Benito. *El hermano bastardo de Dios*. Almadraba Producciones, S.A., 1986. Script: Agustín Cerezales and Benito Rabal based on the novel by José Luis Coll. Photography: Paco Femenia. Music: Juan Pablo Muñoz Zielinski. Starring: Francisco Rabal, Asunción Balaguer, Agustín González, María Luisa Ponte, Mario Pardo, Terele Pávez, Lucas Martín, José Luis Coll, Miguel Angel Rellán, Manolo Zarzo, Juan Diego.

Rivas, Miguel Angel. *Las memorias de Leticia Valle*. 1979. Script: Miguel Angel Rivas, based on the novel by Rosa Chacel. Photography: Carlos Suárez. Starring: Emma Suárez, Ramiro Oliverso, Fernando Rey, Jeannine Mestre, Héctor Alterio, Queta Claver.

Rovira Beleta, Francisco. *No encontré rosas para mi madre*. Hidalgo S.A.; Roma: CP Cinematografic; Paris: Le Productions du Bassan, 1972. Script: Francisco Rovira Beleta, Andrés Velasco, and José Antonio García Blázquez, based on the novel by José Antonio García Blázquez. Photography: Michel Kelber. Music: Piero Piccioni. Starring: Gina Lollobrigida, Danielle Darrieux, Concha Velasco, Susan Hampshire, Renaud Verley.

Sánchez Valdés, Julio. *Luna de lobos*. Brezal, PC, S.A., 1987. Script: J. Sánchez Valdés and Julio Llamazares based on the novel by Julio Llamazares. Photography: Juan Molina. Starring: Santiago Ramos, Antonio Resines, Alvaro de Luna, Kiti Manver.

Suárez, Gonzalo. *Epílogo*. Ditirambo Films, 1984. Script: Gonzalo Suárez, based on his novel. Photography: Carlos Suárez. Starring: Francisco Rabal, José Sacristán, Charo López, Sandra Toral, Manuel Zarzo, Cyra Toledo, José Arranz, Manuel Calvo, Sonia Martínez, Martín Adjemian, Chus Lampreave, David Vélez.

Ungría, Alfonso. *Soldados*. Antonio Gregori, P.C., 1978. Script: Alfonso Ungría and Antonio Gregori, based on the novel *Las buenas intenciones*, by Max Aub. Photography: José Luis Alcaine. Music: F. Schubert. Starring: Marilina Ross, Ovidi Montllor, Francisco Algora, Claudia Gravy, José Calvo, Julieta Serrano, José María Muñoz, Lautaro Murua.

Urbizu, Enrique. *Cuernos de mujer*. Iberoamericana Films, Atrium Films, PROARSA, 1994. Script: Carmen Rico Godoy and Manuel Gutiérrez Aragón, based on the novel by Carmen Rico Godoy. Photography: Juan Amorós. Music: Bingen Mendizábal. Starring: María Barranco, Ramón Madaula Javier Blanco, Santiago Ramos, Pilar Bardem, Marcelina Núñez, Victor Valverde, Julia Martínez, Paloma Lago.

———. *Como ser infeliz y disfrutarlo*. Iberoamericana Films, Atrium Films, PROARSA, 1994. Script: Carmen Rico Godoy and José Luis García Sánchez, based on the novel by Carmen Rico Godoy. Photography: Angel Luis Fernández. Music: Bingen Mendizábal. Starring: Carmen Maura, Antonio Resines, Irne Bau, Francis Lorenzo, Ramón Madaula, Alicia Agut, Fernando Valverde.

Uribe, Imanol. *Días contados*. Aiete and Ariane Films, 1994. Script: Imanol Uribe, based on the novel by Juan Madrid. Photography: Javier Aguirre Sarobe. Music: José Nieto. Starring: Carmelo Gómez, Ruth Gabriel, Candela Peña, Karra Elejalde, Elvira Mínguez, Joseba Apaolaza, Pepón Nieto, Chacho Carreras, Raquel Sanchís, Javier Bardem.

———. *El rey pasmado*. Aite Films, Ariana Films, Arion Productions, Inforfilmes, 1991. Script: Juan Potau and Gonzalo Torrente

Malvido, based on *Crónica del rey pasmado* by Gonzalo Torrente Ballester. Photography: Hans Burmann. Music: José Nieto. Starring: María Barranco, Laura del Sol, Gabino Diego, Juan Diego, Alejandra Grepi, Javier Gurruchaga, Eusebio Poncela, Anne Roussel, Fernando Fernán Gómez, Emma Cohen, Eulalia Ramón.

Zorrilla, José Antonio. *El invierno en Lisboa*. Madrid/Paris: Igeldo, P.C., Impala S.A., Jet Films, Sara Films, 1991. Script: José Antonio Zorrilla and Mason M. Funk, based on the novel by Antonio Muñoz Molina. Photography: Jean-François Gondre. Music: Dizzy Gillespie, arranged by Slide Hampton. Starring: Christian Vadim, Hélène de St. Père, Dizzy Gillespie, Eusebio Poncela, Fernando Guillén, Michel Duperial, Carlos Wallenstein, Isidoro Fernández, Víctor Norte, Mikel Garmendía.

Secondary Works Cited

Abad, Mercedes. "Juan Marsé: 'La película *Si te dicen que caí* contiene demasiado sadismo.'" *Cambio 16* 931 (2 October 1989): 100-101.

Alberich, Ferrán. *Cuatro años de cine español*. Madrid: Comunidad de Madrid, 1991.

Alborg, Concha. "*El sur*, novela y película: dos versiones de un mismo conflicto." *Anuario de cine y literatura en español* 3 (1997): 15-24.

Alcover, Norberto. "*La rusa*." In *Cine para leer, 1987*, 227-229. Bilbao: Mensajero, 1988.

———."*La noche más larga*." In *Cine para leer, 1991*. Bilbao: Mensajero, 1992.

Alewy, Richard. "The Origin of the Detective Novel." Edited by Glenn W. Most and William W. Stowe, 62-78. *The Poetics of Murder. Detective Fiction and Literary Theory*. San Diego: Harcourt Brace Jovanovich, 1983.

Alvares Hernández, Rosa, and Belén Frías. *Vicente Aranda, Victoria Abril: El cine como pasión*. Valladolid: 36 Semana Internacional de Cine, 1991.

Amell, Samuel. *La narrativa de Juan Marsé, contador de aventis*. Madrid: Playor, 1984.

———. "Literatura e ideología: El caso de la novela negra en la España actual." *Monographic Review/Revista monográfica* 3. no. 1-2 (1987): 192-201.

———. "Cine y novela en la España del siglo XX. El caso de Juan Marsé." In *Cine-Lit: Essays on Hispanic Film and Fiction*, edited by George Cabello-Castellet, Jaume Martí Olivella, and Guy H. Wood, 49-54. Corvallis, Oreg.: Oregon State University, Portland State University and Reed College, 1992.

Andrew, J. Dudley. *Concepts in Film Theory*. New York: Oxford University Press, 1984.

———. *The Major Film Theories*. New York: Oxford University Press, 1976.

———. "The Well-Worn Muse: Adaptation in Film History and Theory. In *Narrative Strategies: Original Essays in Film and Prose Fiction*, edited by Syndy M. Conger and Janice R. Welsch. Western Illinois University Press, 1980.

Apaolaza, Jon. "*El palomo cojo* remonta el vuelo." *Cambio 16* 1217 (20 March 1995): 84-85.

Aranda, Vicente. *El amante bilingüe (Guión)*. Madrid: Alma-Plot, 1993.

Arquier, Louis. "Personaje y estructura narrativa en *La colmena*." *Archivum* 27-28 (1977-78): 101-20.

Arribas, Juan. "Mario Camus, *La colmena*." In*Cine para leer, 1982*, 112-114. Bilbao: Mensajero, 1983.

Asís Garrote, María Dolores. *Ultima hora de la novela española*. Madrid: Endema, 1990.

Asún, Raquel. "*La colmena*" de Camilo José Cela. Barcelona: Laia, 1982.

Ayala, Francisco. *El escritor y el cine*. Madrid: Ediciones del Centro, 1975.

Bakhtin, Mikhail. *Problems of Dostoevsky's Poetics*. Translated by Caryl Emerson. Minneapolis: University of Minnesota Press, 1984.

———. *Rabelais and His World*. Translated by Helene Iswolsky. Bloomington, Ind: Indiana University Press, 1984.

Baquero Goyanes, Mariano. *Estructuras de la novela actual*. Barcelona: Planeta, 1970.

Barthes, Roland. *The Pleasure of the Text*. New York: Hill and Wang, 1975.

Bayón, Miguel. "La sosa." *Cambio 16*, 826 (28 September 1987): 138.

Bazin, André. *What is Cinema?* Translated by Hugh Gray. Berkeley, Calif.: University of California Press, 1967.

Beja, Morris. *Film & Literature, an Introduction*. New York: Longman, 1979.

Berger, John. *Ways of Seeing*. London: BBC, 1981.

Besas, Peter. *Behind the Spanish Lens: Spanish Cinema Under Fascism and Democracy*. Denver, Colo.: Arden, 1985.

Bluestone, George. *Novels into Film*. Berkeley, Calif.: University of California Press, 1973.

Blumenberg, Richard. *Critical Focus: An Introduction to Film*. Belmont, Calif.: Wadsworth, 1975.

Bobker, Lee R. *Elements of Film*. New York: Harcourt Brace Jovanovich, 1974.

Boletín informativo del control de taquilla. Datos de 1982. Vol. 10. Madrid: Ministerio de Cultura, 1983.

Boletín informativo del control de taquilla. Datos de 1983. Vol. 11. Madrid: Ministerio de Cultura, 1984.

Boletín informativo del control de taquilla. Datos de 1984. Vol. 12. Madrid: Ministerio de Cultura, 1985.

Booth, Wayne C. *The Rhetoric of Fiction*. Chicago: University of Chicago Press, 1961.

Borau, Pablo. *El existencialismo en la novela de Ignacio Aldecoa*. Zaragoza: Talleres Gráficos "La Editorial," 1974.

Bordwell, David. *Making Meaning: Inference and Rhetoric in the Interpretation of Cinema*. Cambridge, Mass.: Harvard University Press, 1989.

———. *Narration and the Fiction Film*. Madison Wis.: University of Wisconsin Press, 1985.

Boyum, Joy G. *Film as Film: Critical Responses to Film Art*. Boston: Allyn and Bacon, 1971.

———. *Double Exposure: Fiction into Film*. New York: Plume New American Library, 1985.

Branigan, Edward. *Point of View in the Cinema*. New York: Mouton, 1984.

Brown, Jonathan. *Velázquez: Painter and Courtier*. New Haven, Conn.: Yale University Press, 1986.

Carenas, Francisco. "*La colmena*: novela de lo concreto." *Papeles de Son Armadans* 61 (June 1971): 229-55.

Casas, Quim. "*Las edades de Lulú*. Mucho sexo y nada que contar." *Dirigido* 186 (December 1990): 28-31.

———. "*La viuda del Capitán Estrada*. El ejército y el amor." *Dirigido* 194 (September 1991): 62-63.

———. "*El rey pasmado* de Imanol Uribe." *Dirigido* 176 (November 1991): 78-79.

Castellet, José María. "La obra narrativa de Camilo José Cela." In *Camilo José Cela: Vida y obra-bibliografía-antología*. New York: Hispanic Institute, 1962.

Castro, Antonio. "Un 'thriller' rodado con oficio: *Días contados*." *Dirigido* 228 (October 1994): 40-47.

———. "*La noche más larga*: las dificultades de un cine moralista." *Dirigido* 195 (October 1991): 34-36.

———. "[Entrevista con] García Sánchez." *Dirigido* 195 (October 1991): 36-39.

———. "José Luis Cuerda nos habla de *El bosque animado*." *Dirigido por* 152 (1987): 62-65.

Chatman, Seymour. *Story and Discourse: Narrative Structure in Fiction and Film*. Ithaca, N.Y.: Cornell University Press, 1978.

———. *Coming to Terms: the Rhetoric of Narrative in Fiction and Film*. Ithaca, N.Y.: Cornell University Press, 1990.

"Cine en España, El." *Dirigido* (April 1996): 78.

Clark, Katerina, and Michael Holquist. *Mikhail Bakhtin*. Cambridge, Mass: Harvard University Press, 1984.

Cohen, Keith. *Film and Fiction: The Dynamics of Exchange*. New Haven, Conn.: Yale University Press, 1979.

————. "Eisenstein's Subversive Adaptation." In *The Classic American Novel and the Movies*, edited by Gerald Peary and Roger Shatzkin, 245 255. New York: Frederick Ungar, 1977.

Colmeiro, José F. "La narrativa policíaca posmodernista de Manuel Vázquez Montalbán." *Anales de la literatura española contemporánea* 14, no. 1 (1989): 11-31.

Colmena, Enrique. *Vicente Aranda*. Madrid: Cátedra, 1996.

Company, Juan Miguel. "La conquista del tiempo. Las adaptaciones literarias en el cine español." In *Escritos sobre el cine español, 1973-87*, 85-86. Valencia: Generalitat Valenciana, 1989.

Compitello, Malcolm A. "Making *El sur*." *Revista Hispánica Moderna* 46 (1993): 73-86.

————. "Spain's Nueva Novela Negra and the Question of Form." *Monographic Review/Revista Monográfica* 3, no. 1-2: 183-91.

Conrad, Joseph. Preface to *The Nigger of the Narcissus*. London: Dent, 1897.

Cook, David A. *A History of Narrative Film*. New York: W. W. Norton, 1981.

Costas Goberna, José Manuel. "La soledad se inventa espejos: sobre *El amante bilingüe*, de Juan Marsé." *Insula* 46 (June 1991): 25-27.

Cristóbal, Ramiro. "El paraíso como fascinación." *TeleRadio* 20-26 (May 1985): 5, 7.

Defourneaux, Marcelin. *Daily Life in Spain in the Golden Age*. Translated by George Allen. Stanford, Calif.: Stanford University Press, 1970.

De la Fuente, Inmaculada. "Ser padre de Kronen." *El país* (21 May 1995): 12.

Deleuze, Gilles. *Cinema*. 2 vol. Minneapolis, Minn.: University of Minnesota Press: 1986, 1989.

Deveny, Thomas G. *Cain On Screen: Contemporary Spanish Cinema*. Metuchen, N. J.: Scarecrow, 1993.

————. "Cela on Screen." In *Camilo José Cela: Homage to a Nobel Prize*, edited by Joaquín Roy, 90-96. Coral Gables, Fla.: University of Miami Press, 1991.

Dorward, Frances R. "*Réquiem por un campesino español*: Reflections After the Film." *Essays on Hispanic Themes in Honour of Edward C. Riley*, edited by Jennifer Lowe and Philip Swanson, 268-288. Edinburgh: University of Edinburgh Press, 1989.

Dougherty, Dru. "*La colmena* en dos discursos: novela y cine." *Insula* 45, no. 518-19 (February-March 1990): 19-21.

Edel, Leon. "Novel and Camera." In *The Theory of the Novel*, edited by J. Helperin. London: Oxford University Press, 1974.

Editorial Noguer. Letter to the author. 22 February 1990.

Eisenstein, Sergei. "Dickens, Griffith and the Film Today." In *Film Form*, translated by Jay Leyda. New York: Harcourt, Brace, Jovanovich, 1949.

Ellis, John. *Visible Fictions: Cinema, Television, Video*. Boston, Mass.: Routledge, 1982.

Elsaesser, Thomas. *New German Cinema. A History*. New Brunswick, N. J.: Rutgers University Press, 1989.

"Encuesta." *Cambio 16* 830 (26 October 1987): 80-85.

Erlich, Victor. *Russian Formalism: History-Doctrine*. The Hague: Mouton, 1955.

Evans, Peter, and Robin Fiddian. "Víctor Erice's *El sur*: A Narrative of Star-Cross'd Lovers." *Bulletin of Hispanic Studies* 44 (1987): 127-35.

Fajardo, José Manuel. "Auror Rodríguez, la tragedia de la Eva futura. *Cambio 16* 808, 11 May 1987, 130-36.

Fernández Heliodoro, Antonio. *La novela española dentro de España*. Madrid: Antonio Fernández Heliodoro, 1987.

Freixas, Ramón. "*El amante bilingüe*." *Dirigido* 212 (April 1993): 38-41.

———. "*La pasión turca* de Gala revivida por Vicente Aranda." *Dirigido* 230 (December 1994): 34-37.

———. "*Si te dicen que caí*. Retrato de una infancia sin inocencia." *Dirigido* 172 (September 1989): 42-45.

———. "*Tiempo de silencio*. Narración frente a estilo." *Dirigido por* 134 (1986): 30-32.

———, and Joan Bassa. "Entrevista: Vicente Aranda." *Dirigido* 216 (September 93): 46-49.

Frugone, Juan Carlos. *Oficio de gente humilde . . . Mario Camus*. Valladolid: 24 Semana de Cine, 1984.

Gabilondo, Joseba. "Masculinity's Counted Days: Spanish Postnationalism, Masochist Desire, and the Refashioning of Misogyny." *Anuario de cine y literatura en español* 3 (1997): 53-72.

García Domínguez, Ramón. *Miguel Delibes: La imagen escrita*. Valladolid: 38 Semana Internacional de Cine, 1993.

García Fernández, Emilio. *Historia ilustrada del cine español*. Madrid: Planeta, 1985.

García Viñó, Manuel. *Ignacio Aldecoa*. Madrid: ESPESA, 1972.

Géloin, Ghislaine. "The Plight of Film Adaptations in France. Toward a Dialogic Process in the Auteur Film. In *Film and Literature. A Comparative Approach to Adaptation*, edited by Wendell Aycock and Michael Schoenecke, 135-48. Lubbock, Texas: Texas Tech University Press, 1988.

Giddings, Robert. *Screening the Novel: The Theory and Practice of Literary Dramatization*. New York: St. Martin's Press, 1990.

Glassco, David. "Films Out of Books: Bergman, Visconti and Mann." In *Film/Literature*, edited by George E. Toles, 165- 73. Winnipeg, Canada: University of Manitoba Press, 1983.

Glenn, Kathleen M. "Gothic Vision in García Morales and Erice's *El sur.*" *Letras peninsulares* 7, no. 1 (Spring 1994): 239-50.

González, Bernardo Antonio. "Reading *La colmena* through the Lens: From Mario Camus to Camilo José Cela." In *Camilo José Cela: Homage to a Nobel Prize*, edited by Joaquín Roy, 97-103. Coral Gables, Fla.: University of Miami Press, 1991.

Grant, Barry Keith, ed. *Film Genre Reader*. Austin: University of Texas Press, 1986.

Gubern, Román. *1936-1939: La guerra de España en la pantalla*. Madrid: Filmoteca Española, 1986.

Guillot, Vicente. "Las dos colmenas." *Anuario de cine y literatura en español* 1 (1995): 37-46.

Haro Tecglen, Eduardo. "*Pascual Duarte* en su contexto." In *Pascual Duarte*, edited by Emilio M. Lázaro and Elías Querejeta, 18-29. Madrid: Elías Querejeta Ediciones, 1977.

Harvey, David. *The Condition of Postmodernity*. Cambridge: Blackwell, 1990.

Havard, Robert G. "The 'Romance' in Sender's *Requiem por un campesino español.*" *Modern Language Review* 79, no. 1 (January 1984): 87-96.

Henn, David. "Cela's Portrayal of Martín Marco in *La colmena.*" *Neophilogus* 55 (1971): 142-49.

Hernández Les, Juan, and Miguel Gato, eds. *El cine de autor en España*. Madrid: Castellote, 1978.

Holquist, Michael. *Dialogism: Bakhtin and His World*. New York: Routledge, 1990.

Hooper, John. *The Spaniards: A Portrait of the New Spain*. Harmondsworth, England: Penguin, 1987.

———. *The New Spaniards*. London: Penguin, 1995.

Hopewell, John. "Art and a Lack of Money': The Crises of the Spanish Film Industry, 1977-1990." *Quarterly Review of Film and Video* 13, no. 4 (1991): 113-22.

Horton, Andrew, and Joan Magretta, eds. *Modern European Filmmakers and the Art of Adaptation*. New York: Frederick Ungar, 1980.

Hume, Martin. *The Court of Philip IV: Spain in Decadence*. New York: G. P. Putnam's Sons, 1907.

Iser, Wolfgang. *The Implied Reader: Patterns of Communication in Prose Fiction from Bunyan to Beckett*. Baltimore: The Johns Hopkins University Press, 1974.

Jacobs, Lewis. *The Rise of the American Film*. New York: Harcourt, Brace, 1939.

Kaplin, E. Ann. *Woman and Film: Both Sides of the Camera*. New York: Methuen, 1983.

Kazloff, Sarah. *Invisible Storytellers: Voice-Over Narration in American Fiction Film*. Berkeley, Calif.: University of California Press, 1988.

Kenworthy, Patricia. "A Political Pascual Duarte." In *Cine-Lit: Essays on Hispanic Film and Fiction*, edited by George Cabello-Castellet, Jaume Martí Olivella, and Guy H. Wood, 55-59. Corvallis, Oreg.: Oregon State University, Portland State University, and Reed College, 1992.

Keppler, Carl F. *The Literature of the Second Self*. Tucson, Ariz.: University of Arizona Press, 1972.

Kermode, Frank. "Novel and Narrative." In *The Poetics of Murder: Detective Fiction and Literary Theory*, edited by Glenn W. Most and William W. Stowe, 175-196. San Diego: Harcourt Brace Jovanovich, 1983.

Kinder, Marsha. *Blood Cinema: The Reconstruction of National Identity in Spain*. Berkeley, Calif.: University of California Press, 1993.

———. *Refiguring Spain: Cinema/Media/Representation*. Durham, N. C.: Duke University Press, 1997.

Klein, Michael, and Gillian Parker, eds. *The English Novel and the Movies*. New York: Ungar, 1981.

Kovács, K. S. "The Plain in Spain." *Quarterly Review of Film and Video*, 13, no. 4 (1991): 17-46.

Larsson, Donald F. "Novel into Film: Some Preliminary Reconsiderations." In *Transformations in Literature and Film: Selected Papers from the 6th Annual Florida State Conference on Literature and Film*, 69-83. Tallahassee, Fla.: University Presses of Florida, 1982.

Lehman, Peter and William Luhr. *Authorship and Narrative in the Cinema: Issues in Contemporary Aesthetics and Criticism*. New

York : Putnam, 1977.

Linden, George W. "The Storied World." In *Film and Literature. Contrasts in Media,* edited by Fred H. Marcus, 157-63. Scranton, Pa.: Chandler, 1971.

Llopis, Silvia. *"Si te dicen que caí." Cambio 16* 932 (9 October 1989): 126.

López Martínez, Luis. *La novelística de Miguel Delibes.* Murcia: Universidad de Murcia, 1973.

Lotman, Juri. "Point of View in a Text." Translated by L. M. O'Toole. *New Literary History* (Winter 1975): 339-52.

———. *Semiotics of Cinema.* Translated by Mark E. Suino. Ann Arbor: University of Michigan Press, 1981.

MacCabe, Colin. *Theoretical Essays: Film, Linguistics, Literature.* Manchester: Manchester University Press, 1985.

MacFarlane, Brian. *Words and Images: Australian Novels into Film.* Richmond, Australia: Heinemann, 1983.

Mangini González, Shirley. "La novelística de Juan Marsé. " Ph.D. diss. , University of New Mexico, 1979.

Marco, José María. "El espacio de la libertad." *Quimera* 66/67 (n.d.): 48-52.

———. "Julio Llamazares, sin trampa. *Quimera* (August 1988): 22-29.

Marcus, Millecent. *Filmmaking By the Book: Italian Cinema and Literary Adaptation.* Baltimore: Johns Hopkins University Press, 1993.

Marinero, Francisco. *"La colmena:* un fresco histórico." *Diario 16* (12 October 1982): 1, 42.

Márquez-Pribitkin, Yvette. *"Los santos inocentes* visto por Mario Camus años más tarde." *Anuario de cine y literatura en español* 1 (1995): 55-64.

Martialay, Félix. *"La colmena* de Mario Camus." *El Alcazar* (30 October 1982): 30.

Martín, Nieves. "Eduardo Mendicutti." *Cambio 16* 1355 (17 November 1997): 78-79.

Martin-Márquez, Susan. "The Spectacle of Life: Ana Mariscal's Vision of Miguel Delibes' *El camino." Romance Languages Annual* 2 (1990): 469-73.

———. "Bifurcaciones en el camino: cinco directores ante la obra de Miguel Delibes." Ph.D. diss. University of Pennsylvania, 1991.

———. "Desire and Narrative Agency in *El sur."* In *Cine-Lit II. Essays on Hispanic Film and Fiction,* edited by George Cabello-Castellet, Jaume Martí Olivella, and Guy H. Wood, 130-136.

Corvallis, Oreg.: Oregon State University, Portland State University and Reed College, 1995.

Martínez Lázaro, Emilio, and Elías Querejeta. *Pascual Duarte*. Madrid: Elías Querejeta Ediciones, 1977.

Mast, Gerald. *A Short History of the Movies*. New York: Macmillan, 1986.

———, and Marshall Cohen, eds. *Film Theory and Criticism*. 2d ed. New York: Oxford University Press, 1979.

McDougal, Stuart Y. *Made into Movies: From Literature to Film*. New York: Holt, Rinehart, and Winston, 1985.

McHale, Brian. *Postmodernist Fiction*. New York: Methuen, 1987.

McPheeters, D. W. *Camilo José Cela*. New York: Twayne, 1969.

Méndez Leite, Fernando. "El cine español en la transición." In *Cine español 1975-84. Primera semana de cine español. Murcia 1984*. Murcia: Universidad de Murcia, 1985.

Mendoza, Eduardo and Antonio Drove. "Sobre *La verdad del caso Savolta*." Lecture at the Public Theater, New York, 9 May 1994.

Metz, Christian. *Language and Cinema*. Translated by Dona Jean Umiker-Sebeok. The Hague: Mouton, 1974.

———. *Film Language: A Semiotics of the Cinema*. Translated by Michael Taylor. New York: Oxford University Press, 1974.

———. *The Imaginary Signifier: Psychoanalysis and the Cinema*. Translated by Celia Britton. Bloomington, Ind.: Indiana University Press, 1982.

Michener, James. *Iberia*. New York: Random House, 1968.

Miller, J. Hillis. "The Critic as Host." In *Deconstruction and Criticism*. New York: The Seabury Press, 1979.

Miller, Jonathan. *Subsequent Performances*. London: Faber, 1987.

Miró, Pilar. "Diez años de cine español." In *La cultura española en el posfranquismo. Diez años de cine, cultura y literatura (1975-85)*, edited by Samuel Amell and Salvador García Castañeda, 27-32. Madrid: Playor, 1988.

Molina-Gavilán, Yolanda. "Poéticas regionales ante la posmodernidad: dos escritores andaluces." *Lucero* 5 (1994): 106-13.

Monaco, James. *How to Read a Film: The Art, Technique, Language, History and Theory of Film and Media*. Rev. ed. New York: Oxford University Press, 1981.

Montes-Huidobro, Matías. "Análisis fílmico-literario de Los santos inocentes." *Letras peninsulares* 7, no. 1 (Spring 1994): 293-312.

Moreno, Francisco. "*Sinatra*." *Cine para leer*, 1998. Bilbao: Mensajero, 1999: 242-243.

Morris, Barbara, and Lou Charnon-Deutsch. "Regarding the Pornographic Subject in *Las edades de Lulú*." *Letras peninsulares* 6,
no. 2-3 (Fall-Winter 1993-1994): 301-19.

Morrissette, Bruce. *Novel and Film*. Chicago: University of Chicago
Press, 1985.

Mulvey, Laura. "Visual Pleasure and Narrative Cinema." *Screen*
16, no. 3 (1975): 6-18.

Muñoz Molina, Antonio. "Sobre la adaptación cinematográfica."
Public lecture presented at the University of Maryland, College Park, 25 March 1995.

Navajas, Gonzalo. "Modernismo, posmodernismo y novela
policíaca: *El aire de un crimen* de Juan Benet." *Monographic Re-
view/Revista Monográfica* 3, no. 1-2 (1987): 221-30.

Navales, Ana María. *Cuatro novelistas españoles*. Madrid:
Fundamentos, 1974.

Nichols, Bill. *Movies and Methods*. 2 vols. Berkeley, Calif.: University of California Press, 1976-1985.

Olea, Pedro, and Fernando Lalana. *Morirás en Chafarinas,(La
película)*. Zaragoza: Xordica, 1995.

Orloff, Alexander. *Carnival: Myth and Cult*. Worgl, Austria: Perfinger
Verlag, 1981.

Orr, John, and Colin Nicholson, eds. *Cinema and Fiction: New Modes
of Adapting, 1950-1990*. Edinburgh: Edinburgh University Press,
1992.

Ortega, Julio. "El sentido temporal en *La colmena*. *Symposium* 19
(1965), 115-22.

Ostherr, Kirsten. "Margins of Vision: Azarías and Nieves in *Los
santos inocentes*." In *Cine-Lit: Essays on Hispanic Film and Fiction*, edited by George Cabello-Castellet, Jaume Martí Olivella,
and Guy H. Wood, 60-67. Corvallis, Oreg.: Oregon State University, Portland State University and Reed College, 1992.

Paun de García, Susan. "*Los santos inocentes*: Novel to Film. A
Sharper Image of Evil." In *Cine-Lit: Essays on Hispanic Film and
Fiction*, edited by George Cabello-Castellet, Jaume Martí
Olivella, and Guy H. Wood, 68-74. Corvallis, Oreg.: Oregon
State University, Portland State University and Reed College,
1992.

Payan, Miguel Juan. *El cine español de los 90*. Madrid: JC, 1993.

Peary, Gerald, and Roger Shatzkin. *The Classic American Novel and
the Movies*. New York: Frederick Ungar, 1977.

———. *The Modern American Novel and the Movies*. New York:
Frederick Ungar, 1978.

Peña-Ardid, Carmen. *Literatura y cine: Una aproximación comparativa.* Madrid: Cátedra, 1992.

Pérez de León, Vicente. "Los caminos del *Viaje a ninguna parte.*" *Anuario de cine y literatura en español* 1 (1995): 93-100.

Pérez Millán, Juan Antonio. *Pilar Miró: Directora de cine.* Valladolid: 37 Semana internacional de cine, 1992.

Pérez Ornia, José Ramón. "El café de doña Rosa, tienda de antiguedades." *El país,* "Suplemento Artes," 23 January 1982: 4.

Pillado-Miller, Margarita. "Sobre la adaptación cinemato-gráfica de *Beltenebros.*" *Ojáncano* 11 (April 1996): 21-36.

Pipolo, Tony. "The Aptness of Terminology: Point of View, Conciousness, and *Letter from an Unknown Woman.*" *Film Reader* 4 (1979): 166-79.

Polo García, Victoriano. *Un novelista español contemporáneo.* Murcia: Publicaciones de la Universidad, 1967.

Pope, Randolph D. "*Gran sol* a ciegas." In *Cine-Lit: Essays on Hispanic Film and Fiction,* edited by George Cabello-Castellet, Jaume Martí Olivella, and Guy H. Wood, 75-79. Corvallis, Oreg.: Oregon State University, Portland State University and Reed College, 1992.

Porter, Dennis. *The Pursuit of Crime: Art and Ideology in Detective Fiction.* New Haven: Yale University Press, 1981.

Quesada, Luis. *La novela española y el cine.* Madrid: JC, 1986.

Richardson, Robert. *Literature and Film.* Bloomington: Indiana University Press, 1969.

Rodríguez-Fischer, Ana. "Entrevista a Juan Marsé." *Insula* 46 (June 1991): 23-25.

Rogers, Robert. *A Psychoanalytical Study of the Double in Literature.* Detroit: Wayne State University Press, 1970.

Román, Antonio. "Adaptación al cine de *Crónica del alba.*" *Cuadernos de ALDEEU* 5, no. 2 (November 1989): 257-68.

Ross, Harris. *Film as Literature, Literature as Film.* New York: Greenwood, 1987.

Rubio, José Luis. "Los males de *El sur.*" *Cambio 16,* 601 (6 June 1983): 129-30.

Rubio Gribble, Susana. "Del texto literario al texto fílmico: Representación del punto de vista narrativo en tres adaptaciones del cine español de los ochenta." Ph.D. diss. State University of New York at Stony Brook, 1992.

Ruiz, Jesús. "*La colmena*: De lo escrito a lo vivo." *El correo catalán* (17 October 1982): 43.

Samper Pizano, Daniel. "Siempre de fiesta." *Cambio 16* (10 agosto 1991): 11-20.

Santoro, Patricia. "Novel into Film: The Case of *La familia de Pascual Duarte* and *Los santos inocentes.*" Ph.D. diss. Rutgers University, 1989.

Sanz Villanueva, Santos. *Historia de la literatura española 6/2. Literatura actual.* 2d ed. Barcelona: Ariel, 1985.

Scholes, Robert. "Narration and Narrativity in Film." *Quarterly Review of Film Studies,* 1.3: 283-296

Sherzer, William M. *Juan Marsé. Entre la ironía y la dialéctica.* Madrid: Fundamentos, 1982.

Sinyard, Neil. *Filming Literature: The Art of Screen Adaptation.* London: Croom Helm, 1986.

Slade, Joseph W. "Pornography in the Late Nineties." *Wide Angle* 19, no. 3 (July 1997): 1-12.

Smith, Paul Julian. "*Beltenebros (Prince of Shadows).*" *Sight and Sound* 4 (April 1994) : 39.

Sobejano, Gonzalo. "*La colmena*: olor a miseria." *Cuadernos hispanoamericanos* 337-38 (1978), 113-26.

Sobejano-Morán, Antonio. "El proceso creador en *La muchacha de las bragas de oro* y *Epílogo.*" Paper presented at Conference of Foreign Films and Literatures, Villanova University, 2 November 1996.

Soldevila Durante, Ignacio. *La novela desde 1936.* Madrid: Alhambra, 1982.

Spanos, William V. *Repetitions: the Postmodern Occasion in Literature and Culture.* Baton Rouge, Louisiana: Louisiana State University Press, 1987.

Stam, Robert. *Subversive Pleasures: Bakhtin, Cultural Criticism, and Film.* Baltimore: Johns Hopkins University Press, 1989.

Tani, Stefano. *The Doomed Detective: The Contribution of the Decective Novel to Postmodern American and Italian Fiction.* Carbondale, Ill.: Southern Illinois University Press, 1984.

Todorov, Tzvetan. "The Typology of Detective Fiction." *The Poetics of Prose,* 42-52. Translated by Richard Howard. Ithaca, N.Y.: Cornell University Press, 1977.

Tomashevsky, Boris. "Thematics." In *Russian Formalist Criticism.* 2d ed. Translated by Lee Lemon and Marion Reis. Lincoln, Nebraska: University of Nebraska Press, 1969.

Truffaut, François. *Hitchcock.* New York: Simon and Schuster, 1966.

Umbral, Francisco. *Miguel Delibes.* Madrid: E.P.E.S.A., 1970.

Varela, Antonio. "Reading and Viewing *Los santos inocentes.*" *Romance Languages Annual* 1 (1989): 639-44.

Vega, Felipe. "*La colmena* / Mario Camus." *Papeles de cine Casablanca* 25 (January 1983) 52-53.

Vera, Pascual. *Vicente Aranda*. Madrid: JC, 1989.

Vernon, Kathleen. "La Politique des Auteurs: Narrative Point of View in *Pascual Duarte*, Novel and Film." *Hispania* 72, no. 1 (March 1989): 87-96.

———. "Reading Hollywood in/and Spanish Cinema: From Trade Wars to Transculturation." In *Refiguring Spain. Cinema/Media/ Representation*, edited by Marsha Kinder. Durham, N. C.: Duke University Press, 1997.

Villanueva, Darío. "Lectura de *La colmena.*" In Camilo José Cela, *La colmena*. 43d ed. Barcelona: Noguer, 1986.

Wagner, Geoffrey. *The Novel and the Cinema*. Cranbury, N.J.: Associated University Presses, 1975.

Weinrichter, Antonio. "Entrevista [con Vicente Aranda]." *Dirigido por* 134 (1986): 32-35.

Williams, Jay. *The World of Titian*. New York: Time-Life, 1968.

Winks, Robin, ed. "Introduction." In *Detective Fiction. A Collection of Critical Essays*. Englewood Cliffs, NJ: Prentice-Hall, 1980.

Wood, Guy H. "Autobiografía y cinematografía en *Luna de lobos* de Julio Llamazares." In *Cine-Lit: Essays on Hispanic Film and Fiction*, edited by George Cabello-Castellet, Jaume Martí Olivella, and Guy H. Wood, 80-91. Corvallis, Oreg.: Oregon State University, Portland State University and Reed College, 1992.

———. "*El maestro de esgrima* y el canon hollywoodiano." In *Cine-Lit II. Essays on Hispanic Film and Fiction*, edited by George Cabello-Castellet, Jaume Martí Olivella, and Guy H. Wood, 117-29. Corvallis, Oreg.: Oregon State University, Portland State University and Reed College, 1995.

Index

454

About the Author

THOMAS G. DEVENY (B.A., State University of New York at Albany; M.A., University of Florida; Ph.D., University of North Carolina at Chapel Hill) is Professor of Spanish at Western Maryland College in Westminster, Maryland. Professor Deveny is author of *Cain on Screen: Contemporary Spanish Cinema* (Scarecrow Press, 1993). He has written articles on Spanish film, Spanish literature, and Brazilian literature in numerous scholarly journals. He is also the translator of Adelaida García Morales's *The South / Bene* (University of Nebraska Press, 1999).